THE S. MARK TAPER FOUNDATION

IMPRINT IN JEWISH STUDIES

BY THIS ENDOWMENT

THE S. MARK TAPER FOUNDATION SUPPORTS

THE APPRECIATION AND UNDERSTANDING

OF THE RICHNESS AND DIVERSITY OF

JEWISH LIFE AND CULTURE

DENYING HISTORY

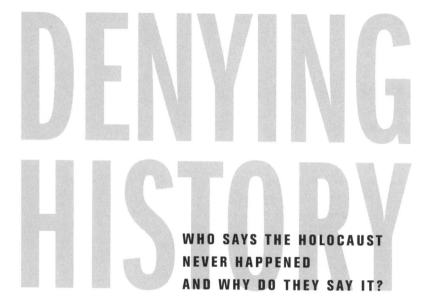

DENYING HISTORY

WHO SAYS THE HOLOCAUST NEVER HAPPENED AND WHY DO THEY SAY IT?

Michael Shermer & Alex Grobman

Foreword by Arthur Hertzberg

UNIVERSITY OF CALIFORNIA PRESS
Berkeley | *Los Angeles* | *London*

The publisher gratefully acknowledges the generous contribution to this book provided by the S. Mark Taper Foundation and by the Jewish Federation Council of Greater Los Angeles.

University of California Press
Berkeley and Los Angeles, California

University of California Press, Ltd.
London, England

© 2000 by Michael Shermer, Alex Grobman, and
the Los Angeles Museum of the Holocaust

Library of Congress Cataloging-in-Publication Data

Shermer, Michael.
    Denying history : who says the Holocaust
never happened and why do they say it? /
Michael Shermer, Alex Grobman ; foreword
by Arthur Hertzberg.
        p.   cm.—(The S. Mark Taper
Foundation imprint in Jewish Studies)
    Includes bibliographical references (p.) and
index.
    ISBN 0-520-21612-1 (cloth : alk. paper)
    1. Holocaust denial.   I. Grobman, Alex.
II. Title.
D804.355.S54   2000
940.53'18—dc21   00-028690

Manufactured in the United States of America

09   08   07   06   05   04   03   02   01   00
10   9   8   7   6   5   4   3   2   1

Contents

Illustrations

Foreword

"Know how to answer" is a command that first appeared among the rabbis two thousand years ago. In the Hellenistic age, pagan intellectuals and confused or heretical Jews who had come under their influence were challenging the Bible. They niggled away at seeming inconsistencies in its text, and they were particularly scathing in asserting that their philosophies contained higher moral truths than those found in the Jewish holy books. The debates raged for generations. Beginning with the third century B.C.E., Judaea was ruled by the successors of Alexander the Great, and the revolt led by the Maccabees in the second century B.C.E. did not end Hellenistic influence in the region. Alexander's successors had planted Greek-speaking colonies that the Maccabees never succeeded in dislodging. So, this foreign and often hostile culture could not be ignored. Its attacks had to be answered. The Talmud is replete with tales of encounters between the rabbis and the "wise men of the pagans," who were always, so the stories go, left nonplused when confronted with the devastating answers that the rabbis offered to the claims of these philosophers.

Unfortunately, such religious debates continued into the Middle Ages. The arguments were now with Christian theologians and prelates, who wanted to establish, above all, that the Hebrew Bible predicted the events that were recorded in the New Testament and that the only proper way to read the Hebrew Bible was as the preamble to Christianity. In answering the Christian contention, Jews were much less free than they had been in Hellenistic times. Anything in Jewish texts that could be read as an attack on the Christian doctrine of the Incarnation was ordered removed by church and civil authorities, and the texts themselves were often burned as purveyors of blasphemous teachings. On occasion during the Middle Ages, representative Jews were forced to appear at disputations with Christian clergy. These dramas were always dangerous. If the Jews made their arguments too gentle, in order to avoid danger, they were likely to be pushed toward immediate conversion to Christianity. If they made them too strong and incisive, these debaters might be punished for lack of respect for the "true faith." Nonetheless, Jewish refutations of Christianity did appear during the Middle Ages. The books that were written in Christian countries were more than somewhat guarded, but the authors who wrote in the diasporas in Muslim lands were free to say what they liked about Christianity.

In the eighteenth century, the age of the Enlightenment, the critique of all religions became much less constrained. The primary attack on Judaism no longer came from Christians. The new enemies were the philosophes, the intelligentsia who accused Judaism of being the progenitor of all they disliked in Christianity. By the middle of the eighteenth century, Jews started to outline and define their responses to the attacks on them by the rationalists of the Enlightenment. In the next century, the new, most vehement attacks on Judaism were made by racialists, who called it the inferior religion of an inferior race, and by some revolutionary socialists, who insisted that the prime meaning of Judaism was to foster capitalism. By the second half of the twentieth century, at the end of World War II and in the aftermath of the Holocaust, attacks on Judaism seemed to be waning. It was becoming widely accepted that any one of the religious faiths, or of the secular philosophical outlooks, taught a form of righteousness and each was right for its believers. Jews were able to think, for an all too brief moment, that they were finally free of having to defend themselves and their beliefs. But it was not to be.

After the murder of six million Jews in Europe for the "crime" of having been born of Jewish ancestry, no one imagined, even in nightmares, that some people would arise to deny that the Holocaust ever took place, but such views are now being broadcast, most insistently. These notions have been advanced not only by avowed neo-Nazis, who have an obvious interest in making their predecessors look better. Some of the Holocaust deniers also promote these ideas in writings supported by the appearance of scholarship, with footnotes and bibliographies. The accounts of Auschwitz, they insist, are wildly exaggerated or even invented. One of their arguments is that the gas chambers were simply not large enough, or efficient enough, to have been the place of execution for many hundreds of thousands of people in a very short time. This claim, along with many others, is based, supposedly, on evidence and on deductions that can be drawn from asserted facts. The pose of objectivity makes this "scholarship" a more dangerous enemy than the obvious incitements by neo-Nazis.

The attack by the Holocaust deniers is, in a very deep sense, the most hurtful that has ever been leveled against Jews. We have long been prepared to defend our religion and our corporate character (to the degree to which it might exist), but the immediate reaction by Jews to the Holocaust deniers is outrage so complete that we cannot think of an appropriate response. How, indeed, can a people answer the charge that it has imagined or invented its greatest tragedy? I do know of one scene that took place before television cameras in London, when the late Rabbi Hugo Gryn confronted one of these pseudo-scholars. Gryn was himself a survivor of the death camps. Gazing directly at his opponent, he said, "Look into my eyes and dare say that it never happened." Rabbi Gryn could speak, effectively and devastatingly, out of his own life, but the Holocaust deniers usually must be answered by people who do not have his biography. Such responses have to be convincing in forums where people have little knowledge of the horrors of the Nazi era.

Michael Shermer and Alex Grobman have performed a great service in this book. They take up the contentions of the Holocaust deniers, point by point, and refute them, down to the smallest detail. I admire their fortitude in making themselves read through all of this enraging literature and the control with which they have demolished the supposed facts and assumptions of these newest denigrators of the Jewish people. This book stands in the saddening, all too long, but very honorable Jewish tradition of providing the refutations to those who attack the credibility of our historic memory. In the deepest sense this book continues the Jewish commitment to defend historic truth and the honor of the Jewish people.

Arthur Hertzberg
Bronfman Visiting Professor of Humanities,
New York University

A Note on Terminology

Why Holocaust "Revisionists" Are Really Deniers

For a long time we referred to the deniers by their own term of "revisionists" because we did not wish to engage them in a name-calling contest (in angry rebuttal they have called Holocaust historians "exterminationists," "Holohoaxers," "Holocaust lobbyists," and assorted other names).[1] We are well aware of David Irving's libel suit against Deborah Lipstadt, which involves, among other things, her calling him a Holocaust denier. We have given this matter considerable thought—and even considered other terms, such as "minimalizers"—but decided that "deniers" is the most accurate and descriptive term for several reasons:

1. When historians talk about the "Holocaust," what they mean on the most general level is that about six million Jews were killed in an intentional and systematic fashion by the Nazis using a number of different means, including gas chambers. According to this widely accepted definition of the Holocaust, so-called Holocaust revisionists are in effect *denying* the Holocaust, since they deny its three key components—the killing of six million, gas chambers, and intentionality. In an ad placed in college newspapers by Bradley Smith, one of the "revisionists" discussed in this book, he even uses this verb: "Revisionists *deny* that the German State had a policy to exterminate the Jewish people (or anyone else) by putting them to death in gas chambers or by killing them through abuse or neglect."[2]

2. Historians are the ones who should be described as revisionists. To receive a Ph.D. and become a professional historian, one must write an original work with research based on primary documents

and new sources, reexamining or reinterpreting some historical event—in other words, revising knowledge about that event *only*. This is not to say, however, that revision is done for revision's sake; it is done when new evidence or new interpretations call for a revision.

3. Historians have revised and continue to revise what we know about the Holocaust. But their revision entails *refinement* of detailed knowledge about events, rarely complete denial of the events themselves, and certainly not denial of the cumulation of events known as the Holocaust.

Holocaust deniers claim that there is a force field of dogma around the Holocaust—set up and run by the Jews themselves—shielding it from any change. Nothing could be further from the truth. Whether or not the public is aware of the academic debates that take place in any field of study, Holocaust scholars discuss and argue over any number of points as research continues. Deniers do know this. For example, they often cite the fact that Franciszek Piper, the head of the Department of Holocaust Studies at the Auschwitz-Birkenau State Museum, has refined the number killed at Auschwitz from four million to a little more than one million, arguing that this proves their case.[3] But they fail to note that at the same time the numbers have been revised up—for example, the number of Jews murdered by the Einsatzgruppen during and after the invasion of the Soviet Union.[4] The net result of the number of Jews killed—approximately six million—has not changed. In the case of Auschwitz and the other camps liberated by the Russians, since the end of the Second World War the Communists' efforts to portray the Nazis in the worst light possible led them to exaggerate the number of the Nazis' victims and the number of extermination camps.[5] Scholars have had to clear through Communist propaganda to get to the truth about what happened. This sifting of data has resulted and will continue to result in Holocaust revision.

Thus, in this book, "Holocaust denial" is a descriptive term that allows for clear and accurate communication about who is being discussed. We adopt as our approach the sage advice of the seventeenth-century philosopher Baruch Spinoza: "I have made a ceaseless effort not to ridicule, not to bewail, not to scorn human actions, but to understand them."

Acknowledgments

First and foremost we thank the Leslie and Susan Gonda (Goldschmied) Foundation for making the publication of this book possible.

We also thank the following people for making this book a reality:

Dr. Samuel Goetz, former Chair, Martyrs Memorial and Museum of the Holocaust

Herbert Gelfand, former President, The Jewish Federation

John R. Fishel, former Executive Vice President and current President, The Jewish Federation

Avner Shalev, Chairman of the Directorate, Yad Vashem

Motti Shalem, Director, International School of Holocaust Studies, Yad Vashem

Marcia Reines Josephy, Director/Curator, The Jewish Federation's Los Angeles Museum of the Holocaust (Martyrs Memorial)

We are grateful to the following individuals for offering advice and feedback on this project: Thomas Blatt, Rabbi Yale Butler, Raul Hilberg, Michael Hirschfeld, Shulamit Imber, Barbara Kamilar, Perla Karney, Ron Kenner, Pat Linse, Cornelius Loen, Yaacov Lozowick, Harvey Lutske, Frank Miele, Safira Rapoport, Israel Shaked, Kim Ziel Shermer, Brian Siano, and Robert Jan van Pelt. And to Masha Loen and Miriam Bell, whose dedication to this book was beyond what we could have anticipated or hoped. Thank you.

We are especially grateful to Reed Malcolm, Sue Heinemann, Yuki Takagaki, and Nicole Hayward of the University of California Press, and to Doug Abram Arava and Elizabeth Knoll for helping to bring this book to the Press.

We also thank the following for reading parts or all of the manuscript: Yehuda Bauer, Aaron Breitbart, Valerie Drees, Henry Friedlander, Bonnie Gurewitsch, Yisrael Gutman, Ephraim Kaye, Amanda Kushnir, Sybil Milton, Michael Tregenza, and Efraim Zuroff. As is always the case in acknowledgments, we take full responsibility for errors and omissions.

Special thanks to the National Archives, the United States Holocaust Memorial Museum, Dr. Franciszek Piper of the Auschwitz State Museum, Director Barbara Distel at Dachau, and at Majdanek the Director Edward Balawajder, Assistant Director Anna Wiszniewska, Curator Tomasz Kranz, Archivist Elzbieta Kielbon, and the late Jozef Marszalak. Also to Johannes Hoegl of the Austrian Gedenkdienst Program, an independent organization that provides Holocaust museums and memorials with qualified young Austrian interns whose work is paid by their government, testifying to Austria's awareness of its participation in the Holocaust.

Special appreciation also goes to Nevin A. Bryant, Supervisor of Cartographic Applications, Image Processing Applications, and Observational Systems Division of the Jet Propulsion Laboratory and NASA for his guidance on interpreting the aerial photographs of Auschwitz, and for the use of their sophisticated and state-of-the-art equipment in enhancing and analyzing these photographs.

We also wish to thank our wives, Kim Ziel Shermer and Marlene Grobman, for being supportive of our trips abroad and for tolerating our endless discussions of the relatively depressing subject of genocide and the bizarre phenomenon of Holocaust denial. For obvious reasons the support of family is important in dealing with this subject. To that end Michael Shermer would also like to acknowledge his parents, Richard and Lois Godbold and Betty and Richard (of Blessed Memory) Shermer, and his in-laws, Harry and Donna Ziel. Alex Grobman would also like to acknowledge the love and support of his parents, Reba and Frank (of Blessed Memory) Grobman, and his in-laws, Belle and Joseph Weisblum.

Introduction:
Who Speaks for the Past?

History and Pseudohistory

I take delight in history, even its most prosaic details, because
they become poetical as they recede into the past. The poetry
of history lies in the quasi-miraculous fact that once, on this
earth, once, on this familiar spot of ground, walked other
men and women, as actual as we are to-day, thinking their
own thoughts, swayed by their own passions, but now all
gone, one generation vanishing after another, gone as utterly
as we ourselves shall shortly be gone like ghost at cock-crow.
This is the most familiar and certain fact about life, but it is
also the most poetical, and the knowledge of it has never
ceased to entrance me, and to throw a halo of poetry around
the dustiest record.

George Macaulay Trevelyan, *An Autobiography*

There we sat, an Orthodox Jew, a professional skeptic, and one of the
world's authorities on Auschwitz face to face with Ernst Zündel, an all-
around Germanophile known for his court cases concerning free speech
in Canada and his media blitzes claiming that the Holocaust never happened. It was a strange experience, the culmination of years of research
that led us through a looking-glass world where black is white, up is
down, and the normal rules of reason no longer apply. We not only met
with those who deny the Holocaust—who deny that during the Second
World War the Nazis and their collaborators carried out the intentional
and bureaucratically administered destruction of about six million Jews,
using gas chambers, crematoriums, and other technologies, and basing
their actions primarily on racial ideology. We also traveled to the camps
themselves, to Dachau, Treblinka, Sobibor, Mauthausen, Majdanek,
Belzec, and Auschwitz (including Birkenau)—to test the claims that no

mass murders, especially by gassing, took place by intention at these camps.

When dealing with the claims of the Holocaust deniers, we believe it is not enough to be ivory-tower academics, attempting to achieve objectivity with distance, when the individuals who make these claims are friendly, eager to talk, and merely a phone call or plane ride away. Historians mostly deal with figures who are no longer alive. But here we are dealing not just with history, but with pseudohistory—*the rewriting of the past for present personal or political purposes.* If we want to know what the proponents of this pseudohistory are like and how they think, what could be more important than meeting and talking to them?

Some have argued that a project such as this is degrading and improper for professional historians (which we are by training). We do not agree. Primary sources are the most important tool of the historian, and what could be more primary in writing a book about Holocaust denial than meeting the deniers themselves, seeing their offices, asking them questions, reading their literature, and, in general, trying to get inside their minds? Others have argued that to meet with the deniers or answer their claims is to validate them, but we believe that to let their arguments go unanswered presents the greater danger. Was it not Joseph Goebbels who observed that if you repeat a lie enough times, people will believe it?

We discovered that most Holocaust deniers are very knowledgeable about very specific aspects of the Holocaust—a gas chamber door that cannot lock, the temperature at which Zyklon-B evaporates, or the lack of a metal grid over the peephole on a gas chamber door—so that anyone who is not versed in these specifics cannot properly question and answer their claims. This problem came to our attention in talking to the top Holocaust scholars in the world. In many cases we have had to go to great lengths during this multiyear project to get answers to our questions. The answers are there, but not in ready-made form. Our book remedies this shortcoming in Holocaust studies. But it does more than this.

The purpose of this book is to reveal the difference between history and pseudohistory by using Holocaust denial as a classic case study in how the past may be revised for present political and ideological purposes. In the process we thoroughly refute the Holocaust deniers' claims and arguments, present an in-depth analysis of their personalities and motives, and show precisely, with solid evidence, how we know the Holocaust happened. We use this case study to consider how we know any past event happened. Finally, we examine how various observers have explained the Holocaust over the past half century and what these different explanations tell us not only about the Holocaust but about ourselves.

One of the deans of Holocaust scholarship, Yehuda Bauer, observed: "I believe that this [denial of the Holocaust] is the work of a growing movement, as for extremely wide circles of people the very phenomenon of the Holocaust is incomprehensible, unintelligible and untenable, and an explanation claiming that it did not happen is accepted with relief."[1] To deal with the untenability of the Holocaust, we have divided this book into four general sections.

In part I we examine two issues that bear on Holocaust denial: free speech and the nature of history. Chapter 1, "Giving the Devil His Due," looks at the freedom of speech that must be considered when dealing with Holocaust denial, and why we need to respond. Chapter 2, "The Noble Dream," investigates the nature of history, the difference between history and pseudohistory, and ways of knowing that anything in the past happened. Over the past couple of decades there have been serious challenges to the notion of truth in history. One step in assessing arguments for the relativity of historical truth and the impossibility of finding out "what really happened" is to ask if the "truth" that the Holocaust happened is equal to the "truth" that it did not happen. In part II we go inside the denial movement to see, in chapter 3, "Who Says the Holocaust Never Happened?" (the personalities and organizations), to find out in chapter 4, "Why They Say the Holocaust Never Happened" (ideological and political motives and the larger social context), and to understand, in chapter 5, "How Deniers Distort History" (the flaws, fallacies, and failings in their arguments). In part III we directly address the three major foundations upon which Holocaust denial rests, including, in chapter 6, "The Crooked Timber of Auschwitz," the claim that gas chambers and crematoria were used not for mass extermination but rather for delousing clothing and disposing of people who died of disease and overwork; in chapter 7, "The Evil of Banality," the claim that the six million figure is an exaggeration by an order of magnitude—that about six hundred thousand, not six million, died at the hands of the Nazis; and in chapter 8, "The Protocols of National Socialism," the claim that there was no intention on the part of the Nazis to exterminate European Jewry and that the Holocaust was nothing more than an unfortunate by-product of the vicissitudes of war. In all three chapters our purpose is twofold: to present the historical facts that refute Holocaust denial, and to show how we know that the Holocaust happened. Many of our arguments draw on specialized research into the claims of the deniers that took us from their headquarters in Newport Beach, California, and Toronto, Canada, to the Nazi extermination camps themselves. Much of the research is the type of work professional historians normally do—digging through primary documents; analyzing ground and aerial photographs; translating memos, orders, and letters—but it also offers new evidence on how we know the Holocaust happened and new interpretations of old theories about the Holocaust. In part IV, in our final chapter, "The Rape of History," we pull back to look at the bigger picture of Holocaust studies and trace explanations of the Holocaust over the past half century to see where the real revision is taking place. We look at the "history wars" in various fields, explore how these "wars" are resolved among historians in particular and the public in general, and how this process differs from what the Holocaust deniers are doing.

Throughout this book we make generous use of both primary and secondary sources that readers will find in the bibliography. We tried to check the accuracy of our assumptions about the deniers by meeting and interviewing the major players of the Holocaust denial movement, attending their conferences and meetings, and reading their literature carefully. All quotes from deniers come either from taped interviews or from their own published literature. To ensure fairness in the representation of both the deniers' claims and the deniers themselves, we even had them read parts of the manuscript in an earlier published form.[2]

Who speaks for the past? In the ancient world it was the scribes and court historians who transmitted a past almost wholly slanted toward the dictates of the ruler or the ruling party. The winners wrote the history of their winnings. In the Middle Ages ideologues also ruled the past, but others laid claim to history, including medieval monks who carried on their tradition of transcribing the past letter by letter, as well as wandering minstrels, poets, and sages who kept the flame of the past burning through the oral tradition. The Modern Age can be said to have begun in 1454 with Johann Gutenberg's invention of movable type and the creation of the printed book.[3] A life that was provincial, rural, and insular was soon after urban, cosmopolitan, and united, in part because of the knowledge and power provided through the written word. Descartes and Spinoza, Cervantes and Milton could speak across the miles, just as Aristotle and Plato, St. Augustine and Cicero could speak across the ages. New intellectual horizons were opened by the vast amount of information that was suddenly available. Authorities were subject to challenge, and cherished ideas could be questioned. Where books were once so rare that the fear of theft kept them chained to posts in libraries, within four decades of Gutenberg's invention there were one thousand printers who produced thirty thousand titles with a total of nine million copies that circulated throughout Europe. Where literacy was once the province of the wealthy and learned, soon over half the European population was reading books, including books about the past. Where only the elite could speak for the past, now almost anyone could.

One problem that arose was the uncritical acceptance of anything in print. "I read somewhere that . . ." has become the doctrine of evidence in the Modern Age that demands proof for claims. And the Internet has accentuated the effect. Where anyone can speak for the past, no one can. Where everyone's opinion is equal to everyone else's opinion, no one's opinion matters. Where all truths share equal billing on the public stage, no truths can emerge with meaning. Fact blends into fiction. Cautious interpretation morphs into wild speculation. Historiography melds into hagiography. History sloughs into pseudohistory.

The problem, as we all know from listening to pundits debate the great (and trivial) issues of our age, is that the facts never just speak for themselves. They must be interpreted through a hypothesis, a model, a theory, a paradigm, or a worldview. And not all hypotheses, models, theories, paradigms, and worldviews are equal. Some *are* better than others. How can we tell which ones carry more veracity? The tools of science, logic, and historiography can help us decide. But who will decide? Scientists, logicians, and historians trained in using these tools can. But so can you. Thanks to that single tool that sparked the Modern Age—the book— everyone has access to the rest of the tools that help us find truth, including the truth about the past. We are all the historians Carl Becker spoke about in his 1931 presidential address to the American Historical Association, "Everyman His Own Historian": "We are Mr. Everybody's historian as well as our own, since our histories serve the double purpose, which written histories have always served, of keeping alive the recollection of memorable men and events. We are thus of that ancient and honorable company of wise men of the tribe, of bards and storytellers and minstrels, of soothsayers and priests, to whom in successive ages has been entrusted the keeping of the useful myths."[4]

Who speaks for the past? We all do. But not equally so. Despite the democratization of knowledge, allowing us to be our own historians, if we want to be taken seriously, we must obey the rules of reason and apply the tools of science and scholarship.

part i

Free Speech and History

However unwillingly a person who has a strong opinion may admit the possibility that his opinion may be false, he ought to be moved by the consideration that however true it may be, if it is not fully, frequently, and fearlessly discussed, it will be held as a dead dogma, not a living truth.

John Stuart Mill,
On Liberty, 1859

1

Giving the Devil His Due

The Free Speech Issue

WILLIAM ROPER: So now you'd give the Devil benefit of law.
SIR THOMAS MORE: Yes. What would you do? Cut a great
road through the law to get after the
Devil?
ROPER: I'd cut down every law in England to do
that.
MORE: Oh? And when the law was down—and
the Devil turned round on you—where
would you hide? Yes, I'd give the Devil
benefit of law, for my own safety's sake.

Robert Bolt,
A Man for All Seasons,
act 1, scene 6

On December 1, 1996, the *New York Times* reported that Benjamin
Austin, a sociology professor at Middle Tennessee State University,
found literature in books on the Holocaust at his college library that more
than implied that the Holocaust did not happen. Not long after he removed the leaflets from the books, Austin discovered that they had been
replaced by more Holocaust denial material. When he looked into the
matter further he came across the same literature placed in Holocaust
books at Davis-Kidd Booksellers, Nashville's largest independent bookstore. The publishers of the literature, he soon learned, were the Institute for Historical Review and National Vanguard Books, a division of
the West Virginia–based National Alliance. The Institute for Historical
Review, in southern California, is the leading Holocaust denial organization in the United States. The National Alliance was founded by
William Pierce (aka Andrew Macdonald), author of the famed *Turner*

Diaries, an inflammatory novel about the bombing of a federal building, similar to that by Timothy McVeigh in Oklahoma City.

Should the Institute for Historical Review be allowed to publish pamphlets, journals, and books denying the Holocaust? Should it be allowed
to place them in public libraries and private bookstores? Should the National Alliance be allowed to publish potentially incendiary books, like
The Turner Diaries, if they appear to offer blueprints for violence and
destruction? At the heart of these questions is one of the most controversial issues any democracy must deal with as it attempts to strike a
healthy balance between freedom of expression and protection of the
rights of its citizens.

THE FREE SPEECH ISSUE

In the United States of America, the First Amendment protects the right
of all citizens to question the existence of anything they like, including
the death of Elvis, the Apollo moon landing, and the single-bullet theory
in the JFK assassination. No matter how much an individual may dislike someone else's opinion—even if it is something as shocking as denying that the Holocaust happened—that opinion is protected by the First
Amendment. In most countries of the world, however, this is not the case.
In Canada there are "anti-hate" and anti-pornography statutes and laws
against spreading "false news" that have been applied to Holocaust deniers. In Austria it is a crime if a person "denies, grossly trivializes, ap-
proves or seeks to justify the national socialist genocide or other national
socialist crimes against humanity."[1] In France it is illegal to challenge the
existence of "crimes against humanity," as defined by the military tribunal at Nuremberg:

> CRIMES AGAINST HUMANITY: namely murder, extermination, enslavement,
> deportation and other inhumane acts committed against any civilian popu-
> lation, before or during the war, or persecutions on political, racial, or reli-
> gious grounds in execution of or in connection with any crime within the ju-
> risdiction of the Tribunal, whether or not in violation of the domestic law of
> the country where perpetrated.[2]

On July 3, 1981, for example, the French Holocaust denier Robert
Faurisson was found guilty in a Paris court of defamation and incite-
ment to racial hatred and violence, based on a law passed July 1, 1972.
Specifically, the court ruled: "In accusing the Jews publicly of being guilty
through cupidity of a particularly odious lie and of a gigantic swindle . . .
Robert Faurisson could not be unaware that his words would arouse in

his very large audience feelings of contempt, of hatred and of violence towards the Jews in France."[3] As recently as April 21, 1998, the journal *Nature* ran a news item on a brewing controversy in France's national scientific research agency—the Centre National de la Recherche Scientifique (CNRS)—involving "the revisionist activities of Serge Thion, a CNRS researcher, as well as those of several other scientists." One of those CNRS scientists was Gabor Rittersporn, who was accused in the German newspaper *Berliner Zeitung* of denying that the Nazi gas chambers had been used for mass homicide. In response Rittersporn successfully sued the paper and cleared his name, but in the trial it came out that in the 1970s and 1980s he belonged to "extreme left-wing groups that favoured free expression for revisionists." The article pinpointed the free speech problem for the CNRS, "which is split between the need to preserve academic freedom and a desire to discipline such individuals."[4]

In Germany the *Auschwitzlüge,* or "Auschwitz-Lie" Law, makes it a crime to "defame the memory of the dead." This statute was the result of a judgment by the Federal German Supreme Court on September 18, 1979, when a student whose Jewish grandfather was killed in Auschwitz sued for an injunction against an individual who had posted signs on the fence of his house proclaiming that the Holocaust was a "Zionist swindle." The Supreme Court ruled in favor of the plaintiff:

> In calling the racist murders by the Nazis an invention, the statements complained of deny the Jews the inhuman fate which they have suffered on account of their origin. . . . This means an attack on the personality of the people who have been singled out by the anti-Jewish persecutions in the Third Reich. . . . Whoever tried to deny the truth of past events, denies to every Jew the respect to which he is entitled.[5]

Switzerland, Belgium, Israel, Italy, New Zealand, Sweden, and Australia have similar laws on the books.[6] These laws are all ambiguous enough to allow courts to interpret various Holocaust deniers' activities as illegal. In December 1982, for example, Sweden arrested Dietlieb Culver Felderer, an associate of a leading Holocaust denier, Willis Carto, when Felderer accused Mel Mermelstein, a Holocaust survivor, of "peddling the extermination hoax." Specifically, Felderer was tried because, as the Swedish prosecutor explained, his "obscene propaganda against Jews abroad and in Sweden is so large that he must have huge financial backing."[7] This was the first time such a prosecution had been undertaken in Sweden.

In Great Britain, the Race Relations Act forbids racially charged speech "not only when it is likely to lead to violence, but generally, on the grounds that members of minority races should be protected from racial insults."[8] In like manner, in Australia, the New South Wales parliament amended the 1989 Anti-Discrimination Act to include a ban on "racial vilification." The sweeping scope of the government's power to determine what constitutes vilification is remarkable:

> The law invests in the Anti-Discrimination Board the power to determine whether a report is "fair," and whether a discussion is "reasonable," "in good faith," and "in the public interest." The Board will pronounce upon the acceptability of artistic expression, research papers, academic controversy, and scientific questions. An unfair (i.e., inaccurate) report of a public act may expose the reporter and the publisher to damages of up to $40,000.[9]

In conflict with more laws of this nature than probably any other historian today, and arguably the most widely known Holocaust denier, David Irving was told by Polish authorities in July 1998 that he would not be allowed to film a documentary at Auschwitz. "They have written refusing even to allow me—an historian of worldwide reputation— at the site," he wrote in an Internet posting. "It is an unprecedented ban."[10] This kind of censure is nothing new to David Irving, who has been banned from numerous countries around the world. While he cannot be legally prohibited from speaking in America, he can be so loudly shouted down that he is, essentially, banned. On Friday, February 3, 1995, for example, Irving was invited by the Berkeley Coalition for Free Speech to lecture at the University of California, Berkeley. The university allowed it, but student groups did not. More than 300 protesters surrounded Latimer Hall to keep Irving from speaking and the 113 ticket holders from entering the building. The police were at first unable to control the crowd, fistfights broke out, and Irving was forced to retreat behind his book table for protection until order was restored.[11]

The event sparked a heated debate at the university and a flurry of letters to the editor and op-ed pieces in the university's newspaper, *The Daily Californian*. Writing in support of the administration's decision to allow Irving to speak, Robert Post, a law professor, explained that its tolerance did not mean "that we ought to have legitimated Irving by engaging in dialogue with him . . . [or including him] in the conversation of our community."[12] Aaron Breitbart, a senior researcher at the Simon Wiesenthal Center in Los Angeles, opined: "The university is a guardian of truth. I do not believe that Mr. Irving belongs on the university campus except as an example of those who murder history." But one student, Gurman Bal, countered: "Protesters have a right to speak also and show their point of view, but I think it's wrong to prevent him from speaking." A graduate student named Nick Virzi accused the protesters themselves of Nazi stratagems: "They're the ones showing actual Nazi tactics. I was called an Aryan Supremacist. I told them I'm an Italian-Hispanic. Long live free speech in Berkeley, right?"[13]

Should free speech live and flourish without restriction? Our position regarding the freedom of speech of anyone on any subject is that while the government should not be in the business of limiting speech, an institution should have the freedom to restrict the speech of anyone at any time who utilizes resources within the jurisdiction of its own institution (such as a school newspaper, classroom, or lecture hall). The Holocaust deniers should have the freedom to publish their own journals and books, and to attempt to have their views aired in other publications, as in college newspaper ads. And colleges, since they own their own newspapers, should have the freedom to restrict the deniers' access to their readership. Walter Reich, former director of the U.S. Holocaust Memorial Museum, has noted that we must not confuse freedom of expression "with the obligation to facilitate that expression."[14] We must never pass a law that says Holocaust deniers may not publish their own literature. But we are not obligated to publish it for them in our own publications. The Holocaust denier Ernst Zündel submitted an advertisement to be run in *Skeptic* magazine (published by one of the authors of this book), but it was declined, even though the editors of *Skeptic* are in favor of free speech.[15] Being in favor of someone's right to freedom of speech is quite different from enabling that speech.

An example of this important distinction concerns the Holocaust denier Bradley Smith, who publishes *Smith's Report,* "America's only monthly Holocaust revisionist newsletter" (according to its subtitle). Smith has his own Web site (www.codoh.com [Committee for Open Debate on the Holocaust]) and is the author of the widely distributed pamphlet entitled *The Holocaust Controversy: The Case for Open Debate.* Smith makes it all sound so banal and innocent: "Students should be encouraged to investigate the holocaust controversy the same way they are encouraged to investigate every other historical controversy. This isn't a radical point of view. The premises for it were worked out some time ago during a little something called the Enlightenment."[16] True enough, the Enlightenment did spawn honest and open debates on all manner of historical questions, including and especially religious, political, and ideological assumptions of centuries past. And the Enlightenment gave birth to the ideas of freedom of speech and freedom of the press. But the Enlightenment also shifted science and rationality to center stage and propounded that logical analysis and empirical evidence must take precedence over personal biases and political ideologies.[17] In the bright light of open discussion the truth will emerge. Let Smith publish his newsletter, make his Internet postings, and distribute his pamphlets. But let's not allow him to do so without a response, without using logical analysis and empirical evidence to show his arguments for what they really are.

How, then, should we respond to Holocaust denial, or any other radical claim? This is a question of strategy: Does one ignore a false claim and hope it goes away, or stand up and refute it for all to see? A decision on this point will be different for different people and different claims. We believe that once a claim is in the public consciousness (as Holocaust denial undeniably is), it should be properly analyzed and, if appropriate, refuted vigorously in the public arena. That is what we intend to do here. Specifically, we hope that our analysis will

Draw a fuller picture of the controversy for those who, because they are unfamiliar with the history of the Holocaust, might be open to the deniers' arguments.

Provide another avenue for people to learn about the Holocaust.

Teach readers how historians use evidence to verify that anything in the past happened.

Demonstrate how anyone can come to believe almost anything because of ideology.

Show how professional historians have already been revising our knowledge of the Holocaust in light of fresh evidence or interpretations that more closely approximate the truth of what happened. The ultimate irony about Holocaust "revisionism" is that historians, not "revisionists," are the ones who have been revising widely accepted views of the Holocaust and will continue to do so as new material on specific events becomes available.

Most Americans will say that they are in favor of free speech and that they believe in the First Amendment. They may even call themselves civil libertarians. But these same people, when their beliefs are challenged, may just as loudly proclaim that their challengers should be censored. We want, again, to make our stance clear: no one, in our opinion, is required to publish or aid in the presentation of the Holocaust deniers' views, but we are against legal attempts to censor those views. Such attempts are what Louis Brandeis called "silence coerced by law—the argument of force in its worst form."[18] The problem was succinctly summarized by Thomas More, who would give the Devil his due for his own safety's sake.

Let us pretend for a moment that the majority of people deny the existence of the Holocaust and that they are in the positions of power. If a mechanism for censorship exists, then the believer in the reality of the Holocaust may now be censored. Would we tolerate this? Of course not. The human mind, no matter what ideas it may generate, must never be quashed. By way of example, when evolutionists were in the minority in Tennessee in 1925 and politically powerful fundamentalists had passed legislation making it a crime to teach evolution in public schools, Clarence Darrow made this brilliant observation in his opening remarks in the Scopes trial:

> If today you can take a thing like evolution and make it a crime to teach it in the public schools, tomorrow you can make it a crime to teach it in the private schools, and next year you can make it a crime to teach it in the church. At the next session you can ban books and the newspapers. Ignorance and fanaticism are ever busy, indeed feeding, always feeding and gloating for more. Today it's the public school teachers, tomorrow the private. The next day the preachers and the lecturers, the magazines, the books, the newspapers. After awhile, your honor, it is the setting of man against man, creed against creed, until the flying banners and beating drums are marching backwards to the glorious ages of the sixteenth century when bigots lighted fagots to burn the man who dared to bring any intelligence, and enlightenment, and culture to the human mind.[19]

THE DUTY TO RESPOND

Not only is it defensible to respond to the Holocaust deniers; it is, we believe, our duty. The Holocaust deniers have succeeded in spreading their beliefs in the media and in the academic world. They are featured on national and local TV and radio talk-shows, are invited to speak on college campuses, and have succeeded in placing full-page paid advertisements in college and university newspapers, including those of Brandeis University, Boston College, Pennsylvania State University, and Queens College. Some of these ads arguing that the Holocaust never happened ran without comment; others generated op-ed pieces by professors and students.

By also publishing a number of professional-looking books, monographs, and a journal, Holocaust deniers attempt to assume the mantle of respectability and credibility. Few would agree that the deniers have achieved their goal, but they have succeeded in getting people to discuss the question of whether the Holocaust occurred. What do they hope to accomplish? Some Holocaust scholars, like Yehuda Bauer, go so far as to argue that deniers are trying to create preconditions to deny the Jewish people the right to live in the post-Holocaust world. In a similar vein Walter Reich asks, "What better way to rehabilitate antisemitism than to make antisemitism arguments seem once again respectable in civilized discourse and even make it acceptable for governments to pursue antisemitic policies than by convincing the world that the great crime for which antisemitism was blamed simply never happened—indeed, that it was nothing more than a frame-up invented by the Jews, and propagated by them through their control of the media? What better way, in short, to make the world safe again for antisemitism than by denying the Holocaust?"[20] This thought reverberates in Pierre Vidal-Naquet's book *Assassins of Memory:* "One revives the dead in order to better strike the living."[21]

Consider this: Some Holocaust deniers, particularly those with extreme right-wing leanings, might gain greater acceptance if the crime attached to fascism had never actually happened. Without the Holocaust perhaps fascism would seem a more acceptable alternative to democracy. Moreover, if people can be convinced that the Holocaust never happened, perhaps they can also be persuaded to believe that slavery is a hoax perpetrated by blacks to coerce Congress to institute affirmative-action programs. Once we allow the distortion of one segment of history without making an appropriate response, we risk the possible distortion of other historical events. For this reason, Holocaust denial is not just a Jewish issue. It is an attack on all history and on the way we transmit the past to the future.

Why, some people ask, do we need to respond at all to the Holocaust deniers? Can't we just dismiss them all as a bunch of antisemitic neo-Nazi thugs? No, we can't. Like all sociopolitical movements, Holocaust denial attracts a wide variety of individuals, each with different motives and intentions, loosely held together by a common set of beliefs and ideologies. The subtleties and complexities of the Holocaust denial movement defy such global labels as "antisemitic" or "neo-Nazi." To resort to labels is to misunderstand what is really going on and therefore to swat down straw men.

We think it is time to move beyond name calling and present the evidence. Failure to do so might create serious consequences. Imagine a student who tells her teacher, "I read in a college newspaper ad that gas chambers were used only for delousing clothing and not for mass murder. How do we know these chambers were used to kill people?" If the teacher responds, "Oh, that ad was placed by an antisemitic neo-Nazi," what is the student to think? First, she gets no answer to her question. Second, she learns that an ad hominem attack is an appropriate response. Third, she may begin to wonder if there is something to the claims she has read because her teacher did not (could not?) provide answers. We must be forthright and honest about what we know and do not know about the Holocaust.

We can no longer ignore the deniers, calling them names and hoping they will go away. They are not going to go away. They are highly motivated, reasonably well financed, and often well versed in Holocaust studies. Like most fringe groups, deniers may seem relatively small and harmless, but remember the adage: For evil to triumph it only requires that the good do nothing. We cannot remain silent anymore. It is time to respond. As the Holocaust historian Robert Jan van Pelt observed, "Academics who choose to ignore Holocaust deniers are like the crew of the Titanic straightening the deck chairs while the ship is going down."[22]

Some may wonder if a book like this does not give credibility to the deniers, in the same way the media might be accused of calling attention to a problem of which few were aware. We believe that the public has a "right to know" about a potential social problem and that it is the duty of informed experts on a subject to share their knowledge. To that end this book is not just for Holocaust scholars and historians, it is for teachers and students, libraries and research facilities, and general readers of all levels interested in history, the Holocaust, and the ways that ideologies and belief systems can distort reality and our view of the past.

It is our belief that truth will always win out when the evidence is made available for all to see. "It is error alone which needs the support of government," Thomas Jefferson wrote in his *Notes on the State of Virginia.* "Truth can stand by itself."[23] The Holocaust as an event has never been only of scholarly interest. Dozens of movies and thousands of popular books have made it highly unlikely that we shall ever forget. But the details of the Holocaust, and how historians know that it happened as it did, are still relatively unknown to most members of the general public. This is why Holocaust denial has had a modicum of success (and more success in America and Canada than in Europe, where too many people know firsthand that these events occurred). The deniers know a great deal about the Holocaust. In conversation, it is easy for them to convince the uninitiated person that there might be something to their claims. To refute the deniers' arguments, we examine Holocaust history, evidence, and methods; present an outline of how the science of history works; and in the process show how truth emerges through rational discourse. As Jefferson explained in his original draft of that greatest of all free speech documents, the Declaration of Independence: "And, finally, that truth is great and will prevail if left to herself; that she is the proper and sufficient antagonist to error, and has nothing to fear from the conflict unless by human interposition disarmed of her natural weapons, free argument and debate; errors ceasing to be dangerous when it is permitted freely to contradict them."[24]

The Noble Dream

How We Know Anything Happened in History

Beyond the noble dream of scientific objectivity and the night-
mare of complete relativism lies the terrain of pragmatic
truth, which provides us with hypotheses, provisional syntheses, imaginative but warranted interpretations, which then
provide the basis for continuing inquiry and experimentation.
Such historical writing can provide knowledge that is useful
even if it must be tentative. It is within that realm that historical truth—like all truth in a world that has moved beyond
the discredited dualisms of both positivism and idealism—
must be made, questioned, and reinterpreted. As historians,
we cannot aspire to more than a pragmatic hermeneutics that
relies on the methods of science and the interpretation of
meanings. But we should not aspire to less.

James Kloppenberg, in *American Historical Review,* 1989

On April 13, 1945, when General Dwight D. Eisenhower arrived at the
Buchenwald concentration camp, he declared that here was "indisputable
evidence of Nazi brutality and ruthless disregard of every shred of de-
cency." Yet with eerie foresight Eisenhower augured how the Holocaust
might come to be denied in the future:

> I visited every nook and cranny of the camp because I felt it my duty to be in
> a position from then on to testify at first hand about these things in case there
> ever grew up at home the belief or assumption that "the stories of Nazi bru-
> tality were just propaganda." Some members of the visiting party were un-
> able to go through the ordeal. I not only did so but as soon as I returned to
> Patton's headquarters that evening, I sent communications to both Washing-
> ton and London, urging the two governments to send instantly to Germany
> a random group of newspaper editors and representative groups from the na-

tional legislatures. I felt that the evidence should be immediately placed before the American and British publics in a fashion that would leave no room
for cynical doubt.[1]

Eisenhower knew his public well. Comments that it was all "just propaganda" and views tinged with "cynical doubt" did indeed emerge from
certain groups at home about the Holocaust. On one level it might be
understandable how the American public *during* the war exerted some
skepticism toward the atrocity stories leaking out of Europe, for they
had become callous after similar stories during the First World War turned
out to be largely the product of British propaganda.[2] But in the closing
weeks of the war, as Allied soldiers liberated concentration camps across
the continent, it became simply impossible to deny what had happened.
Or did it? How is it that so much physical evidence can come to be
doubted? For that matter, how do we know *anything* happened in the
past? Holocaust denial is a harsh lesson in historical skepticism gone
down the slippery slope into nihilism.

WHAT IS HISTORY?

Is history what happened in the past, or is it what we *think* happened in
the past? Further, can we find some meaning in history, or is it just a
chaotic configuration of events? These are some of the most important
and pervasive questions discussed by philosophers of history. And as with
other ageless philosophical conundrums, such as free will versus determinism, there is little consensus on a solution. We have not yet discovered any laws governing the unfolding of events in history; although most
historians would agree that the past is not just one isolated event after
another. And while we can know *something* about the past, we cannot
know *everything* about it. In between these philosophical borders lies
the terrain of historians.

The first dilemma—is history the past events themselves or the inquiry
into those events?—belongs to what is known in the trade as the *analytic
philosophy of history.* The issue is similar to asking: If a tree falls in a forest when no one is around to hear it, does it make a sound? Here, the answer depends on how we define the key term: "sound." If "sound" is
defined as vibrating airwaves, and the tree falls through air, then it makes
a sound. If "sound" is defined as vibrating airwaves falling on an eardrum
that transduces the vibrations into mechanical-neural signals perceived
by a human brain as a falling tree, then it does not make a sound.

If "history" is defined only by our perception of past events, then there is no history of the past without our interpretation of that past. If "history" is strictly the past itself, then those events occurred whether we perceive and interpret them or not. But there is another underlying question here: Can the discipline of history be useful to us? To further our understanding of the past, we believe that as historians we must look at both the historical events and the discovery and description of those events. Trees in the past fell, struck the ground, and caused the air to vibrate, whether humans were there or not, but a fallen tree becomes a historical event for humans when humans discover that it fell. *History is the combined product of past events and the discovery and description of past events.* The real debate among historians is not whether the Holocaust happened—it is about how it happened, what sort of historical facts we use to tell the story about it, and how we tell that story. The history of the Holocaust involves not only the discovery of historical facts about it, but also the description and interpretation of those facts. To come to understand how anyone can deny the event itself, we must examine how major changes in the historical profession in the past century have allowed this and other forms of pseudohistory to thrive.

THE PARADOX OF THE TIERS

To answer the question "What is history?" we must tackle another question: What can we know about history? To answer this second question we have constructed a three-tiered heuristic model, outlining the shifts in the historical profession's thinking over the past century, from *historical objectivity,* to *historical relativism,* to what we hope is *historical science.* Because the tiers contain built-in paradoxes, we call this the *paradox of the tiers.*

The First Tier: Historical Objectivity

By the late nineteenth century, most Western historians believed that history had become an objective science. Writing history was straightforward enough—just present all the facts and let them speak for themselves. This approach, best articulated in the work of the German historian Leopold von Ranke, arose in response to propagandistic history written for political purposes after the French Revolution. According to Ranke, if historians presented the past with severe objectivity and cold neutrality, it would be immune to distortion by the press, ruling classes, or revolutionaries. In Ranke's words, which have become the passe-partout (defining frame) of scientific historicism, the historian's job is to present the past *wie es eigentlich gewesen*—as it actually happened. "He will have no preconceived ideas as does the philosopher," Ranke concluded, "rather, while he reflects on the particular, the development of the world in general will become apparent to him."[3]

This vision of history as absolutely and objectively knowable may be summarized as follows:

1. History exists outside the minds of historians.

2. Historians discover the past as astronomers discover heavenly bodies or chemists discover elements in nature.

3. Historians can know and describe the past.

4. Historians can purge themselves of bias.

5. Contingent events of history had a structural and causal organization.

6. Historians can discover this structure through rational means.

7. Historians' job is to present this discovery of the past "as it actually happened."

Assuming that historical events occur independently of human records and interpretations, and that the recording of those events has been accurate and free from bias, the nineteenth-century objectivist historians believed that pattern and meaning exist in past events and simply await discovery. By taking the millions of pieces of historical facts and laying them out on an intellectual table, historians can begin to piece them together like a jigsaw puzzle. In this process historians ask such questions as: Is there meaning to history? Are there discernible cause-and-effect relationships? Can consistent and repeatable patterns be discovered? Are there lessons to be learned from a study of the past? These questions underlie what is known as the *speculative philosophy of history*. The goal of the objectivist historian is to cast off the veil of mystery and expose the dark past to the light of truth.

The Paradox of the First Tier

On one level all historians *must* believe there is something in the past they can discover and describe in some reasonably objective way. Why else would they write history? Despite this assumption, we now understand that we cannot know with certainty what "actually" happened. The facts do not just speak for themselves. A historical analysis is *an* interpretation, not *the* interpretation (though it may be the accepted interpretation for a while). The paradox is that we cannot stay at this tier without delusion or denial of our own biases and influences. The field of history, after all, is populated by historians subject to the same conditioning and enculturation as everybody else firmly embedded in an era and culture. Histories of the working class, women, minorities, indigenous peoples, and others have made it clear that gaps in historical knowledge are often linked to the fact that histories have usually been written by those in power and that humans write about what interests them and what they think is important at the time.

The irony of this first paradox is that twentieth-century historians suffer from a nearly complete misunderstanding of Leopold von Ranke, the man who they believed best represented a scientific approach to history. From nineteenth-century Germany to twentieth-century America, Ranke literally got lost in the translation. The German word *Wissenschaft* can have two distinct meanings: with an indefinite article, it refers to a body of (systematized) knowledge; with the definite article, it refers—*pars pro toto*—to a single scientist or group of scientists, but not all scientists. Neither of these meanings exactly corresponds to "science." What we call science is what Germans call *Naturwissenschaft,* or natural science. During the nineteenth century they categorized the social sciences and humanities (including philosophy, literature, and theology) as *Geisteswissenschaft.* Whereas *Naturwissenschaft* involves a set of methods including hypothesis testing and mathematical models, *Geisteswissenschaft* uses debate as its primary method to resolve conflicting interpretations. It is possible to argue in English about whether history is a science, but in German "history" is, by definition, *Geisteswissenschaft.* Americans misunderstood Ranke's *Wissenschaft* as implying science, when he really meant *Geisteswissenschaft,* or what we would call the humanities. German historians, then, were shocked when their American counterparts suggested that the methods of *Naturwissenschaft* could be applied to their field. History belonged in the humanistic tradition, not the natural sciences. Yet the latter is precisely where Americans cataloged what they thought was Ranke's philosophy of history. And the process that made him the point man of historical objectivity turned Ranke into the straw man of twentieth-century historical relativism.

The Second Tier: Historical Relativism

In 1902 John Bagnell Bury succeeded John E. E. Dalberg, Lord Acton, as Regius Professor of Modern History at Cambridge. To mark the transition and to accelerate a change in classification of the discipline of history from literature to science, Bury gave an inaugural lecture entitled "The Science of History," in which he firmly embedded the Rankean myth of objectivity in England and ultimately in America. He concluded his address by observing: "If, year by year, history is to become a more and more powerful force for stripping the bandages of error from the eyes of men, for shaping public opinion and advancing the cause of intellectual and political liberty, she will best prepare her disciples for the performance of that task by remembering always that, though she may supply material for literary art or philosophical speculation, she is herself simply a science, no less and no more." Claiming that Rankean objectivity "is a text which must still be preached," Bury noted this transition as "therefore of supreme moment that the history which is taught should be true."[4] Bury's supreme moment, however, was slipping away.

In Germany historians and philosophers such as Friedrich Meinecke charged that history is unscientific to the extent that the spiritual and moral aspects of humanity cannot be understood through scientific means: "Where science fails it is wiser for history to use these suprascientific means than to apply scientific means where their application must lead inevitably to false results." The German sociologist Max Weber's call for value-free social science was found wanting by Meinecke, who explained, "Even the mere selection of value-related facts is impossible without an evaluation. The presentation and exposition of culturally important facts is utterly impossible without a lively sensitivity for the values they reveal."[5]

By the 1920s and 1930s the attacks on historical objectivity were frequent and furious. In 1921, for example, the Italian historian Benedetto Croce illuminated the relationship between a historical narrative and a document: "What were narratives or judgments before are now themselves facts, 'documents' to be interpreted and judged. History is never constructed from narratives, but always from documents, or from narratives that have been reduced to documents and treated as such."[6] History, then, is reconstructed not from the original events, but from the documents that describe them. Further, history is not what happened then; it is what we now think happened then, based on current beliefs and interpretations.

In 1931 Carl Becker told the American Historical Association (AHA), in his now famous presidential address entitled "Everyman His Own Historian," that we cannot know what really happened in the past because "much the greater part of these events we can know nothing about, not even that they occurred; many of them we can know only imperfectly; and even the few events that we think we know for sure we can never be absolutely certain of, since we can never revive them, never observe or test them directly." Thus, there are actually two histories: "the actual series of events that once occurred; and the ideal series that we affirm and hold in memory. The first is absolute and unchanged—it was what it was whatever we do or say about it; the second is relative, always changing in response to the increase or refinement of knowledge."[7] Thus, on one level, the historian is no more objective than Everyman in the remembrance of things past, nor is Everyman any more subjective than the historian in selectively interpreting what really happened. This is the ultimate statement of historical relativism.

Charles A. Beard attempted to go Becker one better in his oft-quoted essay "That Noble Dream." Beard's 1935 essay was in part a response to Theodore Clarke Smith's address to the AHA in celebration of its fiftieth anniversary. Smith had proudly touted the profession's devout fidelity "that presented to the world first in Germany and later accepted everywhere, the ideal of the effort for objective truth."[8] Sensing the decline of Ranke's noble dream, particularly because of challengers like James Harvey Robinson, who had quipped that objective history is just history without an object, Smith fought to buttress the old guard:

> It may be that another fifty years will see the end of an era in historiography, the final extinction of a noble dream, and history, save as an instrument of entertainment, or of social control will not be permitted to exist. In that case, it will be time for the American Historical Association to disband, for the intellectual assumptions on which it is founded will have been taken away from beneath it. My hope is, none the less, that those of us who date from what may then seem an age of quaint beliefs and forgotten loyalties, may go down with our flags flying.[9]

In contrast to Smith, Beard was happy to see the era's flagship sink. He made a plea for defining history as "contemporary thought about the past," arguing that "no historian can describe the past as it actually was and that every historian's work—that is, his selection of facts, his emphasis, his omissions, his organization, his method of presentation— bears a relation to his own personality and the age and circumstances in which he lives." Beard used Einstein's relativistic frame of reference as a metaphor, where "any selection and arrangement of facts pertaining to any large area of history, either local or world, race or class, is controlled inexorably by the frame of reference in the mind of the selector and arranger." In the end, "the validity of the Ranke formula and its elaboration as Historicism is destroyed by internal contradictions and rejected by contemporary thought. The historian's powers are limited. He may search for, but he cannot find, the 'objective truth' of history, or write it, 'as it actually was.'"[10]

This vision of historical relativity may be summarized as follows and compared point by point against the first tier:

1. History exists only in the minds of historians.

2. Historians construct the past much as a sculptor constructs a figure out of marble.

3. Historians know and describe the past only through available documentation, which covers no more than part of "what actually happened."

4. Historians cannot purge themselves of bias any more than those in other fields can, including those studying physical and biological phenomena.

5. There is no complete causal structure of contingent events in the past.

6. In their minds, historians construct a causal structure out of the available documentation.

7. Historians' job is to present this constructed past not "as it actually happened" but as it might have happened in one interpretation only.

The relativism of the 1920s through the 1940s declined in the 1950s as historians tried to shore up the profession. It then came back under a different covering cloth as literary criticism and deconstruction in the late 1960s and has maintained its popularity throughout the 1990s. Dominick LaCapra, for example, points out that in order to understand a document one must understand the context in which it was produced. He sees this as an impossible task because there are at least six contexts: "(1) The relation between the author's intentions and the text. (2) The relation between the author's life and the text. (3) The relation of society to texts. (4) The relation of culture to texts. (5) The relation of a text to the overall literary corpus of a writer. (6) The relation between modes of discourse and texts."[11] If history is just a form of literature, then historians can be no more discriminating about the quality of a historical work than an art critic can be about a work of art. A critic or historian may say "I like this work of art or history better than that one" but not "this one is *truer* than that one." This deconstruction of written sources seemingly undermines the historian's ability to know anything with confidence about the past. As the historian David Harlan bemoans: "It has questioned our belief in a fixed and determinable past, compromised the possibility of historical representation, and undermined our ability to locate ourselves in time."[12]

Here we find a seedbed for pseudohistory and Holocaust denial.

The Paradox of the Second Tier

Karl Marx notes in "The Eighteenth Brumaire" that "Hegel remarks somewhere that all great, world-historical facts and personages occur, as it were, twice. He has forgotten to add: the first time as tragedy, the second as farce."[13] For Marx, sneering at the political history of France, the first was Napoleon I and the second was Louis Bonaparte. For historians, relativism is the tragedy and deconstruction the farce. The paradox of the second tier is that we *must* assume that we can know *something* about the past or we would not, or could not, write history. As with the first tier, historians cannot remain on the second tier for long and practice their profession. In the act of writing history, relativists must step out of their relativism long enough to attempt communication. Like objectivism, relativism has its own agenda, only a nihilistic one—attacks on all forms of knowledge. Logically, the second tier cannot even exist. To enter it is to negate it. By presenting history, whether narrative or analytical, the historian builds a case for "what happened" through documentation and evidence. To attempt to do so is to admit that *something* can be known about the past, thus annihilating relativist nihilism. Like a decaying subatomic particle, as soon as the second tier forms, it disintegrates.

In his 1996 book, *The Killing of History*, the Australian historian Keith Windschuttle documents a perfect example of this paradox when he dismantles Greg Dening's 1992 book, *Mr. Bligh's Bad Language*, acclaimed as one of the great works of postmodern historiography. According to Dening, the numerous retellings of the mutiny on the *Bounty* in literature and film tell us more about the authors' and filmmakers' cultures than they do about the actual mutiny. Charles Laughton's Bligh and Clark Gable's Christian in the 1935 film, says Dening, present a tale of class conflict and of tyranny versus justice, clearly reflecting America in the 1930s. The 1962 film, with Trevor Howard as Bligh and Marlon Brando as Christian, changes the theme to one of naked profit seeking versus humane and liberal ideals, obviously mirroring the values of the period. The 1984 version flirts with a homosexual theme, with Anthony Hopkins's Bligh at once attracted to but outraged by Mel Gibson's Christian, who does not return his affections. According to Dening, history, as revealed in the various mutiny interpretations, is nothing more than an echo of the historian's times, an "illusion" of the past that is really our present. Dening tells his students that "history is something we make rather than something we learn." In the ultimate statement of historical relativism Dening explains, "I want to persuade them that any history they make will be fiction."[14] Does this include the history of the Holocaust?

So what really happened on the HMS *Bounty?* Dening says Bligh's "bad language" was so offensive to the men and so disrupted the hierarchical relationships on the ship that it triggered a mutiny. Imagine that, sailors offended by bad language! By language, however, Dening means more than obscenities. Bligh could not communicate with his men because he could not understand them. He was unable to deconstruct their meanings. Bligh, says Dening, "found it difficult to grasp the metaphors of being a captain, how it could mean something different to those being captained," and he "tended not to hear the good intentions or catch the circumstances and context in the language of others but demanded that others hear them in his."[15] To prove this claim and reject the commonly held hypothesis that the mutiny was triggered by Bligh's draconian punishments, Dening went to the archives and counted the number of floggings given to sailors on British ships in the Pacific in Bligh's era. He discovered that Bligh was far more humane than most captains, including James Cook (another deconstructionist poster boy, in Dening's pantheon).

Dening's historiography, Windschuttle notes in his own deconstruction of this deconstructionist, is interesting for two reasons. First, Dening very much reflects his own postmodern, deconstructionist culture of the 1980s and 1990s, in which textual analysis and theories of language specify how we should "read" history. This is precisely what Dening does in laying the blame on Bligh's language. Of course, Dening says history is nothing more than a reflection of the historian's culture, so we should not be surprised that his own approach reflects this. But, and this is the second point of interest, Dening has a problem. In order to convince readers that his approach is superior to other approaches to history, Dening must reject the earlier theories about the mutiny and prove that his is correct. To do so he presents *objective evidence,* such as the number of floggings Bligh instigated. In other words, Dening must temporarily abandon his own theory of history in order to support it. Windschuttle concludes: "If we accept his version of 'cultural literacy' and disown a realist and empiricist account of history, anything goes. We would have no means of distinguishing between history and myth, between biography and hagiography, between eyewitness reports and fairy tales. Without facts, we would lack one of the most important grounds for debate, for contesting someone else's versions of history."[16]

Consider the case of Michel Foucault, one of the most influential of all deconstructionists. In an oft-quoted passage from his book *The Order of Things,* Foucault claims that "a certain Chinese encyclopedia" classifies animals in the following categories: "(a) belonging to the Emperor, (b) embalmed, (c) tame, (d) suckling pigs, (e) sirens, (f) fabulous, (g) stray dogs, (h) included in the present classification, (i) frenzied, (j) innumerable, (k) drawn with a very fine camelhair brush, (l) et cetera, (m) having just broken the water pitcher, (n) that from a long way off look like flies."[17] This system demonstrates, says Foucault, that the Western taxonomic system is just one among many equally valid ways to classify animals.

Baloney. As Windschuttle reveals, there is no Chinese encyclopedia with such a taxonomy. Foucault's example is pure fiction, created by the poet Jorge Luis Borges. Even worse, Foucault cites Borges but says that the distinction between fact and fiction is unimportant (although those who cite Foucault typically fail to mention the fictional nature of the example). "That a piece of fiction can be seriously deployed to make a case in history or anthropology," Windschuttle concludes, "indicates how low debate has sunk in the postmodern era."[18]

Ironically, it is with issues such as Holocaust denial that all discussion of historical relativism ends. Ask deconstructionists if they think that the belief the Holocaust happened is as valid as the belief that it did not happen, and the debate quickly screeches to a halt. Dening, Foucault, and the other literary critics think that they reside on the second tier, but if they want to write history they must leave it and enter the third tier, the tier where history and science meet.

The Third Tier: Historical Science

The first two tiers—historical objectivity and historical relativism—both give rise to paradoxes that produce either historical "know-everything-ness" or "know-nothingness." A third tier—historical science—is the place practicing historians take up residence. This vision of historical science may be summarized as follows:

1. History exists both inside and outside the minds of historians.

2. Historians both discover and describe the past, just as natural scientists discover and describe natural phenomena.

3. Historians (and natural scientists) can discover and describe a defined portion of the past through the available data.

4. Since, like other human beings, historians cannot purge themselves of bias, the question turns to the quality and quantity of this bias. By what methods and with what evidence do scientists—historical or experimental—arrive at a particular conclusion? And in what cultural context? With whose funds?

5. Given the basic scientific assumption that all effects in the universe have causes, contingent events in the past too must have a causal structure.

6. Recognizing the objective nature of discovery and the subjective nature of description, historians can discover and describe this causal structure.

7. Historians' job is to present this past as a provisional interpretation of "what actually happened," based on current available evidence, much as natural scientists do with evidence from the natural world.

The paradox of history is resolved on the third tier—the tier where all historians reside when they are truly practicing history. Without this tier, there could be no progress of knowledge or advance in our understanding of the past. And it is on this tier where we can more easily distinguish between rational revision and dogmatic denial. Obviously there is a difference between reinterpreting the specific facts of some historical event within the context of the larger historical picture and denying those facts altogether. No one would deny, for example, that Robert E. Lee invaded the North in June 1863, met the Union army at Gettysburg, was beaten, and retreated to the South. We know with great confidence the basic facts of this Civil War battle. There is considerable dispute among Civil War historians, however, on a number of issues, including just how critical this battle was in turning the tide of the war (some would argue that Antietam/Sharpsburg was more important) and whether England would have recognized the Confederacy as a sovereign nation had Lee won (thus allowing the South access to needed supplies by helping to break the naval blockade). Here the facts do not just speak for themselves but must be interpreted. Still, we can use the methods of science to help us resolve such debates through the same methods that other historical sciences solve them—a scholar can marshal the evidence and apply tight logic, tempered with confidence intervals and error bars (to indicate the level of confidence in the findings and the range of probable error). Then, through peer review and discussion, other participants in the debate can register their own degree of confidence in the scholar's conclusions. This process is practiced by all scientists, including those working with data from the past, and has been used by Holocaust historians to revise our understanding of the Holocaust. In contrast, as we shall see, the Holocaust deniers do not use these methods.

James Kloppenberg calls this third-tier approach *pragmatic hermeneutics* and, as cited in this chapter's epigraph, speaks of "pragmatic truth" that provides "hypotheses, provisional syntheses, imaginative but warranted interpretations."[19] Two exemplary models of scientific history in recent years may be found in Frank Sulloway's *Born to Rebel,* in which he uses statistics to test hypotheses about why revolutions succeed or fail and who supports or opposes them, and Jared Diamond's Pulitzer Prize–winning *Guns, Germs, and Steel,* which utilizes the comparison method to understand why cultures developed at different rates around the world over the past thirteen thousand years.[20]

The method we employ in this book is what the nineteenth-century philosopher of science William Whewell called a "consilience of inductions," or what we call a "convergence of evidence." It is the same technique used by other historical scientists, such as cosmologists, geologists, paleontologists, and archaeologists, to prove that anything in the past happened.

A CONVERGENCE OF EVIDENCE: HOW WE KNOW THE HOLOCAUST HAPPENED

In August 1996 a panel of scientists from the National Aeronautics and Space Administration (NASA) announced that it might have discovered life on Mars. The evidence was the Allan Hills 84001 rock, which was believed to have been ejected from Mars by a meteor's impact millions of years ago and to then have landed on the earth. On the panel of NASA experts was the paleobiologist William Schopf, a historical scientist specializing in ancient life. Schopf was skeptical of NASA's claim because, he said, the four "lines of evidence" cited to support the find did not converge on a single conclusion. Instead, they pointed to several possible conclusions.[21]

Schopf's "lines of evidence" analysis reflects William Whewell's insistence on a consilience of inductions. To prove a theory, Whewell believed, scientists must have more than one induction, more than just a single generalization drawn from specific facts. They must have multiple inductions that converge upon one another, independently but in conjunction. Whewell said that if these inductions "jump together" it strengthens the plausibility of a theory: "Accordingly the cases in which inductions from classes of facts altogether different have thus jumped together, belong only to the best established theories which the history of science contains. And, as I shall have occasion to refer to this particular feature in their evidence, I will take the liberty of describing it by a particular phrase; and will term it the Consilience of Inductions."[22] For us, it is a convergence of evidence.

We know about the past through a convergence of evidence. Cosmologists use evidence from astronomy, astrophysics, planetary geology, and physics to tell the history of the universe. Geologists reconstruct the history of the earth through a convergence of evidence from geology and the related earth sciences. Archaeologists piece together the history of civilization using artwork, written sources, tools and weapons, and other site-specific artifacts. The historical theory of evolution gains confirmation by many independent lines of evidence converging on a single conclusion. Independent sets of data from geology, paleontology, botany, zoology, herpetology, entomology, biogeography, comparative anatomy, physiology, and many other sciences each point to the conclusion that life has evolved. Creationists demand "just one fossil transitional form" that shows evolution. But a single fossil cannot prove evolution. Evolution involves a convergence of fossils and many other lines of evidence, such as DNA sequence comparisons across species. For creationists to disprove evolution they would need to unravel all these independent lines of evidence and find a rival theory that can explain them better than evolution. They cannot, without invoking miracles, which are not a part of science.[23]

In a similar way, there is an assumption by deniers that if they can just find one tiny crack in the Holocaust structure, the entire edifice will come tumbling down. This is a fundamental flaw in their reasoning. *The Holocaust is not a single event that a single fact can prove or disprove.* The Holocaust was a myriad of events in a myriad of places and relies on myriad pieces of data that converge on one conclusion. Minor errors or inconsistencies here or there cannot disprove the Holocaust, for the simple reason that these lone bits of data never proved it in the first place. Here is a convergence of evidence that proves the Holocaust happened:

1. *Written documents*—hundreds of thousands of letters, memos, blueprints, orders, bills, speeches, articles, memoirs, and confessions

2. *Eyewitness testimony*—accounts from survivors, Jewish Sonderkommandos (who were forced to help load bodies from the gas chambers into the crematoria in exchange for the promise of survival), SS guards, commandants, local townspeople, and even high-ranking Nazis who spoke openly about the mass murder of the Jews

3. *Photographs*—including official military and press photographs, civilian photographs, secret photographs taken by survivors, aerial photographs, German and Allied film footage, unofficial photographs taken by the German military

4. *The camps themselves*—concentration camps, work camps, and extermination camps that still exist in varying degrees of originality and reconstruction

5. *Inferential evidence*—population demographics, reconstructed from the pre–World War II era: if six million Jews were not killed, what happened to them all?

A powerful example of convergence in practice can be found in the 1996 book on the history of Auschwitz coauthored by the social historian Deborah Dwork and the architectural historian Robert Jan van Pelt.[24] They examined original architectural blueprints, historical photographs, and extant ruins at the camp, which, in conjunction with requisition forms, transportation vouchers, planning permissions, bills of sale, and bills of receipt, corroborated all the eyewitness accounts, confessions, diaries, and letters. Dwork and van Pelt take these independent lines of evidence and weave them into a narrative history that both tells a story and tests a hypothesis. The hypothesis they test is that Auschwitz was originally planned to be an extermination camp. They reject this hypothesis and in its stead present a contingently functional hypothesis—that Auschwitz *evolved* into an extermination camp from its original plans (see chapter 6 below). Dwork and van Pelt's book is a good example of how history can be a science without losing any of its appeal as storytelling.

The Holocaust deniers (conveniently) disregard any convergence of evidence; instead, they pick out what suits their theory and ignore the rest. They divorce their chosen details from the overall context. We contend that instead of revising history, instead of modifying a theory based on new evidence or a new interpretation of old evidence, the Holocaust deniers are engaged in pseudohistory, the rewriting of the past for present personal or political purposes. Historical revision should not be based on political ideology, religious conviction, or other human emotions. Historians are humans with emotions, of course, but if they are true revisionists, and not ideologues, they will weed out the emotional chaff from the factual wheat.

By way of example, in May 1945 a report was submitted to the Congress of the United States entitled *Atrocities and Other Conditions in Concentration Camps in Germany*, as requested by Dwight D. Eisenhower after his visit to the camps. In this report the authors outline their own convergence of evidence:

> Three classes or kinds of evidence were presented to us. The first was the visual inspection of the camps themselves. . . . We saw the barracks, the work places, the physical facilities for torture, degradation, and execution. We saw the victims, both dead and alive, of the atrocities practiced at these camps. We saw the process of liquidation by starvation while it was still going on. We saw the indescribable filth and smelled the nauseating stench before it was cleaned up, and we saw a number of victims of this liquidation process actually die.
>
> The second kind of evidence we obtained was the testimony of eyewitnesses among the prisoners themselves to these atrocities. Many of the prisoners had been in the camps we visited as long as 3 and 4 years. While these prisoners included men from nearly all the countries of central Europe, whose speech, whose station in life, and whose education and previous environment differed widely from one another; yet the testimony of all of these witnesses was substantially the same.
>
> The third kind of evidence was what may be called the common knowledge of the camp, that is to say, evidence of things done in the camp which were not done publicly but which, nevertheless, all prisoners were aware of. These prisoners, from custom and experience, from the conversation with

the guards and among themselves, and from a very plain and almost mathematical kind of circumstantial evidence, have accurate knowledge of certain
things which they have not actually seen with their own eyes. It was the unan-
imous opinion of our committee after talking to hundreds of prisoners that
this third kind of evidence was often as accurate and reliable as the two kinds
of direct evidence.[25]

In the third section of this book—an example of historical science in
practice—we follow a pattern similar to that undertaken by Eisenhower's
committee, using the much greater amount of evidence now available to
show how it all converges on the conclusion that the Holocaust happened.
Our position is that the third tier's process of historical science resolves
the paradox of the tiers. Without this tier there could be no progress of
knowledge or advancement of our understanding of the past. The historical profession, like historical knowledge and understanding, is cumulative in this sense. The objectivists and relativists in our historical
methodological past are the giants upon whose shoulders we stand in
our quest for greater insight into human history. And yet we are obligated to move beyond their methods when we detect their flaws and when
there are new tools available. We are obligated to adopt the third tier as
our operational realm. This is where the noble dream lives.

part ii

Inside the Denial Movement

What makes this inquest significant is that these prisoners . . .
are the living symbols of racial hatreds, of terrorism and
violence, and of the arrogance and cruelty of power. . . .
Civilization can afford no compromise with the social forces
which would gain renewed strength if we deal ambiguously
or indecisively with the men in whom those forces now
precariously survive.

Justice Robert H. Jackson,
"Opening Statement,"
Nuremberg Trials, 1945

Who Says the Holocaust Never Happened?

An Inside Look at the Personalities and Organizations

The SS guards took pleasure in telling us that we had
no chance of coming out alive, a point they emphasized
with particular relish by insisting that after the war the rest
of the world would not believe what happened; there would
be rumors, speculation, but no clear evidence, and people
would conclude that evil on such a scale was just not
possible.

Terrence des Pres, *The Survivor*

In 1990, when he was preparing to run for the presidency, Pat Buchanan wrote a column that included this statement: "Diesel engines do not emit enough carbon monoxide to kill anybody." He went on to speculate that Holocaust survivors were unreliable as eyewitnesses because they were suffering from "group fantasies of martyrdom and heroics," and he concluded that gas chambers were not used at the camps to exterminate Jews.[1] Where did he come up with these claims? Was Pat Buchanan a Holocaust denier?

In the winter 1996 issue of *Reform Judaism* magazine, Charles Allen claimed that Buchanan was indeed a Holocaust denier and reported that he had gotten his information directly from the Institute for Historical Review, the leading Holocaust denial organization in the world. The institute's director, Mark Weber, told Allen: "Pat took all of our findings and worked [them] into his column." Allen proceeded to label Buchanan "the most effective . . . Holocaust denier in America."[2]

Allen's conclusion is something of an exaggeration, as we shall see below, but the story is emblematic of how far and wide such information can disperse across the cultural landscape. When we first encountered this phenomenon ourselves, we became curious about who these people are. Who in their right mind would say the Holocaust never happened? To find out, we met with the deniers in person and allowed them to present their claims in their own words. In general, we found them to be relatively pleasant and willing to talk about the movement and its members quite openly, and they were more than willing to provide a large sampling of their published literature. In history, however, as in all scientific endeavors, the facts never just speak for themselves—they are interpreted through colored lenses. To understand how the deniers' biases influence their interpretation of history, it is constructive to know something about their backgrounds and motivations.

The revisionist movement that eventually gave rise to Holocaust denial—a form of pseudohistory distinct from legitimate historical revision—has a long and complex history dating as far back as the 1930s, when such controversial historians as Harry Elmer Barnes and Sidney Fay challenged the establishment interpretation of World War I, specifically arguing that Germany had not wanted war, and questioned America's involvement in European affairs.[3] After the Second World War revisionism took hold in Germany with opposition to the Nuremberg trials, which were described as the "victor's trials" and seen as unfair and biased.[4] In the 1950s two arguments emerged that disputed German responsibility for the Second World War: (1) that *Weltjudentum* (world Jewry) had declared war on Germany in 1933, and the Nazis, as the ruling party of the nation, had simply reacted to the threat; (2) that because Germany had grown into an industrial and military power under Hitler's leadership in the 1930s, the Western powers had conspired against her by supporting Poland and had thus triggered World War II.[5] From this perspective, such events as the Wehrmacht's invasion of the Soviet Union in June 1941 were seen as defensive maneuvers—Hitler had to attack to preempt Stalin's invasion of Germany. Denial of the Holocaust itself took off in the 1960s and 1970s with Franz Scheidl's 1967 *Geschichte der Verfemung Deutschlands* (History of the ostracism of Germany), Emil Aretz's 1970 *Hexeneinmaleins einer Lüge* (Witches' multiplication of a lie), Thies Christophersen's 1973 *Auschwitz Lüge* (Auschwitz lie), Wilhelm Stäglich's 1973 *Auschwitz-Mythos* (Auschwitz myth), Richard Harwood's 1973 *Did Six Million Really Die?*, Austin App's 1973 *Six Million Swindle*, Paul Rassinier's 1978 *Debunking the Genocide Myth*, and what has become the bible of the movement, Arthur Butz's 1976 *Hoax of the Twentieth Century*. It is out of these volumes that the three pillars of Holocaust denial—no gas chambers, no six million murdered, no master plan—were crafted.

Some evidence has recently come to light that the first person to deny the Holocaust may have been a Scotsman named Alexander Ratcliffe, the leader of the Scottish and later British Protestant League, who was elected a councillor in Glasgow in 1933 on an anti-Catholic campaign.[6] During his service he published a magazine called *Vanguard,* in which he claimed in late 1945 and again in 1946 that the Holocaust was an invention of the Jews. The *Vanguard* statement was based on an earlier pamphlet by Ratcliffe entitled *The Truth about the Jews,* in which he also speculated about the Jewish control of the British government. "What Britain needs is a Hitler," Ratcliffe explained. But what about the Holocaust as a blight on Hitler's otherwise good name? The concentration camps, Ratcliffe answered, were "inventions of the Jewish mind."[7] But what about the newsreel footage of the carnage at Belsen and other camps? The films were "faked in Jewish cinemas." Ratcliffe credited as his source Count G. W. V. Potociki of Poland and the leader of the Imperial Protestant Guard of Great Britain, William John Tracey. Ratcliffe's *Vanguard* articles were cited in *Right Review* and other extreme right-wing publications, and from there found their way around the world. The information on Ratcliffe's Holocaust denial came out in mid-1998 when files on him, previously closed until 2022 (he died in 1947 at age fifty-nine), were opened as part of Scottish TV's *Secret Scotland* series, because of his anti-Catholic activities.

The first influential Holocaust "revisionist" was the French socialist Paul Rassinier, who participated in a pacifistic resistance movement in France during the war. After helping to smuggle Jews into Switzerland, he was arrested by the Gestapo in 1943 and spent the rest of the war in such concentration camps as Buchenwald and Dora. After the war Rassinier took notice of and offense at survivors' inaccuracies in their eyewitness accounts of life at the camps, including the claim that there were gas chambers at Buchenwald. His slide into revisionism and denial came when he made the shift from interpreting these accounts as the normal confabulation and confusion that occurs in all eyewitness testimony, to speculating that these people might be deliberately lying. From this assumption he extrapolated that the number of Jewish victims must also have been exaggerated and published his own estimate that only about one and a half million died in his book *Debunking the Genocide Myth: A Study of the Nazi Concentration Camps and the Alleged Extermination of European Jewry.*

Except for Butz's book, which curiously stays in circulation despite its publication more than two decades ago, these volumes have all given

Figure 1.   The cover of the November–December 1994
issue of the *Journal of Historical Review* features the
speakers at that year's twelfth IHR conference. These
are some of the most active members of the Institute for
Historical Review, including (from left) Robert Faurisson,
John Ball, Russ Granata, Carlo Mattogno, Ernst Zündel,
Friedrich Berg, Greg Raven, David Cole (center), Robert
Countess, Tom Marcellus, Mark Weber, David Irving, and
Jürgen Graf. (Courtesy the Institute for Historical Review)

way to the *Journal of Historical Review* (see figure 1), the voice of the
Institute for Historical Review (IHR). The institute's journal, along with
its annual conference, has become the focal point of the movement,
populated by a handful of highly motivated individuals, including the
director/editor Mark Weber, the author and biographer David Irving,
the ex-professor Robert Faurisson, the publisher Ernst Zündel, and, curiously, a denier of Jewish descent, David Cole.

THE INSTITUTE FOR HISTORICAL REVIEW

In 1978 Willis Carto founded and primarily organized the Institute for Historical Review. Carto published *Right* and *American Mercury* (which Mark Weber has described as ultra-conservative and mildly anti-Jewish magazines)[8] and runs Noontide Press, whose list of controversial books includes ones denying the Holocaust. Carto also runs Liberty Lobby, a right-wing organization that publishes *The Spotlight,* with a circulation in the hundreds of thousands, and has sponsored numerous radio programs such as *This Is Liberty Lobby* and *Radio Free America.* Carto's Populist Party ran former Ku Klux Klan leader David Duke for president in 1988.

In 1980 the IHR landed on the cultural landscape by making headlines with its $50,000 challenge for proof that Jews were gassed at Auschwitz: "The claimant should describe fully his evidence, providing specific names, dates, and locations of incidents, and the names of any other witnesses to such. . . . He should provide supporting documentary evidence such as diaries, photographs, film, official or unofficial documents, and also—some *forensic* evidence . . . if murder is to be proved, there must be the body or parts thereof of a *victim* or *victims,* called a *corpus delicte.*"[9] When the Holocaust survivor Mel Mermelstein responded by providing evidence in the form of his own and others' testimonies, he had to take the IHR to court to collect the reward—a trial that made headlines. Newspapers (and a television movie starring Leonard Nimoy) reported his collection of the award and an additional $40,000 for "personal suffering." The judge in the trial, Thomas T. Johnston, in a Los Angeles County Superior Court on October 9, 1981, took "judicial notice" that Jews were gassed in Auschwitz and therefore Mermelstein was awarded the money.[10] Mermelstein claims he succeeded in both proving the Holocaust and defeating the deniers, but Mark Weber, the IHR's current director, says the institute decided to pay the "nuisance suit" because it did not have the resources for an extended legal battle.[11] Soon after the trial the IHR's first director, William McCalden (aka Lewis Brandon, Sondra Ross, David Berg, Julius Finkelstein, and David Stanford), cofounder of the neo-Nazi British National Party, was fired in 1981 because of conflicts with Carto.[12] He was followed by Tom Marcellus, a field staff member for the Church of Scientology who had been an editor for one of the church's publications. When Marcellus left the institute in 1995, the *JHR* editor, Mark Weber, took over as director and remains there as of this writing.

Since a 1984 firebombing that destroyed its office, the IHR is under-standably cautious about revealing its location to outsiders. Situated in an industrial area, its headquarters has no sign outside, and the build-ing entrance is through a glass door with one-way mirrored coating. Be-cause the door is dead-bolted at all times, visitors must be identified and admitted by the secretary working in a small office in front. There are several offices for the various staff members and considerable shelf space for the voluminous library. In addition, there is a warehouse filled with back issues of the journal, pamphlets, promotional materials, books, and videotapes—part of IHR's catalog business. According to Weber, cata-log sales and subscriptions account for about 80 percent of the institute's revenue.[13] The other 20 percent comes from tax-free donations (it is a nonprofit organization). Whatever funds the organization was receiving through Willis Carto stopped when it became involved in lawsuits with him, which were the result of tensions over the direction the institute should take and what its goals should be.

In February 1994, as the relationship between Carto and the IHR be-gan to falter, the director, Tom Marcellus, did a mass mailing to mem-bers with "AN URGENT APPEAL FROM IHR" because it had "been forced to confront a threat to the editorial and financial integrity . . . that in the past several months has drained, and continues to drain, literally tens of thousands of dollars from our operations." Without the readers' help, the letter claimed, the "IHR may not survive." The letter accuses Carto of becoming "increasingly erratic" both in personal matters and in busi-ness, and of having "involved the corporation in three costly copyright violations." Most interestingly, and in keeping with the attempt to disas-sociate the movement from earlier antisemitic connections and present itself as a collective of objective historical scholars, the letter attacks Carto for changing "the direction of IHR and its journal from serious, non-partisan revisionist scholarship, reporting, and commentary to one of ranting, racialist-populist pamphleteering."[14]

As a result of the battle between Carto and the IHR, the nonprofit corporation's board of directors had voted to sever the ties between the two. Carto apparently did not take this lying down. According to the IHR appeal, not only had Carto "stormed IHR's offices with hired goons," but he had put "out the fantastic lie that the Zionist ADL has been running IHR since last September." The letter concludes with a dra-matic promise by Bradley Smith that if the IHR really is being run by the Anti-Defamation League, "I'll fly to Washington, DC, call a press con-ference, and eat my shorts on the front steps of the Liberty Lobby."[15]

Before this break with Carto, the IHR had leaned heavily on the "Edison money," a total of about $15 million willed by Thomas Edison's granddaughter, Jean Farrel Edison. According to David Irving, about $10 million of that money was apparently lost by Carto "in lawsuits by other members of the [Edison] family in Switzerland," and the remaining $5 million was made available to Carto's Legion for the Survival of Freedom. "From that point on it vanishes into uncertainty," Irving indicates. "Certain sums of money have turned up. A lot of it is in a Swiss bank at present."[16] The complex story remains to be sorted out through the courts. David Cole has predicted that "the IHR is going to have to depend a lot more on journal and book sales" and its right-wing backers:

> In order to keep the IHR in the black they have had to cater to the far right. I think if you were to look at their book sales you would see that some of the more complex, really solid historiographical works probably don't sell as well as Henry Ford's *International Jew* or the *Protocols of Zion* [books that allegedly prove a Jewish conspiracy to run the world], or some of the other things they sell [mostly books denying various aspects of the Holocaust and Germany's role in the Second World War]. If they had to rely on the sales of Holocaust revisionist works alone they'd be screwed. They have to cater to the money. There are a lot of elderly people with money saved or with social security checks, who want to spend the last years of their life fighting the Jews. Bradley [Smith] can get checks for $5,000, $7,000, $3,000. These people are very, very wealthy, and completely anonymous. There is a lot of money to be made by getting a really good ideological mailing list and the IHR has one that caters mainly to people of the far right.[17]

On December 31, 1993, the IHR won a judgment against Carto. It is now trying to recover damages caused by his raid on the IHR offices that destroyed equipment and ended in fisticuffs, as well as other monies that, Weber claims, went "to Liberty Lobby and other Carto-controlled enterprises. Probably the money has been frittered away by Carto but we are trying to track this down."[18] Despite these financial woes, the IHR continues to hold its annual conferences. The *JHR* continues to be published. Promotional literature and the book/video catalog are regularly mailed out. It appears that the IHR will survive the break with Carto— and even if it does not, we must remember that this movement is not a homogenous group held together through this single organization.

Take Ernst Zündel, for example. He says he is "negotiating a deal with an American satellite company who promised me that they can get a signal over Europe that can be picked up on satellite dishes."[19] We are told by some European followers of Zündel that he has had some success in this endeavor.[20] Zündel's goal is to move into the mainstream in Europe and America, where "I think in another fifteen years revisionism will be discussed over pretzels and beer."[21] Perhaps, but in the meantime Zündel's November 15, 1996 newsletter, *Power,* boasts such headlines as: "On direct order from Moscow Russians cancel Zündel 'Voice of Freedom' shows," and "Marxists demonstrate for seven hours outside Zündel headquarters to celebrate the 25th October 1917 Bolshevik Revolution." A photograph shows a protester holding a sign proclaiming "Burn Zündel Down," and Zündel explains that "the Marxist hoodlums . . . shouted in unison: 'Lock the Nazis in—burn the house down!' This happened over and over again, for more than half a day!"[22] It would appear pretzels and beer are not yet the order of the day.

Yet Zündel represents only one aspect of the movement. We must not discount the power and popularity of the (in our eyes) more dangerous comments coming from the mainstream right wing, represented by such figures as Pat Buchanan, whose presidential candidacy was serious enough to result in a near-standoff at the 1990 Republican convention. Moreover, we must keep in mind that the denier movement, like all social movements, is driven by individuals motivated toward a cause. There is no question that those who deny the Holocaust "really believe" in their cause. But what exactly are they denying? What precisely do they think happened or did not happen?

MARK WEBER

Within the denier movement, with the possible exception of David Irving, Mark Weber has the most knowledge of Holocaust history. (Weber's master's degree in Modern European History from Indiana University is not, as some have alleged, faked. We called the university. His degree is real.) Weber arrived on the denier scene with his appearance as a defense witness at Ernst Zündel's "free speech" trial in Canada. At the time Weber denied any racist or antisemitic feelings and claimed: "I don't know anything more about the neo-Nazi movement in Germany than what I read in the papers."[23] Yet Weber was once the news editor of the *National Vanguard,* the voice of William Pierce's neo-Nazi organization, the National Alliance. Some of his sentiments came out in a 1989 interview for the *University of Nebraska Sower,* when he expressed his fear that the United States was becoming "a sort of Mexicanized, Puerto Ricanized country" owing to the failure of "white Americans" to reproduce adequately.[24] More to the point, on February 27, 1993, Weber was the victim of a Simon Wiesenthal Center sting operation in which the researcher Yaron Svoray, calling himself Ron Furey, met with Weber in a café to discuss *The Right Way*, a magazine invented to trick neo-Nazis into identifying themselves. The meeting was secretly filmed by CBS, but Weber quickly figured out that Svoray "was an agent for someone" and "was obviously lying."[25] Weber left not realizing that the Wiesenthal Center would turn this episode into a media event by claiming it had uncovered American connections to European neo-Nazis. Subsequently, Weber was portrayed in an HBO movie about Svoray's investigation of neo-Nazis in Europe and America. Weber claims that the film version of the event, in which Weber is seen inquiring about the magazine and providing information on European neo-Nazis (the Furey character in the movie breathlessly exclaims to his companion, upon answering the phone, "It's Mark Weber," as if it were Hitler himself on the line), is greatly distorted. But why, we might wonder, if Weber is trying to distance himself—as he claims—from the neo-Nazi fringe of denial, did he even agree to such a meeting?

Weber is extremely bright and very personable. He is highly motivated and tightly focused on his goal of exposing the Holocaust for what he thinks it is. He knows history and current politics and is a formidable debater on any number of subjects. One of these topics is "the Jews," whom he generalizes into a unified whole and suggests presents a unified threat to American and world culture. Weber seems not to discriminate between individual Jews, whose actions he may like or dislike, and "the Jews," whose actions he generally dislikes. For example, in an interview Weber justified the IHR's attitude toward "the Jews":

> We focus on the Jews because just about everyone else is afraid to. Part of the reason we exist, and part of the pleasure, is to be able to deal with a subject that others are not dealing with in a way that we feel helps provide information on what is relevant. I wish that the same considerations were given in our society to talking about Germans, or Ukrainians, or Hungarians, that are given to talking about the Jews. We permit and encourage in our society what would be considered vicious stereotypes if applied to other groups, when they are applied to the Germans or the Hungarians. This is a double standard, of which the Holocaust campaign is the most spectacular manifestation. The IHR and those affiliated with us feel a sense of liberation in that we say, in effect, we don't give a damn if you criticize us or not. We're going to say it anyway. We don't have a job to lose because this is our job.[26]

Weber's attitude about his "job" of criticizing Jews was evident at the March 28, 1998, conference of the IHR.[27] Addressing approximately 130 people in Costa Mesa, California, Weber began his presentation by observing that to gain a United States entry visa applicants must declare that they did not participate in the Nazi regime. Weber concluded that it is unfair to single out the Nazis and not target other groups—the Communists, for example. Why, Weber asked, do we have this double standard, where only persecution of the Jews, but no one else, is noted on the visa entry application? Would the Chinese, he wondered, require entering Americans to sign a statement that they did not participate in the Korean War? Why, Weber continued, do we support President Clinton's justification for conflict against Iraq for its crime of defying the United Nations, given that we did not hold Israel to the same standard twenty years earlier, when they defied the U.N. by refusing to withdraw from Lebanon? The bottom line, he summed up, is that "the traditional enemy of truth" (the Jews) receive special status in America, whereas almost everyone else is given an inferior status.[28] Indeed, the catch phrase of the evening was "the traditional enemy of truth," which did not need defining among this group.

But is Weber's own use of this term selective—does he have his own double standard? David Cole, who is his friend, states, "Weber doesn't really see any problems with a society that is not only disciplined by fear and violence, but also where a government feeds its people lies in order to keep them well-ordered." Ironically, says Cole, "revisionists criticize the Jews for lying to its people or the world, and yet a lot of these same deniers will speak very complimentarily of what the Nazis did in feeding their people lies and falsehoods in order to keep morale up and to keep this notion of the master race."[29]

Although Mark Weber comes off as a likable antagonist, when pushed on such issues as "the Jews," he seems tough-minded and pugnacious. In our opinion, he is a true believer in every sense of the phrase and therefore embodies the spirit of the organization he heads—a crusader on an ideological mission.

DAVID IRVING

There is no more paradoxical character in the Holocaust denial movement than the British author David Irving. He aspires to the respect and recognition of the scholarly historical community, while occasionally scorning them for their inability to see in his work the value he perceives there. He accuses academic historians of pomposity and verbosity, but his own comments at times reflect these traits. It seems he would love nothing more than the opportunity to address an audience of World War

II historians, to regale them with tales of his breathless discoveries among the Nazi archives and documents, yet his repeated appearances before Holocaust denial conferences tend to rule out any such opportunity. The elder statesman of German historians, Hans Mommsen, wrote of him in 1978: "It is our good fortune to have an Irving. At least he provides fresh stimuli for historians."[30] Irving proudly displayed the endorsement on his Web site until Mommsen wrote to him on July 21, 1998, requesting its removal: "While I still recognize several among your scholarly contributions in the field of Nazi history, although I altogether reject the turn in your judgement with respect to the Holocaust and other aspects, I certainly do not appreciate to get involved in your internet campaign. Hence, I urge you to omit quotations like the utterance made by me in 1978, the context of which is no longer comprehensible for the public."[31]

The author of World War II histories, *The Destruction of Dresden* and *The German Atomic Bomb,* as well as *The Trail of the Fox* (about Rommel), *Göring, Churchill's War,* and his most controversial book, *Hitler's War,* David Irving is arguably the most historically sophisticated of the deniers. The American publication of his biography of the Nazi propaganda minister Joseph Goebbels was canceled at the last moment because of the controversy generated in the media upon the realization that its author was associated with Holocaust denial. Irving's agent received a terse note from the publisher, St. Martin's Press: "The Work as delivered has been found to be unsatisfactory by the Publisher." But the editor, Irving says, "had not read it" because "the Goebbels manuscript was not mailed to St. Martin's until four weeks after the date of his letter." In the meantime, Irving says that the publisher has tried to retrieve the "six-figure advance," but he maintains that his contract does not allow such an action. The book, lavishly illustrated with color photographs, was subsequently published (in 1996) by Irving's own London-based publishing firm, Focal Point, which maintains most of his works in print.[32]

Irving has no professional training in history, and although he disclaims any official affiliation with the IHR ("you will see that my name isn't on the masthead"),[33] he often speaks at IHR conventions and lectures to denier groups around the world—activity at least suggesting that he is an apologist for the Holocaust deniers, if not for Hitler and the Nazis. (In a 1994 interview with one of us he claimed: "Without Hitler the State of Israel probably would not exist today so to that extent he was probably the Jews' greatest friend.")[34] Irving's attitudes about the Holocaust have evolved, beginning in 1977 with his $1,000 public challenge to historians to produce the long-sought *Führerbefehl*—the order

from Hitler to exterminate the Jews (at this time Irving believed the Holocaust happened but that Hitler did not order it).[35] No document was produced, but Irving gained publicity for his challenge. After reading Fred
Leuchter's *Leuchter Report,* which denies the homicidal use of gas
chambers, Irving began to deny major features of the Holocaust (such
as the use of gas chambers for mass murder), not just Hitler's involvement.[36] In this context, however, his remarks are not always consistent.
In a 1994 interview he estimated that 600,000 Jews were killed in World
War II, but on a July 27, 1995, Australian radio show, Irving admitted
that perhaps as many as four million Jews died at the hands of the Nazis:
"I think, like any scientist, I'd have to give you a range of figures and I'd
have to say a minimum of one million, which is monstrous, depending
on what you mean by killed. If putting people into a concentration camp
where they die of barbarity and typhus and epidemics is killing, then I
would say the four million figure because, undoubtedly, huge numbers
did die in the camps in conditions that were very evident at the end of
the war."[37]

   After Irving testified for the defense in Ernst Zündel's 1988 "free
speech" trial in Canada, various governments filed notices of entry denial and deportation against him. As he recounts on his Web page, his
publishing firm, Focal Point, has received notices from bookstores in England canceling distribution of *Hitler's War* and other titles. "Following
complaints from valued customers we no longer feel able to stock this
title," read one notice from a Sheffield bookstore in July 1992. Also in
the same year, the director of Media House Publications in Johannes-
burg, South Africa, informed Irving that with regard to *Hitler's War,* "I
don't want any copies on our premises. We have had some incidents already. Many of our book buyers are Jewish. It is much easier for [my
staff] now to say, 'We don't stock the book.'"[38]

   Where Irving goes, trouble sometimes follows. In May 1992, for example, Irving told a German gathering that the reconstructed gas chamber at Auschwitz I was "a fake built after the war."[39] The following month
when he landed in Rome, he was surrounded by police and put on the
next plane to Munich, where he was charged under the German law of
"defaming the memory of the dead." He was fined DM3,000. Pugilist
that he appears to be, Irving appealed the conviction, but it was upheld
and the fine increased to DM30,000 (about $20,000), made all the worse
by the fact that at a public meeting in downtown Munich Irving called
the judge a "senile, alcoholic cretin."[40] In late 1992, while in California,
he received notice from the Canadian government that he would not be

allowed into that country. He went anyway to receive a George Orwell award from a conservative free speech organization, whereupon he was arrested by the Royal Canadian Mounted Police. Irving was led away in handcuffs and deported on the grounds that his German conviction made him a likely candidate for future hate speech violations. Erwin Nest, executive director of the Pacific region for the Canadian Jewish Congress, was quoted: "I believe that should David Irving be allowed to travel throughout Canada, personally disseminating his views denying the historical fact of the Holocaust with the attendant publicity arising thereby, this would cause both personal trauma to Holocaust survivors and their families, as well as to other survivors of Nazi concentration camps, and likely cause a noticeable increase in the manifestation of antisemitic incidents in Canada."[41] Irving has been barred from entering Canada, Australia, New Zealand, Italy, Germany, and South Africa, although these bans are not always enforced.

Though his attentions have spanned the scope of the Second World War, particularly from the German perspective, his interest in the Holocaust has grown. "I think that the Holocaust is going to be revised," he states. "I have to take my hat off to my adversaries and the strategies they have employed—the marketing of the very word Holocaust: I half expect to see the little 'TM' after it."[42] For Irving, denial has become a war: "I'm presently in a fight for survival. My intention is to survive until five minutes past D-Day rather than to go down heroically five minutes before the flag is finally raised. I'm convinced this is a battle we are winning."[43] On his Web page are claims (in the third person) that "certain of the world's organizations have targeted him for a campaign of harassment at every level, designed to injure, smear, and if possible ruin him." How will they accomplish this feat? "Their campaign has recruited people at every level, from jobless street-people to dentists, from immigration officials to prime ministers." But Irving will not capitulate: "The Englishman is fighting back with every legal means."[44]

At the 1995 IHR conference in Irvine, California, Irving was the featured speaker before an extremely receptive audience. When not speaking, Irving staffed his own book table, selling and signing his many works. Purchasers of *Hitler's War* received a miniature swastika flag like the one mounted on Hitler's black Mercedes. One conversation Irving had with a couple of fans included his explanation of the worldwide "Jewish cabal" that was trying to prevent his books from being published and impede him from giving talks.[45] He readily makes public comments about what "the Jews" are doing, yet appears surprised and hurt by Jewish groups' reactions to his speech-making. At the 1995 UC Berkeley incident (recounted in chapter 1), for example, Irving was brought in by a student free speech group, but his lecture was picketed by other students and local Jewish groups who attempted to prevent him from speaking. The circumstances of the protest clearly suggest that it was a local and spontaneous reaction rather than a worldwide, planned conspiracy. Irving, however, did not seem to make this distinction.

Irving considers himself an intellectual, but it is his activism that not only generates the greatest attention but obscures much of his scholarly work. In 1995, for example, Irving attended a lecture on Holocaust denial by the Holocaust historian Deborah Lipstadt, who penned a book about the deniers. At the end of the lecture he stood up and announced his presence, whereupon—he claims—he was "swamped" by audience members asking for his autograph (we suspect there may be some hyperbole here).[46] Irving says he had brought a box of copies of his biography *Göring* and gave them away so the students could see "which of us is lying." Yet if, as Irving argues, there were no plan to exterminate the Jews, then what should these students make of this passage from Irving's book?

> Emigration was only one possibility that Göring foresaw. "The second is as follows," he said in November 1938, selecting his words with uncharacteristic care. "If at any foreseeable time in the future the German Reich finds itself in a foreign political conflict, then it is self-evident that we in Germany will address ourselves first and foremost to effecting a grand settling of scores against the Jews."[47]

Since Irving claims that emigration is all the Nazis ever meant by *ausrotten* (extermination) and the Final Solution (see detailed discussion in chapter 8), then just what did Hermann Göring mean here by "the second" plan? And what will these students think about this later passage in Irving's book?

> History now teaches that a significant proportion of those deported—particularly those too young or infirm to work—were being brutally disposed of on arrival. The surviving documents provide no proof that these killings were systematic; they yield no explicit orders from "above," and the massacres themselves were carried out by the local Nazis (by no means all of them German) upon whom the deported Jews had been dumped. That they were *ad hoc* extermination operations is suggested by such exasperated outbursts as that of Governor-General Hans Frank at a Krakau [Kraków] conference on December 16, 1941: "I have started negotiations with the aim of sweeping them [further] to the east. In January there is to be a big conference in Berlin on this problem [the Wannsee conference of January 20, 1942] . . . under SS-

Obergruppenführer [General] Heydrich. At any rate a big Jewish exodus will begin. . . . But what's to become of the Jews? Do you imagine they're going to be housed in neat estates in the Baltic provinces? In Berlin they tell us: What's bugging you—we've got no use for them either, liquidate them yourselves!"[48]

"Berlin," explains Irving, "more likely meant the party—or Himmler, Heydrich, and the SS." The above quotation is Irving's translation and interpretation (Irving reads and speaks fluent German), but we fail to see how Frank's words can be interpreted to support an assertion of *"ad hoc"* nonsystematic killings with no orders from above. This passage, in conjunction with many others (see chapter 8), makes the killings appear very systematic, on orders that did come—directly or tacitly—from above, and the only thing ad hoc about the process was the contingent and incremental development of the Final Solution. What can "liquidate" possibly mean other than exactly what Holocaust historians have always said that it means?

To our minds, one defining factor in Irving's on-again/off-again flirtation with denial is that he earns his living by lecturing and selling books (a difficult challenge for any author). Seemingly, the more he revises the Holocaust, the more books he sells and the more lecture invitations he receives from denier and right-wing groups. The irony is that he appears, in our opinion, to have little respect for the people who constitute his most receptive audience, an audience far outside the mainstream academy. He told the journalist Ron Rosenbaum: "I find it odious to be in the same company as these people. There is no question that there are certain organizations that propagate these theories which are cracked antisemites." But, he adds, "what else can I do? If I've been denied a platform worldwide, where else can I make my voice heard? As soon as I get back onto regular debating platforms I shall shake off this ill-fitting shoe which I'm standing on at present. I'm not blind. I know these people have done me a lot of damage, a lot of harm, because I get associated then with those stupid actions."[49]

Many historians recognize Irving as a first-rate archivist. But he seems, to our minds, to use a lot of selective quoting and creative speculation to support his beliefs. Consider how he has handled a manuscript that appears to several well-regarded authorities to be the memoirs of Adolf Eichmann, one of the prime architects of the Final Solution—a manuscript given to Irving in 1991 while on a lecture tour in Argentina. Immediately following a lecture, Irving recounts, "a guy came out to me with a brown-paper package. And he said, 'You're obviously the correct repository for these papers that we've been looking after since 1960 for the Eichmann family.' See, the Eichmann family panicked when he was kidnapped in the streets. And they took all his private papers which they could find, that had any kind of bearing, put them into brown paper and gave them to a friend. Then he gave them to this man who gave them to me, who gave them to the German government." In the manuscript, Irving explains, Eichmann "refers on many occasions to a discussion he had with Heydrich at the end of September or October, 1941, in which Heydrich says, in quotation marks, these two lines: 'I come from the Reichführer [Heinrich Himmler]. He has received orders from the Führer for the physical destruction of the Jews.'"[50]

It could not be any clearer than that, right? Wrong. Any potentially damaging document is susceptible to spin-doctoring. While admitting that "it rocked me back on my heels frankly because I thought 'Oops!,'" Irving recovered in time to "tell myself, 'Don't be knocked off your feet by this one.'"[51] The easy solution would have been to announce that the Eichmann memoir was a fake, but this would have contradicted the verdict of the German Federal Archives at Koblenz, which determined that the memoir is authentic. In 1992 Irving confessed, "Quite clearly this has given me a certain amount of food for thought and I will spend much of this year thinking about it. They [the memoirs] show that Eichmann believed there was a Führer order." With intellectual honesty, he added: "It makes me glad I have not adopted the narrow-minded approach that there was no Holocaust."[52] As time passed, however, Irving concluded that the memoir is real, but Eichmann lied about the *Führerbefehl*. Why? As he told Ron Rosenbaum in an elaborate rationalization, during the Suez crisis in 1956 Eichmann worried that if Israel conquered Cairo the Israelis might intercept intelligence files on fugitive Nazis in South America, possibly leading to his capture and arrest. Imaginatively, Irving picks up the story: "Eichmann must have had sleepless nights, wondering what he's going to do, what he's going to say to get off the hook. And though he's not consciously doing it, I think his brain is probably rationalizing in the background, trying to find alibis. The alibi that would have been useful to him in his own fevered mind would be if he could say that Hitler—*all* he did was carry out [Hitler's] orders." Eichmann, Irving speculates, inserted into his memoir the phrase "Der Führer hat richt der Ausrottung der Juden befohlen"—"The Führer has ordered the extermination of the Jews"—so that if he were ever captured his defense would be that he was merely following orders.[53] Eichmann was, of course, captured and tried, and his defense included this argument, along with a moral equivalency that made all sides in the war equally guilty

Figure 2.   David Irving, at the 1998 Institute for
Historical Review conference, gestures toward a
poster of Hitler and some of his military staffers
as he sells books. (Courtesy *Skeptic* magazine)

of atrocities. That defense worked about as well as it did at Nuremberg—
Eichmann was executed.

Irving's slant toward the deniers' take on the Holocaust was apparent at the 1998 IHR conference in Costa Mesa, California, at which he
was the keynote speaker. As customary, Irving set up a table at the back
of the room with his numerous books, including his latest works on
Goebbels and new editions of *The Destruction of Dresden* and his book
on the Nuremberg trials. In a box and under glass, Irving featured an
original self-portrait sketch of and by Hitler himself, given to Irving by
one of Hitler's secretaries whom he had interviewed for his research. He
autographed books against a backdrop of large color posters of Hitler
and his generals (see figure 2). He and several attendees conversed in
German, and one elderly gentleman handed him a check "for the fight
against our traditional enemy," with both parties understanding the jargon.[54] Irving began his lecture by, paradoxically, distancing himself from
his audience, saying that what he does is "alternative history," or "real
history," but not "revisionism." He gave out his Web page address to
listeners who wanted updates on his various activities and fights against
"the traditional enemy." He received an enthusiastic applause when he

announced that no matter what the "traditional enemy" did to him, he was in the fight for the duration.

Irving then segued into discussing his next volume on Winston Churchill. There is compelling evidence, Irving claimed, that Churchill knew about the planned attack on Pearl Harbor in time to notify the Americans, but that he chose not to in order to galvanize the American public into joining the British fight against the Nazis. Irving based his conclusion on the now famous "winds" communiqué, a coded message from Japan to the various Japanese embassies, which both the Americans and the British were deciphering. These messages were disguised as weather reports, such as "east wind strong," which meant war against the United States and Great Britain. Irving implied that it is even possible that Roosevelt knew about the attack ahead of time and chose not to alert Pearl Harbor in order to squelch the noninterventionist followers of Charles Lindbergh, who felt that America should stay out of any further European entanglements. The evidence for these claims, however, depends on triangulating numerous diary passages, letters, telegrams, and possibly altered documents, all presented in Irving's book (but not in his lecture). The strongest conclusion we can draw from what Irving has found in the archives still seems to be, at best, a maybe.

In the discussion following the lecture Irving mentioned that he had filed suit against the Holocaust historian Deborah Lipstadt, author of *Denying the Holocaust,* along with the British publishing arm of Penguin Books (which published her book in the United Kingdom), for libel. Irving filed in England because, he explained, British libel laws are much stiffer than they are in America. The specific points Irving considers to be libelous are outlined in his *Action Report* of December 1, 1997, and on his Web page. He comments there: "This trial is not about whether or not Jews were persecuted in WW II (they were), but whether or not Lipstadt . . . peddled her lies about me, on orders from Yad Vashem and various other Holocaust educational trusts."[55]

As of this writing the suit was still going on. Regardless of how it unfolds, Irving sees himself as a soldier in a war, not unlike that of a half-century ago. But this Englishman would appear to identify more closely with his country's enemy of that time. Why?

Irving has had a long fascination with all things German. As a boy born in England in 1938, he recalls the "great deprivations" of the war, including going "through childhood with no toys. We had no kind of childhood at all. We were living on an island that was crowded with other people's armies."[56] In the press, he says, he witnessed the cartoon caricatures of the Nazi leaders: "There was fat old Göring and Hitler with his postman's hat, and there was Dr. Goebbels, who was shorter and had one leg shorter. And it seemed to me at that time, as a youngster, there was something odd in the fact that these cartoon characters were able to inflict so much indignity and deprivation on an entire country like ours." To find out, after the war Irving moved to Germany and worked in a steel factory in order to learn the language. It was here that he first heard about the Allied mass bombing of Dresden (from the German perspective, of course), which eventually led to his book *The Destruction of Dresden,* and his decision to be a writer. His empathy for the plight of the Germans during the war led to his sympathetic portrayal of the Nazi leaders and drew him toward what he calls "the Magic Circle"— the surviving former Hitler confidants.[57]

Sociologists are aware of the problem of a researcher's "co-option" by a group—a cult or New Age religion, perhaps—whereby the scholar, in entering a group and spending considerable time with its members, publishes a paper or book that is not as objective as he or she may believe. In fact, the sociologists Stephen Kent and Theresa Krebs have identified numerous cases of "when scholars know sin," where allegedly nonpartisan, unbiased scholars find themselves the unwitting tools of religious groups striving for social acceptance and in need of the imprimatur of an academic. The problem is not merely one of exposure.[58] The groups want the mainstream credibility that they can get from the academy, and academics want the original research projects that they can get from studying such groups. The process involves a feedback loop between scholar and subject, where the more sympathetic the scholar appears, the more the subject opens up with honest portrayals of the group. It is not enough for the scholar to fake a conciliatory attitude. Humans are good at detecting deception. The best way to beat a lie detector is to believe the lie yourself—that way your body will not betray you.[59] Deception becomes self-deception.

Is it possible that Irving entered the realm of self-deception when he engaged the Magic Circle? "I carried out major interviews with all these people on tape. And what struck me very early on . . . is that you're dealing with people who are educated people." Hitler, he explained, "had attracted a garniture of high-level educated people around him. The secretaries were top-flight secretaries. The adjutants were people who had gone through university or through staff college and had risen through their own abilities to the upper levels of the military service."[60] These

Hitler confidants had thorough professional training, and they spoke highly of their Führer. "Coming as I did with an as-yet-unpainted canvas, this was really the seminal point, the seminal experience—to find twenty-five people of education, all of whom privately spoke well of him. Once they'd won your confidence and they knew that you weren't going to go and report them to the state prosecutor, they trusted you. And they thought, well, now at last they were doing their chief a service." Here, we suggest, was the co-option of David Irving. It is one thing to assert "they trusted you," but what does it mean to say "they'd won your confidence"? Had Hitler's war become Irving's war? It is our opinion that David Irving struck a Faustian bargain and is now paying the price.

ROBERT FAURISSON

Once a senior lecturer in literary criticism at the University of Lyon-2, Robert Faurisson (figure 3) has been dubbed the "Pope of Revisionism" by the Australian Holocaust deniers for his tireless efforts in challenging the first of the three pillars of Holocaust denial: no gas chambers. Throughout the 1980s Faurisson generated numerous works including a 304-page book entitled *Mémoire en défense contre ceux qui m'accusent de falsifier l'histoire* (Memoir of defense against those who accuse me of falsifying history), published by La Vieille Taupe in Paris. In America this work drew considerable attention when it became widely known that the renowned linguist, political activist, and free-speech advocate Noam Chomsky had contributed a preface. Chomsky made it clear he had penned the preface in defense of Faurisson's right to free speech, but some people questioned Chomsky's judgment in aligning himself in any way with Faurisson.[61] For his countless statements, letters, articles, and essays challenging Holocaust historians to "show me or draw me a Nazi gas chamber," as well as his pamphlet "The 'Problem of the Gas Chambers,'" Faurisson lost his job and was physically beaten up; he has been tried, convicted, fined, and barred from holding any government jobs in France.[62] Faurisson's convictions come under the Fabius-Gayssot law (enacted, in part, in response to Faurisson's activities), which makes it a criminal offense "to contest by any means the existence of one or more of the crimes against humanity as defined by Article 6 of the Statutes of the International Military Tribunal, attached to the London Agreement of August 8, 1945, committed either by the members of an organization declared criminal in application of Article 9 of the same

Figure 3. Called the "Pope of Revisionism" by some deniers, Robert Faurisson has become known for his demand to "show me or draw me a Nazi gas chamber." (Courtesy Ernst Zündel)

Statutes, or by a person held guilty of such a crime by a French or International jurisdiction."[63]

Faurisson has focused on the scientific and literary aspects of the Holocaust. Scientifically, he has attempted to show that mass gassings were impossible, by comparing eyewitness accounts with gassings of single prisoners in U.S. executions and with commercial applications of the gas Zyklon-B. Linguistically, he employs the tools of literary deconstruction and textual criticism to examine the internal use of certain words and phrases in documents related to the Holocaust. In a 1987 publication, for example, he claimed that the British Holocaust historian Martin Gilbert had misstated the size of a gas chamber in order to make it fit an eyewitness account of the number of Jews gassed there on a particular occasion.[64] Faurisson failed to take into account the simple fact that eyewitness details may be inadvertently inaccurate (in this case possibly exaggerated) and thus perhaps Gilbert's source was incorrect. He made a similar blunder over his analysis of the famous Gerstein document. Kurt Gerstein was an SS officer involved in ordering Zyklon-B gas used for both delousing and homicide who, before he died in captivity after the war, gave testimony to the homicidal use of the fumigant. Faurisson and others looked for internal contradictions in his confession, claiming, for example, that the number of victims packed into the gas chambers could not have physically fit. It turns out that Faurisson was basing his estimates on the number of people who fit comfortably into a subway car; others (including deniers) have since disproved his estimates.[65]

Faurisson likes to bait his opponents, whom he calls "exterminationists." On a trip to America for the IHR conference in Newport Beach in 1995, Faurisson visited the U.S. Holocaust Memorial Museum and arranged a meeting with one of its directors. As Faurisson later recounted at the IHR conference, he egged his host on about the "lack of proof" that Nazi gas chambers were used for mass murder and managed to trigger an emotional outburst, indicating—Faurisson claimed—that truth had once again triumphed over propaganda.[66] At the conference Faurisson invited one of us (Shermer) to his room to discuss in private the gas chamber story. For half an hour Faurisson held forth, wagging his finger and demanding "one proof, just one proof" that a Nazi gas chamber was used for mass murder. To the repeated counterquestion, "What would you consider *proof?*" Faurisson was unwilling (or unable) to answer. We suspect that the reason for his silence is that Robert Faurisson has no interest in empirical evidence or logical analysis. He is a protagonist, with the apparent goal of pushing a certain point of view. Of all the deniers we met, in fact, Robert Faurisson seems to be the most interested in actively stirring things up, getting in people's faces, and generating controversy. When it comes to the Holocaust, agitation appears to be his raison d'être.

BRADLEY SMITH

In his revealing 1987 book, *Confessions of a Holocaust Revisionist,* Bradley R. Smith describes himself as a fifty-seven-year-old, five-foot ten-inch, 240-pound high school graduate who has "been writing for thirty-five years without making a dime from it and now I am taking money to write for anti-semitic racists." He admits, "I will never be able to disprove these charges," but adds, "I have always written what I wanted and how I wanted." And now "I write what I want" and "I get paid for some of it. Everybody needs an income, even me."[67] More important, we contend, everyone needs a cause, a reason for being, and it appears that Bradley Smith has found his in Holocaust denial. How else would a man in his position find himself featured on such national television programs as *60 Minutes* and *Donahue*, or pictured in such national publications as *Time* magazine?[68]

Smith's denial began when he read Robert Faurisson's "The 'Problem of the Gas Chambers,'" in which the Frenchman points out that soon after the war many camps were said to have contained gas chambers, but it was later discovered that some of these claims were in error. For Faurisson, and subsequently for Smith, this calls into doubt *all* accounts of gas chambers and gassings in *all* camps, including Auschwitz. As he made clear in his appearance, along with David Cole, on *Donahue,* Smith does not deny that there was rampant antisemitism in Europe, that Jews were badly treated and even concentrated in camps where they suffered horribly at the hands of the Nazis. "A thousand-year-old Jewish culture in Eastern Europe was destroyed in three or four years," he has commented. "It doesn't offend me if someone wants to say that was a Holocaust." Like most of the other deniers, Smith disclaims the gas chambers, the six million figure, and the intention of the Nazis to exterminate European Jewry. But more than this, Smith "got interested in the Holocaust business when I discovered that there's a taboo against questioning what's been written about it."[69]

As Smith has explained, he became "crazily preoccupied" with Arthur Butz's book, *The Hoax of the Twentieth Century.*[70] In that book Butz claims that Raul Hilberg's 1961 classic work, *The Destruction of the European Jews,* was fraudulent in its reliance on eyewitness accounts of gassings at Auschwitz. Butz challenged Hilberg to prove his case with additional evidence. Hilberg answered with silence. This reaction bothered Smith more than the subject itself:

> Hilberg had published his book in 1961. Now Butz had replied to it. The ball was in Hilberg's court, but he didn't want to play. Why not? More than that, nobody else had responded to Butz either. . . . Hilberg had the support and respect of every historian in America but he was unwilling to respond to his one critic, Butz. . . . Butz had done the fair thing. He had published his book. He had called the Hilbergs of the world to account. He had called a spade a spade. Hilberg and the intellectuals had refused to answer Butz.[71]

For Smith, it seems, the elitism of the academy (and its attendant refusal to answer him and his companions) is what inflames his passions: "I do not find myself less human than someone that believes the gas chamber stories, less human than Holocaust experts, less human than Jewish survivors." In the vein of "some of my best friends are Jews," Smith says he is not antisemitic because his first wife was Jewish and that he attended her son's bar mitzvah, "which took place on the green lawns at our house where two young rabbis played guitars and sang for us."[72] On the 1994 *Donahue* television talk show he appeared genuinely hurt and offended when accused by Phil Donahue and members of the audience of inciting racial hatred. Yet he seems to have found a comfortable intellectual home in political extremism and Holocaust denial.

Smith is best known for his Herculean efforts to instigate an "open debate on the Holocaust" through his Committee for the Open Debate of the Holocaust (CODODH). Throughout the early 1990s Smith purchased a number of advertisements in college newspapers, such as one in the February 1992 issue of Student Life at Washington University in St. Louis, with the title "THE HOLOCAUST CONTROVERSY: THE CASE FOR OPEN DEBATE." The ad begins contentiously: "No subject enrages campus Thought Police more than Holocaust Revisionism. We debate every other great historical issue as a matter of course, but influential pressure groups with private agendas have made the Holocaust story an exception. . . . Students should be encouraged to investigate the Holocaust story the same way they are encouraged to investigate every other historical event."

Such arguments, of course, sound good at first and usually sit well with college students who have not yet learned to make fine distinctions within the larger principle of freedom of speech (see chapter 1). The ad continues with a lengthy and fairly detailed summary of what "revisionists" believe happened to the Jews in World War II and finishes with a discussion of "Political Correctness and Holocaust Revisionism" in which, once again, the "Thought Police" are invoked as the primary impediment to historical truth:

> Those who take up the Revisionist cause represent a wide spectrum of political and philosophical positions. They are certainly not the scoundrels, liars and demons the Holocaust Lobby tries to make them out to be. The fact is, there are no demons in the real world. People are at their worst when they begin to see their opponents as an embodiment of evil, and then begin to demonize them. Such people are preparing to do something simply awful to their opponents. Their logic is that you can do anything you want to a demon. That logic will not succeed.[73]

Although Smith now lives in Mexico and claims to be struggling financially, he publishes a monthly newsletter, maintains an active Web site, and regularly attends IHR conferences. In November 1999 he released the première issue of *The Revisionist: A Journal of Independent Thought.* This new magazine, says Smith in an editorial, stands for:

> *Accuracy—"The Revisionist* is about correcting the historical record in the light of a more complete collection of historical facts. We be-

lieve in the honest search for historical truth and shall attempt to discredit myths which remain a barrier to peace and goodwill among peoples and nations."

Labeling and sourcing—"If an academic or journalist is not certain that something is accurate, she should either not publish it, or should make that uncertainty plain by clearly stating the source of the information and its possible limits and pitfalls."

No conflicts of interest—"We believe that the content of anything that sells itself as journalism should be free of any motive other than informing its consumers. In other words, it should not be motivated, for example, by the desire to curry favor with an advertiser or to advance a particular political interest."

Accountability—"We believe that academics as well as journalists should hold themselves as accountable as any of those whom they write about. They should be eager to receive complaints about their work, to investigate complaints diligently, and to correct mistakes of fact, context, and fairness prominently and clearly."[74]

Who would disagree with any of these points? But by speaking so generally, Smith has said nothing in particular. Just what does he have in mind, for example, when he states that journalists and academics should not "advance a particular political interest"? Smith's editor-in-chief, George Brewer, explains that this would ensure the freedom "to speak freely about the Holocaust." Today, Brewer contends, "we are unable to say what it really was, unable to question what significance it really has." The purpose of *The Revisionist*, he indicates, "is simply to be the brick that smashes through the crystal palace of the complacency, irrationality, and hypocrisy that has reduced our national intellectual life to little more than the rote maneuvers of linemen at a poultry processing plant." What crystal palace is that? According to Brewer, the magazine "will emphasize the holocaust, and the gas chamber legend, as the means of defending intellectual freedom, though these will not be the only themes we shall engage." Indeed, another target is a favorite among right-wingers: "Whether we will be able to successfully skeet the other clay feet of the hegemonic ideology of liberal Secular Humanism depends on how well we defend the right to think differently about the Jewish catastrophe, as much as anything else."[75]

The articles in the journal's first issue—"David Irving and the Normalization of Gas Chamber Skepticism," "Intellectual Freedom and the Holocaust Controversy," "When Did the Holocaust Begin?" and "The ADL: What They Talk about When They Talk about Hate"—follow Smith's and Brewer's edicts. It remains to be seen how this slim volume of twenty-six pages will differ from its ideological big brother.

With the launching of his new journal, Smith has resurrected his college newspaper advertising campaign, which lay dormant for several years because of financial constraints (not to mention the social constraints imposed by newspaper staffs, which usually, but not always, refused his ads). According to a *New York Times* article, Smith submitted his journal as a twenty-six-page advertisement to *The Chronicle,* the newspaper of Hofstra University. The editors elected to include 5,000 copies of Smith's journal as an insert in the paper, defending this decision in the name of free speech. One editor, Shawna Van Ness, a junior, stated, "Since I've come on as a freshman we've never rejected an ad." In the lively and sometimes emotionally charged debate that ensued, members of the faculty and student body argued that refusing to run an advertisement is not a restriction of someone's free speech. As Nitza Druyan, a literature professor, put it: "The ad is not controversial. It's a lie." Although the decision to run the insert was made by an overwhelming majority, the angry debate alarmed Hofstra's administration, which expressed dismay over not having been alerted to the potential controversy. Smith could not have asked for more since, in our opinion, generating such contention is precisely the purpose of the ads. Here the ad landed Smith squarely in the middle of media attention, in the pages of the *New York Times.*[76]

Smith continues to hope that one day the Holocaust will be the subject of open public debate. He claims, "The politically correct line on the Holocaust story is, simply, it happened. You don't debate 'it.'"[77] On the contrary. The Holocaust story has been debated for fifty years—but by historians using the accepted rules of evidence.

ERNST ZÜNDEL

Among the least subtle of deniers is the pro-German propagandist and publisher Ernst Zündel, whose self-proclaimed goal is "the rehabilitation of the German people" (see figure 4). Zündel freely admitted in an interview with us that he believes, "There are certain aspects of the Third

Figure 4. During a 1985 free speech demonstration held in conjunction with his trial, Ernst Zündel appears in a concentration camp uniform in front of a placard voicing the conspiratorial view of Jews and the media. He added the words at the bottom of the photograph, portraying his cause as a battle between the "Zündelists" and the "Zionists." (Courtesy Ernst Zündel)

Reich that are very admirable [such as eugenics and euthanasia programs] and I want to call people's attention to these."[78] To do so, Zündel publishes and distributes books, flyers, videos, and audiotapes through his Toronto-based Samizdat Publishers. A small donation will net one an assortment of Zündel's paraphernalia, including transcriptions of his trial court proceedings, copies of his publication *Power: Zündelists vs. Zionists* (with articles like "Is Spielberg's 'Schindler' a 'Schwindler'?"), video clips of his many media appearances, a video tour of Auschwitz with

Figure 5.   These stickers are part of media
packages and fundraising mass mailings. (Courtesy Ernst Zündel)

David Cole, and stickers that proclaim "GERMANS! STOP APOLOGIZ-
ING FOR THE THINGS YOU DID NOT DO!" and "TIRED OF THE HOLO-
CAUST?? NOW YOU CAN STOP IT!" (see figure 5).

We visited Zündel at his Toronto home/office several months after it
was firebombed and found him to be at once jovial and friendly, yet
deadly serious about his mission to free the German people "from the
burden of the six million," by convincing the world that the Holocaust
never happened. In front of two Jewish Holocaust scholars, Zündel did
not hesitate to speak his mind on all matters Semitic, including his belief
that in the future the Jews are going to experience antisemitism the like
of which they have never seen. Like other deniers, Zündel finds it irrita-
ting that the Jews are the focus of so much attention:

> Frankly, I don't think Jews should be so egotistical and think they are the navel
> of the universe. They're not. Only a people like them could think themselves

so important that the whole world revolves around them. To me Jews are just like any other person. That already will hurt them. They will be shrieking "Oy vey, that Ernst Zündel said Jews are just like normal people." Well, goddamn it, they are.

What the Holocaust has done to National Socialism, says Zündel, is to "bar so many thinkers from re-looking at the options that National Socialism German style offers." Lift the Holocaust burden off the German shoulders, Zündel seems to be saying, and Nazism suddenly does not look so bad. Sound like a strange argument? Even Zündel admits his ideas are a little extreme:

> I know my ideas might be half-baked—I'm not exactly Einstein, and I know that. I'm not Kant. I'm not Goethe. I'm not Schiller. As a writer I'm not Hemingway. But goddamnit I'm Ernst Zündel. I walk on my hind legs and I have a right to express my viewpoints. I do the best I can in a kind way. My long-term goal is to ring the bell of freedom and maybe in my lifetime I will achieve no more than I have achieved so far, which is not too bad.

Never one to hold his tongue, Zündel fought for his free speech in a Canadian court in 1985 (see figure 6) and has endured countless verbal attacks and even a firebombing of his office. When we arrived shortly after the bombing, bodyguards greeted us at the door. During our interview with him, Zündel voiced a number of his controversial ideas. He estimated, for example, that the number of Jews killed "from all causes, in concentration camps, [was] 300,000." There was more than one Holocaust during the war, he claimed: "To the Germans, Dresden was the Holocaust—burning by fire." Steven Spielberg, he noted, "is celebrating the tribe in Hollywood. This is so arrogant." For a double irony, Zündel admitted, "Because of what has happened to me I now know how it must have felt to be a Jew in Nazi Germany." He added, "Society would do well to listen to its outcasts. These people have a story to tell." Here he included stories about none other than Adolf Hitler, who Zündel describes, with a spark of pride in his voice, as the savior of Germany: "I am an admirer of how this man took a country that was like a beaten child amongst nations and within six years turned that place around and made it into the marvel that National Socialist Germany was in 1938. He was a humble man with wonderful, intuitive gifts. Hitler's contribution to mankind, if he had died in 1939, would be as one of the great statesman of the twentieth century." Of course, Hitler did not die in 1939, and what happened from 1940 to 1945 changed everything.

Figure 6.   Ernst Zündel's Canadian trial in February 1985 became a media event when Zündel turned it into a demonstration for "free speech." (Courtesy Ernst Zündel)

DAVID COLE

The most paradoxical of the deniers is David Cole, a Jew (his mother "was raised as a secular Jew" and his father "was raised Orthodox in London during the Blitz"), who proudly displays his heritage while simultaneously denying its most significant modern historical event.[79] As he said in a 1994 interview with us: "I am damned if I do and damned if I don't. That is, if I don't mention the Judaism I will be accused of being ashamed. If I mention it up front I will be accused of exploiting it." For his views he was physically beaten at UCLA in a debate on the Holocaust; he has received regular death threats from "a small group of people that genuinely hate me with a passion;" and says the Jewish Defense League, the ADL, and Jewish organizations in general "are a little harder on me because I am Jewish." He has been called a self-hating Jew, anti-semitic, a race traitor, and in an editorial in *The Jewish News* he was compared to Hitler, Hussein, and Arafat.[80]

Though Cole's personality seems affable and his attitude sanguine, he sees himself as a rebel in search of a cause. Where other deniers appear to be political and/or racial ideologues, Cole's interests run deeper. He is a meta-ideologue—an existentialist on a quest to understand how ideologues invent their realities. In the process, Cole has joined a variety of organizations, on both ends of the political spectrum:

> I was everywhere. I ran a chapter of the Revolutionary Communist Party. I ran a John Birch Society chapter. I had about five different names, and there was, literally, not a part of the American political spectrum I wasn't involved in. I was a supporter of, and subscriber to, the ADL and the JDL. I have a World Jewish Congress card. I worked for the Heritage Foundation on the right, and the ACLU on the left. My point in doing this was that I felt superior to ideology and to the poor, brainwashed idiots who toil their lives away in pursuit of abstract concepts.

Holocaust denial, then, is just one in a long line of ideologies that have fascinated Cole since he was expelled (as he told us) from Hamilton High, in Los Angeles, for conflicts with the teachers and administration he chose not to elaborate on further in our interview. With no college background, but a parental stipend for self-education, Cole has amassed a personal library that houses thousands of volumes, including a considerable Holocaust section. He knows his subject and, as he says, can "debate the facts until the cows come home." Whereas he indicates that other subjects only held his attention for a few months to a year, the Holocaust "is more about real physical things than some abstract concept that requires faith. We are talking about something for which much of the evidence still exists." And that kind of physical evidence was filmed by Cole on a fact-finding mission over the summer of 1992, financed by the denier Bradley Smith. "I figured I needed $15,000 to $20,000," Cole recalls, "and Bradley set to work—it took him about a month and a half to raise that amount." Cole's stated goal in his research "is to try to move revisionism away from the fringe and into the mainstream." To do so he has tried to reach professional historians. And yet he has also associated closely with deniers, despite his claim to us to the contrary:

> I want to get people who are not right-wingers or neo-Nazis. Right now it [the Holocaust denial movement] is in a very dangerous position because there is a vacuum created by mainstream historians denouncing revisionism. The vacuum has been filled with the likes of Ernst Zündel. Zündel is a very likable human being, but . . . he is not the person I would like to see recognized as the world's leading Holocaust denier.

Still, there is another side to David Cole: he likes to stir things up, and not just for historians. For example, he mentioned how he once brought an African American date to a denier social event, where white supremacists were present, "just to watch them squirm and stare." Even though he disagrees mightily with many deniers' beliefs and most of their politics, he introduces himself to the media as a "revisionist," knowing it will draw scorn and sometimes physical abuse. He wants his video footage to be studied by professional scholars (he says he offered it to Yad Vashem), but at the same time he has edited it into a marketable product and sold it through the IHR's mailing list. His first video of Auschwitz, he says, sold over 30,000 copies.

Where does Cole fit in? On the one hand, he is angry that he has been locked out by historians who, he says, "are not gods, are not religious figures, and are not priests." As he puts it, "We have a right to ask them for further explanations. I am not ashamed to ask the questions I am asking." On the other hand, Cole occasionally runs into conflict with his fellow deniers. In October 1994, for example, on another video research project of Nazi extermination camps, according to his fellow denier Bradley Smith, Cole was at the Natzweiler-Struthof concentration camp examining the gas chamber with Pierre Guillaume (Robert Faurisson's French publisher), Henri Roques (author of *The "Confessions" of Kurt Gerstein*) and his wife, and Tristan Mordrel (a French denier). While the group was inside the building housing the gas chamber, one of the guards, Smith claims, "excused himself, went out, and locked the exit door from the outside. David tells me that when the door was locked it made a loud noise but he didn't think anything of it."[81] After about twenty minutes the guard returned, unlocked the door, and they returned to their cars, whereupon Cole discovered that "a front door window in his car had been smashed and his travel journals, papers, books, personal effects, videotapes and still camera film had all been stolen. In short, all his research. He was cleaned out." Smith claims the trip cost him $8,000 to fund, so he sold an eighty-minute video of David Cole telling his story in order to recoup his expenses. As an ironic twist of fate for those who deny the Holocaust happened, one of Cole's companions in the gas chamber, Henri Roques, denies Cole's story:

> The six of us[82] were never locked from outside the gas chamber in order to be entrapped in it! Simply the guard locked the door from inside and he had to open it once because tourists were knocking at the door, and he told them that the visit was possible only for people with special permission (which was the case for our party). My wife and I remember only one guard. According to the guard and, later on, to the gendarmes in Schirmeck (near Struthof), this kind of theft is unfortunately common, especially in a car with a foreign license plate. Initially, I thought that it could have been a theft directed against denier people but I do not see anything which could substantiate this and, furthermore, the conversations I had with P. Guillaume and T. Mordrel tend to eliminate that possibility. Cole's version could make the readers believe in an anti-denier operation carried out with the complicity of the guards but I don't think it is fair to accuse the guards of having "entrapped" us or even perhaps participated in a theft.[83]

In a doubly ironic twist, in the *Adelaide Newsletter* Robert Faurisson claims that the Natzweiler-Struthof gas chamber was never used for mass homicides,[84] and Cole, to his credit, rebuffed Faurisson:

> What evidence does Faurisson give us to "prove" that no homicidal gassings ever took place at Struthof? He tells us of an "expertise" that has "disappeared," but, "thanks to another piece of evidence," we know what it said. He refers us to a *Journal of Historical Review* article for more info. One would hope to find out in this article just *what* that other piece of evidence is that confirms the existence and conclusions of the "expertise," but sadly Faurisson refuses to enlighten us. So what do we have? A report that has disappeared and a denier who assures us that *he* knows what the report said, without feeling the need to provide us with any further evidence. How would a *denier* respond if an "exterminationist" acted this way? Deniers routinely dismiss documents when the originals have vanished. We don't accept "hearsay," and we certainly don't take exterminationists on their word when it comes to the contents of documents.[85]

"Take nothing on its looks; take everything on evidence," a lawyer in Charles Dickens's *Great Expectations* counsels the hero. It's still good advice.

"HE THAT TROUBLETH HIS OWN HOUSE SHALL INHERIT THE WIND"

A few years ago we learned that David Cole had apparently recanted his denial of the Holocaust. The retraction came in 1998 following a Jewish Defense League Web page article by Robert J. Newman, entitled "David Cole: Monstrous Traitor," in which Newman equated Cole with "a sickness," "a mental disease," and "a human parasite who clings to his ardent Nazi supporters and friends who back his ideas wholeheartedly."[86] The JDL article concludes with an ominous warning: "Don't you think it's time that we flush this rotten, sick individual down the toilet, where the rest of the waste lies? One less David Cole in the world will certainly not end Jew-hatred, but it will have removed a dangerous parasitic, disease-ridden bacteria from infecting society." Following the article was the announcement of a "Reward for Information": "JDL wants to know the location of Holocaust denier David Cole, pictured above. Anyone giving us his correct address will receive a monetary reward."[87]

Subsequently, a "Statement of David Cole," dated January 2, 1998, appeared on the JDL Web page in which Cole stated that everything he had previously believed about Holocaust denial was false and that he now believed the standard history as presented in mainstream Holocaust books. Cole explained, "During my four years as a denier, I was wracked with self-hate and loathing . . . the hate I had for myself I took out on my people . . . I was seduced by pseudo-historical nonsense and clever-sounding but empty ideas and catch-phrases." He concluded: "I am sorry for what I did, and I am sorry for the hurt I caused. This statement is made freely and under no duress, and is quite willingly, even happily, given to Mr. Irv Rubin of the Jewish Defense League for the widest possible distribution."[88] The David Cole signature, says the Web page notice, is notarized.

Something is amiss here. Given the implications in the statement above, if Cole did pen the retraction, is it possible that he did so out of fear for his life? According to Irv Rubin:

> It was not a hit or a contract on him. We just wanted to find out what he was doing and get an update. We didn't know if he had really quit the Holocaust denial movement and we just wondered where he was. We wanted to sit down face to face with him to find out what he was doing. I eventually tracked him down by phone and had numerous conversations with him. He begged me to take him off the Web page, explaining that he was worried that someone would take the Internet posting as a hit or contract on his life. He has moved to Michigan and is taking care of a sick relative and he is worried something bad will

happen. He sent us a couple of hundred dollars to help us get Bradley Smith to quit selling his videos. He says the videos are a fraud and a fake.[89]

Rubin also reported Cole's belief that the IHR would have folded long ago were it not for the sale of over 30,000 copies of a videotaped debate between Mark Weber and Michael Shermer. According to Rubin, Cole indicated: "Shermer is responsible for the continuation of the IHR." Weber's response was unequivocal: "That's ridiculous. We have sold a thousand, maybe two at most. The IHR is sustained by donations from supporters, subscribers to the journal, and the sale of all of our books and tapes. Our bestselling item is Butz's book, *The Hoax of the Twentieth Century.*"[90] When asked if it was possible that Cole wrote the retraction in order to protect himself, Rubin responded:

> I stake my personal credibility on his conversion. It is a result of the fact that someone made him see the light of day. Someone offered him stone cold proof of the Holocaust and so he converted. He realized he was previously distorting. I know it for a fact because I had a fist fight with him at UCLA and he was humiliated. For a guy to turn around and send me $200 cash he must really mean it. He has total contempt for Bradley Smith and Ernst Zündel. I had great trepidation until I saw the notary stamp with the letter. People do make these radical changes. I think the guy is sincere. In correspondence with me he says he quit the denial movement three years ago, and we only put out our materials on the Internet a year ago.

Nevertheless, Rubin concluded his remarks by reiterating that Cole "was deadly afraid for his life, that someone would find him and shoot him." According to the IHR, this interpretation on Cole's part would not be inappropriate, since the FBI once labeled the JDL as a terrorist organization.[91] Rubin says that the FBI has lifted the "terrorist" charge, which they put on the JDL in 1985. It has been suggested in IHR literature that the JDL might be responsible for the 1984 firebombing of their headquarters, although Weber admits this has never been proven. Rubin denies the charge.

After numerous phone messages Cole finally returned our calls, phoning the Skeptics Society office shortly before midnight on April 10, 1998. He asked the *Skeptic* magazine art director Pat Linse to hang up so he could leave a voice message, which he did:

> Now listen up because this is going to be my only communication with you. Originally I didn't plan to answer your calls but after talking with Irv Rubin, whose counsel I have come to trust over the past few months, I've realized that my silence might be misconstrued by you as an attempt to distance my-

self from the statement I gave to the Jewish Defense League making clear my changed position on the Holocaust. So to that end let me make it absolutely crystal clear that that statement is a completely accurate summary of my present views. It was made willingly by me and was in no way the result of threat or blackmail or some kind of contract that was out on me. The people making that claim are either mistaken or are purposefully trying to make trouble for me. My refusal to return your calls was due to my personal opinion of you and your methods. This will be my only communication with you. Please refrain from calling anymore.[92]

David Cole's retraction is so unlike his earlier position that we feel it calls for the gathering of further data, and a healthy dose of skepticism in the interim. Like all social movements that change over time, depending on the vagaries of the personalities involved, the Holocaust denial movement remains in a state of relative flux. Yet it is hardly about to disappear.

As we go to press, the Institute for Historical Review is gearing up for a "renewal and rebuilding" program initiated in an October 1999 letter from *JHR* associate editor Theodore J. O'Keefe, announcing that the six-year legal struggle with IHR founder Willis Carto and his Liberty Lobby is at last coming to an end through an out-of-court settlement, allowing the institute to "get back to doing full time what it does best: fighting for truth in history." In fact, the letter boasts that "Friends of the IHR such as David Irving, Arthur Butz, and Robert Faurisson—and enemies like the Anti-Defamation League, the Simon Wiesenthal Center, and the Harvard Law School's Alan Dershowitz—agree: the IHR is the world's number-one force for historical revisionism." Throughout the six-year ordeal IHR staffers Mark Weber and Greg Raven had to take cuts in salaries (while other staffers were let go), but with the hoped-for donations that the letter requests (the figure cited is $150,000), the institute plans to implement such projects as hosting another revisionist conference, jump-starting Bradley Smith's media campaign and campus crusade for revisionism, updating computers and photocopy machines, and returning the IHR "to the vital work of publishing and publicizing the revisionist classics, as well as the latest in leading-edge revisionist research."[93]

Despite its claimed interest in "historical" revision, we contend the driving force of the Institute for Historical Review and its leaders and supporters will always be denial of the Holocaust. The logical question is why deny the Holocaust?

4

Why They Say the Holocaust Never Happened

The Ideological Agenda

One is astonished in the study of history at the recurrence
of the idea that evil must be forgotten, distorted, skimmed
over. The difficulty, of course, with this philosophy is that
history loses its value as an incentive and example; it paints
perfect men and noble nations, but it does not tell the truth.

W. E. B. Du Bois, *Black Reconstruction,* 1935

The study of history, as a profession, has never approached the level of
scientific sophistication of even the other social sciences, let alone the biological and physical sciences. The reason is twofold: historians are not
trained in the methods of science, in the research protocols and statistical tools that test hypotheses and help determine whether a theory is probably true or definitely false; and historians' search for truth must make
its way through a minefield of human biases and foibles. The facts do not
speak for themselves but are inevitably interpreted through the colored
filters of human minds embedded in cultures and milieus. This obstacle
confronts all scientists, but in most fields the built-in self-correcting mechanisms of science help separate fact from fiction. Not so for most historians, whose subject of study is in the past, making the testing of hypotheses difficult. Historical debates are rarely settled with evidence from
experiments or case studies; most of the time they just fade from our
radar screens as new blips take their place. They usually go out with a
whimper, not a bang. If even the hypotheses of mainstream historians,
who struggle mightily to exculpate themselves from these ubiquitous biases, remain loaded with cultural prejudices and personal preferences,
what are we to expect of the theories from those on the fringe who openly
and proudly display their agendas? The Holocaust deniers are a case in
point—an extreme one to be sure, but emblematic of the larger problem.

Running through almost all denier literature—books, articles, editorials, reviews, monographs, guides, pamphlets, and promotional materials—
is a fascination with Jews and everything Jewish. No issue of the *Journal
of Historical Review* fails to contain something on Jews. The January-
February 1994 issue, for example, features a cover story on who killed
the Romanovs and helped bring the Bolsheviks to power. Guess who?
Yes, Mark Weber explains, it was the Jews: "Although officially Jews have
never made up more than five percent of the country's total population,
they played a highly disproportionate and probably decisive role in the
infant Bolshevik regime, effectively dominating the Soviet government
during its early years." But what about Lenin, who ordered the assassination of the imperial family? Weber's explanation is revealing: "Lenin
himself was of mostly Russian and Kalmuck ancestry, but he was also
one-quarter Jewish."[1] The argument follows a typical denier line of reasoning: the Communists killed the Romanovs and instigated the Bolshevik
Revolution—fact. Some of the leading Communists were Jewish (or had
Jewish ancestors)—fact. Conclusion: the Jews killed the Romanovs and
caused the Bolshevik Revolution. By the same logic, we might say: Ted
Bundy was a serial killer. Ted Bundy was Catholic. Catholics are serial
killers.

The Jewish focus is pervasive. In 1985, for example, the Institute for
Historical Review issued a special report entitled *The Zionist Terror Network: Background and Operation of the Jewish Defense League and
Other Criminal Zionist Groups*. The summer 1980 issue of the *JHR* featured an article by Lewis Brandon (an alias for the then-director of the
IHR, William McCalden), on "The Mendacity of Zion." In the summer
1981 issue Alfred Lilienthal penned "Zionism and American Jews." The
spring 1982 issue included "Zionism's Vested Interest" by Paul Smith.
James Whisker revealed in the spring 1984 issue that Karl Marx was an
antisemite. More recent issues show no attenuation of the Jewish obsession. The first three issues of 1998, for example, include an article on
"The Vexing 'Jewish Question'" (January–February) and two book review articles on "Jewish Power: Inside the American Jewish Establishment" (March–April) and "What Causes Anti-Semitism?" (May–June).
The list goes on and on. Why? David Irving gave this illuminating
explanation:

> I think the Jews are largely to blame for themselves by their knee-jerk re-
> sponses. Every step that they take to try to control antisemitism produces pre-
> cisely the opposite effect in my view. Goebbels himself said that, in fact. I don't
> think it is antisemitism so much as it is xenophobia. And I think it is built in

like the hunting instinct or the mating instinct. It is built into us as one of God's little tricks.[2]

The Jews, it would appear, have brought any antisemitism on themselves—they have only themselves to blame. Here is a classic case of blaming the victims, one of the oldest tactics used against minorities and oppressed peoples in history.

Although the editorial slant toward what "the Jews" have done or are doing, especially with regard to the deniers themselves, can hardly be missed even with only a cursory glance through any issue of the magazine, it turns out that this is not the dominant theme of the *Journal of Historical Review*. To determine that theme, we conducted a content analysis of all 80 issues of the *JHR* from its founding in spring 1980 to spring 1999.[3] With the help of Frank Sulloway, a social scientist and data analyst at the University of California, Berkeley, who has conducted numerous content analyses of historical documents, we established a data grid by thematic category over years, to look for trends and clusters, as well as cumulative totals of articles by subject. We counted 999 articles, essays, book reviews, commentaries, and editorials but did not include letters to the editor and miscellaneous small news items. (By their own count the *JHR* editors tallied 1,526 items, including letters and news items, presented in a retrospective index at the end of 1998.) Our total gave an average of 12.5 items per issue over the past eighteen years. Most of the time the theme of the article, essay, book review, commentary, or editorial was quite clear, as in the numerous pieces on "the Jews" described above. For example, we included a review of Jean-Claude Pressac's *Auschwitz: Technique and Operation of the Gas Chambers*, item number 840 in the *JHR* index, in a category called "Holocaust." Articles like "Reflections of an American World War II Veteran on the Fiftieth Anniversary of the D-Day Invasion" were placed in the category "World War II," covering those items on the war that were not about the Holocaust. Numerous articles dealt with fascists, Nazis, and especially Hitler, so these comprised three separate categories. The category "General" encompassed items dealing with areas of history other than the Second World War, and "Other" contained items we could not classify into our other nine categories.

Two categories of particular interest were "Revisionism" and "Equivalency." In "Revisionism" we included items dealing with the magazine itself, with its editors and contributors, with how deniers are treated by the media and critics, with the numerous "hate-speech" laws around the world that prohibit Holocaust revisionism, and so forth. Among the articles we placed in this category were Mark Weber's "Doug Collins under New Fire for Holocaust Views," described as a "Jewish group brings criminal charges for 'Swindler's List' column" (a reference to an earlier *JHR* satire on the film); David Irving's "My Confrontation with Deborah Lipstadt"; and "'60 Minutes' Takes Aim at Holocaust Revisionism."[4]

The "Equivalency" category helped us understand what is really going on in many *JHR* articles. On the surface, for example, a cover story entitled "The 'Great Emancipator' and the Issue of Race (Abraham Lincoln's Program of Black Resettlement)" sounds innocuous enough, until you read more closely and discover that its deeper argument is that there is an equivalency between American racists (including Lincoln, it is claimed) and German racists (i.e., Nazis). When it is argued in "The 'Jewish Question' in 15th and 16th Century Spain" and "The Spanish Inquisition in Reality and Myth" that there has been a significant exaggeration of the numbers killed in the Inquisition, who is seen as behind this historical distortion? The Jews, of course. A common theme we found in discussions of Pearl Harbor is that Roosevelt knew about the "surprise" bombing and allowed it to happen in order to drag an isolationist America into the war against Hitler. (What Roosevelt knew or did not know about an impending Japanese attack on a U.S. military base is not our point; it is that the *JHR* uses that theme, over and over, to make the equivalency argument that all governments—American or German—execute immoral acts in the name of nationalism, national security, or other psycho-political motives.)[5]

Using these ten categories, we went through the contents of all eighty issues independently, then performed an interrater reliability test to assure we were obtaining consistent results.[6] The ranking of article content by percentage is presented in figure 7, a striking image that tells us instantly what the *Journal of Historical Review* is about.

Some clusters of articles changed over time. For example, 60.1 percent of all the articles on Hitler came in 1984, yet no year before or after saw more than two articles on the Führer. Likewise in 1984 fascists and fascism generated 46.1 percent of the total, with very few items since. The most popular category, "Revisionism," has been steadily rising with 33.3 percent generated since 1995 and 64.9 published since 1993.

Perhaps most significantly, although the overall percentage of articles on Jews was only 6.3 percent for the lifespan of the journal, 52.4 percent have been published since 1995, with five articles that year, ten in the 1996–97 period (six issues), a whopping fifteen in 1998, and three

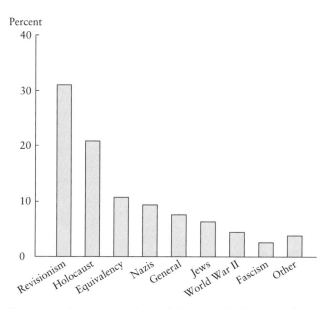

Figure 7. A content analysis of the *Journal of Historical Review* reveals that more than half (51.9 percent) of all articles, essays, book reviews, commentaries, and editorials are about revisionism and the Holocaust, with another fifth (20.2 percent) allocated to the Nazis and the equivalency argument that their government was no different from others. We thus argue that the *JHR* could just as accurately be called the *Journal of Holocaust Revisionism.*

in early 1999. Clearly the IHR's interest in matters Jewish has been accelerating over time. For example, in the final issue of 1998, Robert Faurisson authored "Ah, How Sweet It Is to Be Jewish," which was immediately followed by "A Jewish Appeal to Russia's Jewish Elite" (published without a by-line). In his piece, Faurisson quotes Alain Finkielkraut, a philosophy professor at France's Ecole Polytechnique, who noted the changing fortunes of Jews in the last half of this century: "'Ah, how sweet it is to be Jewish at the end of this 20th century! We are no longer History's accused, but its darlings. The spirit of the times loves, honors, and defends us, watches over our interests; it even needs our imprimatur.'" Faurisson, taking Finkielkraut out of context, then draws the conclusion he seeks: "Obviously, it is 'sweet' to be Jewish in these final years of the century, but only a Jew has the right to say so. In effect, as Finkielkraut acknowledges, it is no longer possible to publish without the imprimatur of organized Jewry. In effect, I might add, the Jew reigns unopposed."[7]

The second article observes, "Most Russians have suffered terribly during the Yeltsin years"—with one exception: "But in the midst of this widespread economic misery, a small minority has grown fabulously wealthy since the end of the Soviet era. Although Jews make up no more than three or four percent of Russia's population, they wield enormous economic and political power in that vast and troubled country."[8]

In conclusion, our content analysis lays bare the implicit agenda of the *JHR* and its sponsoring institute. As our study shows, the journal's major focus over the year has been on revising the Holocaust, and since the Holocaust was, more than anything, the attempt to murder the Jews of Europe, it appears that challenging the veracity of one of the key events in twentieth-century Jewish history is the raison d'être of the institute.

THE CONSPIRATORIAL SIDE OF HOLOCAUST DENIAL

Embedded in the anti-Jewish agenda of Holocaust denial is a strong conspiratorial streak. For example, the *"Holocaust" News,* published by the now-defunct Centre for Historical Review (based in the U.K. and not to be confused with the U.S.-based IHR), carried this headline in its first issue: "HOLOCAUST" STORY AN EVIL HOAX. The article expounded: "We assert that the 'Holocaust' lie was perpetrated by Zionist-Jewry's stunning propaganda machine for the purpose of filling the minds of Gentile people the world over with such guilt feelings about the Jews that they would utter no protest when the Zionists robbed the Palestinians of their homeland with the utmost savagery."[9] It is one thing to debate the politics of the Arab-Israeli conflict over Palestine (a subject under discussion on a regular basis everywhere from college campuses to television political roundtables); it is quite another to suggest that the Holocaust was invented by its victims in order to gain a moral high ground, particularly since the founding of the state of Israel was in the works decades before the Holocaust.

An early example of the conspiratorial thinking that influences the modern denial movement is *Imperium: The Philosophy of History and Politics,* written shortly after the Second World War by Francis Parker Yockey (under the nom de plume of Ulick Varange) and dedicated to Adolf Hitler. The 1994 IHR catalog describes the book as "a sweeping historico-philosophical treatise in the Spenglerian mold and a clarion call to arms in defense of Europe and the West." The book introduced Willis Carto, the founder of the IHR, to Holocaust denial, and he wrote an introduction to a later edition of it when he published it through his Noontide Press. *Imperium* describes an "imperial" system modeled after Hitler's national socialism, in which democracy would wither away, elections would cease, and power would be in the hands of the public because businesses would be publicly owned. The major impediment to this system, in Yockey's opinion, is the Jew, who "lives solely with the idea of revenge on the nations of the white European-American race."[10] A conspiracy theorist of the highest caliber, Yockey has described how the "Culture-Distorters" are undermining the West because of the covert operations of "the Church-State-Nation-People-Race of the Jew."[11] Broadening his net to catch additional targets, Yockey calls the theory of evolution a product of the "materialistic animalization of Culture-man"; he also states that the white race can be contaminated by such "parasites" as "Jews, Asiatics, Negroes, and Communists."[12] Hitler, in Yockey's view, heroically defended the purity of the Aryan race against these inferior racial-cultural aliens and "parasites." It is especially ironic that Yockey rejects the theory of evolution since this theory is typically employed in the service of similar racialism, where in the "survival of the fittest" the "stronger" races will exterminate the "weaker."

Yockey's conspiratorial bent is not uncommon, particularly in the setting of what Richard Hofstader called "the paranoid style in American politics."[13] For conspiracy theorists, all manner of demonic forces have been at work in history, including the Illuminati, the Knights Templar, the Knights of Malta, the Masons, the Freemasons, the Cosmopolitans, the Abolitionists, the Slaveholders, the Catholics, the Communists, the Bilderbergers, the Council on Foreign Relations, the Trilateral Commission, the Warren Commission, the World Wildlife Fund, the International Monetary Fund, the League of Nations, the United Nations, and, most recently, the New World Order.[14] In many of these conspiracy theories, "the Jews" are seen to be at work behind the scenes, deviously conspiring to implement their cabals.

The *Protocols of the Elders of Zion* serves as the classic conspiratorial document of the twentieth century. It supposedly originated in Russia in the nineteenth century and allegedly proves that Jewish elders conspired to gain control of the world through financial and economic means, setting the price of gold and other commodities, as well as dominating the media and political institutions. As several historians have shown, the document is a forgery adapted from an 1864 satirical essay written by a French attorney named Maurice Joly, aimed at Napoleon III and originally entitled *Dialogue in Hell between Machiavelli and Montesquieu, or The Politics of Machiavelli in the Nineteenth Century*.[15] (For publishing his piece, Joly was fined 300 francs and sentenced to over a year in prison.) The document gained popularity in Russia during the 1905 revolution (which itself fueled fears of Jewish machinations), under the guise of a book entitled *The Great in the Small,* written by a czarist supporter named Sergus Nilus. In the 1911 edition Nilus claimed that the *Protocols* had been stolen from the French headquarters of the Zionist world organization, but he changed that reference to an unidentified source inside the Masonic headquarters for the 1917 edition. That edition was the one that made its way to Germany at the close of the First World War. The Germans began to make use of it after the Nazi ideologist Alfred Rosenberg published several pamphlets between 1919 and 1923, citing the *Protocols* as a source about the Jewish conspiracy to take over the world. It has since been used by a variety of antisemitic groups, including Arabs, South Africans, and even American nationals, such as Henry Ford, who serialized it in the *Dearborn Independent,* then reprinted 500,000 copies in book form as *The International Jew: The World's Foremost Problem.* A judge eventually ruled that Ford should discontinue publication, and in 1927 Ford retracted his endorsement of the *Protocols.* The document was ruled a hoax in two trials, one in Port Elizabeth, South Africa in 1934, and the other in Bern, Switzerland in 1934–35. In 1993 the Russian Tancred Golenpolsky, publisher of the Moscow-based *Jewish Gazette,* sued the ultra-nationalist organization Pamyat (memory) for printing antisemitic propaganda, including the *Protocols.* Pamyat struck back with a libel suit, but on November 26, 1993, a Moscow district court judge ruled that the *Protocols* was a fake (though the ruling did not put the screed to rest once and for all: the IHR book catalog lists an edition of it and Mark Weber says it sells very well).

The political ideologue and former Marxist Lyndon LaRouche, whose literature can be routinely found at tables set up by his devoted followers in front of U.S. post offices, thrives on conspiratorial thinking. He and his wife, Helga Zepp LaRouche, are known for their theory that the queen of England is behind the international drug trade. The contents of their newspaper, *The New Federalist,* suggest that they are professional contrarians. For example, in Zepp LaRouche's *Hitler Book* she dismisses Darwinism because it gave rise to Hitlerism (despite the fact that Hitler and the Nazis employed social Darwinism as part of their justification for the extermination of the Jews—see chapter 8).[16] Amid claims that they resolved the wave-particle duality problem in physics, found the error in Karl Marx's thinking (only one?), discovered a new economic system, and conceived the strategic defense initiative, the

LaRouches dismiss the Holocaust as "mythical," claiming the whole thing is "a swindle."[17]

A good example of how someone's ideological bent can distort the historical record comes from a book by the Canadian author James Bacque, *Other Losses: An Investigation into the Mass Deaths of German Prisoners at the Hands of the French and Americans After World War II*. Bacque argues that immediately following the end of the war in Europe, General Dwight D. Eisenhower conspired to withhold food, housing, and supplies from millions of German POWs, "murdering" them through starvation. Carefully selecting German and American sources who claim they witnessed this mass starvation (even when supplies were readily on hand), Bacque concludes that approximately one million Germans were murdered in a conspiracy by the French and Americans—a "holocaust," he claims, on par with what the Germans did to the Jews.[18]

Bacque's statistics are worth noting. Using weekly ledgers of POWs and Disarmed Enemy Forces from the U.S. European Theatre Headquarters, Bacque shows that the prisoner accounting system in these weekly ledgers had such columns as "Previous on Hand," "Discharged," or "Transferred." The most curious, for Bacque, is a column headed "Other Losses," which he takes to mean either escaped or dead. Since the rate of escape was less than one per thousand prisoners, he concludes that about five thousand German POWs died per week. Extrapolating to the length of their encampment, Bacque arrives at his one-million figure. What was Eisenhower's motive? It was revenge, says Bacque, brought on after seeing the Nazi concentration camps, coupled with his pathological hatred of Germans. Why have we not heard about this incredible genocide before? Because, Bacque contends, history is written by the victors, who conspire to cover up their own atrocities, and this was not a story complimentary to the Allied postwar goals.

Bacque's argument is easy to refute. Albert Cowdrey and Stephen Ambrose show the gaping holes in Bacque's book.[19] One of his eyewitnesses, for example, was ninety years old and legally blind when interviewed, and he admitted his memory of the POW experience was fuzzy at best. Other eyewitness testimony seems equally flawed, with conflation of separate memories and confabulation, interweaving fact and fiction, not uncommon. In addition, as Cowdrey and Ambrose reveal, Bacque's statistical analysis of the "other losses" is highly suspect. One million missing Germans are a lot of people. Why were they not noticed for nearly half a century, despite the fact that the Red Cross compiled lists of MIAs (totaling only 41,000 in the European theater)? It turns out the "other losses" assumed by Bacque to mean deaths includes transfers to other commands, normal attrition, desertion, and release without discharge. One cannot help but wonder how Bacque missed this simple explanation, noted by Cowdrey and Ambrose.

THE "REVISIONIST" EXTREME

Occasionally one encounters in studying this movement a peculiar and paradoxical denial of mass extermination along with a hint that Hitler should have finished the job. During a 1960 trial in Germany, for example, the neo-Nazi Bund Heimattreuer Jugend was charged with espousing Nazi views. One of the group's members, Konrad Windisch, quoted the following refrain from a popular Bund chant:

> The gas chambers were too small
> We'll build bigger ones later
> Then there'll be room for you all![20]

Mark Weber and company have actively distanced themselves from what might be termed the extreme fringe of Holocaust denial. Yet how different are these so-called extremists' arguments from those found in the standard Holocaust denial literature? Self-proclaimed "white separatist" and "revisionist" Jack Wikoff, for example, publishes the newsletter *Remarks* from Aurora, New York. The publication is endorsed by the denier Bradley Smith, and Wikoff reviews books for the *JHR*. "Talmudic Jewry is at war with humanity," Wikoff explains. "Revolutionary communism and International Zionism are twin forces working toward the same goal: a despotic world government with the capital in Jerusalem."[21] Wikoff also published this letter from "R.T.K." from California: "Under Hitler and National Socialism, the German troops were taught White racism and never has this world seen such magnificent fighters. *Our job is re-education with the facts of genetics and history.*"[22]

The January 1994 issue of a denier newsletter entitled *Instauration* featured an article on "How to Cut Violent Crime in Half: An Immodest Proposal," with no byline. The author's solution is vintage racialism:

> There are 30 million blacks in the U.S., half of them male and about one-seventh of the males in the 16 to 26 age bracket, the violent sector of the black population. Half of 30 million is 15 million. One-seventh of 15 million is a little more than 2 million. This tells us that 2 million blacks, not 30 million, are committing the crimes. The Soviet Union had gulag populations that ran as high as 10 million at various times during the Stalin era. The U.S. with much more advanced technology should be able to contain and run camps

that hold at least 20% of that number. Negroes not on drugs and with no criminal record would be released from the camps once psychological and genetic tests found no traces of violent behavior. As for most detainees, on their 27th birthday all but the most incorrigible "youths" would be let out, leaving room for the new contingent of 16-year-olds that would be replacing them.[23]

The self-proclaimed Holocaust revisionist Lew Rollins, in his satirical *Lucifer's Lexicon,* offers readers such selections as these:

HOLOCAUST, THE, n. A smoke screen obscuring the atrocities of the Allies and the Israelis. The insurance fraud of the century. A cheap cinematic trick; a filmflam; the Hollywoodcaust; a soap opera.

ZIONIST PROPAGANDA, n. Hebrew-National Baloney.[24]

When these examples of extremism were presented to Weber, he responded: "Why is this relevant? Rollins used to work for the IHR. *Remarks* is on the cusp. They used to be more-or-less denier. But he [Wikoff] is now getting engaged more and more into racialist matters. *Instauration* is racialist. I suppose they're affiliated so far as they agree with some of the things we might put out. But there is no relationship."[25] Fair enough, but what does it mean when deniers like Weber claim to be struggling to extricate themselves from this fringe element yet often seem to be closely aligned? Although it is true that not all participants in the denial movement share the most extreme beliefs, we have found a subtle form of antisemitism that crept into our interviews with them as "Some of my best friends are Jews, but . . . ," or "I'm not antisemitic but . . . ," followed by a litany of all the things "the Jews" are doing. We contend there is a bias that drives deniers to seek and find what they are looking for, and to confirm what they already believe—the very core of pseudohistory.

But a number of those who deny the Holocaust do not bother with subtlety. *Tales of the Holohoax* is one example. Interestingly, this publication has a dedication to Robert Faurisson and Ernst Zündel, and it gives thanks to Bradley Smith and L. A. Rollins. After fourteen pages of crass cartoon characterizations of Jews and the "Holohoax" the unnamed author explains:

The wild fables about homicidal gas chambers loosely grouped under the Orwellian Newspeak heading of the "Holocaust," have become the informal state religion of the West. The government, the public schools and the corporate media promote the imposition of this morbid, funeral-home-of-the-mind on young people, to instill guilt as a form of group-libel/hate propaganda against the German people. There is even a synagogue masquerading as a museum in Washington, D.C. supported by taxpayer funds (the U.S. Holocaust Museum), which represents the first cathedral of the first state-established religion in American history. As in all false religions, those who question the gas chamber cult are labeled demonic.[26]

Cartoons are also used in an advertisement placed in the *Washington Post* by a group calling itself the German-American Anti-Defamation League of Washington, D.C., which claims it "seeks to defend the rights of German-Americans, the forgotten minority."[27] Asking, "How long can the Jews perpetrate the Holocaust myth?" they use offensive characterizations of Jewish media moguls manipulating the press to perpetuate the so-called hoax. The same organization produced an advertisement that queried: "Would *Challenger* have blown up if German scientists had still been in charge?" There is no doubt about the answer. "We don't think so!" exclaims the ad, informing readers that Soviet "Fifth Columnists in the United States" have secretly worked to eliminate German scientists from NASA.[28]

The May 1996 issue of the newsletter of the Adelaide Institute, the voice of the Australian Holocaust deniers, reports this rather bizarre story:

> One of the world's most meticulous researchers on the Holocaust, Professor Udo Walendy, informs in his Historische Tatsachen Nr. 66 that there is no proof of the claim that Auschwitz inmates had a number tattooed on their forearms. If this is correct, then a large number of people have been parading on the world stage as blatant frauds. No wonder that legal sanctions are used to silence those who want to ask simple questions about what happened at this concentration camp called Auschwitz where allegedly millions were killed in homicidal gas chambers, then burned in crematoria ovens which had the miraculous ability to burn a body within ten minutes.[29]

Finally, we cannot ignore the National Socialist German Workers Party, Foreign Organization (NSDAP/AO), hailing from Lincoln, Nebraska. It publishes a bimonthly newspaper entitled *The New Order,* from which readers can order swastika pins, flags, armbands, key holders, and medallions; SS songs and speeches; "White Power" T-shirts; and all manner of books and magazines promoting white power, neo-Nazis, Hitler, and antisemitism. The July–August 1996 issue predicts that at the current rate of AIDS infection and death, "the COMPLETE GLOBAL EXTINCTION of the NEGROID RACE (due to AIDS infection) will occur

For the Next Six Million Years!
Published By Decree of Our State Religion
U.S. Holy Hoax Memorial Council.
Prevent Thought Crime: Worship and Obey the Chosen Pimples

Figure 8.   This antisemitic cartoon sent to
Skeptic magazine had a message on the back:
"To Shermer the Schleptic. Beast wishes!"
(Courtesy *Skeptic* magazine)

NO LATER than the year 2022 AD, and very possibly some years BE-FORE that date!!" A happy face sits below this "news," with the slogan "Have a Nazi Day!" Holocaust denial is a common theme in this publication. Readers find out, for example, that at Auschwitz, "With systematic German precision, each and every death was recorded and categorized. The small number of deaths over a three-year-period is actually a testament to how humane, clean and healthy the conditions were at the SS labor camp in Poland!" The problem, readers are warned, is that "the yids will use the truth to support THEIR evil lies and paranoid persecution complex."[30]

Like all ideologically driven movements, Holocaust denial is complex and multifaceted, featuring diverse motives and personalities, but we maintain that the antisemitic theme returns over and over. It may take an extreme form, as in an antisemitic cartoon (figure 8) sent to *Skeptic* magazine with the following message scrawled on the back: "To Shermer the Schleptic. Beast wishes!" Or it may be cloaked in subtler garb, as in the numerous examples reviewed above from the pages of the *Journal of Historical Review*. But, as we intend to show, it seems difficult to clearly separate the Holocaust denial movement from antisemitic sentiments.

THE PSYCHOLOGY OF EXTREMISM

What drives people in fringe groups to accept spurious beliefs and conspiratorial claims? To answer this question, we turn to John George and Laird Wilcox, scholars of fringe movements, who have outlined a set of characteristics of political extremists and ideological contrarians:

1. Absolute certainty they have the truth.
2. [The belief that] America is controlled to a greater or lesser extent by a conspiratorial group. In fact, they believe this evil group is very powerful and controls most nations.
3. Open hatred of opponents. Because these opponents (actually "enemies" in the extremists' eyes) are seen as a part of or sympathizers with "The Conspiracy," they deserve hatred and contempt.
4. Little faith in the democratic process. Mainly because most believe "The Conspiracy" has great influence in the U.S. government, and therefore extremists usually spurn compromise.
5. Willingness to deny basic civil liberties to certain fellow citizens, because enemies deserve no liberties.
6. Consistent indulgence in irresponsible accusations and character assassination.[31]

Ernst Zündel told us that society should listen to its outcasts. He has a point, but only if those outcasts play by the rules of reason and evidence. According to George and Wilcox, extremists frequently practice "character assassination, name calling and labeling, sweeping generalizations, inadequate proof for assertions, advocacy of double standards, use of buzzwords, assumption of moral superiority over others, doomsday thinking, problems tolerating ambiguity and uncertainty," and they "often feel that the system is no good unless they win." Of course, at one time or another we all succumb to these fallacies of thinking, but as George and Wilcox point out, "the difference between true extremists and others is that this general kind of behavior is the extremist's normal and usual way of relating their values and feelings, and they usually feel no guilt or sense that anything is wrong when they behave this way."[32] Where those in the mainstream question the judgment and reasoning of their opponents, extremists tend to impugn the character and morality of theirs. Where mainstreamers operate within the existing system to change it, extremists may resort to quasi-legal and illegal methods to elicit change, with the justification that the ends justify the means.

These ends often include a level of xenophobia far beyond that of the mainstream. In their book on "right-wing extremists, 'revisionists' and anti-Semites in Austrian politics today," Brigitte Bailer-Galanda and

Wolfgang Neugebauer speculate "that people with fears for their future, those who believe that 'aliens' and other 'enemies' are the personification of that fear, serve as a permanent reservoir for extreme right-wing rat-catchers of all hues."[33] Antisemitism fits this pattern: its nineteenth-century stereotypes of Jews as "God killers" or of the "Talmud Jews" out to eliminate Christians gave way in the twentieth century to the image of the Jews as "subversive," corrupters of philosophy, art, and culture, completely ignoring that Jews made some of the greatest contributions to those fields. The authors note that Holocaust revisionism slid into denial during the *Historikerstreit* of the 1980s, when the intentionalism-functionalism debate was used by some ideologues to imply that instead of debating whether the Holocaust was intended from the beginning or if it was a function of the war, these historians were really arguing over whether the Holocaust happened at all.

Here, in trying to understand the social and cultural context in which the Holocaust deniers fit, it is worth considering the remarks of the sociologist Daniel Bell: "The way you hold beliefs is more important than what you hold. If somebody's been a rigid Communist, he becomes a rigid anti-Communist—the rigidity being constant."[34] The psychologist Milton Rokeach, in a study on the organization of belief systems, commented on the importance of the structure over the content of beliefs: "The relative openness or closedness of a mind cuts across specific content; that is, it is not uniquely restricted to any particular ideology, or religion, or philosophy, or scientific viewpoint." The specific belief may be communism, existentialism, extreme Afrocentrism, radical feminism, or Holocaust denial, and these beliefs may be held in an open or closed manner. "Thus," Rokeach explains, in trying to understand the mindset common to all these beliefs, "a basic requirement is that concepts to be employed in the description of belief systems must not be tied to any one particular system; they must be constructed to apply equally to all belief systems."[35] Insight into the psychology of believers is to be found in the universals of extremist belief systems, not in the details of the claims themselves.

In his book *Turncoats and True Believers: The Dynamics of Political Belief and Disillusionment,* the sociologist Ted Goertzel attempts to show just how important the structuring of the belief system can be. He wants to explain not just why Arthur Butz denies the Holocaust, "but why Jim Jones and Abbie Hoffman committed suicide, Saddam Hussein invaded Kuwait, Ayn Rand seduced her leading disciple, Linus Pauling became a vitamin faddist, and Margaret Mead spun fantastic tales of utopia in the South Seas while Karl Marx prophesied a socialist utopia in industrial

Europe." Goertzel calls the ideologies of these ideologists "life scripts," which "gave meaning to their lives and enabled them to shape the world in which we live."[36] These life scripts are first outlined by the ideology, then written in detail from the facts selected that fit the preconceptions, ignoring those facts that do not fit. Once the script is complete it remains largely intact throughout the person's life, changing only in minor details. If it does change dramatically (in a turncoat's case), the commitment to the new script is typically as intense as it was to the old. Why? Because, Goertzel explains, "a script is a set of guidelines that people develop and use to understand their role in the world around them." Additionally, and more important, ideological scripts give emotional meaning by putting people firmly in a dramatic role in which they matter. As the drama unfolds, instead of sitting in the audience or waiting in the wings, the ideologist has a lead role in the play of life, with all the concomitant benefits, including and especially a sense of identity linked to a cause.

Goertzel identifies a number of ideological scripts, including the *Utopian-Dystopian,* which "seeks to transform the world to prevent disaster and realize an idyllic vision" (Margaret Mead, Jim Jones); the *Survivor,* which "seeks to move with the flow as a cork floating on the river of history" (Jerry Rubin, Bertrand Russell); the *Committed,* which "seeks meaning in life through commitment to a cause" (Lenin, Abbie Hoffman); the *Hawk,* which "seeks strength and security as a defense against outside threats" (Hitler, Hussein); the *Dove,* which "seeks peace and love through conciliation and cooperation with outside groups" (Gandhi); the *Authoritarian,* which "seeks a strictly disciplined world in which everyone must conform to established doctrines or powerful authority figures" (Stalin, Castro); the *Protester,* which "seeks to defend the powerless and oppressed from exploitation by elites" (Trotsky, Betty Friedan).[37] Taking off from Goertzel, we might describe the script of Holocaust deniers as committed and hawkish utopian-dystopian in their commitment to the cause of realizing an idyllic vision by defending against an outside threat. That they are committed no one will dispute. Their cause is the radical revision of the Holocaust into just another unfortunate by-product of the war, with guilt shared equally among the competing nations. Their idyllic vision is a world in which the "truth" will come out about the Holocaust and the Nazis, and concomitantly they wish to reveal the "lies" and "distortions" of history perpetrated by the Jews and their willing accomplices—historians and other academics, the victorious Allied nations, and the media.

We all write our own ideological scripts, of course, so what is the difference between our scripts and the scripts of extremists? If we assume that the underlying beliefs of all extremists are false, we have to admit that at some point in our lives most of us qualify as extremists. But, Goertzel explains, the "true beliefs" of extremist ideological thinking are often so amorphous and ambiguous that it is difficult to refute them. Further, when these beliefs form the basis of group cohesion, when they create in their followers a passionate, almost obsessional attachment to them, that is another sign of extremism, as is the polarization of the world into unambiguous categories, biased rhetorical and semantic argumentation, all-inclusive systems that offer the key to wisdom and truth, the dogmatic use of texts where the leader's words become hallowed, and the denial of contradictory information. Each of these characteristics is a necessary but not sufficient delimiter of extremist ideology. It is the combination of many of these indicators that makes an ideology extreme. The belief that the Holocaust did not happen, for example, is most certainly cohesive for the denier movement—the entire ideology revolves around it. The followers are deeply passionate, indeed, almost obsessive about their belief. They have polarized their world into Jews and non-Jews, exterminationists and revisionists, lies and truth. Their bias, as we shall see, drives them to select evidence, analogies, and documents that fit their belief and ignore those that do not.

An interesting puzzle sociologists have been working on is what is called the phenomenon of "left-wing authoritarianism," which, as Goertzel notes, should be a contradiction in terms: "Leftist protesters are usually compassionate people who empathize deeply with the suffering of others, while authoritarians, such as the Nazis and their apologists, have only hatred and disdain for society's victims. Despite this difference in their feelings, protesters and authoritarians have a great deal in common in the way they think about the political world. In both ideological scripts, the world is polarized between good and evil forces."[38] The puzzle is solved when we go to a deeper level of analysis and consider not the content of the ideology, but the psychology of it. At this deeper level of analysis we see a key to understanding the extremism of ideological polarization—the need for opposition.

THE NEED FOR ENEMIES

The one thing an extremist needs more than anything else is an enemy. An external enemy clears away internal strife. An enemy in life, like an opponent in sports, gives focus and meaning—someone to defeat, something to overcome. An enemy helps define a cause, delineating good from bad, black from white, as Richard Nixon explained: "It may seem melodramatic to say that the U.S. and Russia represent Good and Evil, Light and Darkness, God and the Devil. But if we think of it that way, it helps to clarify our perspective of the world struggle."[39]

Of course, it's not only extremists who make use of "enemies." Politicians live by the bipolarity of political rhetoric, and religious leaders have their own versions of a bifurcated morality. Billy Graham, for example, employed the oldest enemy in Western culture to explain who he thinks is the real enemy behind the Soviet Union: "My own theory about communism is that it is masterminded by Satan. I think there is no other explanation for the tremendous gains of communism in which they seem to outwit us at every turn, unless they have supernatural power."[40] Apparently Russia lost her satanic and supernatural powers in 1989. With the collapse of communism the enemy slipped from view. Other outlets for our collective fears will emerge, under other guises. Saddam Hussein perhaps?

The point is that many of our enemies seem more powerful than they really are. Although there may be real threats, more often than not political and ideological expedients exaggerate them, to justify our behavior against them. There is some suggestive evidence, for example, that during the height of the Cold War the Pentagon significantly exaggerated the military might of the Soviet Union, in part to justify its own defense spending.[41] Now that the Cold War is over new enemies must be found. The Iraqis occasionally fit the bill, along with domestic enemies like drugs, cancer, and poverty (couched in military rhetoric: the "war on drugs," the "war on cancer," and the "war on poverty"). The Harvard political scientist Samuel P. Huntington suggests that the newest source of conflict will not be ideological or economic, but cultural. "Nation states will remain the most powerful actors in world affairs, but the principal conflicts of global politics will occur between nations and groups of different civilizations. The clash of civilizations will dominate global politics. The fault lines between civilizations will be the battle lines of the future." Our own Western culture will square off against Islamic, Confucian, Japanese, Hindu, Slavic-Orthodox, Latin American, and African cultures, requiring "the West to maintain the economic and military power necessary to protect its interests in relation to these civilizations."[42] On a more local level, "waving the red meat" at a fund-raising rally for some cause usually entails explaining why the audience not only *should* want to but absolutely *must* make a donation in order to stave off the enemy. The more dastardly the enemy, the more coins in the collection basket.

Every IHR conference, for example, features a fund-raising effort to fight "for the truth" and against "our traditional enemy." A July 1998 letter from the IHR director Mark Weber to the mailing list thanks friends of the IHR for their "steadfast support" that "has meant the difference between *life and death* for the Institute and its vital work—a fact that our enemies certainly understand." According to this letter, the Anti-Defamation League "attacked" the IHR by asking the IRS to revoke its tax-exempt status, and Willis Carto has drained IHR resources through his "relentless *smear campaign*" and lawsuits.[43] Thus, Weber explains, "we're grappling with a real crisis." The IHR had to cut both expenses and salaries "to the *bare minimum*" and was forced to "*postpone or eliminate key IHR projects.*" Therefore, "we must once again turn for help *to you* and others who have generously supported the Institute and its work in the past. We really need the *most generous* donation you can afford. And we need it *now.*" Like a military commander exhorting his troops, Weber concluded his letter: "With victory now dimly in sight, this is no time to slacken or falter. As we close in on the finish line, we need your support to keep alive this precious, time-tested *beacon of truth* in history." For as long as we have been tracking the IHR, it has sent out such letters. This type of appeal works.

The psychologist David Barash, in his provocative book *Beloved Enemies,* suggests that a need for enemies may have evolved in the human species from our earliest social bondings into tribes and clans, which eventually gave rise to our modern classes and states, religions and races. The anthropologist Clifford Geertz says these "primordial alliances" are at the very heart of the tendency to see ourselves as members of a group and others as not in that group.[44] The Same and the Other. Us and Them. Friend and Enemy. Good and Bad. "Hatred against a particular person or institution might operate in just the same unifying way," Freud suggested, "and might call up the same kind of emotional ties as positive attachment."[45] Barash said it more succinctly: "In enmity, there is unity."[46] This proclivity to cleave people into collectives may be so ingrained in human nature and culture that we not only feel directionless if we do not belong to a group, we feel empty without another group with whom to contrast ourselves. The poet Constantine Cavafy suggested as much in his poem "Waiting for the Barbarians":

Why this sudden bewilderment, this confusion?
(How serious people's faces have become.)

Why are the streets and squares emptying so rapidly,
everyone going home lost in thought?
Because night has fallen and the barbarians haven't come.
And some of our men just in from the border say
there are no barbarians any longer.
Now what's going to happen to us without barbarians?
Those people were a kind of solution.[47]

If our natural gregariousness leads many of us to join groups, what differentiates those who join extremist groups? Loren Christensen, a nationally recognized expert on skinhead gangs and a police officer in Portland, Oregon—once dubbed the "Skinhead Capital of the United States"—came on a curious phenomenon as he observed the gangs on his beat in the 1990s: "Just when you think you have it figured out, something new will come along to shoot down your perceived truth." As his files on local gangs and their national connections to other groups grew in size and number, he realized that "the antiracist skinhead becomes involved in a gang for all the same psychological and sociological reasons as the racist skinhead. While they have a different philosophy and political stance, the individuals who form the different skinhead factions have the same basic needs and wants." Young males in particular need to belong, Christensen discovered, but what matters is not which gang they are in. What matters is to *belong*. "We had a white male gangster who was an active member in the black gang known as Bloods," Christensen explained. "He hung out with them, drank with them, and was even involved in a drive-by shooting against a Crip. A few months later, we documented him as a white supremacist because he was running with neo-Nazi skinheads and had formed a right-wing organization known as the National Socialist Front. Even in that capacity, he continued to communicate with individuals associated with the Blood gang." The process of belonging may cross even the sharpest lines of all forms of group classification—race. Switching sides is acceptable (to a point), as long as you belong to something. "Antiracist skinheads frequently change sides and become racist skins for a while, then switch back to become antiracist. One racist skinhead who had switched back and forth several times told us he was also bisexual. Does that make him bi-gangual as well?" Being in a gang, in fact, embodies the very essence of enemy-formation and ideological polarization (see figure 9). A gang "conspires to commit, or commits, crimes against individuals or groups based on color, race, religion, sexual preference, national origin, or against rival gang associations; uses a name or common identifying sign or symbol; has a

Figure 9.   Skinhead gang poster for recruit-
ing new members. (Reprinted with permission
from *Skinhead Street Gangs,* by Loren Christensen [Paladin Press, 1994])

high rate of interaction among members to the exclusion of other groups;
claims a neighborhood and/or geographical territory; wears distinctive
types of clothing, exhibits distinctive appearance, or communicates in a
peculiar or unique style." People join gangs, Christensen says, for the
same reasons they join any organization: "because of the excitement of
gang activity, peer pressure, attention, respect, strength, sense of family,
and survival." Gang membership becomes dangerous, however, when it
turns to the process of enemy formation. "An individual skinhead becomes strong within a gang, because as a member he sees everything as
'us against them.' It's rare for a skinhead to act out by himself." And as
Christensen notes with sarcastic humor, "It can get lonely being right,
when a person believes only he is right and everyone else is wrong. But
when he is with others who believe the same way as he does, he feels
stronger and more confident that his belief is a valid one." The power
to defeat the enemy comes out of group cohesiveness, "especially when
members have a sense of righteousness about the belief and the knowledge that others will stand with them to defend it."[48]

The process is the same on a national level, albeit with far greater consequences. In what would turn out to be a prophetic statement about his own people, Friedrich Nietzsche noted that in many ways enemies are more important than friends in uniting a new nation: "Our spiritualization of hostility . . . consists in a profound appreciation of having enemies." Writing in 1880 of the recent unification of Germany under Bismarck, he warned that "a new creation—the new Reich, for example, needs enemies more than friends: in opposition alone does it feel itself necessary."[49] The Third Reich, of course, found its external enemy in communism, and since the Jews were also linked to the communists, they became both external and internal enemies.

The enemy can come in any form, but the extremists we are concerned about here have chosen the Jews, as expressed in the following passage from *Die Kameradschaft*, the publication of the veterans' association for former members of the Waffen-SS, describing the eternal danger from the Jew who "crouches in the background, hardly recognizable, a danger just as great. It emanates from that race-conscious minority which from its formation as a people in the brutal laws of the desert has survived throughout the centuries. By using its inimitable craftiness and constant doggedness, this minority is determined to subjugate the world to its will."[50]

How many times have we heard this before? Throughout history there has been a plethora of allegations: that the Jews caused the French Revolution and the Russian Revolution; that they were the driving force behind Darwinism and Marxism; that they control the world's gold and the world's press; that they are socialists, anarchists, communists; that they create financial panics and economic depressions; and that they meet in secret cabals to plot the takeover of the world. Whether the threat is real or illusory does not matter. As the sociologist Lewis Coser explains, "If people define a threat as real, although there may be little or nothing in reality to justify this belief, the threat is real in its consequences— and among these consequences is the increase of group cohesion."[51] As a group, Holocaust deniers need the Jews as their enemy—in fact, they routinely refer to Jews as "the traditional enemy." Willis Carto, in a private letter written to a right-wing extremist (discovered by a Liberty Lobby employee and turned over to the FBI), sums up what he perceives as the ultimate problem: "Hitler's defeat was the defeat of Europe and America. How could we have been so blind? The blame, it seems, must be laid at the door of the international Jews. It was their propaganda, lies, and demands which blinded the West to what Germany was doing.

If Satan himself . . . had tried to create a permanent . . . force for the destruction of all nations, he could have done no better than to invent the
Jews."[52]

Here, in one summary statement by one of the modern founders of
Holocaust denial, we have two of the oldest enemies in Western culture:
Satan and the Jews. It does not matter if nothing in reality justifies such
a belief, the threat is real in its consequences because the deniers *believe*
it is. And this belief gives them the cohesion they need to continue their
mission. This, we contend, is the ultimate reason why they say the Holocaust did not happen. The deniers need the Jews much as Captain Ahab
needed the white whale:

> The White Whale swam before him as the monomaniac incarnation of all those
> malicious agencies which some deep men feel eating in them, till they are left
> living on with half a heart and half a lung. . . . He pitted himself, all muti-
> lated, against it. All that most maddens and torments; all that stirs up the lees
> of things, all truth with malice in it; all that cracks the sinews and cakes the
> brain; all the subtle demonisms of life and thought; all evil, to crazy Ahab,
> were visibly personified, and made practically assailable in Moby Dick. He
> piled upon the whale's white hump the sum of all the general rage and hate
> felt by his whole race from Adam down; and then, as if his chest had been a
> mortar, he burst his hot heart's shell upon it.[53]

5 How Deniers Distort History

Flaws, Fallacies, and Failings in the Deniers' Arguments

The first, the Retort Courteous; the second, the Quip Modest;
the third, the Reply Churlish; the fourth, the Reproof Valiant;
the fifth, the Countercheck Quarrelsome; the sixth, the Lie
with Circumstance; the seventh, the Lie Direct.

William Shakespeare, *As You Like It*

To construct a veritable past, avoiding fictional whole cloth, we must recognize that not all histories are equally plausible. Some are certain, some less certain, and some simply impossible. "Debunking" is a strong word, but it seems an appropriate reaction to such an extraordinary claim as denial of the Holocaust. As a segue into the specific arguments and refutations of the next part, we sift through flaws, fallacies, and failings in the deniers' arguments in the larger context of how they distort history. It is an exercise in the difference between history and pseudohistory, historiography and hagiography, genuine revision and denial.

We do not mean to imply that there is some impenetrable canon of truth about the Holocaust (as many deniers believe). In fact, when researchers delve into the study of the Holocaust, especially when they attend conferences, lectures, and debates among Holocaust historians, they learn that there is plenty of inside arguing (even fighting) about significant issues of the Holocaust. The major brouhaha over Daniel Goldhagen's book *Hitler's Willing Executioners* and the debate about Ron Rosenbaum's biography *Explaining Hitler* show that Holocaust historians are anything but in agreement.[1] But, please note, they *do* agree that the Holocaust happened. Here is one of the primary differences between historians and pseudohistorians.

HOW DENIERS REDEFINE THE HOLOCAUST

When historians ask, "How can anyone deny the Holocaust?" and deniers respond, "We're not denying the Holocaust," there is obviously a difference in definition. What deniers are explicitly denying are three points found in most definitions of the Holocaust:

1. A *highly technical,* well-organized extermination program, using *gas* chambers and crematoria, among other instruments and methods, was implemented to kill millions of Jews.

2. An estimated *six million* Jews were killed.

3. There was an *intention* to commit genocide of Jews based primarily on racial ideology.

Deniers agree that there was rampant antisemitism in Nazi Germany, and that Hitler and many of the Nazi leaders hated the Jews. They also agree that Jews were deported, their property and wealth were confiscated, and they were rounded up and forced into concentration camps where, in general, they were very harshly treated and made the victims of overcrowding, disease, and forced labor. Specifically what the deniers say—as outlined in Bradley Smith's advertisement in college newspapers, as well as in other sources—is this:

1. The main causes of death of Jews in the camps were disease and starvation generated primarily by the Allied destruction of German supply lines and resources at the end of the war. There were shootings and hangings (and maybe even some experimental gassings), and the Germans did overwork Jews in forced labor in the war effort, but this accounts for a very small percentage of the dead. Gas chambers were used for delousing clothing and blankets only, and the crematoria were used to dispose of the bodies of those who had succumbed to these other forms of death, especially disease.

2. Anywhere from 300,000 to one or two million Jews died or were killed in ghettos and camps.

3. There was no Nazi policy to exterminate European Jewry. The "Final Solution" to the "Jewish question" was deportation out of the Reich. Because of early successes in the war, the Reich was

...ping more Jews than it could deport. Because of later fail-
... the war, the Reich concentrated Jews into ghettos, and

2

...ated in the introduction, when we refer to the Holocaust, we
... *the systematic bureaucratically administered destruction by the
Nazis and their collaborators during the Second World War of an estimated six million Jews based primarily on racial ideology.* Therefore, we
respond to these claims as follows:

1. Gas chambers and crematoria were only one mechanism of extermination in the "Final Solution," and they evolved from an
   earlier Nazi euthanasia program aimed at eliminating the physically and mentally retarded. If the Nazis were willing to kill their
   own people, it is reasonable then to assume they could kill people
   whom they considered alien and whom they viewed as a cancer
   on society—the Jews. Regardless of the mechanism of murder,
   however, murder is murder. We know that, in occupied Soviet territories, the Nazis also killed well over one million Jews by means
   other than gassing, and these means are as much a part of the
   Holocaust as the gas chambers.

2. Six million Jews killed is a general estimate, but a sound one. The
   figures are derived through population demographics, based on
   the number of Jews registered as living in countries throughout
   Europe before the war, the number who emigrated, the number
   reported transported to camps, the number who died of natural
   causes, the number killed in the camps, the number liberated from
   the camps, and the number remaining after the war. Historians
   use several methods of calculation to corroborate the figures for
   each location.

3. The destruction by the Nazis and their collaborators of six million Jews evolved over many years, beginning in the early 1930s
   with the expulsion of Jews from German social and economic life,
   continuing in the late 1930s with deportation of Jews from an
   expanding Germany. From June 1941, with the invasion of Russia, through early 1945, the Final Solution was implemented, that
   is, Jews were systematically deported, concentrated in ghettos and
   camps, and murdered. While policy intentions are difficult to

prove, policy outcomes are not. The outcome of Nazi policy against the Jews was millions of dead Jews. There is no legitimate way to deny the fact that it happened.

In part three of this book we address these three points in detail and provide the historical evidence to support each claim.

FALLACIES OF DENIERS' METHODS AND REASONING

In examining the deniers' history and literature we observe a striking similarity between their methodologies and those of other fringe groups, such as militias, cults, and religious extremists.[3] Perhaps, since there is no reason to assume the resemblance is deliberate, what we see is the ideological pattern of a fringe group as it tries to move into the mainstream:

1. Early in the development of a movement, the very remoteness of the group's cause allows a relative diversity of thought and membership, bringing together different people from the fringes of society. Initially, the group has little success in entering the mainstream. (Holocaust denial in the early 1970s.)

2. As the movement grows, its more conservative members try to disassociate themselves and their organization from the radical fringe and to establish scientific or scholarly credentials. (In the late 1970s, the Institute for Historical Review and the *Journal for Historical Review* are founded, and in the 1990s IHR breaks with its founder, Willis Carto, who has ties to the extreme right [see chapter 3]).

3. During this drive toward acceptability emphasis shifts away from anti-establishment views, toward a more positive statement of beliefs. (Today, some deniers have tried to divorce themselves from the most extreme elements of their past. David Irving, for example, has publicly stated his intention to break from the IHR [see chapter 3].)

4. To enter public institutions such as schools and public access television, American fringe groups will use the First Amendment and claim violation of their "freedom of speech" if they are not allowed to be heard. (Bradley Smith raised this cry in his ad campaigns in college newspapers in the 1990s.)

5. To draw the public's attention the groups shift the burden of proof from themselves to the establishment, demanding specific pieces of evidence for general phenomena not normally proved through single facts. (The deniers demand "just one proof" that Jews were killed in gas chambers or to see "the" order from Hitler to exterminate the Jews.)

The parallels between the fallacies of the reasoning of Holocaust deniers and other fringe groups are also eerily similar:

1. They rarely say anything definitive about their own position and instead attack their opponents' weak points or mistakes. (Deniers hammer away at the inconsistencies among eyewitness accounts of the Holocaust.)

2. They find errors made by scholars and historians and exploit these as if *all* the historians' conclusions are wrong. (Pointing to the number killed at Auschwitz, deniers underline "the incredible shrinking Holocaust.")[4]

3. They quote, usually out of context, leading mainstream figures to buttress their own position. (Deniers have cited historians, such as Raul Hilberg and Yehuda Bauer, as well as historical figures, such as leading Nazis.)[5]

4. They consciously turn debates among scholars on specific issues into debates about the veracity of the entire field. (When historians ask if the Nazis intended to exterminate the Jews from the beginning, or if this was a function of the war, deniers claim that historians are arguing about whether the Holocaust happened.)[6]

5. They focus on what is *not* known and ignore what is known, carefully selecting data that fit and ignoring data that do not fit their preconceived ideas. (Deniers stress what we do not know about the gas chambers and disregard eyewitness accounts, as well as photographs of the chambers in operation.)[7]

THE MORAL EQUIVALENCY ARGUMENT

Ironically, after denying that the Nazis intended to exterminate the Jews, deniers argue that what the Nazis did to the Jews is really no different from what other nations do to their perceived enemies. David Irving,

Figure 10.   Adolf Eichmann at the time
of his 1961 trial in Jerusalem. (Photo: Yad
Vashem, Jerusalem, Israel; courtesy United
States Holocaust Memorial Museum)

for example, points out that the U.S. government obliterated two Japanese cities and their civilian populations with atomic weapons—the only government in history to do so.[8] Furthermore, Mark Weber notes, Americans concentrated Japanese Americans in camps, much as Germans did to their perceived internal enemy—the Jews.[9] These examples and others, such as Irving's citation of the mass bombing of Dresden, have a not-so-hidden agenda: to implicate America and Britain as equally guilty, along with Germany, in the mass destruction of the Second World War.

But what is missing in this comparison? First, there is a big difference between two nations fighting one another, both using trained soldiers, and the systematic, state-organized killing of unarmed, unsuspecting people—not in self-defense, not to gain territory or wealth (although these may accrue as a beneficial by-product), but because of antisemitism. Scholars and the general public debate the morality of the atomic bombing of Hiroshima and Nagasaki, the internment of Japanese Americans in concentration camps, and the mass bombing of Dresden. But historians do not try to equate these actions with the Holocaust.[10] If we take the mass bombing of Dresden, for instance—although it was admittedly one of the worst acts against the Axis powers by the Allies, it resulted in about 35 thousand deaths, not the 250 thousand first claimed by the Germans, and nowhere near the 6 million of the Holocaust.[11]

At his trial in Jerusalem Adolf Eichmann, SS-Obersturmbannführer of the RSHA (lieutenant colonel of the Reich Security Main Office) and one of the chief planners and organizers of the Final Solution (see figure 10), tried to make the moral equivalency argument. The judge, however, did not accept his rationalizations, as this sequence from the trial transcript shows:

JUDGE BENJAMIN HALEVI TO EICHMANN: You have often compared the extermination of the Jews with the bombing raids on German cities and you compared the murder of Jewish women and children with the death of German women in aerial bombardments. Surely it must be clear to you that there is a basic distinction between these two things. On the one hand the bombing is used as an instrument of forcing the enemy to surrender. Just as the Germans tried to force the British to surrender by their bombing. In that case it is a war objective to bring an armed enemy to his knees.

On the other hand, when you take unarmed Jewish men, women, and children from their homes, hand them over to the Gestapo, and then send them to Auschwitz for extermination it is an entirely different thing, is it not?

EICHMANN: The difference is enormous. But at that time these crimes had been legalized by the state and the responsibility, therefore, belongs to those who issued the orders.

HALEVI: But you must know surely that there are internationally recognized Laws and Customs of War whereby the civilian population is protected from actions which are not essential for the prosecution of the war itself.

EICHMANN: Yes, I'm aware of that.

HALEVI: Did you never feel a conflict of loyalties between your duty and your conscience?

EICHMANN: I suppose one could call it an internal split. It was a personal dilemma when one swayed from one extreme to the other.

HALEVI: One had to overlook and forget one's conscience.

EICHMANN: Yes, one could put it that way.[12]

Please note that Eichmann never denied the Holocaust. His argument was that "these crimes had been legalized by the state" and therefore the people who "issued the orders" are responsible. This was, in fact, the classic defense used at Nuremberg by most of the Nazis—denial of responsibility, not denial of the crime.

CONSPIRACIES, REPARATIONS, AND THE SECRET NATURE OF GENOCIDE

Why, we might ask the deniers, if the Holocaust did not happen would any group concoct such a horrific story? Because, some deniers claim, there was a conspiracy by Zionists to exaggerate the plight of Jews during the war in order to finance the state of Israel through war reparations.[13]

Our answer here is straightforward. The basic facts about the Holocaust were established before the state of Israel was founded in 1948 and before it began receiving reparations in the 1950s. When reparations were made, the amount Israel received from Germany was based not on numbers killed but on the cost to Israel of absorbing and resettling Jews who had fled Germany and German-controlled countries before the war, as well as survivors of the Holocaust who came to Israel after. In March 1951, when Israel requested reparations from the Four Powers, it claimed:

> The government of Israel is not in a position to obtain and present a complete statement of all Jewish property taken or looted by the Germans, and said to total more than $6 thousand million. It can only compute its claim on the basis of total expenditures already made and the expenditure still needed for the integration of Jewish immigrants from Nazi-dominated countries. The number of these immigrants is estimated at some 500,000, which means a total expenditure of $1.5 thousand million.[14]

If reparations were based on the total number of survivors, wouldn't it make sense for any Zionist conspirators to claim a much higher number of survivors? If we pretend the deniers are right and say that only a few hundred thousand Jews died, then surely Germany owes Israel far more in reparations, for at least a sizable portion of those six million survivors would have gone to Israel.

The deniers' paradoxical spin on conspiracy theories is of note in this regard. First, they deny that the Nazis had a clear plan (a conspiracy) to exterminate the Jews. They reinforce this argument by pointing out how extreme conspiratorial thinking can become (as in John F. Kennedy conspiracy theories). From historians, they demand powerful evidence before drawing any conclusion that a Nazi/Hitler conspiracy to exterminate European Jewry existed.[15] This insistence on evidence is fine. But they cannot then claim that the idea of the Holocaust is a Zionist conspiracy to demand reparations from Germany in order to fund the new state of Israel, without meeting similar demands for proof.

In furthering their argument, deniers claim that if the Holocaust really happened, then it would have been widely known during the war. It would be as obvious as, say, the D-Day landing. Plus, the Nazis would have discussed it among themselves, as they made their plans for mass, systematic murder.[16]

But, we counter, the D-Day landing was not widely known until after the event began. For obvious reasons, D-Day was kept a secret. Might not a similar need for secrecy apply to the Holocaust? It was not something that was casually discussed on an everyday basis between fellow Nazis, as Albert Speer noted in his *Spandau Diary*:

> *December 9, 1946.* It would be wrong to imagine that the top men of the regime would have boasted of their crimes on the rare occasions when they met. At the trial we were compared to the heads of a Mafia. I recalled movies in which the bosses of legendary gangs sat around in evening dress chatting about murder and power, weaving intrigues, concocting coups. But this atmosphere of back room conspiracy was not at all the style of our leadership. In our personal dealings, nothing would ever be said about any sinister activities we might be up to.[17]

As an example of this, SS guard Theodor Malzmueller described his introduction to the idea of mass murder upon his arrival at the Kulmhof (Chelmno) extermination camp:

> When we arrived we had to report to the camp commandant, SS-Haupsturmführer [captain] Bothmann. The SS-Haupsturmführer addressed us in his living quarters, in the presence of SS-Untersturmführer [second lieutenant] Albert Plate. He explained that we had been dedicated to the Kulmhof extermination camp as guards and added that in this camp the plague boils of humanity, the Jews, were exterminated. We were to keep quiet about everything we saw or heard, otherwise we would have to reckon with our families' imprisonment and the death penalty.[18]

As Shumel Spector has shown, the Nazis had an organized plan, known as Aktion 1005, to eradicate all traces of their killing actions.[19] Begun in mid-1942, the process continued to the last days of the war. Aktion 1005 unfolded in two major stages: the removal of the bodies in the extermination camps and the removal of the bodies from the mass graves. The program was directed by SS-Standartenführer (colonel) Paul Blobel, who took over after heading the Sonderkommando 4a of the Einsatzgruppe ("special force") C.[20] At his trial at Nuremberg Blobel explained that Adolf Eichmann had assigned him the task of obliterating all traces of mass murder, especially at the extermination camps and the numerous locations of the murderous actions of the Einsatzgruppen in the east (with which he was quite familiar).[21] Under orders from the Reich security's main office, Blobel had bodies from the mass graves in Chelmno exhumed and burned. From there Blobel went to Auschwitz, where he instructed Rudolf Höss, the commandant, to use the same procedure in a literal holocaust of 107,000 bodies. Belzec, Sobibor, and Treblinka were next, where over 500,000 bodies were burned.[22] From the camps, Blobel went to Kiev where he began the arduous task of mopping up after the Einsatzgruppen actions. Jews were used to dig up and burn the bodies—then these Jews were killed as well. After the German defeat at Stalingrad in 1943—when the German army began to retreat to the west—this process began to intensify. In the end, however, there were too many graves, too many bodies, and not enough time. Furthermore, many Jewish prisoners escaped Aktion 1005 and lived to tell about their experiences.

Also, contrary to the deniers' claims, Allied intelligence apparently did know about many actions of Nazi genocide during the war. The Holocaust historian Richard Breitman recently discovered files proving that British intelligence agents knew as early as the summer of 1941 that the Nazis were committing regular atrocities against the Jews as they swept into eastern Poland and Russia following the June invasion of the Soviet Union. These included such decoded messages as these: July 18: "1,153 Jewish looters shot." August 27: "Regiment South shot 914 Jews; the special action staff with police battalion 320 shot 4,200 Jews." August 31: "2,200 Jews shot." In another message dated August 7, 1941, Nazi General von dem Bach-Zelewsky makes it clear just how extensive the mass murders were: "The action of the SS cavalry brigade proceeds. By noon today, a further 3,600 were executed, so that the total number by Cavalry Regiment Eastern is 7,819. Thereby, the number of 30,000 in my area has been exceeded."[23] But why didn't the British publicize this information? The answer is simple: they believed that if they released this information the Germans would then know that their codes had been broken, thus jeopardizing the war effort and possibly extending the war (and thus the Holocaust itself).

THE YELLOW STAR AND THE PURPOSE OF THE CAMPS

Some deniers argue that Jews were made to wear the yellow star to ensure the safety of German soldiers, because Jews engaged in espionage, terrorism, black market operations, and arms trafficking. In other words, the yellow star was a warning sign to Germans that an enemy was in their midst. Along the same line, deniers have argued that Jews and others were placed in concentration camps for protection "where they could not hurt the new regime and where they could be protected from the public anger."[24] Additionally, deniers claim, the camps were places where Jews could be rehabilitated for eventual reintroduction into German life.

None of this is fact. Not only were Jews forced to wear a symbol of their difference, so were other groups, such as homosexuals, gypsies, political dissidents, and others. Jews, however, were forced to wear the yellow star in public, whereas the other groups' discrimination was mostly confined to concentration camps. As for the camps offering protection, even most deniers now admit that they were miserable places for anyone to be.[25] Moreover, to say that the camps provided rehabilitation goes against Nazi philosophy. Nazis believed strongly in biological determinism—the position that most of the variation among people and groups is genetic. Therefore, group differences are biological differences, not to be overcome through cultural training or socialization or anything short of a "final solution," mass extermination.[26]

PUBLIC DISCOURSE AND PRIVATE DOUBTS: DENIERS ON *DONAHUE*

It is one thing to analyze the literature of deniers or to interview them face to face; it is quite another process to confront them in a public forum, where their skills at rhetoric and debate can trip up even seasoned scholars and historians. On March 14, 1994, the television talkshow host Phil Donahue featured two Holocaust deniers (David Cole and Bradley Smith) as part of a program on his daily series, this one dealing with Holocaust denial. Many of the major shows had considered doing something on the subject, but for a variety of reasons *Donahue* was the first. Montel Williams actually taped a program on April 30, 1992, but it was pulled from major markets because, according to deniers, they looked too good and the Holocaust scholar offered nothing better than ad hominem attacks.

One of us (Shermer) appeared on the show under the guidance of the other (Grobman), who provided numerous documents and photographs to be used in rebuttal. The *Donahue* producer had promised there would be no skinheads or neo-Nazis, and the show would not be allowed to erupt into violence or mere shouting. The deniers were promised they would be allowed to make their claims, and we were promised that time and opportunity would be allotted to properly refute them. Edith Glueck, who had been in Auschwitz, albeit for only a couple of weeks, also appeared on the show, along with a close friend, Judith Berg, who had been in Auschwitz for seven months; both were seated in the studio audience. We instructed them not to exaggerate or embellish anything, and to just tell the audience exactly what they remembered. (Most survivors know very little about the Holocaust outside of what happened to them half a century ago, and deniers are skilled at tripping them up when they get dates wrong, or worse, claim they saw someone or something they could not have seen.)

Donahue opened the show with these words: "How do we know the Holocaust really happened? And what proof do we have that even one Jew was killed in a gas chamber? Those questions are being asked and causing furors on campuses all across America, provoked by an ad which is offered by a person that you're about to meet who suggests that the Holocaust needs revisiting." As the producers rolled stock footage from Nazi concentration camps, Donahue continued the narration:

> In just the last six months fifteen college newspapers across the country have run advertisements that call for an open debate of the Holocaust. The ad claims that the United States Holocaust Memorial Museum in Washington, D.C., has no proof whatever of homicidal gassing chambers, and no proof that even one individual was gassed in a German program of genocide. The ads have caused an uproar everywhere, sparking protests from students and boycotts of the papers. The man who placed all the ads, Bradley Smith, has been called anti-Semitic and a neo-Nazi because of the challenges of the Holocaust. Smith claims he simply wants the truth to be told—that Jews were never placed in gas chambers and that the figure of six million Jewish deaths is an irresponsible exaggeration. And he is not alone in his beliefs. A recent poll by the Roper organization found that 22 percent of all Americans believe it's possible the Holocaust never happened. Another 12 percent say they don't know. So in a time when over 5,000 visitors are crowding the new Holocaust museum everyday, and the film *Schindler's List* is reducing jaded movie-goers to tears, the question should be asked, How can anyone claim the Holocaust was a hoax?[27]

It was obvious from the start that Donahue was in over his head. Turning to Bradley Smith, who was the first guest to be introduced and brought on stage, he immediately tried to reduce the discussion to accusations of antisemitism. "You do not deny that antisemitism in Europe in the thirties, most especially Germany, Poland, and environs, was visceral and that Hitler—"

SMITH: We're not talking about any of that. Listen—
DONAHUE: Please don't be upset with my questions.
SMITH: I'm not upset. But the question is outside the parameter of the issue. I'm running an advertisement that says the museum—

DONAHUE: We're three minutes into this program and you don't like my question.

SMITH: The question has nothing to do with what I'm doing.

DONAHUE: Let's accept your point here. May I ask you the courtesy of responding to this question?

SMITH: Yeah, sure.

DONAHUE: Do you believe that there was engineered by Hitler and the Third Reich a strategy of eliminating Jews called the Final Solution? Do you believe that?

Finally we got to a question with some substance. It looked as though Donahue were going to zero in on one of the deniers' major points—the moral equivalence argument that claims in times of war all people are treated badly and that the Nazis were no worse than the other major combatants in this and other wars.

SMITH: I don't believe it anymore. I used to. But that's not what I'm talking about. If you don't understand what I'm talking about you won't ask the right question. The question is this. We have a $200 million museum in Washington, D.C. It's in America. It's not in Europe. And the whole museum is dedicated to the proposition that Jews were killed in gas chambers. They don't have any proof in the museum that Jews were killed in gas chambers. As a matter of fact, they are so sure of guys like you will never ask them the question . . . nothing personal.

DONAHUE: Guys like me? [Audience laughter]

This sort of patter went on for another fifteen minutes, with Donahue continually returning to the issue of antisemitism and Smith and David Cole, brought on stage shortly after Smith, trying to make their points. Cole showed some of his video footage from Auschwitz and Majdanek and discussed the issue of Zyklon-B trace deposits and other technical matters (see chapter 6). Knowing that this was probably over the heads of his audience, Donahue turned to Cole's personal life, trying to associate him with Ernst Zündel (see chapter 3). But it backfired in a big way:

DONAHUE: Let me just talk personal. How old are you?

COLE: No, wait a minute. I want to put the issue in some perspective, especially for the audience. When the war was over in 1945 it was claimed that there were twenty-two camps that had gas chambers in them—twenty-two. By the 1950s, sixteen of those camps had been officially revised by the Americans, the Israelis, the British, the Soviets, and now it is only claimed that six camps in Poland had gas chambers. In other words, what happened was the camps

that were in Germany and Austria, they were able to be investigated by Americans, freely investigated by historians. But the
camps in Poland were not made available until recently to Western researchers—

DONAHUE: It's an hour show.

COLE: Well, yeah, but it's a complex topic.

DONAHUE: It certainly is. David, you are familiar, and know, and have traveled with Ernst Zündel. Is that so?

COLE: No, I have not traveled with Ernst Zündel.

DONAHUE: Did you meet him in Poland?

COLE: I met him in Poland. I met him twice in my entire life.

DONAHUE: All right, what did you do, have a beer? I mean, what's travel mean?
[Audience laughter] You met him in Poland. He is a neo-Nazi. You
don't deny that?

DONAHUE: No, I'm sorry Phil. This is not about who I've met in my life. I just
met you. Does that mean I'm Marlo Thomas? [Huge audience
laughter] This is about physical evidence. This is about Zyklon-B
residue. This is about windows in a gas chamber. One clip they
didn't show, with me standing in front of the Majdanek gas chamber with a big plate glass window in it that was not barred or covered in anyway.

DONAHUE: Were you bar mitzvahed David?

COLE: I'm an atheist. I made that clear to your production staff.

DONAHUE: Well, but you may not have been at age thirteen.

COLE: I've always been an atheist.

This kind of banter went on for several more minutes until a commercial break. The producer, page, makeup artist, and microphone tech-
nician now all escorted Shermer from the green room into the studio. It
had the feel of a prize fighter going into the ring: "Okay Shermer," the
producer encouraged, "we're counting on you to nail these guys." "Do
it." "Good luck." And so on. The producer said to stay away from the
technical matters and stick to analyzing the deniers' methods. Unfortunately, during this segment Donahue failed to show the photographs and
quotes we had provided him. Instead, he blundered, showing film footage
from Dachau, now known not to be an extermination camp. Cole
promptly nailed him.

COLE: I'd like to ask Dr. Shermer a question. They just showed the Dachau
gas chamber in that footage. Is that gas chamber ever claimed to
have killed people?

SHERMER: No. And in fact, the important point here. . . .

DONAHUE: There is a sign at Dachau notifying tourists of that fact.

COLE: That it was not used to kill people. So why did you just show it in the clip?

DONAHUE: I'm not at all sure that was Dachau.

COLE: Oh, that was Dachau. Now wait a minute. You're not sure that was Dachau? *You* show a clip on *your* show and you're not sure it was Dachau?

SHERMER: History is knowledge, and like all knowledge it progresses and changes. We continually refine our certainty about claims, and so we once thought there was human soap—the human soap story was true—now we know it's not. And that's what historical revision is all about.

Soon after this, David Cole left the studio in disgust that he was not allowed to discuss the gas chamber story as promised. The producer yelled at him, but Donahue said, "Let him walk!" The show then turned to questions from the audience and callers. One wanted to know why Smith was "doing this" to the Jews. The ensuing exchange demonstrates why it is so important to know how to deal with the specific claims of the deniers.

SMITH: One of the problems here is we have a feeling that if we talk about this issue nobody is involved but Jews. Germans are involved. For instance, if we tell . . . there is something vulgar about lying about Germans and thinking that it's proper. For example, it was a lie that Germans cooked Jews to make soap from them. It was a lie—

SHERMER: No, not a lie. It's a mistake—

JUDITH BERG [sitting in front row]: It was true. They made lampshades and they cooked soap. That's true.

SMITH: Ask the professor.

SHERMER: Excuse me, historians make mistakes. Everybody makes mistakes. We're always refining our knowledge, and some of these things come down and they don't turn out to be true. But let me tell you what I think is going on here—

SMITH: Ask why they're doing that to this woman. Why have they taught this woman to believe that the Germans cooked and skinned—

BERG [jumps out of seat, screaming]: I was seven months in Auschwitz. I lived near the crematorium as far as I am from you. I smelled . . . you would never eat roast chicken if you had been there. Because I smelled—

SMITH: Let's get to the bottom of one thing. She says soap and lampshades. The professor says you're mistaken.

BERG: Even the Germans admit it. They admit it that they had lampshades—

DONAHUE [to Smith]: Do you have any empathy at all . . . are you concerned about the pain that you cause this woman?

SMITH: Sure, but why should we ignore the Germans, who are accused of this despicable story?

BERG [in a very emotional voice, pointing finger at Smith]: I was seven months there. If you are blind someone else can see it. I was seven months there—

SMITH: What does that have to do with soap? No soap, no lampshades. The professor says you're wrong, that's all.

BERG: He wasn't there. The people there told me not to use that [soap] because it could be your mother.

SMITH: A doctor of history, Occidental College. He says you're mistaken.

SHERMER: They burned bodies in mass graves. . . .

As chaos ensued, Donahue broke for a commercial. In the green room Judith Berg had said she saw the Nazis burning large numbers of bodies in an open field. We had provided *Donahue*'s producers a photograph of this (see chapter 6) and the producer was prepared to flash it on the screen. Somewhere between the green room and the studio, however, the burning bodies became human soap. So much for the reliability of Holocaust survivors' composure on national television. Eyewitness testimony, as psychologists and lawyers know, must be used selectively and checked against other testimony and corroborative evidence. The results of this problem were evident in this segment of the show. Some accounts have probative value, others do not. Berg provided a perfect setup and Smith capitalized on it. Donahue, having exhausted his knowledge of the Holocaust, returned to the free speech issues and, once again, antisemitism and ad hominem attacks on Smith's character and credentials.

The human soap story that proved so disastrous for the *Donahue* show is, as it turns out, one of the most misunderstood topics in all of Holocaust scholarship. Knowing this, the deniers use it to their advantage to imply to the general public that perhaps all of the Holocaust story is exaggerated or wrong. Just what is the truth behind this story?

THE HUMAN SOAP CONTROVERSY

During the Second World War rumors spread that the Nazis were turning some of their victims into soap. The rumor started when the Germans distributed bars of soap with the initials "RIF" stamped into them. Some misread this as "RJF" and thought it stood for *Rein Judisches Fett*, or "pure Jewish fat." The story spread throughout Europe during the war and has persisted to this day. Mel Mermelstein, the subject of a made-for-TV movie about his lawsuits against the Holocaust deniers—*Never*

Forget—claims that soap made from murdered Jews is factual.[28] On the *Donahue* program on Holocaust denial, Judith Berg insisted she had learned first-hand that the Germans made soap from Jews at Auschwitz. Yet most historians do not believe it. Deniers exploit this confusion, claiming it is a clear example of Holocaust myth-making, the unreliability of eyewitness testimony, and poor historiography. For this reason we want to address this controversy and clarify what we know and do not know.

During the First World War rumors were rampant of atrocities allegedly committed by the Germans against the Allies, especially in Belgium. After the war it was discovered that most of these horrors were simply not true and that some were constructed by the British to help draw America into the war.[29] This situation helps explain why Americans found it difficult at first to believe the stories coming out of Nazi Germany of the mass execution of Jews and others.

There is some evidence that at a site near the camp at Stutthof (about twenty-two miles east of Gdansk [Danzig]) the Nazis may have manufactured soap from human remains. Cakes are on display at the museum there and witnesses have testified that soap was made at Stutthof from the fat of dead persons. At the war crime trials Sigmund Mazur, laboratory assistant at the Danzig Anatomic Institute, testified that the institute conducted experiments in producing soap from human bodies. The professors collected bodies, bones, and human fat in "a laboratory for the fabrication of skeletons, the burning of meat and unnecessary bones." The chief, Professor Spanner, gave Mazur the soap recipe: 5 kilos of human fat are mixed with 10 liters of water and 500 or 1,000 grams of caustic soda. All this is boiled two or three hours and then cooled. The soap floats to the surface while the water and other sediment remain at the bottom. A bit of salt and soda is added to this mixture. Then fresh water is added, and the mixture is again boiled two or three hours. After it has cooled, the mixture is poured into molds. Mazur described the process:

> I boiled the soap out of the bodies of women and men. The process of boiling alone took several days—from 3 to 7. During two manufacturing processes, in which I directly participated, more than 25 kilograms of soap were produced. The amount of human fat necessary for these two processes was 70 to 80 kilograms collected from some 40 bodies. The finished soap then went to Professor Spanner, who kept it personally. The work for the production of soap from human bodies has, as far as I know, also interested Hitler's Government. The Anatomic Institute was visited by the Minister of Education, Rust; the Reichsgesundheitsführer [Reich health minister], Doctor Conti; the Gauleiter [party regional leader] of Danzig, Albert Forster; as well as pro-

fessors from other medical institutes. I used this human soap for my personal needs, for toilet and for laundering. For myself I took 4 kilograms of this soap.[30]

Two British POWs, part of the forced labor that built the camp and observed some of the activities there, gave the prosecution staff convincing testimony on the soap experiments. One of them stated:

> Owing to the preservative mixture in which they were stored, this tissue came away from the bones very easily. The tissue was then put into a boiler about the size of a small kitchen table. . . . After boiling the liquid it was put into white trays about twice the size of a sheet of foolscap and about 3 centimeters deep. . . . Approximately 3 to 4 trayfuls per day were obtained from the machine. A machine for the manufacture of soap was completed some time in March or April 1944. The British prisoners of war had constructed the building in which it was housed in June 1942. The machine itself was installed by a civilian from Danzig by the name of AJRD. It consisted, as far as I remember, of an electrically heated tank in which bones of the corpses were mixed with some acid and melted down. This process of melting down took about 24 hours. The fatty portions of the corpses and particularly those of females were put into a crude enamel tank, heated by a couple of Bunsen burners. Some acid was also used in this process. I think it was caustic soda. When boiling had been completed, the mixture was allowed to cool and then cut into blocks for microscopic examination.[31]

The prosecutor showed the court soap samples.

Similar testimonies and anecdotes abound. During the course of research on the human soap story, for example, the Sobibor survivor Thomas Blatt found several eyewitnesses, including Dr. Stanislaw Byczkowski, head of the Department of Toxicology at the School of Medicine in Gdansk nearby, who reported seeing these activities. But Blatt discovered little in the way of concrete documentation, concluding: "I found no evidence of mass production of soap from human fat, but indeed, there is without any doubt enough evidence of the experimental cannibalism in soap making in the cellars of the former Institute of Hygiene in Gdansk."[32]

The Holocaust historian Raul Hilberg summarized the soap controversy this way:

> A lot of these rumors originated during the war and, in fact, reached the United States long before the war was over. And human soap is one example. There are a couple of others. You will find the soap story in the *New York Times* mentioned by Rabbi Stephen Wise. Whether or not human soap was actually made is completely doubtful. In my opinion it was not. But there is a story— call it a rumor if you wish—that there was one particular SS unit of societal

rejects who got their last chance by joining that particular outfit, and according to the rumor, in the Lublin district quite early (before there were extermination camps) these guys amused themselves in ways totally unimaginable. They first engaged in some sort of sexual practice and then supposedly also made soap out of human bodies. That was a rumor. And rumors start based on some modicum of fact and get transmogrified, they get enlarged. But in the whole pattern of the process there is no indication that soap was made.

Interestingly, there is a report from Himmler who, after hearing the rumor in the *New York Times,* wrote to one of his subordinates, and apparently hearing it for the *first time* through the *New York Times,* cautioned his underling that under no circumstances is an improper use to be made of corpses. What is fascinating here is that Himmler himself is unsure whether that rumor is true. That gives you an indication of what goes on in this kind of rumor formation. There were other rumors: people killed by electric current in water, which turned out not to be correct. Or people gassed aboard trains, which also turned out not to be correct. Skin was apparently tattooed and taken from concentration camp inmates, though it is highly unlikely it was taken from Jews because it was tattooed. There were some human skin lampshades exhibited at the Nuremberg trials but these were one little tiny bizarre development, which is to be expected in a massive undertaking of this sort. Somebody is bound to be a little bit abnormal.[33]

What can we conclude about this story? Soap was never manufactured on an industrial scale from victims' bodies, but it may have been done experimentally. As in the case of the renegade SS unit abusing corpses, there may have been isolated cases of turning human fat into soap, but certainly not an organized plan to do so on any scale. We agree with the Holocaust historian Yisrael Gutman, who concludes that "it was never done on a mass scale."[34]

HOW DENIERS RATIONALIZE THE EVIDENCE

Our discussion of the soap story reveals how history can be appropriately revised. But what about the deniers' calls for revision throughout Holocaust historiography? Are they looking impartially at the evidence, to see where it leads, or do they insist on a prior interpretation? Let us reconsider the "convergence of evidence," discussed in chapter 2, as it applies to the Holocaust, and typical ways that deniers twist the data to support their claims. First, a survivor reports he heard about the gassing of Jews while he was at Auschwitz. A denier might counter that survivors exaggerate and that their memories are unsound. Next, another survivor tells another story, different in details but with the core similarity that Jews were gassed at Auschwitz. The denier replies that rumors floated through the camps and many survivors incorporated them into their memories. An SS guard then confesses (after the war) that he actually saw people being gassed and cremated. The denier claims that such confessions were forced out of the Nazis by the Allies. But now a member of the Sonderkommando—Jews who were forced to help the Nazis load bodies from the gas chambers into the crematoria—says he not only heard about the gassing, not only saw it happening, but actually *participated* in the process. The denier explains this away by saying that the Sonderkommando accounts make no sense—their figures of numbers of bodies are exaggerated and their dates are incorrect. What about the camp commandant, who confessed after the war that he not only heard, saw, and participated in the process but helped *orchestrate* it?! He was tortured, says the denier. But what about his autobiography written after his trial, conviction, and sentencing to death, when he had nothing to gain by lying? No one knows why people confess to ridiculous crimes, explains the denier, but they do.[35]

No single testimony says "Holocaust" on it. Yet, together, these testimonies form a body of evidence that challenges the deniers' defense. Instead of the presentation of "just one proof," here are five pieces of historical data, gathered through five different sources and converging to one conclusion, that deniers must disprove.

But there is more. We have blueprints of gas chambers and crematoria (see chapter 6). The gas chambers were used strictly for delousing, claim the deniers, and thanks to the Allies' war against Germany, the Germans were never given the opportunity to deport the Jews to their own homeland, and instead had to put them into overcrowded camps where disease and lice were rampant. What about the huge orders of Zyklon-B gas? It was strictly used for delousing all those diseased inmates. What about speeches by Hitler, Himmler, Frank, and Goebbels talking about the "extermination" of the Jews? They really meant "rooting out," as in deporting them out of the Reich. What about Eichmann's confession at his trial? He was coerced. Hasn't the German government confessed that the Nazis attempted to exterminate European Jewry? Yes, but they lied so they could rejoin the family of nations.

Now the deniers must rationalize no fewer than fourteen different bits of evidence that converge on a specific conclusion. But the convergence continues. If six million Jews did not die, where did they go? They are in Siberia and Peoria, Israel and Los Angeles, reply the deniers. But why cannot they find one another? They do—haven't we all heard the occasional stories of long-lost siblings making contact with each other after many decades? What about those photos and newsreels of the liberation of the camps with all those dead bodies and starving, dying inmates? Those people were well taken care of until the end of the war when the Allies mercilessly bombed the German cities, factories, and supply lines that fed those camps—the Nazis tried valiantly to save their prisoners but the combined strength of the Allies was too much. What about all those accounts by prisoners of the brutality of the Nazis at such camps as Auschwitz, Majdanek, and Sobibor—the random shootings and beatings, the deplorable conditions, the freezing temperatures, the death marches? That is the nature of war, say the deniers. The Americans put Japanese Americans in camps. The Japanese imprisoned Chinese. The Russians tortured Poles and Germans. War is hell. The Nazis are no different from anyone else.

We are now up to eighteen proofs all converging on one conclusion. The deniers are desperately swinging away at them all, steadfastly determined not to give up their belief system. They rely on what might be called *post hoc rationalization*—an after-the-fact reasoning to justify contrary evidence. In addition, the deniers shift the burden of proof to historians by demanding that *each* piece of evidence, independently and without corroboration among them, prove the Holocaust. Yet no historian has ever claimed that one piece of evidence proves the Holocaust. We must examine the collective whole.

Are we exaggerating these examples? No. This is not a hypothetical situation. Every one of these examples, and hundreds more, are readily available in the various denier sources cited in the bibliography. We specifically discuss and refute them in the next section.

part iii
Arguments and Refutations

The historian should be fearless and incorruptible; a man of independence, loving frankness and truth; one who, as the poet says, calls a fig a fig and a spade a spade. He should yield to neither hatred nor affection, but should be unsparing and unpitying. He should be neither shy nor deprecating, but an impartial judge, giving each side all it deserves but no more.

Lucian,
How History Should Be Written,
circa A.D. 170

6 The Crooked Timber of Auschwitz

How Concentration Camps Became Extermination Camps

If we are to hope to understand the often violent world in
which we live, we cannot confine our attention to the great
impersonal forces, natural and man-made, which act upon
us. The goals and motives that guide human action must
be looked at in the light of all that we know and understand;
their roots and growth, their essence, and above all their
validity, must be critically examined with every intellectual
resource that we have.

Isaiah Berlin, *The Crooked Timber of Humanity*, 1991

Isaiah Berlin's last book was inspired by the German philosopher Immanuel Kant, who, in one of the great one-liners of philosophy, summarized the history of civilization in this way: "Out of timber so crooked as that from which man is made nothing entirely straight can be built."[1] The grain of the past, Kant and Berlin understood, is twisted and full of knots. Rarely do historical events of any magnitude or import match the linear progression of cardboard textbook histories. Instead, the past is quirky and nonlinear, as one of the foremost proponents of this view of history, Stephen Jay Gould, explains:

> Life's history is massively contingent—crucially dependent upon odd particulars of history, quite unpredictable and unrepeatable themselves, that divert futures into new channels, shallow and adjacent to old pathways at first, but deepening and diverging with the passage of time. We can explain the actual pathways after they unroll, but we could not have predicted their course. And if we could play the game of life again, history would roll down another set of utterly different but equally explainable channels.[2]

FROM EUTHANASIA TO MASS MURDER

Gould is right. Life's history *is* massively contingent—all facets of it: the history of civilization, the history of war, the history of the Holocaust, and the history of the Nazi concentration camps. Holocaust deniers seem unaware of this contingency. They think that because extermination camps like Auschwitz and Majdanek do not look like perfectly designed killing machines no one used them for genocide. However, history is a product of both planned and unplanned events. Rarely do historical events unfold as expected. What typically happens is that plans change as events cascade, one upon another. As these plans and events interact and change, they create a feedback loop that constantly alters the events as they develop, often driving them further and further away from original intentions. A brief history of the evolution of the extermination camps in general, and Auschwitz in particular, supports this contingent view of history.

Long before they herded prisoners into gas chambers and killed them with Zyklon-B or carbon monoxide, the Nazis had developed a program of systematic and secret murder of targeted peoples. As we detail below, it began with the sterilization programs of the early 1930s, evolved into the euthanasia programs of the late 1930s, and escalated into mass murder in the extermination camps from 1941 to 1945. Although the idea of gassing masses of prisoners in a chamber seems shocking, psychologists have indicated how easy it is to get people to do almost anything when the steps leading to it are small and incremental.[3] We contend that after the Nazis had murdered tens of thousands of "inferior" Germans (see below), the idea of attempting to annihilate the Jewish people did not appear unimaginable. The demonization, exclusion, expulsion, sterilization, deportation, and euthanasia of targeted peoples made the step to mass murder seem a small one.

The Third Reich passed sterilization laws in late 1933. Within a year 32,268 people had been sterilized. In 1935 the figure jumped to 73,174, with the official reasons including feeblemindedness, schizophrenia, epilepsy, manic-depressive psychosis, alcoholism, deafness, blindness, and malformations. So-called sex offenders were simply castrated—no fewer than 2,300 in the first decade of the program.[4]

In 1935 Hitler told the leading Reich physician, Gerhard Wagner, that when the war began he wanted to make the shift from sterilization to euthanasia. True to his word, in the summer of 1939 the Nazis began killing physically handicapped children, then quickly moved on to mentally handicapped children, and soon after to adults with either handi-cap. The murders were initially committed through large doses of "nor-mal" medication given in tablet or liquid form, so as to look like an ac-cident (families were notified of the death). If the patients resisted, injections were used. When the numbers chosen for death became cum-bersomely large, however, the operations were moved into special killing wards instead of isolated units.[5]

In 1939 the Germans had expanded their operation into an office com-plex set up at a confiscated Jewish villa in Berlin, located at Tiergarten Strasse no. 4. The program then became known as Operation T4, or just T4, the "Reich Work Group of Sanatoriums and Nursing Homes."[6] T4 doctors decided who would live and who would die: economic status was one of the common criteria—individuals unable to work or able to perform only "routine" work could be put to death. Historians estimate that approximately 5,000 children and 70,000 adults were murdered in the euthanasia program before August 1941.[7]

As the numbers increased so too did the complications of murder on such a scale. Mass murder requires a mass murder process, and med-ication and injections did not suffice. According to the euthanasia doc-tor, Dr. Karl Brandt (also a member of the Führer's Chancellery), he and Hitler discussed various techniques and decided on gas as "the more hu-mane way."[8] Indeed, throughout the euthanasia program Hitler was kept informed of its progress. In 1939, on Chancellery stationery carrying the emblem of the National Socialist party, Hitler issued a written order call-ing for certain physicians to have the authority to grant a "mercy death" to patients "considered incurable" (see chapter 8).[9]

The T4 administrators set up their first killing center at an old jail building in the city of Brandenburg. Sometime between December 1939 and January 1940, a two-day series of gassing experiments was con-ducted there and deemed successful. Five more killing centers were soon established, including one each at Grafeneck in Württemberg, Hartheim near Linz, Sonnenstein in Saxony, Bernburg in the Prussian province of Saxony, and Hadamar in Hessen. The gas chambers were disguised as showers, the "handicapped" patients herded in, and the gas adminis-tered. One observer, Maximilian Friedrich Lindner, recalled the process at Hadamar:

> Did I ever watch a gassing? Dear God, unfortunately, yes. And it was all due to my curiosity. . . . Downstairs on the left was a short pathway, and there I looked through the window. . . . In the chamber there were patients, naked people, some semi-collapsed, others with their mouths terribly wide open, their

chests heaving. I saw that, I have never seen anything more gruesome. I turned away, went up the steps, upstairs was a toilet. I vomited everything I had eaten. This pursued me days on end.[10]

According to Lindner, the gas was ventilated from the chamber with fans; the bodies were disentangled and removed from the room; the corpses, marked with an "X" on back, were looted for gold in their teeth, then cremated. The entire process—from arrival at the killing center to cremation—took less than twenty-four hours. Henry Friedlander, who traced this evolutionary process, concludes: "The success of the euthanasia policy convinced the Nazi leadership that mass murder was technically feasible, that ordinary men and women were willing to kill large numbers of innocent human beings, and that the bureaucracy would cooperate in such an unprecedented enterprise."[11]

In the T4 killing centers we see all the components of the extermination camps like Auschwitz. Through time the Nazi bureaucracy evolved along with the T4 killing centers, setting the stage for the conversion of concentration and work camps into extermination camps. By 1941–42 this conversion was just another incremental step in the contingently evolving system that became the Final Solution.

The contingent history of the euthanasia program also helps us understand another mystery: what happened to "the" order from Hitler to exterminate the Jews? In our opinion, one of the reasons there is no record of a written order by Hitler is that he once authorized in writing the euthanasia of handicapped patients and this fact came back to haunt him when the press ran critical stories about the euthanasia program.[12] Hitler, it appears, realized that such actions needed to be taken in secret, and certainly not ordered in writing. Furthermore, it seems that as a general principle Hitler preferred not to sign orders himself. There is no order signed by Hitler, for example, to start the war.

PROVING GAS CHAMBERS AND CREMATORIA WERE USED FOR GENOCIDE

In the controversial book *Why Did the Heavens Not Darken?* the Princeton diplomatic historian Arno Mayer concludes: "Sources for the study of the gas chambers are at once rare and unreliable."[13] Mayer surely had no idea this single sentence would win him so much notoriety among Holocaust deniers. Read out of context, this statement by a mainstream and highly respected historian seemingly reinforces what deniers have always believed. But to quote out of context—however encouraging or tantalizing the notion—can be misleading. The *entire* paragraph reads:

> Sources for the study of the gas chambers are at once rare and unreliable. Even though Hitler and the Nazis made no secret of their war on the Jews, the SS operatives dutifully eliminated all traces of their murderous activities and instrument. No written orders for gassing have turned up thus far. The SS not only destroyed most camp records, which were in any case incomplete, but also razed nearly all killing and cremating installations well before the arrival of Soviet troops. Likewise, care was taken to dispose of the bones and ashes of the victims.[14]

Clearly Mayer is not suggesting, as deniers do, that gas chambers were not used for mass extermination. Indeed, how can anyone deny that the Nazis used gas chambers and crematoria? Don't these facilities still exist in many camps? To debunk the deniers can't we just go there and see them for ourselves? The answer, of course, is "yes." But deniers do not deny the *existence* of gas chambers and crematoria. They claim that the gas chambers were used strictly for delousing clothing and blankets and that the crematoria were used to dispose of the bodies of those who died of "natural" causes in the camps. How can we distinguish between gas chambers used for delousing and gas chambers used for mass murder? How can we prove that the bodies disposed of in crematoria were murdered and had not just died of so-called natural causes like disease, starvation, and overwork?

To find out, we went to Europe to conduct research at the camps, in particular at Mauthausen, Majdanek, Treblinka, Sobibor, Belzec, Dachau, Auschwitz, and Auschwitz-Birkenau. We wanted to see for ourselves just what evidence there is at the camps and to take the opportunity to examine firsthand the claims of David Cole, Robert Faurisson, and other deniers who specialize in this area. As we discovered, there is far more to the story than meets the eye through books and films alone.

Before we look at the evidence from the camps, consider in general how we might prove through a convergence of evidence from various sources that the Nazis used gas chambers and crematoria for mass murder:

1. *Written documents*—orders for Zyklon-B (the trade name of hydrocyanic acid, which is embedded in diatomaceous earth pellets), architectural blueprints, and orders for building materials for gas chambers and crematoria

2. *Zyklon-B gas traces*—on the walls of the gas chambers at several camps

3. *Eyewitness testimony*—survivor testimonies, Jewish Sonderkommando diaries, and confessions of guards and commandants

4. *Ground photographs*—not only of the camps, but also of bodies burning (photos taken secretly and smuggled out of Auschwitz)

5. *Aerial photographs*—indicating prisoners being moved toward the gas chamber/crematorium complexes, and matching those of ground photographs corroborating the structure of the gas chambers and crematoria

6. *The extant ruins of the camps*—examined in light of the above sources of evidence

In presenting these six lines of evidence, we are not saying that each or even any particular one proves that gas chambers and crematoria were used for genocide. Rather, we are arguing that these lines of evidence converge on this conclusion. As we shall see, there were six extermination camps—with gas chambers and crematoria—involved in the Final Solution, resulting in a total of approximately 3,062,000 killed (see table 1).[15]

TABLE I

ESTIMATED JEWISH LOSSES
AT THE EXTERMINATION CAMPS

Camp	Number Killed	Killing Method
Auschwitz-Birkenau, 1942–44	1,100,000	Zyklon-B
Treblinka, 1942–43	900,000	Carbon monoxide
Belzec, 1942	600,000	Carbon monoxide
Sobibor, 1942–43	250,000	Carbon monoxide
Chelmno, 1941–42	152,000	Carbon monoxide
Majdanek, 1942–44	60,000	Zyklon-B and carbon monoxide

What the Nazis learned in the T4 program, along with subterfuge and secrecy and the methods of mass murder, was that the public would not tolerate such activities on German soil—for example, on August 3, 1941, Bishop Clemens Galen delivered a sermon in Münster in which he spoke out against the euthanasia program. As a result of public outcry, the Nazis located these six camps in the East, far from the watchful eyes of the German public and press. But the evidence to convict the murderers has not escaped history.

ZYKLON-B TRACES

One of the most controversial claims the deniers have presented concerns evidence from the traces of Zyklon-B left in the gas chambers. This issue began with the publication in 1989 of *The Leuchter Report,* by Fred Leuchter, who subtitled it *An Engineering Report on the Alleged Execution Chambers at Auschwitz, Birkenau, and Majdanek, Poland.* According to Leuchter, not only did gassings not take place, but they *could not* have taken place. Under "Synopsis and Findings" in his report, Leuchter concludes, "The author finds no evidence that any of the facilities normally alleged to be execution gas chambers were ever used as such and finds, further, that because of the design and fabrication of these facilities, they could not have been utilized for execution gas chambers."[16]

The *Leuchter Report* was followed by a report by Germar Rudolph, a German chemist who was at the Max Planck Institute at the time. Like Leuchter before him, Rudolph contends, "The mass gassing procedures [at Auschwitz], as reported by witnesses interrogated by the courts, as established in the quoted judgements, and as described in scientific and literary publications, in whatever building one picks at Auschwitz at all, are irreconcilable with the laws of physical science." As for the other extermination camps, Rudolph similarly states, "On chemical-physical grounds, the mass gassings as described, using hydrocyanic acid in the alleged gas chambers, could not have taken place."[17]

An Austrian engineer named Walter Lüftle, former president of the Austrian Federal Engineering Association, then published a paper allegedly proving the impossibility of murdering people with Zyklon-B and carbon monoxide.[18] These three reports by Leuchter, Rudolph, and Lüftle became the staple of "scientific proof" in support of the deniers' claim that gas chambers were not used for mass homicide. Yet Leuchter's report in particular has been severely criticized in the anthology *Truth Prevails,* edited by Shelly Shapiro; further, Jean-Claude Pressac and Robert Jan van Pelt's report on "The Machinery of Mass Murder at Auschwitz" demonstrates how the physical evidence supports the use of poisonous gas.[19]

Leuchter's connection to the Holocaust deniers was apparent in 1991, when he testified for the defense in the Canadian trial of Ernst Zündel. Leuchter is a self-described "engineer," although he lacks an engineering degree. Since Leuchter had for a number of years worked servicing and selling execution devices, Zündel paid him $30,000 to perform an analysis on brick and cement samples obtained without permission from

concentration camp ruins—samples that had been exposed to the elements
since 1945.[20] Subsequently, Serge and Beate Klarsfeld, along with a Mass-
achusetts survivors group, brought an action against Leuchter for practicing engineering without a license. The trial became a media event and
Leuchter was forced to sign a consent decree barring him from using the
title "engineer."[21] According to a taped interview distributed by Ernst
Zündel, because of the bad publicity surrounding the trial, Leuchter's "career" as an engineer is over and he has been struggling to make ends meet
ever since.[22] In 1991 Leuchter went to Germany to appear as a guest on
a TV program about capital punishment, but he was arrested in the studio before taping began, on "suspicion he would use the TV show to in-
cite racism and to slander the memory of Holocaust victims."[23]

One of Leuchter's claims is that the Nazis who dropped Zyklon-B pellets into the chambers would have themselves died from exposure, and
therefore they could not have used the gas for mass murder. But in Zündel's trial, during Leuchter's testimony, the judge challenged him on this
point:

Q: So this stuff you told us about people on the roof who dropped the gas
     down and how they would be committing suicide, it would take a matter
     of minutes before the gas got to them, wouldn't it?
A: Unquestionably.
Q: So, if they closed the vent and got off the roof, there would be nothing to
     concern them, would there?
A: If they got off the roof. But at some point they have to do an inspection to
     determine whether the parties are deceased.
Q: They send in the Sonderkommandos to do that, sir, and they don't care
     what happens to them.
A: Right, all right.
Q: So, if someone's on the roof with a gas mask, you agree that they've got
     all kinds of time to get off the roof after they've closed the vent?
A: Perhaps.[24]

Not surprising, Leuchter's recantation is not often cited in deniers' literature, although David Irving characterized Leuchter's research in this
regard as the work of "an archaeologist with a sledge hammer."[25]

In support of their claims, Leuchter, Faurisson, and Cole note that at
some sites the Zyklon-B traces are stronger in the delousing chambers
than in those used for homicide.[26] This finding, they contend, makes no
sense if the chambers were used to kill millions of people because then
they would have been in operation nearly twenty-four hours a day and
the gas would have left deep blue staining.

But is that true? To begin with, millions did not die in any one gas chamber. Many, perhaps one-third to one-half of the six million, died from a variety of other causes, including the Einsatzgruppen (special group forces') shootings, as well as beatings, overwork, starvation, disease, and the general unsanitary conditions at the camps—murder is murder regardless of the method. Furthermore, the gas chambers were never in operation continuously, around the clock, 24 hours a day, 365 days a year, as is sometimes believed. Finally, what about the darker stains in the delousing chambers? Consider this: lice take much longer to succumb to Zyklon-B than humans do, who absorb it through their lungs and die in a matter of minutes (the delousing of clothing took twelve to eighteen hours). And minutes after the prisoners died, the gas was let out of the chambers (and the bodies removed), preventing any long-term buildup of residue in most cases.[27]

Faurisson and Leuchter claim that use of Zyklon-B gas in a chamber not far from the crematoria would have caused an explosion.[28] This idea is ludicrous. The crematoria were brick structures with sealed doors. The flames that burned the corpses were not in the open air or anywhere Zyklon-B gas could have wafted through and ignited. Additionally, the level of Zyklon-B used to kill humans was far lower than that needed to reach the explosion level. Specifically, it takes 300 parts per million (ppm) of hydrocyanic acid to kill human beings; it takes 56,000 ppm to cause an explosion—a 186-fold difference.[29]

Faurisson indicates that there are traces of Zyklon-B in general buildings that were fumigated as well as in the gas chambers; so he concludes that traces of Zyklon-B prove nothing about the homicidal use of gas chambers.[30] According to the pharmacist and extermination camp expert Jean-Claude Pressac, however, Faurisson's defense does not make sense since buildings and morgues are normally disinfected with antiseptics, whether solid (lime, lime chloride), liquid (bleach, cresol), or gas (formaldehyde, sulfur anhydride).[31] Neither the general buildings, nor the morgues, would have been disinfected with an insecticide or vermin killer like the hydrocyanic acid Zyklon-B. In other words, Faurisson's claim that traces of Zyklon-B were found in general buildings appears to be false. (This is not surprising since much of his analysis depends on the findings of *The Leuchter Report*, which relied on highly questionable data collection techniques.)

Finally, we must ask how accurate any findings of Zyklon-B traces can be. Keep in mind that the gas chambers at Auschwitz-Birkenau, where the deniers have conducted their analyses, were completely destroyed by the Nazis as the Russians were closing in on the camp in late 1944. The deniers make it sound as if anyone could go there, walk into the gas chamber, pick up a brick, and test it for Zyklon-B traces. There is nothing but rubble there, completely exposed to the elements for over half a century. The partially reconstructed undressing rooms, gas chambers, and crematoria at Auschwitz-Birkenau are part of the recent restoration of the camp as a museum.

David Cole, in his unpublished "Forty-six Important Unanswered Questions Regarding the Nazi Gas Chambers," acknowledges that the extant ruins have been exposed to the elements but then wonders why Zyklon-B blue staining remains on the outside of the brick gas chamber at Majdanek, against which the Nazis beat clothing and blankets to remove the gas residue.[32] Wouldn't these blue stains have washed away in the weather as at Auschwitz? His question sounds reasonable, but when we visited Majdanek we could see that the blue staining on the outside bricks is minimal. Moreover, a roof overhang has protected the bricks from rain and snow, so that the bricks at Majdanek are nowhere near as weathered as the open rubble at Auschwitz. In addition, Cole gives no citations for some of his claims. When he says, for example, "the buildings which used to serve as the camp delousing facilities still have extremely high traces of the gas" and "the Auschwitz camp barracks and offices, which were fumigated with the Zyklon-B from time to time, show similarly minute traces of the gas, and no blue staining,"[33] is this just his opinion or does he have solid evidence? Before we even bother to respond to such claims, then, we need to test their accuracy. In this case, there are no references to back up Cole's statements—a shortcoming that seems to happen all too often in deniers' "research." When a question or statement has no grounding in evidence, it becomes just a rhetorical device and requires no answer. Consider, as yet another example, Cole's claim that at Mauthausen the door of the gas chamber does not lock. True, the present door does not lock, but that is irrelevant because it is not the original door. All we had to do to find out that fact was ask.

What about the "evidence" that Cole, Leuchter, and Faurisson do present, such as their "finding" that the residue from Zyklon-B in the gas chamber at Crematorium I at Auschwitz I (the original camp converted from a Polish army barracks) does not reach a level consistent with extermination?[34] Significantly, they fail to mention in their writings that this building was reconstructed using both original materials and those

Figure 11.   This label, taken from a canister found at Majdanek, documents the poisonous (*Gift*) nature of Zyklon-B manufactured by the German firm Degesch. (Courtesy Yad Vashem, Jerusalem, Israel)

from other buildings.[35] Who knows what they actually "tested" in their research? The deniers are only too happy to point out that the gas chamber is a reconstruction but conveniently drop the subject when it comes to their testing of the bricks. David Cole, in his video documentary of his visit to Auschwitz, dramatically proclaims that he got the museum director to "confess" that the gas chamber was a reconstruction and thus a "lie" thrust upon an unwitting public. We see this as classic denier hyperbole and ideological flag waving. No one at Auschwitz—from the guides to the director—denies that the gas chamber there is a reconstruction. A visitor has only to ask.

CORROBORATION FROM DOCUMENTS AND GROUND PHOTOGRAPHS

As noted, no one element alone of the six lines of evidence presented above proves that gas chambers and crematoria were used for mass murder—but the convergence of these sources leads to this conclusion. How might we connect what we know about the use of Zyklon-B gas with other lines of evidence to show that the gas chambers were used for mass murder? Can we, for example, corroborate the orders for Zyklon-B gas and the remains of Zyklon-B canisters (see figure 11) with eyewitness accounts and photographs? We have dozens of accounts of survivors describing the unloading and separation process of prisoners at Auschwitz, for example,[36] and we have photographs of at least the first steps in the process (figure 12). We also have eyewitness accounts of the Nazis forcing prisoners to undress and march into the gas chambers, and of the Nazis burning bodies in open pits,[37] and we have photographs of both processes, taken secretly by a Greek Jew named Alex (figures 13 and 14).

In addition to such photographs, we have documents regarding the

Figure 12. These two photos of prisoners support eyewitness accounts of the arrival of a train of Hungarian Jews at Auschwitz-Birkenau and the sorting out by gender. A further subdivision would send them either toward the gas chambers or into the camp barracks. (Photos: Yad Vashem, Jerusalem, Israel; courtesy United States Holocaust Memorial Museum)

Figure 13. These two photographs show naked women on their way to Crematorium V and the burning of bodies in an open pit after gassing (the crematoria often broke down). A Sonderkommando at Auschwitz-Birkenau took them secretly; Alter Fajnzylberg, another Sonderkommando, described what happened: "On the day on which the pictures were taken we allocated tasks. Some of us were to guard the person taking the pictures. At last the moment came. We all gathered at the western entrance leading from the outside to the gas chamber of Crematorium V: we could not see any SS men in the watch-tower overlooking the door from above the barbed wire, nor near the place where the pictures were to be taken. Alex, the Greek Jew, quickly took out his camera, pointed it toward a heap of burning bodies, and pressed the shutter. This is why the photograph shows prisoners from the Sonderkommando working at the heap" (in Swiebocka's *Auschwitz: A History in Photographs* [1993], 42–43). (Top photo: Yad Vashem, Jerusalem, Israel; left photo: National Museum of Auschwitz-Birkenau, courtesy United States Holocaust Memorial Museum)

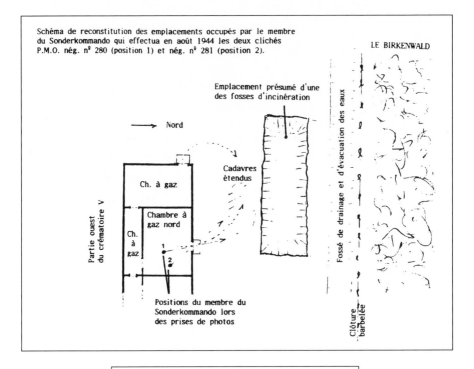

Figure 14. In his 1989 book, *Auschwitz: Technique and Operation of the Gas Chambers,* Jean-Claude Pressac reconstructed in schematic form where the photographer stood to take the pictures in figure 13. (Courtesy Beate Klarsfeld Foundation)

construction of the gas chambers. In a letter dated January 29, 1943, from SS-Sturmbannführer (Major) Bischoff, of the Auschwitz construction department, to SS General Heinz Kammler, the major reports: "Crematorium No. 2. The completed furnaces have been started up in the presence of Engineer Prüfer from Messrs. Topf (of Erfurt). The planks cannot yet be moved from the ceiling of the mortuary cellar on account of frost, but this is not important, as the gassing cellar can be used for that purpose. The ventilation plant has been held up by restrictions on rail transport, but the installation should be ready by February 20th."[38]

On March 6, 1943, Bischoff refers to a gas-tight door for Crematorium III, similar to that of Crematorium II, which was to include a peephole of thick glass. Bischoff's order reads: "order of 6/3/1943 concerning the delivery of a gas-tight door 100×192 cm for cellar I of Crematorium III, to be produced to the identical pattern and dimensions as the cellar door of Crematorium II which is situated opposite, with peephole of double 8 mm glass, with rubber sealing strip and frame."[39] Why would they need a peephole with thick glass if all that was happening in this room was the delousing of clothing? Although in itself the existence of the peephole does not "prove" anything, it is one more finding that dovetails with the idea that these chambers were used for killing people.

EYEWITNESSES TO MASS MURDER

Additional evidence comes from the confessions of guards such as SS-Unterscharführer (Sergeant) Pery Broad, captured on May 6, 1945, by the British in their zone of occupation in Germany. Broad began work at Auschwitz in 1942 in the "Political Section" and stayed there until the liberation of the camp in January 1945. After his capture, he worked as an interpreter for the British and, in the process, wrote a memoir that was passed on to the British Intelligence Service in July 1945. That December, he declared under oath that what he wrote was true. On September 29, 1947, the document was translated into English and presented at the Nuremberg trials as evidence of the use of gas chambers as mechanisms of mass murder. Later that year Broad was released. In April 1959 Broad was called to testify at a trial of captured Auschwitz SS members and acknowledged the authorship of the memoir, confirmed its validity, and retracted nothing.[40]

The reason for this background to Broad's memoir is that deniers tend to dismiss any damning Nazi confession as being coerced or made up for bizarre psychological reasons, while simultaneously accepting statements by those who support their position. Broad was never tortured, and he had nothing to gain and everything to lose by confessing. When given the opportunity to recant, which he certainly could have done in the later trial, he did not. Instead, he described in detail the gassing procedure, including the use of Zyklon-B, the early gassing experiments in Block 11 of Auschwitz, the temporary chambers set up at the two abandoned farms at Birkenau (Auschwitz-Birkenau, or Auschwitz II), which he correctly called by their jargon name of "Bunkers I and II." He also recalled the construction of Crematoria II, III, IV, and V at Birkenau, accurately depicting (by comparison with blueprints) the design of the undressing room, gas chamber, and each crematorium. He then described the actual process of gassing in gruesome detail:

> The disinfectors are at work . . . with an iron rod and hammer they open a couple of harmless looking tin boxes, the directions read Cyclon [sic] Vermin Destroyer, Warning, Poisonous. The boxes are filled with small pellets which look like blue peas. As soon as the box is opened the contents are shaken out through an aperture in the roof. Then another box is emptied in the next aperture, and so on. After about two minutes the shrieks die down and change to a low moaning. Most of the men have already lost consciousness. After a further two minutes . . . it is all over. Deadly quiet reigns. . . . The corpses are piled together, their mouths stretched open. . . . It is difficult to heave the interlaced corpses out of the chamber as the gas is stiffening all their limbs.[41]

Deniers point out that Broad's four minutes for the total process is at odds with the statements of others, such as the commandant Höss who said it was more like twenty minutes.[42] Because of such minor discrepancies, deniers dismiss Broad's account entirely. A dozen different accounts give a dozen different figures for time of death by gassing, so deniers believe that no one was gassed at all. Does this make sense? No. The time required for the gassing process would vary according to the room's temperature (hydrocyanic acid's evaporation from the pellets depends on the air temperature), the number of people there, the room's size, and the amount of Zyklon-B poured into the apertures—not to mention the psychological differences in time perception experienced by different observers.[43] Indeed, if the estimation of times were exactly the same, we would have to be suspicious that they were all taking their stories from a single account. Such minor discrepancies actually back up the veracity of Broad's statement.

Deniers make a similar argument about the confession of SS-Obersturmbannführer Rudolf Höss, commandant of Auschwitz from May 20, 1940, to November 11, 1943. Höss made his statement on April 5, 1946, probably unaware of Pery Broad's memoir (and vice versa). Further, the Nuremberg tribunal, when trying Höss, was also unaware of the Broad document. Even if deniers completely discount the Höss testimony, which they do, they still have the problem of explaining why the two accounts coincide so well. Höss, like Broad, talks about the temporary gassing experiments at Auschwitz I, the two "Bunkers" at Birkenau, the construction of the four large structures at Birkenau that included undressing rooms, gas chambers, and crematoria. Moreover, after Höss was found guilty and sentenced to death, he wrote a 250-page autobiographical manuscript that corroborates both his previous testimony and Broad's statement. On the gassing procedure, for example, compare Höss's account with Broad's above:

> Then, very quickly, the door was hermetically sealed, and a can of gas was immediately thrown onto the floor, through an opening connected to an air duct in the ceiling of the gas chamber, by the disinfectors, who were standing ready. This led to the immediate release of the gas. Through the peephole one could see that those who were near the air duct died immediately. It can be said that about a third died within a moment's notice. The others began to struggle, to scream, to choke. But very quickly the cries became death rattles, and, after a few minutes, all were on the ground. After a maximum of twenty minutes, nobody moved.[44]

As far as we know, Broad and Höss never saw each other before Höss's capture on March 11, 1946 (ten months after Broad's). But even if we fantasize a secret meeting between the two before Broad was captured, why would they spend time fabricating a story that was likely to convict them? Besides, theirs are not the only accounts. Compare, for example, this testimony from the Auschwitz camp physician, Dr. Johann Paul Kremer:

> September 2, 1942. Was present for first time at a special action at 3 A.M. By comparison Dante's Inferno seems almost a comedy. Auschwitz is justly called an extermination camp!
> September 5, 1942. At noon was present at a special action in the women's camp—the most horrible of all horrors. *Hschf.* Thilo, military surgeon, was right when he said to me today that we are located here in the *anus mundi* [anus of the world].

Deniers claim that Kremer says "special action," not gassing, but at the trial of the Auschwitz camp garrison in Kraków in December 1947 Kremer clarified exactly what he meant by "special action":

By September 2, 1942, at 3 A.M. I had already been assigned to take part
in the action of gassing people. These mass murders took place in small cottages situated outside the Birkenau camp in a wood. The cottages were called
"bunkers" in the SS-men's slang. All SS physicians on duty in the camp took
turns to participate in the gassings, which were called *Sonderaktion* [spe-
cial action]. My part as physician at the gassing consisted in remaining in
readiness near the bunker. I was brought there by car. I sat in front with the
driver and an SS hospital orderly sat in the back of the car with oxygen ap-
paratus to revive SS-men, employed in the gassing, in case any of them should
succumb to the poisonous fumes. When the transport with people who were
destined to be gassed arrived at the railway ramp, the SS officers selected
from among the new arrivals persons fit to work, while the rest—old people,
all children, women with children in their arms and other persons not
deemed fit to work—were loaded onto lorries and driven to the gas chambers. There people were driven into the barrack huts where the victims undressed and then went naked to the gas chambers. Very often no incidents
occurred, as the SS-men kept people quiet, maintaining that they were to
bathe and be deloused. After driving all of them into the gas chamber the
door was closed and an SS-man in a gas mask threw the contents of a Cy-
clon [*sic*] tin through an opening in the side wall. The shouting and screaming of the victims could be heard through that opening and it was clear that
they were fighting for their lives. These shouts were heard for a very short
while.[45]

The convergence of the accounts from Broad, Höss, and Kremer is
additional proof that the Nazis used gas chambers and crematoria for
mass extermination. And these are only the three most famous accounts.
There are many others, such as the following extract from a sworn statement by Stefan Kirsz taken in Belzec on October 15, 1945 (where carbon monoxide was used instead of Zyklon-B). In 1942 Kirsz was a
twenty-nine-year-old Belzec villager employed by the Polish State Railways as an assistant locomotive driver on the line between Rawa Ruska
and Belzec. In other words, Kirsz was a witness with no particular agenda
when describing what he saw:

The transports which I drove from Rawa Ruska to Belzec were divided into
three parts in Belzec whereby each part (20 wagons) was rolled onto a siding
on the area of the camp. As soon as the wagons came to a stop on the siding
on the area of the camp they were emptied of Jews. Within 3–5 minutes the
20 wagons were completely emptied of people and luggage. I saw that besides the living people, corpses were also taken out. These people were ordered to place their luggage on one side and to completely undress themselves.
Their clothes were laid on one side and their shoes on the other and then they
went, undressed, one after the other, into a barrack which stood near the siding, from where they were pushed into the gas chambers [*von wo sie in die*

Gaskammer geschoben wurden]. I was able to see this because I entered the camp area and pretended that I had to shovel coal nearer to the furnace door. The Germans allowed no one to see the camp area. Whenever I was in a locomotive near the extermination camp I tried to see something more, but I did not hear the screams of the Jews driven in.[46]

The power of this eyewitness account speaks for itself, as does the following statement of Hans Stark, registrar of new arrivals at Auschwitz:

> As early as autumn 1941 gassings were carried out in a room in the small crematorium which had been prepared for this purpose. The room held about 200–250 people, had a higher-than-average ceiling, no windows and only a specially insulated door, with bolts like those of an airtight door. There were no pipes or the like which would lead the prisoners to believe that it was perhaps a shower room. In the ceiling there were two openings of about 35 cm in diameter at some distance from each other. The room had a flat roof which allowed daylight in through the openings. It was through these openings that Zyklon-B in granular form would be poured. . . .
>
> At another, later gassing—also in autumn 1941—Grabner ordered me to pour Zyklon-B into the opening because only one medical orderly had shown up. During a gassing Zyklon-B had to be poured through both openings of the gas chamber room at the same time. This gassing was also a transport of 200–250 Jews, once again men, women and children. As the Zyklon-B—as already mentioned—was in granular form, it trickled down over the people as it was being poured in. They then started to cry out terribly for they now knew what was happening to them. I did not look through the opening because it had to be closed as soon as the Zyklon-B had been poured in. After a few minutes there was silence. After some time had passed, it may have been ten to fifteen minutes, the gas chamber was opened. The dead lay higgledy-piggledy all over the place. It was a dreadful sight.[47]

The historian Michael Tregenza has provided us with translations of primary documents for a book he is writing on Rudolf Reder, who spent three months in Belzec before escaping in November 1942. The sworn affidavit from Reder, about his experiences in the Lemberg ghetto in Poland from November 1941 to mid-August 1942 and the months in the Belzec extermination camp, is revealing. Here is just one especially gruesome account of a gassing and mass burial soon after Reder's arrival in Belzec:

> On 17 August 1942, I was deported to the Belzec extermination camp. We were unloaded and had to strip naked. Specialists were asked to step forward. I reported as a mechanic. Only eight men were left behind; the rest were immediately gassed. There were about 4,500 people on the transport. All the prisoners were taken to a big barrack where the women had their heads shaved

bald. Then they were driven into a narrow corridor; there was a door there with the inscription, "Bade und Inhalationsräume" [bath and inhalation room]. In front of the door hung a flowerpot with some flowers. As one opened the door there was another corridor; to the right were three doors, and to the left three doors, which led into six gas chambers. Each chamber could hold 750 people. The building was of concrete. I know from my own observation that the gassing took no more than 20 minutes. The gas was fed through pipes from an engine in a small hut. I operated a machine which dug the earth out of pits which served as graves for those gassed. I additionally had to drag the corpses out of the gas chambers and drag them to the pits. I dragged the corpses in this way: I placed a belt around a wrist and a second worker did the same, and thus we carried the corpses to the pits. There were about 30 graves, each grave was 100 metres long, 25 metres wide and 15 metres deep. In my opinion, about 100,000 corpses could be buried. The corpses were stacked up to about 50 centimetres above the edge of the pit, because the corpses later settled.[48]

We could cite many more, similar eyewitness accounts, but we hope it is clear by now how these add to the overwhelming convergence of evidence for mass gassings.

AERIAL PHOTOGRAPHS

In 1992 the Holocaust denier John Ball published a book analyzing the aerial photographs of Auschwitz and other camps, entitled: *Air Photo Evidence: Auschwitz, Treblinka, Majdanek, Sobibor, Bergen Belsen, Belzec, Babi Yar, Katyn Forest.* The cover blurb reads: "World War II photos of alleged mass murder camps! Does evidence confirm or dismiss eye witness stories? Were gas chamber marks put on by CIA workers?" The book is a high-quality publication printed on glossy paper in order to hold the detail of the aerial photographs. Ball spent tens of thousands of his own dollars producing the book and admits that the project cost him more than just his savings, negatively affecting his personal life and marriage in many ways.[49] But he remains dedicated to the project and spends much of his spare time (when he is not working as a self-employed geologist) on his research, now centered on making detailed four-color maps of Auschwitz.

According to Ball, the aerial photographs, including the negatives, of Auschwitz were tampered with, marked, altered, or faked. By whom? By the CIA, he says, in order to match the story as depicted in the 1970s television miniseries *Holocaust.*[50] Ball's book is a response to a 1979 CIA report on the aerial photographs—*The Holocaust Revisited: A Retro-*

spective Analysis of the Auschwitz-Birkenau Extermination Complex—
in which the two authors, Dino A. Brugioni and Robert G. Poirier, claim
that these aerial photographs taken by the Allies prove extermination
activities. On February 15, 1979, after the report was published, newspapers proclaimed:

> "Photos of Auschwitz Extermination Unit Produced" (*New York Times*)
>
> "'44 Photos Showed Auschwitz Camp" (*Washington Post*)
>
> "'44 Photos Showing Auschwitz Camp Spur Questions on Failure to Bomb It" (*Los Angeles Times*)
>
> "The World Knew—and Kept Silent" (*Washington Post*)

Ball does not accuse Brugioni and Poirier of doctoring the photographs;
rather, he argues that they were interpreting already altered photos,
marked to show extermination activity.

What do these aerial photographs really tell us? Brugioni and
Poirier's claim that their analysis of the photographs shows extermination activity is overstated. By themselves the photographs in their
report do not show mass murder. But that does not mean they are useless. As corroboration for other forms of evidence, including eyewitness accounts, blueprints, extant ruins, and ground photographs, they
have much to tell us. Enhanced with new digital techniques, the photographs reveal more detail than Brugioni and Poirier were able to see.
Brugioni and Poirier were using analog technology (just enlarging the
photographs from the negatives), but—thanks to Dr. Nevin Bryant,
supervisor of Cartographic Applications and Image Processing Applications at NASA's Jet Propulsion Laboratory in Pasadena, California
(operated by the California Institute of Technology)—we were able to
get these photographs analyzed by digital technology. The photographic negatives were converted to digital data in the computer, then
enhanced with software programs used by NASA for aerial and satellite imaging.

The photographs of Auschwitz were shot in sequence as a plane flew
over the camp (on a bombing run toward its ultimate target—the IG Farben industrial works a few miles from the camp).[51] The rolls of film are
long, containing hundreds of large-format photographs, most of which

Figure 15.   This aerial photograph of Auschwitz was taken by an Allied bomber from 30,000 feet on June 26, 1944. At the top is Auschwitz-Birkenau (Auschwitz II) with Auschwitz I, the original camp, just below. The town of Auschwitz is in the center. Just to the left of the river in the center of the photograph is Auschwitz III, or Auschwitz-Monowitz, where the IG Farben industrial works were located. (Courtesy National Archives)

are of farms and countryside and contain nothing significant to see. Photographs of the camp itself are few and far between, and for each of the five dates there exist one, two, or three photographs at most. Since there is more than one photograph of the camp, and each is taken a few seconds apart, stereoscopic viewing of two photographs shows movement of people and vehicles. Such viewing also provides greater depth perception of the size of buildings, as explained in the captions for figures 15 to 22.

In figure 15 we see the entire Auschwitz complex, including Auschwitz-Birkenau (top), Auschwitz I (the original camp, just below Birkenau),

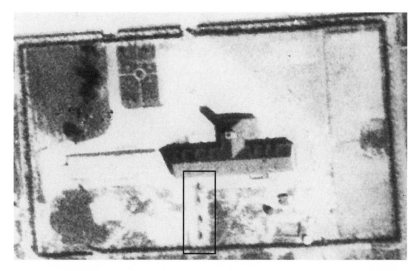

Figure 16.   This aerial photograph from August 25, 1944, shows the distinct features of Crematorium II (including the long shadow from the chimney) and the adjacent gas chamber (bottom center, at a right angle to the crematorium). On the roof of the gas chamber, note the four staggered shadows, openings through which the Zyklon-B pellets could be poured, as described in eyewitness accounts. (Courtesy National Archives)

Figure 17.   Note two sides of the rectangular underground gas chamber structure that protrudes a few feet above the ground, directly below the chimney of Crematorium II. On the gas chamber roof are four small structures that match the shaded markings in the aerial photograph in figure 16. (Courtesy Yad Vashem, Jerusalem, Israel)

Figure 18.   This photograph of prisoners disembarking from a train at
Auschwitz-Birkenau shows in the background Crematorium II (left chimney)
and Crematorium III (right chimney). (Courtesy Yad Vashem, Jerusalem,
Israel)

and the IG Farben industrial center (next to the river). Figure 16 is an
aerial photograph of Crematorium II at Birkenau, showing the crematorium chimney and four shadows on the adjacent gas chamber roof,
created (as we will demonstrate) by the four small roof structures
through which the SS poured the Zyklon-B gas pellets. Compare this with
figure 17, a ground shot of the back of Crematorium II, in which four
small structures are visible on the roof of the gas chamber, matching the
four shaded markings in the aerial photograph. A different perspective
is offered by figure 18, a ground photograph of prisoners being unloaded
from a train, with Crematoria II and III in the background (see chimneys, left and right). This photograph in turn sheds light on the five aerial shots in figures 19 and 20, portraying the movement of groups of
people on the ground. Finally, figure 21 appears to be a group of people
moving toward Crematorium V, offering yet another important piece of
direct physical evidence, corroborating other evidence that indicates the
reality of mass murder (see also figure 22).

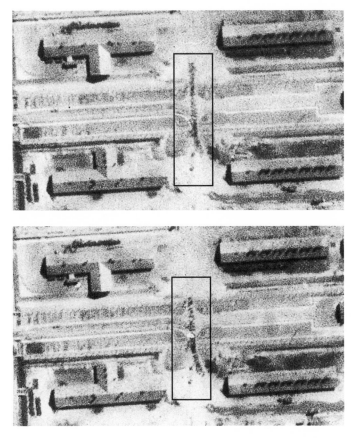

Figure 19.   These two aerial photographs of Auschwitz were
shot seconds apart by the same plane on a bombing run on the IG
Farben plant on August 25, 1944. They show a group of people
moving in marching fashion into a registration building; in the
second photo, the back of the line has advanced significantly. This
is a common problem in marching untrained groups of people:
military marches are synchronized; untrained civilian marches are
not synchronized. The Holocaust denier John Ball has claimed that
this "zigzag" line was drawn in by the CIA to make their report fit
the Holocaust story. However, on the original negative, the line is
extremely small and would be impossible to draw on. Ball theo-
rizes that the negative was enlarged about 800%, marked, then
reduced and reshot into a negative. Yet the original negatives are
not separate; they are still on a giant roll in the archives at Yad
Vashem, connected with hundreds of other aerial photographs.
In addition, with high-resolution equipment and photographic
enhancement, we were able to discern shades of gray between the
so-called zigzag lines. The zigzag is produced by a "moiré effect"—
the sizes of the heads in this particular photograph are about the
size of the grains in the emulsion of the film, generating an "inter-
ference" pattern. (Courtesy National Archives)

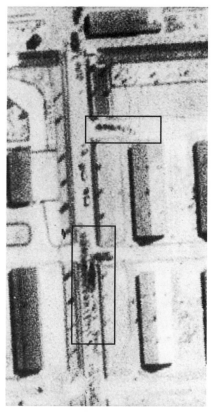

Figure 20. In this set of photographs from the August 25 bombing mission, the three shots are taken a few seconds apart each. Note the movement of both people and vehicles on the ground (compare movement with stationary structures, such as the roof structures next to the moving vehicles). (Courtesy National Archives)

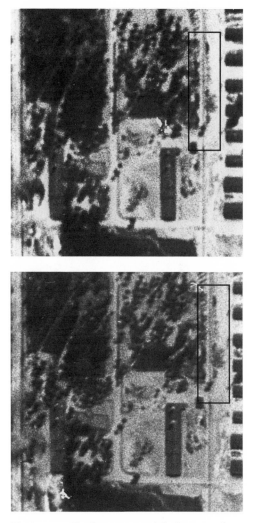

Figure 21.   In these two aerial photographs, taken on May 31, 1944, image enhancement enables us to decipher a group of people seemingly being marched into Crematorium V. The front of the long line (to the right in the photographs) is turning into the crematorium grounds through an opening in the fence; comparison of the two shots reveals some movement in the line into the crematorium grounds. (Courtesy National Archives)

Figure 22. This ground photograph shows Crematorium V, with the gas chamber at the far end of the building and the double chimneys for the crematorium. (Courtesy Yad Vashem, Jerusalem, Israel)

Interpreting the Aerial Photographs

As mentioned above, there has long been a myth that, at camps like Auschwitz, the Nazis exterminated masses of prisoners 24 hours a day, 365 days a year. That did not happen. Gassings began in 1941, and Himmler witnessed his first gassing on July 18, 1942. Through March 1943, a total of only 280,000 Jews from all over Europe were shipped to Auschwitz. By June 1943, all four crematoria at Birkenau were operational, with a theoretical capacity of 4,736 corpses per 24 hours. This level of activity was not needed, however, as from April 1943 to March 1944 no more than 160,000 Jews were deported to Auschwitz, and not all of these were killed (the strongest were "selected" to labor for the Reich).[52]

On March 19, 1944, however, the picture changed. The Nazis invaded Hungary and soon afterward half a million Jews were deported to Auschwitz. On May 16 the killing of the Hungarian Jews began and lasted through June. In preparation Crematoria IV and V, which had not been used since September 1943, were reactivated, and SS-Obersturmführer (Lieutenant Colonel) Werner Jothann ordered ventilation systems installed in them (to remove the gas when the job was completed), as well as elevators in Crematoria II and III to move the bodies from the gas chamber to the crematoria on small rail cars (see figure 24 below). In addition, pits were dug for open-air burning (see figure 13), as the crematoria could not practically handle so many bodies in such a short period of time. In the two months of May and June 1944, one-third of the total number killed in the entire history of Auschwitz were exterminated.[53]

In addition to the major mass exterminations, there were sporadic smaller killings, so that between 1942 and the end of 1944, a little over one million prisoners were killed at Auschwitz, nearly all of them Jewish. On October 7, 1944, members of the Jewish Sonderkommando at Birkenau revolted and blew up Crematorium IV. By the end of November, with the Russians closing in, Himmler ordered that gassing be halted and the crematoria destroyed. On January 18, 1945, most of the camp was evacuated, and on January 20 the SS dynamited the remaining crematoria. On January 27, the Russians arrived and liberated what was left of the camp.[54]

Looking more closely at Auschwitz, we learn that the camp, like war itself, was filled with long periods of slow suffering and short periods of terror. Deniers claim that between April and October 1944 there is not one aerial photograph that shows extermination activity. First of all, we do have photographs of people in long lines being marched toward Crematorium V, where the gassing would have taken place. But, as for direct evidence, what could we realistically expect to see? The undressing, gassing, and cremation were all done inside the crematoria buildings. It was highly unlikely that an Allied plane would have flown over at the same time as smoke was coming out of chimneys or from an open-pit burning. Indeed, it would be an extraordinary coincidence if we had such a photograph.

The existing aerial photographs were taken on only five dates—April 4, May 31, June 26, August 25, and September 13, 1944. These dates are easy to check for extermination activity. Danuta Czech's *Auschwitz Chronicle: 1939–1945* gives a day-by-day description of all significant activities at the camp. It was compiled from the twenty-one volumes of documents from the trial of Rudolf Höss, seven volumes of documents from the Kraków trial of forty members of the Auschwitz SS, transport registers, prisoner records, smuggled notes and letters from the resistance movement, survivor testimonies, and thousands of other Nazi documents recovered after liberation.[55]

On April 4, 11 prisoners from Katowice (in Silesia) received numbers 179576–179586; 53 female Jewish prisoners selected from an RSHA transport from Trieste and Istria received nos. 75460–76512; 32 prisoners sent in a group transport received nos. 179666–179697; and a small transport of deportees arrived from Trieste, 103 of whom were killed in the gas chambers, according to the *Auschwitz Chronicle*. Since the process would have taken less than an hour, it is, as we noted, not surprising that the few seconds an Allied plane was flying over Auschwitz that day did not correspond with the time the victims would have been burned in the crematoria.

The entry for May 31 includes 100 Jews selected from an RSHA transport from Hungary who received nos. A-10741–A-10840; others were reported as "killed in the gas chambers." It also notes that 1,000 male Jews received nos. A-10841–A-11840 and 1,000 female Jews received nos. A-6039–A-7038 from another RSHA transport from Hungary. The rest were reported as "killed in the gas chambers." For this day we do not know how many Jews were killed in the gas chambers, what time they were killed, or if they were cremated that day or the next day. It is reported that between May 16 and May 31 the SS acquired eighty-eight pounds of gold and white metal from false teeth, so it is possible that the bodies were not cremated until after this process was completed, which would have been after May 31 for those arriving that day. But in an enhanced portion of the aerial photographs from this date we can see a large group of people going toward Crematorium V (figure 21). That fits with reports of prisoners being marched into the crematoria for gassing that day. These may be the Hungarian Jews from an RSHA transport, some of whom were selected for work, the rest for extermination. Deniers claim the gas chambers in these crematoria were simply morgues. Why would you march living prisoners into a morgue other than to kill them?

On June 26 no one was gassed, according to the *Chronicle*. Four prisoners received numbers; 778 prisoners were transferred from Auschwitz to Buchenwald; and the camp received four sieves for sifting through human ashes to find unburned human bones for incineration.

No one was gassed on August 25 either. The *Chronicle* reports only prisoners receiving numbers, and, interestingly, "750 Polish and Russian prisoners are transferred from Auschwitz II to the Bremen A.C., which belongs to Neuengamme." In one August 25 photograph a train is visible, with thirty-three cars stationed near the loading and unloading ramps, and lines and groups of prisoners. These may very well be the same 750 Polish and Russian prisoners, but since we do not know the exact time they were moved, we cannot be certain this is the activity in the photograph.

Finally, on September 13, no one was gassed.

These photographs are a good example of how, in order to make proper interpretations, we must review the physical evidence in conjunction with written documents and eyewitness testimonies. Sometimes we can make logical inferences, but other times we cannot draw final conclusions. The historian, however, is willing to wait for further evidence. In contrast, deniers seem anxious to prove that because nothing appeared to happen on one particular day at one particular moment, then nothing happened at other times on other days as well—an example of the fallacy of pseudohistorical thinking.

THE CONTINGENT HISTORY OF AUSCHWITZ

On April 21, 1990, David Irving addressed a large audience at the Löwenbräu Hall in Munich, Germany, proclaiming: "By now we know, and I am sure I don't need to point this out as anything more than an aside, that there were never any gas chambers in Auschwitz." But are there not extant gas chambers at the camp for everyone to see? Yes, Irving admits, but "we believe that, just as the gas chambers which the Americans put up here in Dachau [outside Munich] in the first few days after the war were fakes, those gas chamber facilities which tourists can now sightsee in Auschwitz were set up by Polish authorities after the Second World War."[56]

Could Auschwitz be a fake? Holocaust deniers assume that because historians have determined that Auschwitz ended up being an extermination camp, we should be able to show it was originally designed as an extermination camp. Since the layout, design, and function of Auschwitz do not match what we might expect to find in a perfectly designed extermination camp, deniers then argue that it was not an extermination camp at all. In general, this argument is flawed because historical outcomes rarely match historical intentions. In particular, it is flawed because we can trace the changes that occurred at Auschwitz, as they did at Majdanek and the other extermination camps.

The architectural historian Robert Jan van Pelt, in a brilliant essay entitled "A Site in Search of a Mission," has demonstrated through a chronology of blueprints and architectural designs of Auschwitz, that modern myths about the camp have erased the historical contingencies of its origin and development:

> Banished from the world of description, analysis, and conclusion, Auschwitz has become a myth in which the assumed universality of its impact obscures the contingencies of its beginning. I use the word myth in the sense that

[Roland] Barthes gave to it in his essay "Myth Today." Mythification, he argued, occurs when language empties a narrative of its historical contingency to fill it with an unchanging nature. "In passing from history to nature, myth acts economically: it abolishes the complexity of human acts, it gives them simplicity of essences." The result is an account of "blissful clarity" in which there are no contradictions because statements of fact are interpreted as explanations; "things appear to mean something by themselves." Few events can rival the mythic power of "Auschwitz."[57]

In his essay, and even more poignantly in his 1996 book coauthored with Deborah Dwork, van Pelt unravels the contingencies that constructed the necessity that became the Auschwitz we know today. The problem is that we are trying to understand the early stages of Auschwitz by what now remains. The original intention of Auschwitz, however, was quite different: "Auschwitz was not preordained to become the major site of the Holocaust. It acquired that role almost by accident, and even the fact that it became a site of mass murder at all was due more to the failure to achieve one goal than to the ambition to realize another."[58] The focus on the final stage of Auschwitz as a killing machine has prevented us from understanding its contingent history, as well as how anyone could assume the role of mass murderer. Dwork and van Pelt put Auschwitz and its operators in historical context, observing: "This almost comfortable demonization [of a place of preordained mass murder] relegates the camp and the events that transpired there to the realm of myth, distancing us from all too concrete historical reality, suppressing the local, regional, and national context of the greatest catastrophe western civilization both permitted and endured, and obscuring the responsibility of the thousands of individuals who enacted this atrocity step by step. None of them was born to be a mass murderer, or an accomplice to mass murder. Each of them inched his way to iniquity."[59]

Auschwitz, it seems, was to be a district capital, a center of mass industry, and a model city that would project the image of an ideal future city for the Thousand-Year Reich. The Nazis believed that Poland was rightfully theirs and therefore they were liberating it. In an SS handbook entitled *The Struggle for the German Eastern Border*, SS men were told: "The German East was for centuries the German people's space of destiny. It will remain so for the following centuries."[60] Concentration camps were originally designed as instruments of terror to control resistance to the Nazi Party (Dachau is the classic case), but in time, as they evolved, they furnished labor for productive work, especially after 1939. Before the war the free labor of the camps would have competed with German businesses and thus increased unemployment, which went against Nazi policy. When the war began, however, the camps took on two new functions: providing a source of labor and housing prisoners of war. And, as more and more of Germany's productive labor joined the fighting line, these two new functions blended into one, with prisoners providing the free labor.

In 1940 Himmler began to make plans for the future of Auschwitz. The industrial giant IG Farben would have a plant in Auschwitz, all Jews and Poles would be removed from the region, and Auschwitz itself would become "a paradigm of the settlement in the East."[61] Within two months, a master architectural plan to reconstruct and enlarge the camp was completed: it included an SS garden city and a center for agricultural experimentation. Nestled at the confluence of three major rivers, Auschwitz was to be the model Aryan city. Dwork and van Pelt detail this evolution in blueprints and plans, including the first master plan for the expansion of Auschwitz, which specified the location of the IG Farben industrial area, the Nazi Party headquarters, and, of course, the concentration/labor camp. The plans were all in keeping with Nazi architectural aesthetics as envisioned by Hitler and his chief architects Paul Troost and Albert Speer.

These plans, however, changed on Sunday, June 22, 1941, when the Nazis invaded the Soviet Union. Contingencies once again altered future necessities, and the crooked timber of Auschwitz took another twisted turn. With the initial successes of the Wehrmacht and the Luftwaffe, Russian prisoners of war came pouring into Auschwitz, suddenly transforming the camp into an instrument of war. Conditions were brutal and thousands of Russians died monthly from disease and starvation: in October, November, and December 1941 respectively, 1,255, 3,726, and 1,912 died.[62] Barracks were hastily thrown up to house the POWs, and new crematoria had to be added to dispose of the bodies. The model-city-turned-POW-camp was, de facto, rapidly on its way to becoming an extermination camp. After the Russian armies began to hold the line against the Germans and it became clear that Operation Barbarossa—the German invasion of the Soviet Union—was going to become a protracted operation, Auschwitz was further expanded to house up to 100,000 prisoners, primarily for labor. After Stalingrad and the turning of the tide in the East, the supply of free Russian labor began to dry up. Himmler needed a replacement, and he found it in the Jews. The evolution of

Auschwitz toward its final end as an extermination camp now took a dramatic leap.[63]

At the Wannsee Conference, where plans for the Final Solution were coordinated (see chapter 8), SS-Obergruppenführer Reinhard Heydrich declared, "Under appropriate direction the Jews are to be utilized for work in the East in an expedient manner in the course of the final solution. In large (labor) columns, with the sexes separated, Jews capable of work will be moved into these areas as they build roads."[64] Six days later, Himmler sent the following telegram to the inspector of concentration camps, Richard Glücks: "As no Russian prisoners of war can be expected in the near future, I am sending to the camps a large number of Jews who have emigrated from Germany. Will you therefore make preparation to receive within the next four weeks 100,000 Jews and up to 50,000 Jewesses in the concentration camps? The concentration camps will be faced with great economic tasks in the coming weeks."[65]

Indeed they were. Three weeks later, the first transport of Jews arrived, whereupon the young and healthy were put to work and the old and infirm were gassed and cremated.[66] When this procedure became cumbersome, given the confines of the camp's original design, it was moved three kilometers away, from Auschwitz I to Auschwitz II (Auschwitz-Birkenau), where new crematoria were constructed and the killing escalated as the war intensified. Yet all the while, says van Pelt, "the extermination of the Jews was meant to be a transient phenomenon in the history of the camp." Plans were continued to convert the camp yet again after the war, but "that other future never materialized. Thus the name Auschwitz became synonymous with the Holocaust, and not with Himmler's model town."[67]

A trace of this contingent history appears in photographs taken by the authors at Auschwitz. Figure 23 shows the railway tracks leading in to Auschwitz-Birkenau, as well as the arrival platform visible in the wartime photographs in figures 12 and 18. Figure 24 presents the blueprints for Crematorium II, including the undressing room (left), the gas chamber (bottom), and the crematorium (right), housing the five separate furnaces, each with a set of rail tracks leading to it. Pictured in figure 25 is what remains of the undressing room and gas chamber of Crematorium II, which was dynamited by the Nazis just before the camp was evacuated. Figure 26 shows the inside of the gas chamber with the supporting pillars and roof and the remains of the crematorium, as well as the rail lines leading to the crematorium, on which ran small rail cars moving the bodies of people recently killed in the gas chamber.[68]

Figure 23. The entrance to Auschwitz-Birkenau with the railway spur coming in through the gate and tower and proceeding to the arrival platform. Compare these contemporary photographs with the historical photographs in figure 12. (Authors' collection)

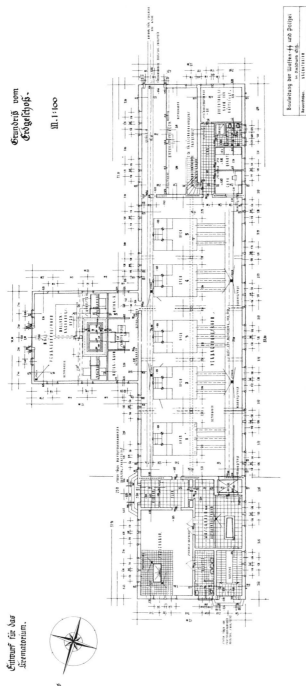

Grunдriß vom Erdgeſchoß.

M. 1:100

Entwurf für das Krematorium.

Figure 24. The original ground plan of Crematorium II, dated January 1942, is from the Auschwitz-Birkenau State Museum (box BW[B] 10/1, file BW 30/2). The axonometric drawing on the next page by Kate Mullin is based on this plan. (Both, courtesy Deborah Dwork and Robert Jan van Pelt)

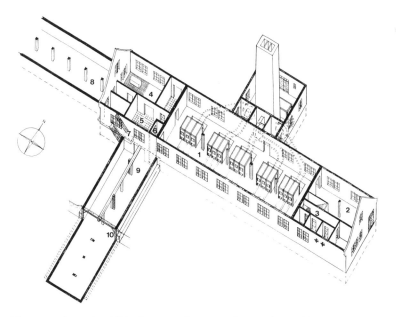

Figure 24 (*cont.*). This drawing shows (1) five triple-muffle furnaces and short rail tracks leading to each, (2) storage room for fuel, (3) workers' room, (4–5) dissection rooms, (6) elevator for transporting bodies from gas chamber to crematorium, (7) staircases to outside and chute for corpses, rooms designed to be morgues, then converted to undressing room (8) and gas chamber (9–10).

Figure 25. The Crematorium II undressing room (left) and gas chamber (right) remain in a state of rubble today, after the Nazis destroyed them just before liberation in January 1945. The extant hole in what remains of the gas chamber may be one of the openings through which the SS guards poured Zyklon-B gas pellets. (Authors' collection)

Figure 26. The floor of what remains of the location of Crematorium II (left) with a close-up of the railway tracks that led directly into the ovens. (Authors' collection)

THE CONTINGENT HISTORY OF MAJDANEK

As we reconstruct the historical sequence of Majdanek, the parallels to Auschwitz are revealing. On July 21, 1941, Heinrich Himmler ordered the plans for the construction of the Majdanek camp to house 25,000 to 50,000 Soviet prisoners of war "with a view to employing them in the workshops and on building sites of the SS and police." As with Auschwitz, Himmler's plans for the colonization of the East called for a centralized labor camp from which prisoners would work in the Lublin area. Thus, he appointed a "plenipotentiary for the organization of SS and police stations in the new eastern territories" as "settlements for the whole families of SS and police functionaries." The Research Center for Settlement in the East consisted of a group of architects who would design the plans for the model German cities. In Lublin, where Majdanek was constructed, squares and streets were Germanized and the "old German town" was considered an "intermediary between the West and the East and the final pillar of the great German Reich."[69]

The original plan was for Majdanek to serve as a labor source for the construction of the SS district, to include building and operation of the building supply and the clothing works, a supply storehouse for the higher SS, a military economic storehouse, and large workshops in the camp. Initially, there were four districts of occupied Poland under SS and police administration: Kraków, Warsaw, Lublin, and Radom; each was commanded by an SS-und Polizeiführer with the rank of SS-Brigadeführer, under the overall command of the Höhre-SS-und Polizei-führer in Kraków. After the invasion of Russia, the district of Galicia was added.

The formal order to construct the camp was issued on September 22, 1941, by Heinz Kammler (under the direction of Himmler), who five days later noted the comparison with Auschwitz: "In Lublin and Auschwitz, camps for prisoners of war will be set up immediately, as of 1 October, with the possibility of accommodating 50,000 prisoners of war each." As in Auschwitz, the lure of free labor in the form of Russian POWs was irresistible (already by September 325,000 Soviet prisoners were available). The camp was quickly expanded to accommodate more prisoners as well as take on a new function—in April 1942 Himmler ordered that "the POW camp in Lublin is to serve at the same time as a concentration camp." The standard camp facilities included "a big laundry, a de-lousing station, a crematorium, and large workshops."[70]

The construction of the gas chambers began in August 1942 and was completed in October. According to Pressac, in all there were seven gas chambers used for killing at Majdanek, some of which were equipped with more than one killing method, including both Zyklon-B and carbon monoxide. However, "for want of a precise technical study," Pressac warns, "we still don't know much about these gas chambers, for many questions about how they worked remain unanswered."[71]

The first two gas chambers, which apparently used both Zyklon-B and carbon monoxide, were built in the middle of the camp, near a laundry and crematorium, and housed in a wooden shack. The SS estimated the crematorium's capacity at one hundred bodies per twelve hours, comparable to the capacity of Auschwitz's crematoria.[72] Since the extant building now has windows in the gas chambers, Pressac believes these were later converted for use in delousing clothing, which would explain the location near the laundry as well as the crematorium. The Majdanek historian Michael Tregenza describes these gas chambers this way:

> Built of concrete they have a bigger floor area than the two chambers in "Desinfektion I" (approximately double the capacity) and used both HCN [Zyklon-B] and CO [carbon monoxide] gas, although this has not been officially confirmed. The walls are stained blue which confirms the use of Zyklon-B. Entry to the chambers is through a large room with a cement floor and has several windows. Current theory, however, tends to favor these chambers as disinfection facilities only—mainly because they are too big to have been used as extermination chambers; such large numbers as may be accommodated there were never gassed in Majdanek at one time.[73]

But this theory does not explain the use of carbon monoxide, which is useless against lice. Its only plausible use is against human beings.

The building housing the main gas chambers (it is open to the public today) was labeled "Bad und Desinfektion" (bath and disinfection) I. The original block measures 9.2 meters by 3.62 meters by 2.05 meters high. Casual inspection of the large gas chamber room shows that its use was for delousing clothing and blankets, not for mass extermination, since the doors to it open in, they do not (and cannot) lock, and there is a large glass window (about 30 by 60 centimeters, or 1 by 2 feet) that could easily be broken. The window frame appears to be original, since the wood from which it is constructed is saturated with blue Zyklon-B stains (as is the rest of the room). But this room is significantly different from the two gas chambers at the back of the building, which were built later and for a different purpose. These rooms measure 4.8 meters by 3.6 meters by 2 meters and are connected to a small room, where an SS man could pump gas through a small opening. They were built of ceramic brick, covered with a ferroconcrete roof, and had a cement floor. The doors of these chambers, constructed by the Berlin firm Auert, are made of solid iron, lock with two bolts and iron bars, are airtight, and feature both a peephole (with glass and protective plate) and a gas detection device. The walls are made of thick concrete and are soaked in blue Zyklon-B stains. According to Tregenza, during the war these were separate structures, and they were later combined under one roof for preservation purposes. "The outside appearance of both of these barracks bears little resemblance to their wartime appearance," he indicates. "Most of Majdanek was demolished after the war when the Red Army came in. Some buildings were burnt, some were demolished."[74] Nevertheless, the interior structures are extant, with Zyklon-B traces, allowing comparisons to be made.

Given two types of rooms, each with Zyklon-B stains, we can infer that they were used for two different purposes. In our opinion, the contingent history of this and other camps like Auschwitz indicates that the initial purpose of the large gas chamber was to disinfect clothing and blankets, and the deep blue staining in this large room backs this up. As the war progressed, laboring prisoners died not only from starvation and overwork but, as they became unfit, from mass shootings as well.[75] For prisoners not fit for labor, gassing became an economical option. Jozef Marszalek, the Polish historian of Majdanek, believes the Nazis may have even tried some experimental gassings of prisoners in the disinfection room, but the window in the wall makes this idea seem doubtful.[76] The SS then built the two smaller concrete gas chambers with iron doors (in the back of the building and at that time separate from the other rooms), and these additions, we believe, were for the express purpose of gassing prisoners. Why else would the SS have built these new rooms that featured peepholes and locking doors, components not found in *any* delousing chamber? The small delousing chambers (too small to fit people in) in Bad und Desinfektion II, a converted barracks building next to this one, do not have these features, so this helps us differentiate between delousing and gas chambers. Finally, we know that carbon monoxide was employed in the Bad und Desinfektion I gas chambers, pointing to their use for mass homicide.[77]

According to Marszalek, gassing at Majdanek began in October 1942 and continued sporadically through the evacuation of the camp on April 1, 1944.[78] An estimated 360,000 prisoners (mostly Jews) died or

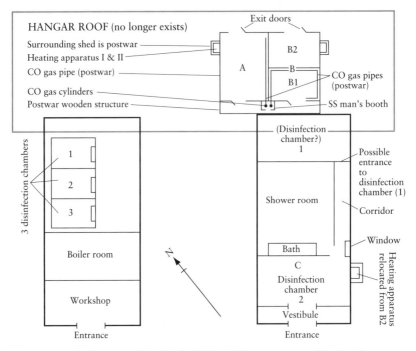

Figure 27.   A diagram of the Desinfektion I–II structures at Majdanek.
(Courtesy Michael Tregenza)

were killed at Majdanek by various means, including starvation, disease, overwork, beatings, shootings, and gassings. Marszalek provides
massive documentary evidence for the construction of the camps, the
gas chambers, and the crematoria, as well as the orders for Zyklon-B
gas, and he cites extensive eyewitness accounts of these various causes
of death. Yet of the Jewish prisoners who died it is estimated only about
60,000 were killed by gassing (see table 1). Tregenza concludes, "Majdanek was not a major gassing camp on the order of camps like
Auschwitz. At Majdanek the gassings were rather irregular. An odd
transport of Jews came in specifically for gassing who were prisoners
deemed unfit for work, but I hesitate to say that there was a regular
gassing program there."[79] The contingencies of the war changed the final
outcome of Majdanek.

Figure 27 is a diagram of Desinfektion I and II by Tregenza, indicating what was original during the war and what exists today. As Tregenza
describes it:

Area B was divided into two equal sized chambers (marked B1 and B2). Only area B1 was equipped for killing human beings with CO gas—the gas was introduced into the chamber via a perforated metal pipe laid 30 cm above the floor along three walls and part of the fourth. The pipe was fixed to two steel cylinders containing pure CO gas in liquid form under pressure. The cylinders were placed in a small shed between the two entry doors and had a small observation window through which the gassing process could be observed in one chamber only—B1. There was no observation window into chamber A. An opening was made in the ceiling of area B and the stove which had heated area B was moved to service area C instead.

Area A was also fitted with a CO gas pipe, but of a smaller diameter than the pipe in area B1; the CO gas was also pumped in from a cylinder in the booth outside, but through a single pipe only along the dividing wall between the two areas.

A had an area of 36 square meters for groups of 250–350 people, and B1 had an area of 18 square meters for groups of 125–175 people, figures often quoted by Majdanek survivors. Also, compare these figures with Nazi estimates. For example, SS-Obersturmbannführer Walter Rauff, in a report of June 5, 1942, states: "The normal capacity of the [gas] vans is 9–10 persons per square meters." Reports have also noted that transports occasionally arrived at Belzec with 200 people per wagon, and each wagon had a floor area of 20 square meters, or 10 people per square meter.[80]

Figure 28 shows the Bad und Desinfektion I building, as well as the large delousing gas chamber inside the building, with Zyklon-B stains on the walls and on the window frame. The patched round hole in the wall was an opening to a small shack outside containing the heating generator, used to heat the room so the Zyklon-B gas would evaporate.

Figure 29 includes a small delousing chamber found in the Bad und Desinfektion II building immediately to the west of building I. At the back of Bad und Desinfektion I, after passing through the large delousing chamber shown in figure 28, a visitor encounters two smaller concrete gas chambers, one of which is pictured in figure 29. The latter includes a locking steel door with peephole and gas detector, and the room itself contains floor-to-ceiling Zyklon-B staining. On the left wall is an opening to an adjoining shack containing a heating generator (to trigger the evaporation of the Zyklon-B gas from the diatomaceous earth pellets). Speaking of this chamber and its companion, Tregenza notes that "these two chambers were adapted yet again for use with CO gas, which can only be used for extermination purposes—CO is useless for disinfection purposes, and is fatal only for warm-blooded animals."[81] What we are looking at, then, is a chamber where people, not clothes, were gassed.

Figure 28.   The outside of Majdanek's Bad und Desinfektion I is shown with the interior of a delousing chamber with a window (a room incorrectly labeled as a gas chamber used for homicide). The patched hole (on the right) led to a small room that housed a heating unit, used to help evaporate the Zyklon-B. (Authors' collection)

Figure 29. These gas chambers (top and bottom left) used for homicide are found in the rear of Majdanek's Bad und Desinfektion I. Note the locking door with peephole, metal protective grid, and gas detector (bottom left). Compare these with the delousing chamber (bottom right), located in the Bad und Desinfektion II building next to building I. (Authors' collection)

THE GAS CHAMBER AT MAUTHAUSEN

On April 12, 1995, the French Holocaust denier Robert Faurisson wrote to one of the authors, "I am waiting for you to SHOW me or to DRAW me a gas chamber . . . along, of course, with its technique and operation."[82] Faurisson is famous for his "show me or draw me a Nazi gas chamber" challenge. We presume, of course, that he means by this a Nazi gas chamber used for mass murder. No one denies there were gas chambers. Such proof, as we have seen, is plentiful in its indirect form and when corroborated with other pieces of evidence. There is, however, no film of people being gassed or any blueprint on which it says "gas chamber for killing prisoners." Many historical events are by their nature inferential—and are not therefore any less true. (John Wilkes Booth's gun does not say "for killing Lincoln" on it, nor is there a film or photograph of the assassination. But we know he did it nonetheless.)

Consider the gas chamber at Mauthausen. According to Obersturmführer (Lieutenant) Franz Ziereis, the commandant of Mauthausen: "In the concentration camp of Mauthausen, a gas chamber was built camouflaged as a shower room under the direction of Dr. Krebsbach, the former local doctor. Prisoners were gassed in this camouflaged shower room. Additionally, a specially constructed vehicle went back and forth between Mauthausen and Gusen in which the prisoners were gassed during the trip."[83] Our own photographs from Mauthausen reveal a basement shower room and disinfection chamber (figure 30); a crematorium, dissection room, and morgue (figure 31); and a gas chamber with features that indicate it was used to kill prisoners (figure 32). The Holocaust denier David Cole makes a point of the fact that the peephole on the door of this gas chamber is not covered with a metal screen to prevent the victims from punching out the glass and letting the air escape.[84] The point is moot, for the gas chamber's original door is now in a museum. But even if that were not the case, the peephole is about one inch in diameter, with glass almost half an inch thick. To break the glass, someone would need a hammer, not a common item among prisoners about to be gassed. Moreover, since gas chambers were not under pressure, the gas would not rush out even if a victim did manage to break the glass. And if this chamber were only a shower, as deniers claim, of what use would a heavy steel door with a peephole be?

Regardless of the door's condition, figures 30 to 32 illustrate the difference between a shower, a delousing chamber, and a gas chamber for killing. In the basement of a barracks building (figure 30), to the right

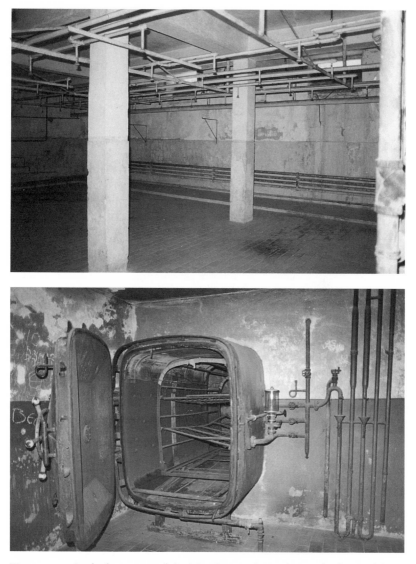

Figure 30.   In the basement of the Mauthausen barracks (at the front of the camp) is a large shower room (top), outfitted with operative showerheads and a complete piping system, and a small delousing chamber (bottom), large enough for clothing and blankets, but not people. (Authors' collection)

Figure 31.   In the basement of another barracks
building at Mauthausen is a crematorium (top), a
dissection room (*Sezierraum;* middle), and a morgue
(*Leichenraum;* bottom), with short walkways between
each. It makes no sense to argue (as deniers do) that
the gas chamber was either a shower room or a delousing chamber, since these already existed elsewhere in
the camp. (Authors' collection)

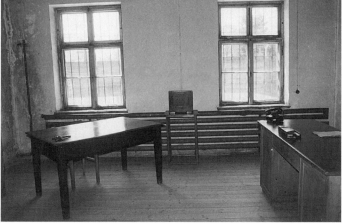

Figure 32. The Mauthausen gas chamber (top) features a ventilation system hole (covered by a metal plate; in center of photograph), fake showerheads, and pipes to heat the room and hasten
the rapid evaporation of the hydrocyanic acid gas from the Zyklon-
B pellets. Compare the set of pipes on the wall to that in an office
at Auschwitz (bottom). (Authors' collection)

just inside the main gate at the front of the camp, is a Desinfektion room housing a small chamber, large enough to delouse clothing and blankets but not to contain people. The nearby shower room is large and outfitted with dozens of operative showerheads and a complete piping system. Prisoners brought into the camp were showered, and their clothing deloused, all in the basement of this building. By contrast, in the basement of another barracks building (figure 31)—toward the back of the camp (far from the entrance)—is a crematorium, a dissection room, and a morgue where bodies were stacked—all neatly connected with short walkways between them.

It makes little sense to argue (as deniers do) that the adjoining gas chamber (figure 32) was either a shower room or a delousing chamber. First, a shower and delousing chamber already existed at the front of the camp (where we would expect to find them); second, why would the Nazis have placed either a delousing room or a shower room next to a dissection room and crematorium? The gas chamber in figure 32 has a ventilation system, fake showerheads, and a system of pipes (compare it to the heating system in an Auschwitz office). The pipes in the gas chamber appear to have been installed to heat the room to hasten the rapid evaporation of the hydrocyanic acid from the Zyklon-B pellets. No other explanation for this room arrangement and all these artifacts is plausible other than that the room was used to gas people.[85]

This chapter has revealed how history is often quirky and unpredictable and how final outcomes rarely match original intents. History is contingent. Coordinating blueprints, drawings, photographs, and documented eyewitness accounts to test the historical hypothesis that the Nazis used gas chambers and crematoria as part of the Final Solution, we use the evidence to demonstrate that the proof is in the convergence of evidence. All the evidence from these various sources points to this macabre conclusion. It is not enough for deniers to concoct an alternative explanation that amounts to nothing more than denying each piece of freestanding evidence. They must proffer a theory that not only explains all of the evidence but does so in a manner superior to the present theory. This they have not done. Our conclusion stands on this bedrock of scientific history.

7

"For God's Sake—Terrible"

The Scope and Scale of the Holocaust

Schacht objects to being made to look at film as I ask him to
move over; turns away, folds arms, gazes into gallery. (Film
starts.) Fritzsche already looks pale and sits aghast as it starts
with scenes of prisoners burned alive in a barn . . . Keitel
wipes brow, takes off headphones . . . Funk covers his eyes,
looks as if he is in agony, shakes his head . . . Ribbentrop
closes his eyes, looks away . . . Sauckel mops brow . . . Frank
swallows hard, blinks eyes, trying to stifle tears . . . Funk
now in tears, blows nose, wipes eyes, looks down . . . Frick
shakes head at illustration of "violent death"—Frank mutters
"Horrible!" . . . Speer looks very sad, swallows hard . . .
Defense attorneys are now muttering, "for God's sake—
terrible."

> Dr. G. M. Gilbert, prison psychologist, describing Nazi
> leaders' reactions to a film of concentration camps liberated
> by Americans, International Military Tribunal, Nuremberg,
> November 29, 1945

This raw description at the Nuremberg trials of some Nazi leaders' shock
and horror at the scope and scale of the Holocaust gives us some indication of just how far beyond belief the mass murder was even to the
perpetrators. So vast in scope and complex in scale was the Holocaust
that no one individual—with the possible exceptions of Hitler and
Himmler (who had taken their own lives before capture) or Eichmann
(who was still at large in late 1945)—knew what had gone on throughout the Reich. One purpose of the Nuremberg trials was to determine
how many people were killed in order to assess culpability and, where
appropriate, punishment for these crimes against humanity. The specific
question at hand was not how many people died in the course of the war,

since battle deaths are a normal and (however grimly) acceptable part of war. Instead, what the prosecutors wanted to know was, how many people did the Nazis murder? As the trial unfolded and more information came in from camps throughout Europe, it became apparent that one group of people in particular was singled out more than any other. So the question became, how many Jews did the Nazis murder?

HOW MANY JEWS DIED AND HOW WE KNOW

How many Jews died at the hands of the Nazis? The second major axis around which Holocaust denial turns is the number of victims. Paul Rassinier concluded in his 1978 book, *Debunking the Genocide Myth: A Study of the Nazi Concentration Camps and the Alleged Extermination of European Jewry,* that "a minimum of 4,419,908 Jews succeeded in leaving Europe between 1931 and 1945."[1] Therefore, he argued, far fewer than 6 million died at the hands of the Nazis. Most Holocaust scholars, however, using reliable figures (see below) and cross-checking them with other sources, place the total between 5.1 and 6.3 million Jewish victims.[2] And, of course, there were many millions more killed by the Nazis, including gypsies, Poles, Serbs, Czechs, Soviet civilians, mentally and physically handicapped patients, political prisoners, Soviet POWs, and the countless civilians in towns and villages throughout Europe who simply got in the way.

While estimates vary, there is independent corroboration among historians, using different methods and different source materials. Indeed, the variation adds credibility to the figure of around six million, for it would be more likely that the numbers were "cooked" if they all came out the same. The fact that they do not come out the same but are within a reasonable range of error variance gives us assurance that somewhere between the earlier estimates of five million and more recent estimates of six million Jews died in the Holocaust. Whether it is five or six million is central to the victims, but from the point of view of whether the Holocaust took place it is irrelevant. Either figure represents a large number of people. In any case, it was not several hundred thousand, or "only" one or two million, as some deniers suggest.[3] More accurate estimates will be made in the future as new information from Russia and formerly held Soviet territories continues to surface. The overall figure, however, is not likely to change by more than a few tens of thousands, and certainly not by millions.

To challenge the deniers we can begin with a simple question: If six million Jews did not die, where did they all go? A denier might say they are living in Siberia, Peoria, and similar places, but the occasional Holocaust survivor who does turn up is the source of astonished publicity. It goes against logic to expect millions of Jews to appear suddenly out of the hinterlands of Russia or America (especially given the intensely restrictive immigration laws at the time). The number of Jews in both countries is well established; we cannot believe that millions of Jews have consistently eluded the census takers there and in other countries.[4] Interestingly, the Nazis themselves estimated that at least six million were murdered, if not more. On November 26, 1945, at the first Nuremberg trial, the Nazi physician Dr. Wilhelm Hoettel testified:

> In the various concentration camps approximately four million Jews had been killed, while about two million were killed in other ways, the majority of these having been killed by the action squads of the security police.
> Himmler had not been satisfied by the report, since in his opinion the number of Jews killed must have been greater than six million. Himmler had declared that he would send Eichmann a man from his Office of Statistics so that he could make a new report, on the basis of Eichmann's sources, in which the exact number would be worked out.
> I must assume that the information Eichmann gave me was correct, since of all the people who might come into consideration, he would have had the best knowledge of the number of Jews murdered. First of all, he so to speak "delivered" the Jews to the death camps with his special commandos and, therefore, knew this number precisely, and second as department head in Section IV of the RSHA, which was responsible for Jewish matters, he certainly knew best the number of Jews who had died in this manner.[5]

As historical scientists, however, we realize that even such powerful statements by the perpetrators must be corroborated. The German historian Wolfgang Benz, for example, comments on the problem of depending only on confessions of Nazis: "But historic research is not dependent on confessions of the perpetrators. Original and undeniable sources are available for the research and calculation of the dimension of the genocide, but there are massive difficulties still. A major part of the murder actions was secret, covered through euphemistic expressions like the Final Solution, and proofs for the crimes had been destroyed during a last effort of the NS regime. Thus it will never be possible to quote an absolute figure that counts every single human, but it is possible to position the measure beyond every speculation."[6] Table 2 presents estimates of Jewish losses in the Holocaust by country, as compiled by Benz, using his own as well as other sources, including those from Gerald Reitlinger's *The Final Solution*, Raul Hilberg's *The Destruction of the Eu-*

ropean Jews, and Yisrael Gutman and Robert Rozett's article in the *Encyclopedia of the Holocaust.* Benz describes two methods of calculation: "the direct estimating method which sums up the number of victims in concentration camps, extermination camps, through killing squads plus all additional material about killed people; [and] the indirect method of statistical comparison [although] there is a lack of useful statistics (mainly in the east European countries) and the often changed borders make some of them incomparable."[7] By combining the two methods and looking for a convergence of evidence on one range of figures versus another, we can estimate figures with a high degree of confidence.

Reitlinger, Hilberg, and Gutman and Rozett derive their figures by various methods, including population demographics before the war, the number reported transferred to camps, the number reported killed, the number estimated killed, the number liberated from the camps, the number killed in "special actions" by the Einsatzgruppen, and the number remaining after the war. Hilberg cautions that "margins of error may be wider than they seem" and that "exactness is impossible."[8] But these margins are not so wide that, for example, six million would become six hundred thousand. Indeed, the range of estimates is typical for scientific data, necessary when figures have been estimated and cannot be stated with certainty. In the physical and biological sciences, for example, estimates often include error bars to show the range of possible error variance, not unlike those social scientists use for polling data. In our example, the error variance is about 8.5 percent, or about half a million. Moreover, a convergence of evidence provides us with a high degree of certainty that the figure lies near six million.

One method used in compiling these estimates is the "addition" method, which arrives at the number of victims by counting the number killed through (1) general privation (starvation and disease), especially in the ghettos; (2) shooting, especially by the Einsatzgruppen; and (3) imprisonment in the camps, especially the extermination camps like Auschwitz-Birkenau, Sobibor, Majdanek, Belzec, and Treblinka. We have voluminous data on privation, as Jewish councils as well as the Germans themselves kept statistics for the purpose of rationing food and space. The RSHA kept detailed records of Einsatzgruppen actions, including the number of victims, and much of this material still exists. We also have many deportation lists for the camps, with rosters of names— lists that were sometimes compiled so the security police could be properly billed. Working from the other end, the "subtraction" method uses prewar demographics and subtracts emigrations, numbers remaining in

TABLE 2
HISTORIANS' ESTIMATES
OF JEWISH LOSSES IN EACH COUNTRY

Country	Reitlinger	Hilberg	Gutman and Rozett	Benz
Poland	2,350,000–2,600,000	3,000,000	2,900,000–3,000,000	2,700,000
Soviet Union	700,000–750,000	900,000	1,211,000–1,316,500	2,100,000
Hungary	180,000–200,000	<180,000	550,000–569,000	550,000
Romania	200,000–220,000	270,000	271,000–287,000	211,214
German Reich	160,000–180,000	<120,000	134,500–141,000	160,000
Czechoslovakia	233,000–243,000	260,000	146,150–149,150	143,000
Netherlands	104,000	<100,000	100,000	102,000
France	60,000–65,000	75,000	77,320	76,134
Austria	60,000	<50,000	50,000	65,459
Yugoslavia	58,000	60,000	56,200–63,300	60,000–65,000
Greece	57,200	60,000	60,000–67,000	59,185
Belgium	25,000–28,000	24,000	28,900	28,518
Italy	8,500–9,500	1,000	7,680	6,513
Luxembourg	3,000	>1,000	1,950	1,200
Norway	>1,000	762	762	758
Denmark	>100	60	60	116
Total	4,578,800	5,109,822	5,859,622	6,269,097

NOTE: Where ranges are given, the higher numbers are used in the totals. Most historians believe the most recent figures (from Gutman and Rozett and Benz) are the most accurate. Figures compiled from Gerald Reitlinger, *The Final Solution* (New York: Beechhurst Press, 1953 [1978]); Raul Hilberg, *The Destruction of the European Jews* (Chicago: Quadrangle Books, 1961); Yisrael Gutman and Robert Rozett, "Estimated Jewish Losses in the Holocaust," *Encyclopedia of the Holocaust*, vol. 4, edited by Yisrael Gutman (New York: Macmillan, 1990); Wolfgang Benz, *Dimension des Volkermords: Die Zahl der Jüdischen Opfer des Nationalsocialismus* (Munich: Deutscher Taschenbuch Verlag, 1991).

the camps at liberation, and numbers remaining in areas after the war to estimate the number killed. The "recapitulation" method employs both the addition and the subtraction methods, cross-checking numbers and comparing figures.

One important source of data is the Korherr report, a sixteen-page document compiled by the SS statistician Dr. Richard Korherr, dated March 23, 1943, and written for Heinrich Himmler. The document is something of a progress report on the Final Solution, in which Korherr estimates the number of Jews before the German takeover in the "Incorporated Territories" and "Generalgouvernement" to be 2,790,000. He then estimates the remaining population in these areas on December 31, 1942, to be 531,124. About 1,496,283 were "evacuated," leaving 762,593 "excess of deaths and emigration over births" (that is, 762,593 either died a natural death or emigrated).[9] Of those "evacuated," Korherr makes it clear they went to camps like Auschwitz and Treblinka, not Siberia or Peoria.

Although Hilberg cautions against relying too heavily on the Korherr report (or any single source for that matter), he shows how a cross-checking of sources presents a fairly reliable estimate of the overall losses.[10] Might these figures change as new data emerge? Of course. How much might they change? Gutman has confidence in the *Encyclopedia of the Holocaust* figures, which are much higher than those of Hilberg: "I don't think they will change in a substantial way. There are places where we know exact numbers; we know about Poland, we know about Belgium. But we don't know enough about Russia because we did not have clear figures on the Soviet Jews during the Second World War."[11] Gutman believes the encyclopedia's estimate could vary by a few hundred thousand, but not an order of magnitude difference. Moreover, as we can see in the most recent figures—those from Benz—revisions, based on more accurate data, have increased, rather than decreased, the estimate.

THE VICTIMS AND PERPETRATORS SPEAK OUT

Deniers claim that no extermination camp victim has given eyewitness testimony of gassings. If so many millions of Jews were exterminated, surely someone could tell us what happened, Butz insists.[12] Indeed, we do have lots of eyewitness accounts, not only from the SS and Nazi doctors, but from the Sonderkommandos who dragged the bodies from the gas chambers into the crematoria. Specifically, after the war six diaries and fragments of notes were found buried near the Auschwitz-Birkenau crematoria. Three of them, by Zalman Gradowski, Zalman Leventhal, and Dayan Leyb Langfus, documented "the heart of hell," providing "rich material for the historian."[13] Gradowski is eloquent: "The dark night is my friend, tears and screams are my songs, the fire of sacrifice is my light, the atmosphere of death is my perfume. Hell is my home."[14] He goes on to describe the arrival of a transport, the undressing room, the gassing, and the cremation. With some rancor he describes the helplessness with which his fellow prisoners went to their deaths.

Langfus speaks of the execution of 600 Jewish children and 3,000 Jewish women, as well as of Polish prisoners gassed between October 9 and 24, 1944, their bodies burned in Crematoria II, III, and V. He exhorts his fellow Sonderkommandos to give up their grisly work and kill themselves: "We have burned enough Jews! Let us destroy everything, and go together to sanctify God's name!" There is a touching description of a child who approached a member of the Sonderkommando and said: "You are a Jew! How can you drive such sweet children in to be gassed, just so you can stay alive? Is your life among a band of murderers really dearer to you than the lives of so many Jewish sacrifices?"[15]

Even more dramatic is the account given by Filip Müller, also a member of the Sonderkommandos, in his *Eyewitness Auschwitz: Three Years in the Gas Chambers*. He describes the gassing and deception process as follows:

Two of the SS men took up positions on either side of the entrance door. Shouting and wielding their truncheons, like beaters at a hunt, the remaining SS men chased the naked men, women and children into the large room inside the crematorium. A few SS men were leaving the building and the last one locked the entrance door from the outside. Before long the increasing sound of coughing, screaming and shouting for help could be heard from behind the door. I was unable to make out individual words, for the shouts were drowned by knocking and banging against the door, intermingled with sobbing and crying. After some time the noise grew weaker, the screams stopped. Only now and then there was a moan, a rattle, or the sound of muffled knocking against the door. But soon even that ceased and in the sudden silence each one of us felt the horror of this terrible mass death.

Once everything was quiet inside the crematorium, Unterscharführer [Sergeant] Teuer, followed by Stark, appeared on the flat roof. Both had gasmasks dangling round their necks. They put down oblong boxes which looked like food tins; each tin was labeled with a death's head and marked *Poison!* What had been just a terrible notion, a suspicion, was now a certainty: the people inside the crematorium had been killed with poison gas.

On these occasions [gassings] a camp curfew was declared. To break it meant to risk being shot. For that same reason those of us prisoners who had been forced to participate in preparations for the extermination of Jews as well as in covering up all traces of the crimes were divided into two groups. This was to prevent us from pooling our information and obtaining detailed knowledge of the extermination methods. Prisoners of the second working party, the crematorium stokers, turned up only after we had swept and thoroughly cleaned the yard. By the time they arrived the gas chamber had already been aired and the gassed were lying there as if they had just fallen naked from the sky.

The ceiling of the changing room was supported by concrete pillars to which many more notices were fixed, once again with the aim of making the unsuspecting people believe that the imminent process of disinfection was of vital importance for their health. Slogans like *Cleanliness brings freedom or One louse may kill you* were intended to hoodwink, as were numbered clothes hooks fixed at a height of 1.5 metres. Along the walls stood wooded benches, creating the impression that they were placed there to make people more comfortable while undressing. There were other multi-lingual notices inviting them to hang up their clothes as well as their shoes, tied together by their laces, and admonishing them to remember the number of their hook so that they might easily retrieve their clothes after their showers. There were further notices on the way from the changing room to the gas chamber, directing people to the baths and disinfecting room.

The whole get-up of these subterranean rooms, cunning camouflage and clumsy deception at one and the same time, was horrifying. I began to fear that what I had experienced so far was child's play to what awaited me. Every single detail was carefully aimed at allaying the victims' suspicions and calculated to take them quickly and without trouble into the gas chamber.[16]

From these accounts we can see how multiple eyewitness testimonies can be used to corroborate a historical event. Additional eyewitness accounts, from a 1970 film documentary entitled *History of the SS*, speak for the victims who cannot speak for themselves.[17] In the film SS members and others recall on camera the gruesome details of the extermination process. Their remarks are not coerced confessions or statements resulting from torture; they are simply part of their conversations with the filmmaker. One interview is with Joseph Elber, who joined the SS in 1939 and from 1940 on served as a sergeant in the Gestapo office in Auschwitz, where he was responsible for receiving new arrivals. Elber recollects: "I worked at Birkenau, not far from the platform. There I checked the number of prisoners who had arrived, and handed over a receipt. When the transport leader and the guard had left, the people were formed up into rows. So they put them in front of the doctor and then he selected those who were to go to the camp, and those who must be gassed." According to Elber, those selected for labor worked until they were no longer useful; many were then disposed of through injection.

One of the men who administered the injections was Joseph Klehr, an SS medical orderly. A carpenter by trade, Klehr had joined the SS in 1932. In 1934 he became a nurse in a mental asylum. During August 1939, he enrolled in the Waffen-SS and in October 1941 went to Auschwitz as a medical orderly. In the film Klehr describes the process of extermination by lethal injection and compares that to death by gassing:

> They died at once, as soon as they were injected. As I have said before the man was already dead even before the whole of the injection had been given. This death was not so gruesome as the gassing. That was a gruesome death. It was like in a beehive. They came into the gas chamber and when they were ready he went up and gave the order. And the gas was released into the chimney. And then there was a buzzing—umm, umm, umm, umm—and the tomb got quieter and quieter, and you couldn't hear anything more. It was a gruesome death.

Since the SS guards did not volunteer for these duties, why did they carry them out? Alfred Spiess, chief senior state prosecutor in the trial of some of the Treblinka SS guards, has offered this revealing explanation:

> On the one hand obviously there was the order, and also a certain willingness not to refuse the order. But this readiness was naturally promoted psychologically in that these people were given privileges. Let me put it this way, a lot of carrot and a little stick—that was more or less how the system worked. And the carrot consisted of, first, there was more to eat, and second, which was most important, one couldn't be sent to the front. There was a note to this effect in their pay books. Third, one had the chance of getting into a rest home run by T4, and not least of all, good rations, plenty of alcohol, and last, and not least of all, the opportunity of helping themselves to many valuables which had been taken from the Jews.[18]

There is a myth that the SS were forced to perform these executions. At Nuremberg, in addition to trying the major Nazi war criminals, the British and Americans held trials of a number of concentration camp staff, Gestapo officials, and members of the Waffen-SS. A total of 1,500 were tried; 420 were sentenced to death, 29 received reprieves, and the rest were given various prison sentences. Many of the SS men pleaded that they were only following orders and that they would have been executed had they not done this. Investigations after the Nuremberg trials, however, failed to turn up a single case where someone had been killed for refusing to carry out an order. In his books *The Path to Genocide* and *Ordinary Men,* Christopher Browning shows that many people, including and especially SS guards, consciously, knowingly, and willingly participated in the mass murder of Jews.[19]

Finally, there are the dramatic testimonies captured on film by Claude
Lanzmann, in his documentary *Shoah: An Oral History of the Holocaust*.
At Treblinka, for example, SS-Unterscharführer (Sergeant) Franz Su-
chomel recalls that the horror began before the Jews even arrived at the
camp: "While five thousand Jews arrived in Treblinka, three thousand
were dead in the cars. They had slashed their wrists, or just died. The
ones we unloaded were half dead and half mad." Upon his arrival at the
camp he was given a tour by a fellow Unterscharführer, who "showed
us the camp from end to end. Just as we went by, they were opening the
gas-chamber doors, and people fell out like potatoes. Naturally, that
horrified and appalled us. We went back and sat down on our suitcases
and cried like old women. Each day one hundred Jews were chosen to
drag the corpses to the mass graves. In the evening the Ukrainians drove
those Jews into the gas chambers or shot them. Every day!"[20] The victims and the perpetrators have spoken.

THE EINSATZGRUPPEN PROVE THE HOLOCAUST HAPPENED

The death camps were just one instrument in the Final Solution. The Einsatzgruppen were mobile SS and police units used for special missions in
occupied territories, such as cleaning out towns and villages of Jews and
other unwanted persons, and killing them after occupation by the Germans. We want to emphasize that the method of murder is irrelevant to
the moral consequences of how many were murdered. Murder is murder, whether it is done by gas or by gun. Gitta Sereny put it well:

> [F]or most of the world, including most Jews, the term "Final Solution" has
> mainly or entirely been identified with gas chambers in occupied Poland, or
> even more narrowly, those in Auschwitz. For almost half a century, the mur-
> der by shooting of between one and a half million and two million Jews in
> the occupied Soviet territories has somehow been treated differently. Gro-
> tesquely, more often than not, these murders by shooting have been neatly
> classified as "acts of war," an extraordinary misconstruction of history which
> plays straight into the hands of the so-called revisionists.[21]

Well over one million, and possibly as many as two million, were murdered by non-gassing techniques. For example, during the winter of
1941–42, Einsatzgruppe A reported killing 2,000 Jews in Estonia, 70,000
in Latvia, 136,421 in Lithuania, and 41,000 in Belorussia. On November 14, 1941, Einsatzgruppe B reported an additional 45,467 shootings,
and on July 31, 1942, the governor of Belorussia reported 65,000 Jews

Figure 33.   This photograph of a mass execution of
Russian Jews by Einsatzgruppe D in the Ukraine in
1942 does not by itself prove the Holocaust. But as
one piece of data in a convergence of evidence it helps
prove the mass extermination of European Jewry.
(Photo: YIVO Institute for Jewish Research, New York;
courtesy United States Holocaust Memorial Museum)

had been killed in the previous two months. Einsatzgruppe C estimated
it had killed 95,000 by December 1941. Finally, on April 8, 1942, Einsatzgruppe D reported a total of 92,000 killed, for a grand total of 546,888
dead, or more than half a million in less than one year (see figure 33).[22]

As a specific example of an Einsatzgruppen killing action, a report from
Lithuania was submitted to Reinhard Heydrich by Karl Jäger, commander
of Einsatzkommando 3 in Einsatzgruppe A, and regional head of the Special Security Force. The report is labeled "Secret Reich Business" and titled "Comprehensive Tabulation of Executions Carried out in the EK3

Area up to 1 December 1941." For just two of the days, November 25
and 29, rather than transport Jews to the Kovno ghetto, the commando
unit took them to fort number 9 near the city and executed them, as the
Jäger report notes:

| 25.11.41 | Kauen-F. IX—1159 Juden, 1600 Jüdinnen, 175 J.-Kind. (Umsiedler aus Berlin, München u. Frankfurt a. M.) | 2,934 |
| 29.11.41 | Kauen-F. IX—693 Juden, 1155 Jüdinnen, 152 J.-Kind. (Umsiedler aus Wien u. Breslau) | 2,000 |

Kauen is Kovno, Lithuania, and *Breslau* is Wrocław, the chief city
of Silesia. *Juden* are Jewish men, *Jüdinnen* are Jewish women, and
J. Kind are Jewish children. *Unsiedler* means transferred.[23]

Not everyone was shot. Some were gassed in special gas vans. In a
letter to SS-Haupsturmführer (Captain) Walter Rauff from the automo-
tive organization of the security police, labeled "Top Secret!" and dated
June 5, 1942, orders are given to make adjustments to the vans to make
them more effective. Some of the points include:

Since December 1941, ninety-seven thousand have been processed, using three
vans, without any defects showing up in the vehicles. The explosion that we
know took place at Chelmno [known in German as Kulmhof, it was the first
camp at which mass executions were carried out by gas] is to be considered
an isolated case. The cause can be attributed to improper operation. In order to avoid such incidents, special instructions have been addressed to the
services concerned. Safety has been increased considerably as a result of these
instructions.
   Previous experience has shown that the following adjustments would be
useful:

(1) In order to facilitate the rapid distribution of CO, as well as to avoid a
    buildup of pressure, two slots, ten by one centimeters, will be bored at
    the top of the rear wall. The excess pressure would be controlled by an
    easily adjustable hinged metal valve on the outside of the vans.
(2) The normal capacity of the vans is nine to ten per square meter. The ca-
    pacity of the larger special Saurer vans is not so great. The problem is
    not one of overloading but of off-road maneuverability on all terrains,
    which is severely diminished in this van. It would appear that a reduc-

tion in the cargo area is necessary. This can be achieved by shortening the compartment by about one meter. The problem cannot be solved by merely reducing the number of subjects treated, as has been done so far. For in this case a longer running time is required, as the empty space also needs to be filled with CO. On the contrary, were the cargo area smaller, but fully occupied, the operation would take considerably less time, because there would be no empty space.[24]

There were a total of seven recommendations. Although the term "gassing" people is not used, "treating subjects" with "CO" can only mean murder by gas. In *Anatomy of the SS State,* Helmut Krausnick et al. show that when the Einsatzgruppen were created in May 1941, members were "told about the secret decree on shooting by word of mouth. According to the testimony of Otto Ohlendorf, who was in command of Einsatzgruppe D, the 'liquidation order' (as he called it) meant 'putting to death all racially and politically undesirable elements among the prisoners, where these might be thought to represent a threat to security.'"[25]

Numerous eyewitness accounts from the Einsatzgruppen can be found in a remarkably graphic book entitled *"The Good Old Days": The Holocaust as Seen by Its Perpetrators and Bystanders.* Here, for example, is a statement by the teleprinter engineer Kiebach from Einsatzgruppe C:

> In Rovno I had to participate in the first shooting. . . . Each member of the firing-squad had to shoot one person. We were instructed to aim at the head from a distance of about ten metres. The order to fire was "Ready to shoot, aim, fire!" The people who had been shot then fell into the grave. I myself was detailed to the firing-squad; however, I only managed to shoot about five times. I began to feel unwell, I felt as though I was in a dream. A private or lance-corporal from the Wehrmacht, I don't know which unit, took my carbine from me and went and took my place in the firing-squad.[26]

In an emotional, personal letter to his wife, "My dear Soska," dated Sunday, September 27, 1942, SS-Obersturmführer (Lieutenant Colonel) Karl Kretschmer apologizes for not writing more but notes he is feeling ill and in "low spirits" because "I'd like to be with you all. What you see here makes you either brutal or sentimental." His "gloomy mood," he explains, is caused by "the sight of the dead (including women and children)." Which dead? Dead Jews: "As the war is in our opinion a Jewish war, the Jews are the first to feel it. Here in Russia, wherever the German soldier is, no Jew remains. You can imagine that at first I needed some time to get to grips with this." In a subsequent letter, not dated, he explains to his wife that "there is no room for pity of any kind. You women and children back home could not expect any mercy or pity if the enemy got the upper hand. For that reason we are mopping up where necessary but otherwise the Russians are willing, simple and obedient. There are no Jews here anymore." Finally, on October 19, 1942, in another letter from Kretschmer, signed "You deserve my best wishes and all my love, Your Papa," he shows how easy it is to slip into the banality of evil:

> If it weren't for the stupid thoughts about what we are doing in this country, the Einsatz here would be wonderful, since it has put me in a position where I can support you all very well. Since, as I already wrote to you, I consider the last Einsatz to be justified and indeed approve of the consequences it had, the phrase: "stupid thoughts" is not strictly accurate. Rather it is a weakness not to be able to stand the sight of dead people; the best way of overcoming it is to do it more often. Then it becomes a habit.[27]

HANS FRANK PROVES THE HOLOCAUST HAPPENED

On October 7, 1940, in a speech to a Nazi assembly, Hans Frank, head of the Generalgouvernement (the governmental administration over Poland's four districts of Kraków, Warsaw, Radom, and Lublin), summed up his first year: "My dear Comrades! . . . I could not eliminate [*ausrotten*] all lice and Jews in only one year. But in the course of time, and if you help me, this end will be attained."[28] To those deniers who claim that by *ausrotten* Frank merely meant deportation, we counter: Did Frank, then, mean to "deport" all the lice? Only one translation makes sense here.

On December 13, 1941, Frank told a cabinet session at his Kraków headquarters: "As far as the Jews are concerned, I want to tell you quite frankly that they must be done away with in one way or another. . . . Gentlemen, I must ask you to rid yourself of all feeling of pity. We must annihilate the Jews."[29] "Annihilate" is a strong word; it is not a word that would be used if all they were doing was transporting Jews to a new homeland. On December 16, 1941, Frank addressed a government session in the office of the governor of Kraków, in conjunction with the upcoming Wannsee conference:

> Currently there are in the Government Generalship [Generalgouvernement] approximately 2 1/2 million, and together with those who are kith and kin and connected in all kinds of ways, we now have 3 1/2 million Jews. We cannot shoot these 3 1/2 million Jews, nor can we poison them, yet we will have to take measures which will somehow lead to the goal of annihilation, and that will be done in connection with the great measures which are to be dis-

cussed together with the Reich. The territory of the General Government must be made free of Jews, as is the case in the Reich. Where and how this will happen is a matter of the means which must be used and created, and about whose effectiveness I will inform you in due time.[30]

If the Final Solution meant only deportation out of the Reich, why does Frank refer to attaining "the goal of annihilation" of Jews through means other than shooting or poisoning? The phrase "die irgendwie zu einem Vernichtungseriolg führen" underlines the murderous intent.

JOSEPH GOEBBELS PROVES THE HOLOCAUST HAPPENED

Joseph Goebbels (figure 34) was the Reich minister of propaganda, the Reich plenipotentiary for total war effort, and the party regional leader of Berlin (the Nazi Party divided Germany into 42 units [*Gaue*]; in each region the Gauleiter was responsible for all political and economic activity, and for mobilizing labor and civil defense). And so his diary entries are especially revealing. The following three passages need no further commentary.

> *August 8, 1941,* concerning the spread of spotted typhus in the Warsaw ghetto: "The Jews have always been the carriers of infectious diseases. They should either be concentrated in a ghetto and left to themselves or be liquidated, for otherwise they will infect the populations of the civilized nations."

> *August 19, 1941,* after a visit to Hitler's headquarters: "The Führer is convinced his prophecy in the Reichstag is becoming a fact: that should Jewry succeed in again provoking a new war, this would end with their annihilation. It is coming true in these weeks and months with a certainty that appears almost sinister. In the East the Jews are paying the price, in Germany they have already paid in part and they will have to pay more in the future."

> *February 24, 1942,* after a visit with Hitler in Berlin: "The Führer again voices his determination to remorselessly cleanse Europe of its Jews. There can be no sentimental feelings here. The Jews have deserved the catastrophe that they are now experiencing. They shall experience their own annihilation together with the destruction of our enemies. We must accelerate this process with cold brutality; by doing so we are doing an inestimable service to humanity."[31]

Figure 34.   Propaganda Minister Joseph Goebbels at
the assembly of the SA's 28th Horst Wessel brigade
in Berlin, August 25, 1935. (Courtesy United States
Holocaust Memorial Museum)

In a speech of September 23, 1942, to sixty German newspaper editors,
in the throne room of the Propaganda Ministry in Berlin, Goebbels made
it clear that the press must keep silent about what they all knew was the
outcome for the remaining Berlin Jews: "There are still 48,000 in Berlin.
They know with deadly certainty that as the war progresses they will be
packed off to the east and delivered up to a murderous fate. They already feel the inevitable harshness of physical extermination and therefore they harm the Reich whenever possible whilst they yet live."[32]

This speech, discovered in the British Public Record Office in London by Sol Littmann, a Canadian representative of the Simon Wiesenthal Center, was transcribed and passed along by the Polish resistance
to the British Foreign Office in May 1943. It was read by the entire British
Foreign Office hierarchy in 1943, including Foreign Secretary Anthony
Eden, but it was not made public, nor was it shared with Jewish leaders

in Britain or the United States. Why? David Irving contends: "It is a very dubious document, which needed a lot more digesting before it was put out to the startling and marveling world the way that it was put out a few weeks ago [when Littmann rediscovered it]. The speech was actually on English paper typed on an English typewriter in the English archives. A lot of work had to be done on it—I found the actual Polish origins of it, and the people who have provided it, the Polish Intelligence Service. I think it is a second-hand report, not a direct verbatim transcript in any sense."[33] Although we agree with Irving's assessment that this document is not a verbatim transcript, that does not invalidate the gist of the speech. The transcriber makes it clear that he is "reproducing his [Goebbels's] remarks impartially, just as I heard them, from my shorthand notes, which make no claim to textual exactitude." He adds: "I ask you to read Dr. Goebbels' speech very carefully, for in the opinion of all of us this was the most important internal speech that we had heard since the beginning of the war."[34] The speech is four pages long (typed single space) and mentions the Jews only in the three sentences quoted above. Goebbels is most concerned about the ability of the German people to endure a protracted war and the role of the press in helping to sustain optimism in the face of military uncertainties.

Is it possible the document was forged, or the transcriber badly misjudged what Goebbels said or meant? It is possible but not likely. To avoid the *snapshot fallacy,* we must examine the context for this document. In this case, the context is Goebbels's other speeches and diary entries, and the fact that the speech came just eight months after the Wannsee conference of January 20, 1942, and the acceleration of the Final Solution. Significantly, Irving admits: "We have much better sources than that [the transcribed speech] on Goebbels and his role in this particular crime. Goebbels' true diaries leave no doubt at all that he knew perfectly well what was going on."[35] What crime? What was going on? Here the Holocaust seems implicitly confirmed by one of its sometimes deniers.

Irving, after all, is Goebbels's biographer and knows as much as anyone about the primary sources, especially Goebbels's diary. In his controversial 1996 book about the "Mastermind of the Third Reich," Irving tells how Goebbels lunched with Hitler on February, 18, 1942, after which he dictated to his diary: "'The Führer once again expresses his ruthless resolve to make a clean sweep of the Jews out of Europe. One can't go getting all sentimental about it. The Jews have richly deserved the catastrophe they are suffering today.'" The next month, on March 27, Goebbels dictated what Irving calls a "spine-chilling entry into his diary which confirmed that he at least was now in little doubt": "'Beginning with Lublin the Jews are now being deported eastward from the Government-General. The procedure is pretty barbaric, and one that beggars description, and there's not much left of the Jews. Broadly speaking one can probably say that sixty percent of them will have to be liquidated, while only forty percent can be put to work.'"[36]

In an article on Goebbels in the *Journal of Historical Review,* Irving rationalizes this quote as follows: "It's a very ugly passage, and it's easy to link this diary passage with everything we've seen in the movies and on television since then. He's describing 'Schindler's List' here—or is he? I don't know. All he's actually saying here is that the Jews are having a pretty rigorous time. They're being deported, it's happening in a systematic way, and not many of them are going to survive it."[37] "A pretty rigorous time" seems an extraordinarily loose interpretation of "liquidated." But the passage is even more prescient than Irving realizes. On March 7, 1942, Goebbels noted in his diary that there were still eleven million Jews in Europe.[38] If, as he notes twenty days later, sixty percent of these "will have to be liquidated," we have a close approximation of the six million figure, from just about as high a leader in the Nazi regime as can be found.

Interestingly, and contrary to the bad publicity Irving and his book received when it was about to be published,[39] Irving makes no attempt to rehabilitate Goebbels in the following passage, concerning one of Goebbels's diary entries: "The Jews had had it coming to them for a long time, he [Goebbels] added, and cited yet again Hitler's prophecy of 1939, and the need to eschew all mawkish sentimentality. 'It's a life-and-death struggle between the Aryan race and the Jewish bacillus,' he concluded, adopting Hitler's favorite analogy. 'Here too,' he dictated to his poker-faced stenographer, 'the Führer is the staunch champion and promoter of a radical solution.'"[40] In a "life-and-death struggle," what could "a radical solution" mean other than mass murder? In conjunction with Goebbels's other remarks about "annihilation" and "liquidation," we see a convergence of evidence on the conclusion that the Final Solution had come to mean mass murder.

HEINRICH HIMMLER PROVES THE HOLOCAUST HAPPENED

Himmler's speeches are no less potent as evidence of the Holocaust. He too talks about the *ausrotten* of the Jews, and deniers once again return to their semantic game of arguing that he meant deportation. But two quotes negate that argument.

(1) In a lecture on the history of Christianity in January 1937, Himmler told his SS-Gruppenführers (lieutenant generals): "I have the conviction that the Roman emperors, who exterminated [*ausrotteten*] the first Christians, did precisely what we are doing with the communists. These Christians were at that time the vilest scum, which the city accommodated, the vilest Jewish people, the vilest Bolsheviks there were." *Ausrotten* meant murder.[41]

(2) In June 1941 Himmler told Rudolf Höss, the commandant of Auschwitz, that Hitler had ordered the *Endlösung,* or Final Solution of the Jewish Question, and that Höss would play a major role at Auschwitz:

> It is a hard, tough task which demands the commitment of the whole person without regard to any difficulties that may arise. You will be given details by Sturmbannführer Eichmann of the RSHA who will come to see you in the near future. The department taking part will be informed at the appropriate time. You have to maintain the strictest silence about this order, even to your superiors. The Jews are the eternal enemies of the German people and must be exterminated. All Jews we can reach now, during the war, are to be exterminated without exception. If we do not succeed in destroying the biological basis of Jewry, some day the Jews will annihilate the German *Volk* [people].[42]

Similar speeches from Himmler are no less damning. One of the most notorious is the October 4, 1943, speech to the SS-Gruppenführer in Poznan, which was recorded on a red oxide tape (you can actually hear the speech—it is Himmler's voice).[43] Himmler was lecturing from notes, and early in the talk he stopped the tape recorder to make sure it was working. He then continued, knowing he was being recorded, speaking for three hours and ten minutes on a range of subjects, including the military and political situation, the Slavic peoples and racial blends, German racial superiority that would help them win the war, and the like. Two hours into the speech Himmler began to talk about "the extermination of the Jewish people" (figure 35). He compared this action with the June 30, 1934, blood purges against traitors in the Nazi Party and underscores the necessity of such executions, no matter how difficult:

> I also want to refer here very frankly to a very difficult matter. We can now very openly talk about this among ourselves, and yet we will never discuss this publicly. Just as we did not hesitate on June 30, 1934, to perform our duty as ordered and put comrades who had failed up against the wall and execute them, we also never spoke about it, nor will we ever speak about it. Let us thank God that we had within us enough self-evident fortitude never to

Ich will hier vor Ihnen in aller Offenheit,
auch ein ganz schweres Kapitel erwähnen. Unter
uns soll es einmal ganz offen ausgesprochen sein,
und trotzdem werden wir in der Offentlichkeit
nie darüber reden. Genau so wenig, wie wir am
30. Juni 1934 gezögert haben, die befohlene
Pflicht zu tun und Kameraden, die sich verfehlt
hatten, an die Wand zu stellen und zu erschießen,
genau so wenig haben wir darüber jemals gespro-
chen und werden je darüber sprechen. Es war
eine, Gottseidank in uns wohnende Selbstver-
ständlichkeit des Taktes, dass wir uns unter-
einander nie darüber unterhalten haben, nie
darüber sprachen. Es hat jeden geschaudert
und doch war sich jeder klar darüber, dass er
es das nächste Mal wieder tun würde, wenn es
befohlen wird und wenn es notwendig ist.

Ich meine jetzt die Juden evakuierung, die
Ausrottung des jüdischen Volkes. Es gehört zu
den Dingen, die man leicht ausspricht. - "Das
jüdische Volk wird ausgerottet", sagt ein jeder
Parteigenosse, "ganz klar, steht in unserem
Programm, Ausschaltung der Juden, Ausrottung,
machen wir." Und dann kommen sie alle an, die
braven 80 Millionen Deutschen, und jeder hat
seinen anständigen Juden. Es ist ja klar, die
anderen sind Schweine, aber dieser eine ist ein
prima Jude. Von allen, die so reden, hat
keiner zugesehen, keiner hat es durchgestanden.
Von Euch werden die meisten wissen, was es
heisst, wenn 100 Leichen beisammen liegen, wenn
500 daliegen oder wenn 1000 daliegen. Dies
durchgehalten zu haben, und dabei - abgesehen
von Ausnahmen menschlicher Schwächen - anstän-
dig geblieben zu sein, das hat uns hart gemacht.
Dies ist ein niemals geschriebenes und niemals
zu schreibendes Ruhmesblatt unserer Geschichte,
denn wir wissen, wie schwer wir uns täten, wenn
wir heute noch in jeder Stadt - bei den Bomben-
angriffen, bei den Lasten und bei den Entbehrun-
gen des Krieges - noch die Juden als Geheim-
saboteure, Agitatoren und Hetzer hätten. Wir
würden wahrscheinlich jetzt in das Stadium
des Jahres 1916/17 gekommen sein, wenn die Juden
noch im deutschen Volkskörper säßen.

Figure 35.   The original
German for Himmler's Poznan
speech (translated in the text).
(Courtesy National Archives)

discuss it among us, and we never talked about it. Every one of us was
horrified, and yet every one clearly understood that we would do it next time,
when the order is given and when it becomes necessary.

I am now referring to the evacuation of the Jews, to the extermination of
the Jewish people. This is something that is easily said: "The Jewish people
will be exterminated," says every Party member, "this is very obvious, it is
in our program—elimination of the Jews, extermination, will do." And then
they turn up, the brave eighty million Germans, and each one has his decent
Jew. It is of course obvious that the others are pigs, but this particular one is

a splendid Jew. But of all those who talk this way, none had observed it, none had endured it. Most of you here know what it means when 100 corpses lie next to each other, when 500 lie there or when 1,000 are lined up. To have endured this and at the same time to have remained a decent person—with exceptions due to human weaknesses—has made us tough. This is an honor roll in our history which has never been and never will be put in writing, because we know how difficult it would be for us if we still had Jews as secret saboteurs, agitators and rabble rousers in every city, what with the bombings, with the burden and with the hardships of the war. If the Jews were still part of the German nation, we would most likely arrive now at the state we were at in 1916/17 [here Himmler refers to the difficult conditions in Germany in the middle of the First World War].[44]

In an interview with Irving, his response to this quote was surprising because he seemed to gainsay all of his previous rationalizations with this exchange, though leaving himself one final out:

IRVING: I have a later speech he made on January 26, 1944, in which he is speaking to the same audience rather more bluntly about the *ausrotten* of Germany's Jews, when he announced that they had totally solved the Jewish problem. Most of the listeners sprang to their feet and applauded. "We were all there in Poznan," recalled a rear admiral, "when that man [Himmler] told us how he'd killed off the Jews. I can still recall precisely how he told us. 'If people ask me,' said Himmler, 'why did you have to kill the children too, then I can only say I am not such a coward that I leave for my children something I can do myself.'" Quite interesting—this is an admiral afterwards recording this in British captivity without realizing he was being tape-recorded, which is a very good summary of what Himmler actually said.

SHERMER: That sounds to me like he means to kill Jews, not just transport them out of the Reich.

IRVING: I agree, Himmler said that. He actually said "We're wiping out the Jews. We're murdering them. We're killing them."

SHERMER: What does that mean other than what it sounds like?

IRVING: I agree, Himmler is admitting what I said happened to the 600,000. But, and this is the important point, nowhere does Himmler say "we are killing millions." Nowhere does he even say we are killing hundreds of thousands. He is talking about solving the Jewish problem, about having to kill off women and children too.[45]

To focus on what we don't know and ignore what we do know opens the door to fallacious reasoning—Himmler never exactly said millions, therefore deniers maintain he really meant thousands. But Himmler never said thousands either. Irving infers what he wants to infer. The actual numbers come from other sources that, in conjunction with Himmler's speeches (and many other pieces of evidence), converge as evidence for the conclusion that he meant millions would be killed. And millions were killed.

This conclusion should not surprise us. Himmler not only knew what was going on, he helped orchestrate it. On June 21, 1944, he told top military and SS leaders at Sonthofen: "The war we are waging is chiefly and essentially a race war. It is first and foremost a war against the Jew, who incited other nation-states, such as England and America, to enter the war against us, and it is, second, a war against Russia. The war against Jewry and the Asiatics is a war between two races."[46]

ADOLF HITLER PROVES THE HOLOCAUST HAPPENED

An interesting report of December 29, 1942, from Himmler to Hitler, on the operation of Einsatzgruppen C and D, links Himmler and Hitler together (figure 36) to the Holocaust. Signed by Himmler and initialed by Hitler (to show that he read it), the report begins: "51st report of Himmler to Hitler, 29 December 1942, concerning 'results in combatting partisans from 1 September to 1 December 1942,' containing statistics showing the execution of over 300,000 people, the capture of weapons and ammunition, villages searched or burned down, German casualties, and related matters."[47] The document is a long one but records these figures for the number of Jews shot in the Ukraine, South Russia, and the city of Białystok, in Poland:

August 1942	31,246
September 1942	165,282
October 1942	95,735
November 1942	70,948
Total	363,211

Keep in mind that these are the operations of just two groups in four months. Over one and possibly as many as two million Jews were murdered by mobile killing squads of the Einsatzgruppen throughout the war, accounting for perhaps a third of the total Jewish deaths in the Holocaust.[48] Hitler and Himmler communicated on a regular basis about these and a number of other related issues, including what should be done and what was being done about the Jews. For example, Felix Kersten, Hitler's masseur, reports that Himmler told him on November 11, 1943,

Figure 36.   Heinrich Himmler and Adolf Hitler, architects of the Final
Solution. (Photo: Estelle Bechhoefer; courtesy United States Holocaust
Memorial Museum)

that the annihilation of Poles and Jews "happened on a legal basis. Because the Führer decided in Breslau [Wrocław] in 1941 that the Jews should be annihilated. And the order of the Führer is the highest law in Germany."[49] Hitler even told the Hungarian head of state:

> In Poland this state of affairs has been . . . cleared up: if the Jews there did not *want* to work, they were shot. If they *could* not work, they were treated like tuberculosis bacilli with which a healthy body may become infected. This is not cruel if one remembers that even innocent creatures of nature, such as hares and deer when infected, have to be killed so that they cannot damage others. Why should the beasts who wanted to bring us Bolshevism be spared more than these innocents?[50]

David Irving makes it sound as if there were no smoking gun. In fact, there is an entire battery of smoking guns. In Hitler's speech of January 30, 1939, for example, he said: "Today I want to be a prophet once more: If international finance Jewry inside and outside of Europe should succeed once more in plunging nations into another world war, the consequence will not be the Bolshevization of the earth and thereby the victory of Jewry, but the annihilation of the Jewish race in Europe." In September 1942 Hitler recalled: "In my Reichstag speech of September 1, 1939 [actually January 30], I have spoken of two things: first, that now that the war has been forced upon us, no array of weapons and no passage of time will bring us to defeat, and second, that if Jewry should plot another world war in order to exterminate the Aryan peoples in Europe, it would not be the Aryan peoples which would be exterminated but Jewry." At a public speech in Munich, November 8, 1942, Hitler told his audience:

> You will recall the session of the Reichstag during which I declared: If Jewry should imagine that it could bring about an international world war to exterminate the European races, the result will not be the extermination of the European races, but the extermination of Jewry in Europe. People always laughed about me as a prophet. Of those who laughed then, countless numbers no longer laugh today, and those who still laugh now will perhaps no longer laugh a short time from now. This realization will spread beyond Europe throughout the entire world. International Jewry will be recognized in its full demonic peril; we National Socialists will see to that.[51]

On December 1, 1941, Hitler told dinner guests at his headquarters: "Many Jews are quite unaware of the destructive nature of their very existence. But whoever destroys life courts death, and that is exactly what is happening to them!"[52] Alfred Rosenberg, Nazi Party ideologist and head of the foreign policy department, recalled a conversation with Hitler on December 14, after which he reflected: "I am of the opinion that one ought not to discuss the extermination of the Jews. The Führer agrees with that standpoint."[53]

From his earliest political ramblings to the final Götterdämmerung in his Berlin bunker, Hitler was obsessed with the Jews. On April 12, 1922, in a Munich speech later published in the Nazi Party newspaper *Völkischer Beobachter,* he stated: "The Jew is the ferment of the decomposition of people. This means that it is in the nature of the Jew to destroy, and he must destroy, because he lacks altogether any idea of working for the common good. He possesses certain characteristics given to him by nature and he never can rid himself of those characteristics. The Jew is harmful to us."[54] Twenty-three years later, on February 13, 1945, with his world collapsing around him, Hitler recalled: "Against the Jews I fought open-eyed and in view of the whole world. At the beginning of the war I sent them a final warning. I did not leave them in ignorance that, should they once again manage to drag the world into war, they would this time not be spared—I made it plain that they, this parasitic vermin in Europe, will be finally exterminated."[55] Even as he faced his own death, on April 29, 1945, at 4:00 A.M., just one day before his suicide, Hitler commanded his successors in his political testament to carry

on the fight: "Above all I charge the leaders of the nation and those under them to scrupulous observance of the laws of race and to merciless
opposition to the universal poisoner of all peoples, International Jewry."[56]

How many more quotes do we need to prove that Hitler ordered,
or at least approved proposals submitted by others, to implement the
Holocaust—one hundred more, or a thousand more? Ten thousand
more? The convergence of evidence is overwhelming. The banality of evil
reveals the evil of banality.

8 The Evil of Banality

The Protocols of National Socialism

I remember that at the end of this Wannsee conference,
Heydrich, Müller, and my humble self settled down comfortably by the fireplace, and that then for the first time I saw
Heydrich smoke a cigar or a cigarette, and I was thinking:
today Heydrich is smoking, something I have not seen before.
And he drinks cognac—since I had not seen Heydrich take
any alcoholic drink in years. After this Wannsee conference
we were sitting together peacefully, and not in order to talk
shop, but in order to relax after the long hours of strain.

> Adolf Eichmann, after the Wannsee conference on the
> *Endlösung der Judenfrage,* quoted in J. Robinson,
> *And the Crooked Shall Be Made Straight*

At the Israeli trial of Adolf Eichmann—one of the chief orchestrators of
the Final Solution—Hannah Arendt, covering the trial for the *New
Yorker,* spoke of the "banality of evil." Expecting to see the raw vi-
ciousness of evil in the face of Eichmann—seated in a bulletproof glass
box like a caged predatory beast—she instead gazed upon a sad and pa-
thetic-looking man who recounted in cold language and with dry statistics the collection, transportation, selection, and extermination of millions of human beings. Most surprising of all, Eichmann seemed like a
relatively normal human being—not a monster, not mentally deranged,
not so different from many paper-pushing bureaucrats who go about
their daily tasks like automatons. He actually seemed like the type of
person who could share a smoke and a brandy with a good friend and
colleague—Reinhard Heydrich—after a hard day at the office. The difference is that Heydrich's and Eichmann's bureaucratic duties included
the processing of humans, not just paper.

In an all-encompassing study of human violence and cruelty, entitled simply *Evil*, the psychologist Roy Baumeister demonstrated that for most people killing one human being is repulsive, but killing millions can become routine: "The essential shock of banality is the disproportion between the person and the crime. The mind reels with the enormity of what this person has done, and so the mind expects to reel with the force of the perpetrator's presence and personality. When it does not, it is surprised. Yet the magnitude gap provides one explanation for the surprise and disappointment at evil's banality. The enormity of the crime is apparent from the victim's perspective, but often to the perpetrator it was far less enormous. It might seem quite fitting and appropriate to be a rather ordinary, banal person, if the crime is viewed from the perpetrator's perspective."[1] Maximillian Grabner, the head of the Political Department at Auschwitz and an associate of the camp commandant Rudolph Höss, explained the crime of the Holocaust from a perpetrator's perspective: "I only took part in this crime because there was nothing I could do to change anything. The blame for this crime lay with National Socialism. I myself was never a National Socialist. Nevertheless, I still had to join the party. . . . I only took part in the murder . . . out of consideration for my family. I was never an anti-Semite and would still claim today that every person has the right to live."[2] This is the evil of banality.

THE SEARCH FOR HITLER'S ORDER OF THE HOLOCAUST

How did Hitler and the Nazis make the shift from normal human repulsion against violence to the routineness of evil? How did evil become banal? We examine this question from several perspectives in this chapter. To begin we can ask, specifically: When did Hitler decide that he wanted the Jews of Europe exterminated? Was it during the First World War, as he lay in a hospital bed blinded by a gas attack? Was it in the 1920s, following the draconian Versailles Treaty and the "stab in the back" the Jews allegedly delivered to Germany in the form of economic hardships and international disdain? Was it in the early 1930s, when his party came to power and he could take legal action on his racist ideologies? Was it in the late 1930s, after he gained confidence in the success of the legal expulsion of Jews from German culture and society? Was it in the 1940s, during the maximum securities and minimum restrictions of the Second World War? In 1977, as historians debated this issue, David Irving weighed in with his opinion that Hitler did not even know about the Holocaust. Specifically, in *Hitler's War,* Irving concluded, "No documentary evidence exists that Hitler was aware of what was befalling the Jews." His evidence for this is a quote from Hitler, recorded by Bormann's adjutant Henrich Heim late in the day of October 25, 1941:

> From the rostrum of the Reichstag I prophesied to Jewry that if war could not be avoided, the Jews would disappear from Europe. That race of criminals already had on its conscience the two million dead of the Great War, and now it has hundreds of thousands more. Let nobody tell me that despite that we cannot park them in the marshy parts of Russia! Our troops are there as well, and who worries about them! By the way—it's not a bad thing that public rumor attributes to us a plan to exterminate Jews.[3]

Shortly after the publication of his book, Irving publicly announced his $1,000 challenge to any historian who could produce a written order as documentary proof that Hitler ordered the Holocaust.

The challenge exemplifies what we call the *snapshot fallacy.* In *Hitler's War* Irving reproduces Himmler's telephone notes of November 30, 1941, after Hitler requested a meeting with him, showing that the SS chief telephoned Reinhard Heydrich (head of the RSHA) at 1:30 P.M. "from Hitler's bunker at the Wolf's Lair [*Wolfschanze*], ordering that there was to be 'no liquidation' of Jews" (see figure 37). Taking this "snapshot" out of its historical context, Irving concludes: "the Führer had ordered that the Jews were not to be liquidated."[4] But let's re-view this snapshot in the sequence of frames around it. As Raul Hilberg points out, a more accurate translation of the log is "Jewish transport from Berlin. No Liquidation." In other words, Himmler is referring to *one particular transport,* not *all* Jews. And, ironically, says Hilberg (and Irving concurs in *Hitler's War*), "that transport was liquidated! That order was either ignored, or it was too late. The transport had already arrived in Riga and they didn't know what to do with these thousand people so they shot them that very same evening."[5] Moreover, for Himmler to declare "No Liquidation" implies that liquidation was something that was ongoing and, in fact, happened to this very transport as planned. Why bother to say anything if there were no plan to exterminate Jews? Combined with the evidence presented in the last chapter, the notes shown in figure 37 belong as part of the convergence of evidence that we believe answers David Irving's and Robert Faurisson's demands for "proof." If this order came from Hitler, as Irving says it did,[6] then this further confirms that it was Hitler, not Himmler (or Goebbels), who ordered the Holocaust. As Albert Speer observed regarding Hitler's role: "I don't suppose

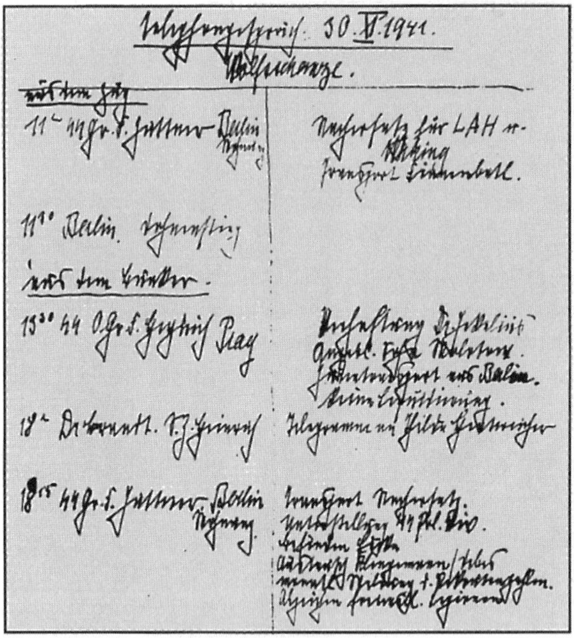

Figure 37. Heinrich Himmler's telephone notes of
November 30, 1941, when the SS chief telephoned
Reinhard Heydrich from Hitler's bunker with the order,
"Jewish transport from Berlin. No Liquidation." For
Hitler to veto an order for liquidation implies that liqui-
dation was something that was ongoing—or why would
he feel the need to halt the extermination of a particular
transport? (Courtesy Yad Vashem, Jerusalem, Israel)

he had much to do with the technical aspects, but even the *decision* to
proceed from shooting to gas chambers would have been his, for the
simple reason, as I know only too well, that no major decisions could be
made about *anything* without his approval."[7]

For years scholars have searched in vain for a signed document by
Hitler authorizing the Final Solution. Now there is a consensus among
Holocaust historians that such a document probably never existed. A possible reason for this stems from Hitler's experience with his euthanasia
program, as we noted in chapter 6. In fall 1939 Hitler signed a letter,
prepared on his own personal stationery, authorizing the killing of the
handicapped in Germany. Specifically, the letter states:

> Reich Leader [Philip] Bouhler and Dr. med. [Karl] Brandt are charged with
> the responsibility of enlarging the competence of certain physicians, designated

by name, so that patients who, on the basis of human judgment, are considered incurable, can be granted mercy death after a discerning diagnosis.[8]

Functionaries at the Nazi Party leader's chancellery (the KdF), who directed the killing operation, had asked Hitler for such written authorization. They knew that a 1930s commission established to revise the penal code had rejected the idea of legalizing euthanasia, so they wanted some reassurance that they and their collaborators would not be prosecuted.

The KdF held the original letter in a safe, and a copy was sent to the Reich minister of justice, Franz Gürtner. Copies were shown to those needing reassurance.[9] In August 1941, however, Hitler gave a "stop" order ending the first phase of the killings of the adult handicapped. The reason is that the Nazis' plan to keep the killing operations secret was unraveling. Rumors were spreading among the general population, leading many to ask local officials and clergy what was really going on. For example, people in Hadamar began to notice that the windows of buses going into the facilities were painted over and that the chimneys of the "euthanasia" facilities were constantly bellowing smoke. Pupils at one school called the buses "killing crates" and threatened each other, "You'll end up in the Hadamar ovens!" Families began to notice the near-identical wording of condolence letters, and some even received two urns while others got empty urns. One family was told that the cause of death of their loved one was acute appendicitis, but the "patient" had had his appendix removed many years before. In another instance a death notice was delivered for a patient still alive, as verified by the family.[10]

Such rumors and slip-ups led people to query local officials, who in turn questioned their superiors, and this eventually made its way to the top. For example, on July 9, 1940, Pastor Braune, vice president of the Central Committee of the Interior Missions of the German Evangelical Church, wrote a memorandum to the Reich Chancellery recounting such stories. Two letters dated August 11 and 16, 1940, from the archbishop of Freiburg, Conrad Cröber, addressed to the Reich interior minister, the head of the Reich Chancellery, and the interior minister of Baden, made similar queries. We can also trace one such letter that found its way to Himmler—dated November 25, 1940, it was written by Frau Elsa von Löwis to the wife of Walter Buch, presiding judge of the Nazi party's own highest court, who in turn passed it to the head of the SS.[11]

A significant step toward halting the killing machine came on July 28, 1941, when the bishop of Münster, Clemens August, Count von Galen, filed murder charges against persons unknown at the public prosecutor's office. When these went unacknowledged, he delivered a public sermon at St. Lambert's Church on August 3, 1941, calling the euthanasia program murder and those who practiced it murderers. Later that month, in response to "public knowledge and popular disquiet," Hitler issued the order to suspend the T4 killing operation, and it came to an official halt on August 24.[12]

Given this precedent, it seems doubtful that Hitler would have committed his signature to any similar document, such as one ordering the Final Solution. From then on any orders to kill people would probably have been verbal. But, even without a written order, we can implicate Hitler in the decision making. After all, there is no written order from Hitler to start the war either. Such decisions do not need to be spelled out. As Yisrael Gutman explains: "Hitler interfered in all main decisions with regard to the Jews. All the people around Hitler came with their plans and initiatives because they knew that Hitler was interested [in solving the 'Jewish question'] and they wanted to please him and be the first to realize his intentions and his spirit."[13] This spirit was made plain in his speeches and writings. Raul Hilberg agrees that the Holocaust "was not so much a product of laws and commands as it was a matter of spirit, of shared comprehension, of consonance and synchronization."[14]

As an example of this spirit, eleven days after the Wannsee Conference Adolf Eichmann sent a circular to the appropriate state police offices, stating, "The evacuation of Jews to the East which has recently been carried out in specific areas represents the beginning of the Final Solution to the Jewish Question in the Altreich (1937 Germany), the Ostmark [Austria] and in the Protectorate of Bohemia and Moravia."[15] "Evacuation to the East" is a euphemism for the deportations of German, Czech, Austrian, and Luxembourg Jews to ghettos in Lodz, Minsk, Riga, and Kovno—journeys that ended in death for most of these Jews. The "evacuation" process had begun the previous summer, in the euphoria following the initial successes of the invasion of the Soviet Union. Indeed, Peter Witte believes the order to deport these Jews should be considered "a document of vital importance in the initial phase of the Final Solution of the Jewish Question."[16] The document, dated September 18, 1941, is a letter from Heinrich Himmler to Gauleiter Greiser, the party leader for the region where the Lodz ghetto was located:

> The Führer wishes the *Altreich* and the Protectorate to be cleared of and freed from Jews from West to East as soon as possible. Consequently, I shall endeavor, this year if possible, and initially as a first stage, to transport the Jews of the *Altreich* and the Protectorate to those Eastern territories which became

part of the Reich two years ago, and then deport them ever further eastwards next spring. My intention is to take approximately 60,000 Jews of the *Altreich* and the Protectorate to spend the winter in the Litzmannstadt [Lodz] ghetto which, I have heard, still has available capacity. I ask you not only to understand this step, which will certainly impose difficulties and burdens on your *Gau,* but to do everything in your power to support it in the interests of all of the Reich. SS-*Gruppenführer* [Lieutenant General] Heydrich, whose task it is to carry out the transfer of the Jews, will contact you in good time, directly or through SS-*Gruppenführer* Koppe.[17]

Witte believes that this letter "removes any possible doubt that the decision to set in motion the deportations and hence the 'Final Solution' in the Reich and in the Protectorate was presented to Hitler personally and was taken by him personally." But what about Himmler's choice of words, "the Führer wishes," as opposed to "the Führer orders"? According to Witte, "in 1941 the Reichsführer-SS and Chief of the German Police was not yet in a position to give orders to the Gauleiters. The phrase shows that Hitler was making use of Himmler (who was responsible for the 'resettlements') to pass on his orders without putting anything in writing. Moreover, the choice of 'wish' used by a third party is, in content, absolutely identical to a command from the Führer, as members of Hitler's staff confirmed after the war." Witte also points out that the deportations were described as a "first stage" in the letter. The following spring they were to be "deported even further eastwards." Witte concludes: "This terminology already virtually represents the death sentence for those Jews due for deportation, irrespective of the fact that at this point there were no extermination camps ready."[18] By the following spring, however, the camps were ready for the *ausrotten,* or extermination, of the Jews.

THE *AUSROTTEN* OF THE JEWS

Another piece of evidence in our pantheon is a word that appears in numerous Nazi documents referring to the Jews—*ausrotten,* which means "to extirpate or exterminate." In *Hitler's War* David Irving claims that *ausrotten* really means "stamping out" or "rooting out." For instance, he translates a conversation between Hitler and Alfred Rosenberg, the Nazi Reich minister for the eastern occupied territories. In Rosenberg's discussion of handling the Jews, Irving takes *ausrotten* to mean "stamping out" and then concludes that Rosenberg meant transporting Jews out of the Reich.[19] But modern dictionaries say *ausrotten* means "to exterminate, extirpate, or destroy." Irving's response to this is, "The word *ausrotten* means one thing now in 1994, but it meant something very different in the time Adolf Hitler uses it."[20] Yet a check of historical dictionaries shows that *ausrotten* has always meant "exterminate."[21] Irving's rejoinder sounds like a post hoc rationalization:

> Different words mean different things when uttered by different people. What matters is what that word meant when uttered by Hitler. I would first draw attention to the famous memorandum on the Four-Year Plan of August 1936. In that Adolf Hitler says, "we are going to have to get our armed forces in a fighting state within four years so that we can go to war with the Soviet Union. If the Soviet Union should ever succeed in overrunning Germany it will lead to the *ausrotten* of the German people." There's that word. There is no way that Hitler can mean the physical liquidation of eighty million Germans. What he means is that it will lead to the emasculation of the German people as a power factor.[22]

How do we know he did not mean actual liquidation? "Because," says Irving, "no one is going to say that if Russians take over Germany they are going to liquidate eighty million people." Yet that is precisely how the word appears to be used in document after document. For example, in a December 1944 conference regarding the Ardennes attack against the Americans, Hitler ordered his generals "to *ausrotten* them division by division." Was Hitler giving the order to *transport* the Americans out of the Ardennes division by division?! "No," Irving admits:

> But compare that with a speech he made in August 1939, in which he says, with regard to Poland, "we are going to destroy the living forces of the Polish Army." This is the job of any commander—you have to destroy the forces facing you. How you destroy them, how you "take them out" is probably a better phrase, is immaterial. If you take those pawns off the chess board they are gone. If you put the American forces in captivity they are equally neutralized whether they are in captivity or dead. And that's what the word *ausrotten* means there.[23]

An unlikely reading. In a memo (figure 38) SS-Sturmbannführer (Major) Rudolf Brandt tells Reich physician Ernst Robert Grawitz in Berlin about the *"Ausrottung der Tuberkulose"* (tuberculosis) "as a disease affecting the nation." Clearly he is using *ausrotten* to indicate the eradication or elimination—the killing off—of TB. Irving himself translates a report this same Rudolf Brandt wrote in March 1943 to Ernst Kaltenbrunner, Heydrich's successor as chief of the RSHA, as "I am transmitting herewith to you a press dispatch on the accelerated extermination [*ausrotten*] of the Jews in Occupied Europe."[24] The same man is using

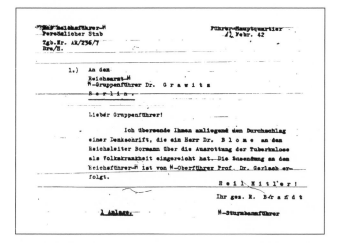

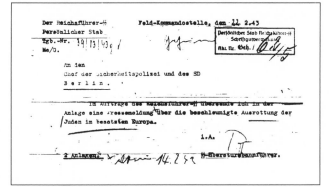

The Reichsführer SS   Field Command Post
Personal Staff   Secret   Feb.22, 1943
(Diary Entry No.)

To: Chief of Sicherheitspolizei [Security Police] and
    SD [Security Service]
    Berlin

As ordered by the SS Reichsführer, I am sending you the outline
of a press announcement concerning the accelerated extermination
of the Jews [Ausrottung der Juden...] in occupied Europe.
                              On behalf of

                              SS Obersturmbannführer

Two Enclosures

Figure 38.   The February 12, 1942, memo from SS Sturm-
bannführer Rudolf Brandt to Reich physician Ernst Robert
Grawitz, in which he uses the same word—*ausrotten*—to
discuss the extermination of TB and of Jews. (Courtesy
National Archives)

the same word to discuss the same process of extermination for both TB and Jews.

Finally, consider this excerpt from the sworn testimony given in Nuremberg on January 2, 1946, by Haupsturmführer (Captain) Dieter Wisliceny, Adolf Eichmann's deputy, who organized the mass deportations of the Jews in Slovakia, Greece, and Hungary between 1942 and 1944. Wisliceny not only spells out the mass murder of the Jews but makes it clear the order came from the very top:

> At the end of July or beginning of August (1942) I went to Berlin in order to visit Eichmann and I once again pleaded with him to accede to the Slovakian government's request. I told him that there were rumors coursing through foreign countries that all the Jews were being murdered in Poland. I reminded him that the Pope had intervened on their behalf with the Slovakian government. I informed him that such a thing, if it were really true, would do great damage to our image, that is, Germany's image in foreign countries. For all these reasons I asked him to permit the inspection in question. After a long discussion Eichmann told me that this request to visit the Polish ghettos could not be granted under any circumstances. In answer to my question of "why?" he said that most of those Jews were no longer alive. I asked him who had given such instructions and he referred me to an order of Himmler's. Thereupon I asked him to show me this order, since I could not believe that it really existed in written form.
>
> He took a small bundle of documents out of his safe and showed me a letter of Himmler's to the chief of the security police and the SD [security service]. The essential contents of the letter were as follows:
>
> The Führer had ordered the final solution to the Jewish question; the chief of the security police and the SD and the inspector of the concentration camps were given authority to carry out this so-called final solution. All Jewish men and women who were capable of working were temporarily freed from the final solution and were to be used for work in the concentration camps.
>
> Eichmann continued to explain to me what this meant. He said that the planned biological destruction of the Jewish race in the eastern territories was camouflaged under the concept and the expression of "final solution." It was fully clear to me that this order meant the death of many millions of human beings. I said to Eichmann: "May God provide that our enemies will never have the opportunity to do the same to the German people," whereupon Eichmann answered that I shouldn't be sentimental, it was an order given by the Führer and had to be carried out.[25]

Wisliceny added that at his last meeting with Eichmann at the end of February 1945, when the war was coming to an end, Eichmann "said that he would go to his grave with a smile on his face because the feeling that he had five million human beings on his conscience would be a source of particular satisfaction for him."

INTENTION AND FUNCTION ON THE ROAD TO THE HOLOCAUST

Throughout the 1980s historians, especially German historians, debated the "intentionalism" versus the "functionalism" of the Holocaust, as part of what was known as the *Historikerstreit,* or the "Historical Dispute," or more commonly the "History Wars." Among the issues discussed were the crimes committed by the Wehrmacht in Poland and other countries swept up by the Nazis in their thrust to the east, particularly after the invasion of the Soviet Union in June of 1941. Some historians argued that there were actually two wars: the unfortunate and regrettable war in the west, which should have been avoided, and the necessary war in the east against the Soviet Union, which some maintained was fought to thwart a potential invasion of Germany by Stalin (for which the evidence is slim) and which helped save Europe from communism. Churchill and the Allies, some contended, did not understand the seriousness of the threat that communism posed for European civilization, but Hitler did and thus he should be seen in a new light that includes the good he did for the western world. These historians also debated the relative guilt of the German people as a whole (not just Nazis) for supporting Hitler politically and putting him in a position of power in the first place. In our opinion, these debates were mostly within the realm of legitimate revision (although sometimes barely) and are not examples of denial; they evidenced a movement toward normalizing the German war experience that, while extreme, was still within the boundaries of the tragedy that is modern war.

On subjects more directly related to the Holocaust, *intentionalists* argued that Hitler intended the mass extermination of the Jews from early in the party's history (possibly as early as the 1920s), Nazi policy was programmed toward this end, and the invasion of Russia and the quest for *Lebensraum* (living space) was directly planned and linked to the Final Solution.[26] *Functionalists,* by contrast, contended that the Nazis' original plan for the Jews was expulsion from the Reich and that the Final Solution evolved as a result of circumstances of the war.[27] Uwe Adam, for example, said that mass murder was the direct result of a decision by Hitler, whereas Karl Schleunes, Martin Broszat, and Hans Mommsen claimed that the Holocaust was the result of a cumulative cultural and conditional momentum instead of any one decision by a single individual.[28] The Holocaust historian Raul Hilberg feels that this is an artificial distinction: "In reality it is more complicated than either of these interpretations. I believe Hitler gave a plenary order, but that order was it-

self the end product of a process. He said many things along the way
which encouraged the bureaucracy to think along certain lines and to
take initiatives. But on the whole I would say that any kind of systematic shooting, particularly of young children or very old people, and any
gassing, required Hitler's order."[29]

Hilberg's reasoning makes sense from a psychological perspective.
Hitler was the supreme commander and, as such, behind all orders (figure
39). As he himself put it in 1933: "Every bullet that is now fired from
the barrel of a police pistol is my bullet. If that is called murder, then I
have committed murder, for I have ordered it all; I take the responsibility for it."[30] Indeed, the Holocaust historian Leni Yahil asks: "Did
[Hitler's] totalitarian system mean that his wishes were the moving spirit
behind everything that happened in the complex entity known as the
Third Reich?" While admitting that Hitler could not have controlled
every tiny detail, Yahil insists: "At the same time, there is also no doubt
that until his death in the bunker beneath his Berlin chancellery, Hitler
was absolute master of Germany. He held both legislative and executive
power; after the slaughter of the leaders of the SA [storm troopers] on
June 30, 1934, he also assumed the mantle of supreme judge, with the
authority to pass the death sentence. Time and again in the course of the
years, his absolute authority was reaffirmed by his party."[31] Clearly Hitler
could not control every the minutia of the Reich, yet the historical record
shows that his influence was pervasive in all matters of political, economic, social, and military significance.

Ronald Headland argues in favor of a functionalist interpretation
based on the realities of the inefficiencies of a large bureaucracy like the
one the Nazis ran in Germany: "Perhaps the greatest merit of the functionalist approach has been the extent to which it has delineated the
chaotic character of the Third Reich and the often great complexity of
factors involved in the decision-making process."[32] This perspective does
not discount the possibility of an intentional "blueprint" for murder,
as Gutman has called it.[33] Another value of a functional view is that
history, especially a historical event as complex as the Holocaust, rarely
unfolds as historical actors intend. In *Jews for Sale?* Yehuda Bauer, one
of the most senior Holocaust scholars, documents the complicated and
contingent evolution of the Final Solution: "In prewar Germany, emigration suited the circumstances best, and when that was neither speedy
enough or complete enough, expulsion—preferably to some 'primitive'
place, uninhabited by true Nordic Aryans, [such as] the Soviet Union

Figure 39.   Adolf Hitler in command (Photo: Richard
Freimark; courtesy United States Holocaust Memorial
Museum)

or Madagascar—was the answer. When expulsion did not work either,
and the prospect of controlling Europe and, through Europe, the world
arose in late 1940 and early 1941, the murder policy was decided on,
quite logically, on the basis of Nazi ideology. All these policies had the
same aim: removal." Bauer argues that even the Wannsee Conference
was but one more contingent step down the road from original expulsion to final extermination: "The public still repeats, time after time,
the silly story that at Wannsee the extermination of the Jews was arrived at. Wannsee was but a stage in the unfolding of the process of mass
murder."[34]

    For many, the history of Auschwitz typifies the entire Holocaust: one
long but very crooked road from early stages to the final aim. But as Yahil

notes, early intent and final aim are not always the same: "The exclusion of the Jews from the economic, cultural, and social life of Germany
was not accomplished according to a definite, preconceived plan, but
steadily expanded and became more rigorous in the wake of broader de-
velopments within the country."[35] Sybil Milton shows how the expulsion
of Polish Jews in 1938–39 was an important step in the development of
subsequent Nazi policy because "it was the first sizable deportation of
Jews requiring the coordination of railways, police, diplomats, and treas-
ury officials. Furthermore, the expulsion led to the assassination of vom
Rath and provided the Nazis with an excuse for the subsequent violence
of the Kristallnacht"—the "night of broken glass," November 9, 1938,
when the Nazis attacked Jewish businesses and synagogues.[36] And these
were just a few of the steps among thousands that eventually led to the
Final Solution.

The functional sequence goes from *eviction* of the Jews from German
life (including the confiscation of most of their property and homes), to
expulsion from Germany and German territories, to *concentration and
isolation* in ghettos (leading to crowding, filth, disease, and death), accompanied by economic exploitation in concentration and labor camps
(often resulting in overwork, starvation, and death), to *extermination* by
shooting, starvation, and gassing in the camps. Gutman confirms this contingent interpretation: "The Final Solution was an operation that started
from the bottom, from a local basis, with a kind of escalation from place
to place, until it was a comprehensive event. I don't know if I would call
it a plan. I say it was a blueprint. Physical destruction was the outcome
of a series of steps and attacks against the Jews. It was a culmination of
a long series of steps."[37]

In such complex social phenomena as the Holocaust, various conditions interact in an autocatalytic feedback loop (where the components
automatically catalyze each other, causing an acceleration of the system).
Yahil sums up how this feedback loop operated in the Third Reich: "This
unique combination of methodical planning and opportunism, of tight
control and improvisation, of rational preparation and intuitive action
was characteristic not only of Hitler himself but of the way in which the
Nazis rose to power, exercised power, and then fell from power."[38]
Christopher Browning agrees:

> In short, for Nazi bureaucrats already deeply involved in and committed to
> "solving the Jewish question," the final step to mass murder was incremen-
> tal, not a quantum leap. They had already committed themselves to a politi-
> cal movement, to a career, and to a task. They lived in an environment al-

ready permeated by mass murder. This included not only programs with which they were not directly involved, like the liquidation of the Polish intelligentsia, the gassing of the mentally ill and handicapped in Germany, and then on a more monumental scale the war of destruction in Russia. It also included wholesale killing and dying before their very eyes, the starvation in the ghetto of Lodz and the punitive expeditions and reprisal shooting in Serbia. By the very nature of their past activities, these men had articulated positions and developed career interests that inseparably and inexorably led to a similar murderous solution to the Jewish question.[39]

History involves a vast complexity of influencing variables, but within this complexity resides a simplicity of forces derived from the actions of individuals that can direct these social conditions and historical trends. What began as an intention to resettle Jews in time evolved into a functional solution of mass extermination. Hitler, Himmler, Goebbels, Frank, and others were quite serious in their intention to solve the Jewish "question," mainly because they were virulently antisemitic, and resettlement was a real and (at the time) viable solution. But the roads of history are paved with both good and bad intentions because intentions can, at best, produce only a general direction for the road. We believe that history's ultimate pathways are finally determined by the *functions* of any given moment, as they interact with the intentions that came before, in what we call *intentional functionalism*.

INTENTIONAL FUNCTIONALISM IN ALBERT SPEER

At the Nuremberg trials following the war, Hitler's chief architect and minister of armaments, Albert Speer, said that he did not know about the extermination program. Deniers are only too happy to point this out, but they conveniently overlook such passages as this from Speer's *Spandau Diary:*

> December 20, 1946. Everything comes down to this: Hitler always hated the Jews; he made no secret of that at any time. He was capable of tossing off quite calmly, between the soup and the vegetable course, "I want to annihilate the Jews in Europe. This war is the decisive confrontation between National Socialism and world Jewry. One or the other will bite the dust, and it certainly won't be us." So what I testified in court is true, that I had no knowledge of the killings of Jews; but it is true only in a superficial way. The question and my answer were the most difficult moment of my many hours on the witness stand. What I felt was not fear but shame that I as good as knew and still had not reacted; shame for my spiritless silence at the table, shame for my moral apathy, for so many acts of repression.[40]

Deniers also ignore Speer's actual participation in the Final Solution. Matthias Schmidt, in *Albert Speer: The End of a Myth*, demonstrates that Speer organized the confiscation of 23,765 Jewish apartments in Berlin in 1941; he was present in 1943 at Dora, the German concentration camp, when preparations were made to execute inmates as a warning against sabotage in the construction of A-4 rockets; he was apparently present at the October 4, 1943, speech of Heinrich Himmler, the SS-Reichsführer (head of the Schutzstaffel, or security organization), who, with regard to killing Jewish women and children, said "we had to reach the difficult decision of making this nation vanish from the face of the earth"; and in 1977 he confessed in a newspaper interview: "I still see my guilt as residing chiefly in the approval of the persecution of the Jews and the murder of millions of them."[41]

In *Albert Speer: His Battle with Truth* Gitta Sereny, a journalist specializing in the Third Reich, goes even further in implicating Speer. She tracked down Nazi Germany's greatest fighter pilot, General Adolf Galland, who told her in 1987: "The first indication I had, which made me think seriously of genocide was while flying over Russia, around March 1942, with Himmler and Speer. Himmler pointed down where we could see a lot of people moving about, and he said, 'Last year we had decided to kill them all—this year we need them for the *Rüstung* [armament production].' That remark jolted me. I thought, what does he mean '*kill* them all'? And of course, if it was Speer who was there with us, then he heard that too."[42]

In 1977 Speer was asked to testify against the publishers of a Holocaust denial work entitled *Did Six Million Really Die?* Speer's three-page document concludes dramatically: "to this day I still consider my main guilt to be my tacit acceptance [*billigung*] of the persecution and the murder of millions of Jews." Speer confirmed in a footnote for a translation of this document that by *billigung* he meant "looking away, not by knowledge of an order or its execution. The first is as grave as the second."[43] Yet, according to our German-English dictionary, *billigung* really means "approval," just as *missbilligung* means "disapproval." In this sense, then, Speer approved of the persecution and murder of millions of Jews, which is a far stronger reaction than a mere tacit acceptance. Sereny asked him the obvious question: "Why did you say this so directly now, after denying it for so long?" He answered: "For this purpose, and with these people, I didn't wish to—I couldn't—hedge." Sereny then concludes her book: "If Speer had said as much in Nuremberg, he would have been hanged."[44]

INTENTIONAL FUNCTIONALISM IN THE WANNSEE PROTOCOL

The work Speer testified against in 1977, *Did Six Million Really Die?*, was one of the most widely read Holocaust denial publications at the time. It was written by Richard Harwood, a nom de plume for Richard Verral, the editor of the British publication *Spearhead*, the voice of the right-wing National Front. This twenty-six-page booklet was sent to all members of the British Parliament, key journalists and academics, and top figures in the Jewish community. Since its publication over one million copies have circulated around the globe. On the first page Harwood warns readers:

> . . . the accusation of the Six Million is not only used to undermine the prin-
> ciple of nationhood and national pride, but it threatens the survival of the
> Race itself. It is wielded over the heads of the populace, rather as the threat
> of hellfire and damnation was in the Middle Ages. Many countries of the An-
> glo-Saxon world, notably Britain and America, are today facing the gravest
> danger in their history, the danger posed by the alien races in their midst. Un-
> less something is done in Britain to halt the immigration and assimilation of
> Africans and Asians into our country, we are faced in the near future, quite
> apart from the bloodshed of racial conflict, with the biological alteration and
> destruction of the British people as they have existed here since the coming
> of the Saxons. In short, we are threatened with the irrecoverable loss of our
> European culture and racial heritage.[45]

Harwood maintains that immigration and assimilation lead to racial impurity and the destruction of Western culture, an argument of racist ideology found in many European countries and parts of America today. Brigitte Bailer-Galanda and Wolfgang Neugebauer, for example, describe similar arguments in Austria: "Neo-Nazi groups spread openly racist ideas in this context, the majority of the extreme Right and part of the FPÖ [a right-wing group] conceal such racist prejudice behind appar-ently harmless phrases—preserving Austria's national identity, her cul-tural inheritance, etc. Such phrases are now part of the extreme Right's strategy to update its vocabulary . . . the words Volk and Rasse are re-placed by Kultur, 'cultural mixture' is employed instead of 'racial mix-ture.' Similarly, 'Ethnopluralism' is presented as a concept antagonistic to different peoples and cultures coming together (multicultural society) and is basically just a new expression for traditional racist view."[46]

Where have we heard this before? It is hardly surprising that some Holocaust deniers have acquired the label of neo-Nazis. To us, Harwood's argument sounds like the basic Nazi eugenic ideology. But the Nazis did not invent eugenics. In his book *The Holocaust in History*, Michael Marrus observes: "Extensive investigation of the beginnings of Hitlerian and Nazi antisemitism has failed to uncover any particular originality in this field—any new twist or turn in thinking about Jews. Virtually every commentator concludes that, despite his efforts to portray himself as an independent thinker and creative genius, Hitler expressed nothing that was not part of the popular culture of Vienna or Munich in the period of his youth. And the Nazi party, similarly, offered voters no anti-Jewish plank that could not be found elsewhere in political life."[47]

If Marrus is right, then we must look before and beyond the Nazis and the ideologies of National Socialism if we are to understand the origins of their anti-Jewish policy. This policy has many causes and reaches back decades, even centuries before the regime. Specifically relevant to our discussion is one particular connection—to the nineteenth-century anthropological idea of a first race (the "pure" Aryan race) and linguistic idea of a first language (a "pure" Aryan language) that, when linked to a certain vicious type of eugenics program (better living through selective breeding and extermination), leads from social Darwinism to the Wannsee Protocol. Seen in this light, the Wannsee Protocol, we believe, offers further evidence that Hitler ordered the Final Solution.

Penned by Adolf Eichmann, the Wannsee Protocol, which defines the Jews of Europe and outlines policies against them, was the product of the Wannsee Conference held on January 20, 1942, in the wealthy Berlin suburb of Wannsee. The meeting took place in a two-story mansion, Am Grossen Wannsee no. 56–58, owned by Reinhard Heydrich and nestled among trees along the Haval River, which runs peacefully around the western outskirts of Berlin. (During the war this building was being used as a guest house for visiting police and SS officers; Heydrich planned to retire there but was assassinated in 1943.) The setting was ideal for a day of concentrated work followed by an evening of relaxation. Heydrich called the meeting to inform his colleagues that Göring had assigned him the task of preparing the Final Solution. Himmler's "General Plan for the East" included the compulsory resettlement of thirty million Slavs. The question at hand, however, was what to do with the eleven million Jews remaining. The purpose of the conference, then, was to coordinate a more efficient execution of the Final Solution of the Jewish question.

There were fifteen high-ranking SS officers and ministerial bureaucrats present, plus, it is believed, a secretary to take the minutes of the meeting. Unfortunately no record exists of who this secretary was, or what happened to the minutes. Fortunately Adolf Eichmann transcribed his own summary of the meeting, and this is what has come to us as the Wannsee Protocol, discovered in the files of the German Foreign Office in Bonn in 1947 and used in subsequent war trials as evidence for the planning of the mass extermination of Jews.[48] Deniers, of course, argue that there is nothing incriminating in the document; still others suggest the meeting may not have taken place; and a German denial publication argues that the document is a forgery.[49] The director of the Gedenkstätte Haus der Wannsee-Konferenz (the Wannsee Conference house of remembrance), Dr. Wolf Kaiser, has explained that the original document was retyped in the late 1940s with some errors, and it is *this* transcription that the deniers claim is a forgery.[50] There is no question of the authenticity of Eichmann's original document, which he verified and elaborated on during his 1961 trial in Israel.[51]

By the time the meeting was held the question was not whether to implement the Final Solution—that had already begun in the second half of 1941 with the actions of the Einsatzgruppen in the East and the early experimental gassings of prisoners. Rather, the issue was how best to carry this out. The conference was just one step in many along the crooked road to Auschwitz and the other death camps. The Wannsee Conference was important, but not the *only* or even *the* step that triggered the Nazis' change of intentions. Twelve of the fifteen present at the meeting were well informed about the regional deportations and killing operations already in progress in various parts of the Reich (see below). Chelmno, the first of the extermination camps, had already been in operation for six weeks. Auschwitz-Birkenau was under construction, as were other camps. And Jews in the eastern territories that came under the control of the Nazis after they routed the Soviet armies, were being routinely rounded up and killed by the Einsatzgruppen squads.

Part I of the protocol is a listing of who "took part in the conference on the Final Solution (*Endlösung*) of the Jewish question."[52] The list is a veritable who's who of the Nazi hierarchy, with no less than eight of the fifteen holding doctorates (all but two in law). These men were the very best of their profession:

1. Reinhard Heydrich, chief of security police and security service, was given the nod by Himmler in July 1932 to organize the service for the monitoring of political opponents. In 1936 he was appointed head of the Reich security main office (RSHA), and in June 1941 he organized the Einsatzgruppen purges of Eastern European Jews.

2. Adolf Eichmann, then head of the Reich security main office, was involved in emigration, deportation, and evacuation of Jews from as early as the fall of 1934; he was so effective that Heydrich relied heavily on him for the detailed implementation of the Final Solution.

3. Dr. Rudolf Lange, from the security police and security service, had considerable experience working in the Gestapo and the SS, including directing Special Commando II, which by the end of 1941 had murdered nearly 60,000 Latvian, German, and Austrian Jews.[53]

4. Dr. Eberhard Schöngarth, from the security police and security service, was one of the first to join the Nazi Party in 1922 and moved up the ranks, becoming head of the Gestapo in Dortmund, Bielefeld, Münster, and Erfurt.

5. Heinrich Müller, from the Reich security main office, was both an SS major general and a police brigadier general, specializing in the "special treatment" of political prisoners.

6. Otto Hofmann, from the SS race and settlement main office, was responsible for German settlements in occupied Poland (after the inhabitants were booted out), as well as the "Germanization" of Polish children.

7. Wilhelm Kritzinger, from the Reich chancellery, had experience in drafting decrees against "parasites" (*Volksschädlirge*)[54] as well as implementing the legal justification for the confiscation of the property of German Jews during their deportation.

8. Dr. Gerhard Klopfer, from the Nazi Party chancellery, was an expert on matters of race and national characteristics.

9. Martin Luther, from the German Foreign Office, was a key liaison between the Foreign Office and the SS, in particular to the "Section for Jewish Affairs" of the Reich security main office.

10. Dr. Josef Bühler, from the office of the governor-general at Kraków (near Auschwitz), worked on the establishment of Jewish ghettos, participated in the introduction of distinguishing marks for Jews, and was involved in the "special pacification operation" that resulted in the mass murder of 3,500 Polish intellectuals in May–June 1940.[55]

11. Dr. Roland Freisler, from the Reich Ministry of Justice, was present as a representative of Undersecretary Franz Schlegelberger.

12. Erich Neumann, from the office of the plenipotentiary for the Four-Year Plan, was an expert on economic matters, such as the "Aryanization" of the economy, the isolation of Jews, and the exploitation of oil resources in occupied territories of the Soviet Union.

13. Dr. Wilhelm Stuckart, from the Reich Ministry of the Interior, was coauthor of the highly influential Nuremberg Racial Laws, worked to deprive Jews of their citizenship, and participated in a conference on the "Germanization" of the occupied territories of the Soviet Union.

14. Dr. Georg Leibbrandt, from the Reich Ministry for the Occupied Eastern Territories, specialized in the "Section East" department of the Nazi Foreign Policy Department and was in charge of anti-Communist and anti-Soviet Russian propaganda.

15. Dr. Alfred Meyer, from the Reich Ministry for the Occupied Eastern Territories, was an undersecretary to the Nazi propagandist Alfred Rosenberg.

Taken as a whole, this group could not have had better preparation for planning what would turn out to be one of the largest mass exterminations in human history.

Part II explains that "the meeting opened with the announcement by the Chief of the Security Police and the SD, SS-Obergruppenführer Heydrich, of his appointment by the Reich Marshal [Hermann Göring] as Plenipotentiary for the Preparation of the Final Solution of the European Jewish Question." The remainder of this section gives a brief history of what had been accomplished thus far, including "forcing Jews out of the various territories for living [*Lebensgebiete*] of the German people" and "forcing the Jews out of the living space [*Lebensraum*] of the German people," as well as all the financial and logistical problems that had been encountered. Eichmann makes it clear that these two stages were inadequate: "Financial difficulties—such as increases ordered by the various foreign governments in the sums of money that immigrants were required to have and in landing fees—as well as lack of berths on ships and continually tightening restrictions or bans on immigration, hampered emigration efforts very greatly."[56]

In part III we glimpse a smoking gun. Eichmann announces that a new plan has been devised: "Another possible solution of the problem has now taken the place of emigration, i.e., the evacuation of the Jews to the

> Unter entsprechender Leitung sollen nun
> im Zuge der Endlösung die Juden in geeigneter Wei-
> se im Osten zum Arbeitseinsatz kommen. In großen
> Arbeitskolonnen, unter Trennung der Geschlechter,
> werden die arbeitsfähigen Juden straßenbauend in
> diese Gebiete geführt, wobei zweifellos ein Groß-
> teil durch natürliche Verminderung ausfallen wird

> Der allfällig endlich verbleibende Rest-
> bestand wird, da es sich bei diesem zweifellos um
> den widerstandsfähigsten Teil handelt, entsprechend
> behandelt werden müssen, da dieser, eine natürliche
> Auslese darstellend, bei Freilassung als Keimzelle
> eines neuen jüdischen Aufbaues anzusprechen ist.
> (Siehe die Erfahrung der Geschichte.)

Figure 40.   These two paragraphs from the Wannsee Protocol, part III,
call for "suitable treatment" of any Jews who survive the rigors of hard labor
and the "natural selection" (*natürliche Auslese*) of a potential "germ-cell" of
a new Jewish revival (see translation in text). (Courtesy Gedenkstätte Haus
der Wannsee-Konferenz)

East."[57] Evacuation is a not-so-veiled code for sending them to their death
in the eastern camps. Why make this assumption? Eichmann had just described the first two attempts at solving the Jewish question, both of which
he said were inadequate, followed by "another solution." And what is
that solution?

> Under appropriate direction the Jews are to be utilized for work in the East
> in an expedient manner in the course of the final solution. In large (labor)
> columns, with the sexes separated, Jews capable of work will be moved into
> these areas as they build roads, during which a large proportion will no doubt
> drop out through natural reduction.
>
> The remnant that eventually remains will require suitable treatment; be-
> cause it will without doubt represent the most resistant part, it consists of a
> natural selection [*natürliche Auslese*] that could, on its release, become the
> germ-cell of a new Jewish revival. (Witness the experience of history.) [For
> the original German, see the figure 40][58]

The "evacuation of the Jews" Eichmann describes cannot mean
simple deportation to live elsewhere, since the Nazis had already been

deporting Jews to the east, and Eichmann indicates this was inadequate. Instead, he outlines a new solution. Shipment to the east will mean, for those who can work, work until death, and (as we know from other sources) for those who cannot work, immediate death.[59] What about those who can work and do not succumb to death? "*The remnant that eventually remains will require suitable treatment.*" Suitable treatment can only mean murder. Why? Eichmann explains that a natural selection (*natürliche Auslese*) in the Darwinian sense will make these Jews the most resistant (to death by exhaustion), meaning they will be the fittest—the strongest, healthiest, smartest, etc. Should this new population of naturally selected Jews survive, they might (Eichmann fears) "become the germ-cell of a new Jewish revival." History, Eichmann points out, supports this theory of social Darwinism. Commenting on Eichmann's reference to social Darwinism, the Harvard paleontologist Stephen Jay Gould remarks: "*Natürliche Auslese* is the standard German translation of Darwin's 'natural selection.' To think that the key phrase of my professional world lies so perversely violated in the very heart of the chief operative paragraph in the most evil document ever written!"[60]

The remainder of part III outlines what must be done to prevent this "germ-cell" from multiplying: "Europe is to be combed through from West to East in the course of the practical implementation of the final solution."[61] Part IV, the last part, describes in precise detail what constitutes a Jew and how to handle *Mischlinge* (those of mixed race). The Nuremberg Laws, Eichmann explains, will "form the basis" for classification. *Mischlinge*—the offspring of one Jew and one Aryan—will be counted as Jews. Quarter-breeds (offspring of a half-breed and an Aryan) will be counted as Germans. But there are exceptions to this simple taxonomy:

(a) First-degree *Mischlinge* married to persons of German blood, from whose marriages there are children (second-degree *Mischlinge*). Such second-degree *Mischlinge* are essentially in the same position as Germans.

(b) First-degree *Mischlinge* for whom up to now exceptions were granted in some (vital) area by the highest authorities of the Party and the State.[62]

Of course, such exceptions carry a price: "The first-degree *Mischling* exempted from evacuation will be sterilized in order to obviate progeny and to settle the *Mischling* problem for good." The quarter-breed second-

degree *Mischlinge* also are at risk of being classified Jewish if they fall
into specific categories:

(a)   Descent of the second-degree *Mischling* from a bastard marriage
      (both spouses being *Mischlinge*).

(b)   Racially especially unfavorable appearance of the second-degree
      Mischling, which will class him with the Jews on external
      grounds alone.

(c)   Especially bad police and political rating of the second-degree
      Mischling, indicating that he feels and behaves as a Jew.[63]

But if "the second degree *Mischling* is married to a person of German
blood," then she or he is spared. These exceptions and provisos go on
for another seven paragraphs, outlining the gray areas: marriages between
full Jews and persons of German blood, marriages between first-degree
Mischlinge and persons of German blood (with and without children),
marriages between first-degree *Mischlinge* and first-degree *Mischlinge* or
Jews, and marriages between first-degree *Mischlinge* and second-degree
Mischlinge. The entire section is taxonomic insanity.

The protocol finishes with who should do what, noting the observations by Gauleiter Dr. Meyer and Secretary of State Dr. Bühler, that such
actions might cause concern among local populations and therefore
"preparatory work for the final solution should be carried out locally in
the area concerned, but that, in doing so, alarm among the population
must be avoided."[64] The conference ended with a call from the chief of
the security police and the SD for the full support of all those involved
in the Final Solution.

THE OBVIOUS AND THE OBSCURE

The language of the Wannsee Protocol, like that of most Nazi documents
in dealing with the "Jewish question," is obfuscated by innocuous-sound-
ing jargon—action, special action, large-scale action, reprisal action,
pacification action, radical action, cleaning-up or cleansing action,
cleared or cleared of Jews, freeing the area of Jews, Jewish problem solved,
handled appropriately, handled according to orders, liquidated, over-
hauling, rendered harmless, ruthless collective measures, severe measures,
special treatment or special measures, executive tasks, elimination, evac-

uation, eradication, relocation, and, of course, Final Solution (*Endlö-sung*). The Holocaust historians Henry Friedlander and Sybil Milton have documented the difference between the Nazis' public and bureaucratic languages. The former served "to guide the followers, convince the sub-jects, and intimidate the opponents," the latter was the "hidden language, the language of the technicians." When it came to the Jews, however, the language was unmistakable. For Hitler, the Jews were "the enzyme of decomposition" (*Ferment der Dekomposition*). Jews were parasites, "international maggots and bedbugs" (*Völkermaden und Völkerwanzen*). "World Jewry"—*Weltjudentum*—became *Alljuda*, "universal Jewry," against which Germany was fighting a defensive war. Language, in part, helped the Nazis justify genocide as a form of defensive fighting in the "Jewish War."[65] So common was the use of such terms that Heinrich Himmler became concerned about security. On April 9, 1943, he penned this top secret letter to Ernst Kaltenbrunner, who had succeeded Rein-hard Heydrich as chief of security police and SD:

> Reichsführer-SS Field HQ
> April 9, 1943
> Top Secret!
>
> To the Chief of the Security Police and SD Berlin:
>
> I have received the Inspector of Statistics' report on the Final Solution of the Jewish Question.
>
> I consider this report well executed for purposes of camouflage and poten-tially useful for later times.
>
> For the moment, it can neither be published nor can anyone be allowed sight of it.
>
> The most important for me remains that whatever remains of Jews is shipped East. All I want to be told as of now by the Security Police, very briefly, is what has been shipped and what, at any points, is still left of Jews.
>
> Hh[66]

The next day SS-Obersturmbannführer Rudolf Brandt passed along to Richard Korherr, Himmler's inspector for statistics, a message that the "special treatment" (*Sonderbehandlung*) language was to be changed:

> The Reichsführer-SS has received your report about the Final Solution of the European Jewish Question. His instruction is that the word Sonderbehand-lung is to be eliminated from the report. Thus page 9, point 4, is to be amended to read as follows:

Transport of Jews from the Eastern Provinces to the Russian East: . . .

Sluiced through the camps in the General Government: . . .

Through the camps in the Warthegau: . . .

No other wording is permitted. I am returning the copy already initialed by the Reichsführer-SS, which you will be good enough to amend as directed and return.[67]

If there could be any doubt about what was going on here, at his trial Eichmann clarified exactly what he meant in the Wannsee Protocol: "What I know is that the gentlemen convened their session, and then in very plain terms—not in the language that I had to use in the minutes, but in absolutely blunt terms—they addressed the issue, with no mincing of words. . . . The discussion covered killing, elimination, and annihilation."[68] Hitler gives us another clue to this harsh reality. Three days after the Wannsee Conference, he met with Himmler to discuss the fate of the Jews. We do not have a record of this meeting, but later that same day Hitler told his underlings:

The Jew must clear out of Europe. Otherwise no understanding will be possible between Europeans. It's the Jew who prevents everything. When I think about it, I realize that I'm extraordinarily humane. I restrict myself to telling them they must go away. If they break their pipes on the journey, I can't do anything about it. But if they refuse to go voluntarily, *I see no other solution but extermination.*[69]

FROM A STATE OF MIND TO CONCRETE REALITY

In 1972 the historian Geoffrey Barraclough pondered the connection between ideas and actions: "it is a long way from a state of mind to the concrete reality of Belsen and Auschwitz, and the road is not quite so direct, or well signposted as people seem to assume."[70] Where did the Nazis get their ideas about racial purity and eugenics? What are some of the signposts that show us how states of mind become concrete reality? According to Walter Laqueur, "the doctrine of Hitler's movement was neither a mere propaganda trick nor the outpouring of a small group of unbalanced minds. On the contrary, Nazism is based on a body of intellectual doctrine that goes back for at least a century."[71] George Mosse, in his meticulous study of Nazi culture, demonstrates that National Socialism and the Nazi rise to power "would have all come to naught if the world view itself had not reflected already existing prejudices among the people. The bourgeois ideas which had become rooted in the German mind during the nineteenth century were combined with an omnipresent nationalism, and both were built into the ideology of race, blood, and soil."[72]

Nazi racial ideologies can indeed be traced back to the end of the nineteenth century, to the linking of social Darwinism and eugenics that burst on the scene in Germany, arriving from England, where the "science" of eugenics was founded by Charles Darwin's cousin Francis Galton. In America, a similar commitment to social Darwinism resulted in mass sterilizations of the "feebleminded" and other "undesirables."[73] The Germans, however, put their own perverse twist on eugenics, creating a type of racial eugenics that led to Auschwitz. Here are just two rather startling examples of the kind of racist ideology found in Germany, wherein we can see the seeds of the Wannsee Protocol.

(a) In his March 6, 1895, Reichstag speech in favor of legislation to close Germany's borders to "Israelites who are not citizens of the Reich," entitled "The Semitic versus the Teutonic Race," Hermann Ahlwardt concluded: "It is certainly true that there are Jews in our country of whom nothing adverse can be said. Nevertheless, the Jews as a whole must be considered harmful, for the racial traits of this people are of a kind that in the long run do not agree with the racial traits of the Teutons. Every Jew who at this very moment has not as yet transgressed is likely to do so at some future time under given circumstances because his racial characteristics drive him on in that direction. We hold the view that the Jews are a different race, a different people with entirely different character traits."[74]

(b) *The Racists' Decalogue,* also called the "Ten German Commandments of Lawful Self-Defense" (or *Antisemiten-Katechismus*), published in 1893, spells out loud and clear how Jews were to be treated:

1. Be proud of being a German and strive earnestly and steadily to practice the inherited virtues of our people, courage, faithfulness, and veracity, and to inspire and develop these virtues in thy children.
2. Thou shalt know that thou, together with all thy fellow Germans, regardless of faith or creed, hast a common implacable foe. His name is Jew.
3. Thou shalt keep thy blood pure. Consider it a crime to soil the noble Aryan breed of thy people by mingling it with the Jewish breed.
4. Thou shalt be helpful to thy fellow German and further him in all matters not counter to the German conscience, the more so if he be pressed by the Jew.
5. Thou shalt have no social intercourse with the Jew.

6. Thou shalt have no business relations with the Jew.
7. Thou shalt drive the Jew from thy own breast and take no example from Jewish tricks and Jewish wiles. . . .
8. Thou shalt not entrust thy rights to a Jewish lawyer, nor thy body to a Jewish physician, nor thy children to a Jewish teacher lest thy honor, body, and soul suffer harm.
9. Thou shalt not lend ear nor give credence to the Jew. Keep away all Jewish writings from thy German home and hearth lest their lingering poison may unnerve and corrupt thyself and thy family.
10. Thou shalt use no violence against the Jews because it is unworthy of thee and against the law. But if a Jew attack thee, ward off his Semitic insolence with German wrath.[75]

Nineteenth-century eugenics offered scientific justification for sterilization programs based on racist ideology. Germany was not the only place where eugenics became linked with racist ideology. America had set a precedent. Craniometric measurements of head size—thought to measure intelligence—were used by such scientists as the American physician Samuel George Morton as empirical data in support of the ideology of racial ranking, with blacks on the bottom, Indians in the middle, and northern European whites on top. Morton and others, such as H. H. Goddard, believed the "feebleminded"—those at the bottom of the intellectual heap—to be draining the gene pool and pulling the country down.[76] The combination of difficult economic times, new immigrants who would work for less, obvious "others" such as blacks and Jews, and science in the service of ideology, led to a call for sterilization, and from 1907 to 1928, almost 9,000 Americans were sterilized.[77] The most famous case of sterilization justified in the name of eugenics was that of Carrie Buck, who lived, along with her mother, in Virginia's Colony for Epileptics and Feebleminded. Carrie and her mother were both classified as feebleminded. When Carrie gave birth to an illegitimate daughter, also believed to be feebleminded, it was determined that Carrie should be sterilized, since three successive generations of feeblemindedness (in the science of the day) constituted evidence of hereditary cause. The decision was challenged and went to the Virginia Supreme Court where it was upheld in 1925. Challenged again, the case was argued before the United States Supreme Court, where the justices voted in favor of sterilization. Supreme Court Justice Oliver Wendell Holmes passed judgment on Carrie Buck with these chilling words, which were later used by the Nazis to justify the T4 program:

> We have seen more than once that the public welfare may call upon the best citizens for their lives. It would be strange if it could not call upon those

who already sap the strength of the State for these lesser sacrifices, often not felt to be such by those concerned, in order to prevent our being swamped with incompetence. It is better for all the world, if instead of waiting to execute degenerate offspring for crime, or to let them starve for their imbecility, society can prevent those who are manifestly unfit from continuing their kind. The principle that sustains compulsory vaccination is broad enough to cover cutting the Fallopian tubes. Three generations of imbeciles are enough.[78]

Carrie Buck was sterilized, along with a thousand others at the Virginia institution, pushing the total in America to about 20,000 sterilizations by the mid-1930s.

In Germany, the Reichstag passed the Eugenic Sterilization Law soon after Hitler came to power in 1933. Surpassing the American law, the German one made sterilization compulsory for everyone who fit the criteria, not just the institutionalized. The Reich Ministry of the Interior office proclaimed: "We want to prevent . . . poisoning the entire bloodstream of the race. We go beyond neighborly love; we extend it to future generations. Therein lies the high ethical value and justification of the law."[79] Starting January 1, 1934, physicians were required to report anyone who was "unfit" to the Hereditary Health Courts. The courts made the decisions on sterilization, which were carried out by the Nazi doctors. As the program grew so did the bureaucracy to administer it, giving rise to the T4 program. The Nazi program also topped the American one in numbers by an order of magnitude—within three years, it sterilized about 225,000 people. By 1939 sterilization gave way to euthanasia, with another 70,000 murdered.[80]

The racial theories of social Darwinism gave the Nazis and others the scientific sanction they needed to make their racist ideology seem wholly rational and their actions justifiable in defense against what they considered to be a real threat to their nation and their culture. Consider these passages from *Mein Kampf*'s chapter on nation and race:

The whole of nature is a powerful struggle between the strong and the weak, an eternal victory of the strong over the weak. . . .

A stronger race will drive out the weak, for the vital urge in its ultimate form will, time and again, burst all the absurd fetters of the so-called humanity of individuals, in order to replace it by the humanity of Nature which destroys the weak to give his place to the strong. . . .

[I]n every mingling of Aryan blood with that of lower peoples the result was the end of the cultured people. North America, whose population consists in by far the largest part of Germanic elements who mixed but little with the lower colored peoples, shows a different humanity and culture from Cen-

tral and South America, where the predominantly Latin immigrants often
mixed with the aborigines on a large scale. . . .

The Aryan gave up the purity of his blood and therefore he also lost his
place in the Paradise which he had created for himself. He became submerged
in the race-mixture, he gradually lost his cultural ability till . . . he began to
resemble more the subjected and aborigines than his ancestors . . . Blood-
mixing, with the lowering of the racial level caused by it, is the sole cause of
the dying-off of old cultures; for the people do not perish by lost wars, but
by the loss of that force of resistance which is contained only in the pure blood.
All that is not race in this world is trash.[81]

This racist ideology did not spring from a conquered nation defending itself against a foreign invader. Germans were sterilizing and killing
fellow Germans. By classifying Jews as *untermenschen* (subhumans)—as
"colored" and therefore not pure white, or Aryan—and linking eugenics
to an already virulent antisemitism, the Nazis arrived at the Final Solution. The road to Auschwitz may have been long and indirect, but over
the course of a half century it joined racist theories to advanced technology and the aims of the Nazi state. It led to the deaths of six million Jews.

part iv
Truth and History

Such is the irresistible nature of truth that all it asks,
and all it wants, is the liberty of appearing. The sun
needs no inscription to distinguish him from darkness.

Thomas Paine,
The Rights of Man,
pt. 2, 1791

9 The Rape of History

Denial, Revision, and the Search for a True and Meaningful Past

[T]here can be no history of "the past as it actually did happen"; there can only be historical interpretations, and none of them final; and every generation has a right to frame its own. . . . But this does not mean, of course, that all interpretations are of equal merit. First, there are always interpretations which are not really in keeping with the accepted records; secondly, there are some which need a number of more or less plausible auxiliary hypotheses if they are to escape falsification by the records; next, there are some that are unable to connect a number of facts which another interpretation can connect, and in so far "explain." There may accordingly be a considerable amount of progress even within the field of historical interpretation.

Karl Popper, *The Open Society and Its Enemies*, 1950

On December 13, 1937, the Japanese army overran the Chinese city of Nanking, delivering a crushing defeat to Chiang Kai-shek's forces and capturing the prized capital of Nationalist China. It was the culmination of a war of aggression that began in 1931 and did not end until the defeat of Japan in 1945. The military occupation of the city was quickly followed by brutalities that can, in legal terms, best be described as crimes against humanity—brutalities that have come to be known as the "Rape of Nanking." Over the course of seven weeks somewhere between 260,000 and 350,000 Chinese noncombatants were tortured, raped, and ultimately murdered at the hands of Japanese soldiers.[1] Five years before the gas chambers and ovens of Auschwitz were fired up, tens of thousands of Chinese men served as targets for bayonet practice and decapitation contests; somewhere between 20,000 and 80,000 Chinese women were raped, and many of these were hung, shot, disemboweled, or had their breasts cut off; fathers were forced to rape their daughters in front of their families; men were often castrated; people were burned or buried alive; and German shepherds were encouraged to rip apart people buried in sand to their waists. One Nazi in the city described the massacre as "bestial machinery."[2]

Nanking was only one of many atrocities committed by the Japanese between 1931 and 1945, in what Iris Chang has called "the forgotten holocaust of World War II," the subtitle of her disturbing book *The Rape of Nanking*. Chang carefully documents the Japanese "Three-all" policy— "loot all, kill all, burn all"—implemented against the Chinese people in Nanking and other locations. "I have received orders from my superior officer that every person in this place must be killed," wrote one Japanese colonel in his diary.[3] As in the Nazi mass murder of the Jews, totals of the numbers killed vary, ranging from 1,578,000 to 6,325,000, with a mid-range moderate estimate of 3,949,000 people exterminated as a direct result of Japanese crimes against humanity (i.e., noncombatants). When total Chinese deaths are calibrated to include Japanese military actions through looting, starvation, bombing, medical experimentation, and battle deaths, historians estimate that the figure may be as high as 19 million.[4] As is evident from Chang's copious documentation of primary sources and shockingly graphic photographs of decapitations and disembowelments (including heads lying on the ground, a woman strapped to a chair for multiple rapes, and another woman with a bayonet driven deeply into her vagina), the Nazis did not hold a monopoly on human cruelty. There seems nothing the Nazis did to Jews that would have shocked their Japanese counterparts.

The question we would like to address here is not how these atrocities came about or what drove its perpetrators to such repugnant extremes of evil, but why so few people know about it. "Sixty years later the Japanese as a nation are still trying to bury the victims of Nanking," writes Chang, "not under the soil, as in 1937, but into historical oblivion."[5] Nanking has become part of Japanese denial of atrocities. Officially the Japanese government has refused to acknowledge most of the crimes against humanity it committed in Nanking and other places, let alone apologize for them (the exception being the sex slaves). Extremists in Japan accuse the Chinese government and other anti-Japanese forces around the world of exaggerating Chinese losses and fabricating stories of Japanese atrocities that never took place. According to Chang, even within mainstream Japanese circles, including the media, the academy, and especially the government administration, there are no signs of contrition. Whereas Germany has paid out approximately $60 billion in reparations to its wartime enemies and Israel, Japan has paid virtually nothing (with the exception of reparations paid to the sex slave victims and their families).

It is significant that the Rape of Nanking was front-page news around the world, not just in the fringe and alternative press but in such august publications as the *New York Times*. This "second rape" of denial, as Chang calls it, began at the top and worked its way down. The denial of atrocities on the part of the Japanese government has resulted in historical interpretations of the Rape of Nanking ranging from declarations that it involved only the isolated acts of a few out-of-control soldiers to flat-out denial that it even happened. Such denial, as we have seen, usually begins with revision, and in Japan this has taken the form of reinterpreting the underlying causes of the Second World War. From this perspective, which can still be found in many Japanese history textbooks, Japan fought to free Asia from the West's imperialist machinations and exploitative capitalistic ways, as well as to ensure its own survival against anti-Japanese sentiments in the geopolitical arena. Ultranationalists in the country not only endorse this view, they "have threatened everything from lawsuits to death, even assassination," says Chang, "to silence opponents who suggest that these textbooks are not telling the next generation the real story."[6] One leading member of Japan's conservative Liberal Democratic Party, Ishihara Shintaro, for example, told *Playboy* magazine in a 1990 interview: "People say that the Japanese made a holocaust there [in Nanking], but that is not true. It is a story made up by the Chinese. It has tarnished the image of Japan, but it is a lie."[7]

The comparison to Holocaust denial is obvious, as Yoshi Tsurumi noted in a *New York Times* article in response to Ishihara's *Playboy* comments: "Japan's denial of the rape of Nanjing would be politically the same as German denial of the Holocaust." Ishihara fired back with the argument that the International Military Tribunal of the Far East exaggerated the events at Nanking in order to obtain convictions of the charged war criminals and that the *New York Times* correspondent Frank Tillman Durdin, who reported on China in 1937, never witnessed any atrocities. Durdin, now aging and retired in San Diego, held a press conference to rebut Ishihara and explained that his reporting predated the massacre. As the rhetoric got hotter, Ishihara ratcheted up his revisionism to argue that the Chinese concocted the story about Nanking in order to galvanize the American government into the atomic bombing of Hiroshima and Nagasaki. He concluded by stating that although the German government had acknowledged and apologized for its crimes against the Jews, Japan would never take such actions.[8]

In a clear example of official denial (one that echoes the Holocaust deniers in their techniques and arguments), the Japanese minister of education, Fujio Masayuki, told *Bungei Shunju* magazine in 1986 that the Rape of Nanking was "just a part of war," that the numbers killed had been highly exaggerated, and that the Tokyo War Crimes Trial was nothing more than "racial revenge" intended to "rob Japan of her power." In 1988 Okuno Seisuki, then the third most senior member of the cabinet and a former minister of justice and minister of education, told reporters during his visit to a war shrine in Tokyo: "There was no intention of aggression. The white race made Asia into a colony, but only Japan has been blamed. Who was the aggressor country? It was the white race. I don't see why Japanese are called militarists and aggressors." Similar remarks were made in 1994 by General Nagano Shigeto, upon his appointment to the cabinet-level position of minister of justice. Claiming that "I was in Nanking immediately afterwards," he told the newspaper *Mainichi Shimbun,* "I think the Nanking Massacre and the rest was a fabrication." Nagano also asserted that the Korean sex slaves were actually "licensed prostitutes" and that Japan entered the war because it was "in danger of being crushed."[9]

The denials made by prominent Japanese politicians were also reflected in the textbooks read by Japanese children. All textbooks must be approved by the Japanese Ministry of Education, with social science and history books among the most scrutinized. Throughout the 1960s and 1970s little to no mention was made that Japan had even been at war with China, with most children just learning that the Americans had firebombed Tokyo and other Japanese cities and were the first to use atomic weapons, accompanied by photographs of obliterated Japanese cities. When textbook authors began introducing the Nanking story, the Ministry of Education insisted on revisions to indicate that there were only a few atrocities and these were committed in the heat of battle and in retaliation against Chinese aggression. Invoking the equivalency argument so favored by Holocaust deniers, Japanese textbooks in the 1970s and 1980s explained that in all wars atrocities are committed by both sides. Responding specifically to a description of the Rape of Nanking in a textbook, one examiner for the Ministry of Education demanded that it be rewritten because "the violation of women is something that has happened on every battlefield in every era of human history. This is not an issue that needs to be taken up with respect to the Japanese Army in particular."[10]

The textbook debate, however, heated up, and in the early 1980s Chinese and Korean officials filed formal protests. Eventually the Japanese government was forced to capitulate a bit to those who had recognized a classic case of pseudohistory, where denial of the past is used for present political or ideological reasons. Yet the debate was not over. "How long must we apologize for the mistakes we have made?" the military historian Noboru Kojima complained in 1991. One answer comes from a Tokyo University professor, Fujioka Nobukatsu, who argues that the number of victims at Nanking has been greatly exaggerated and that those who were killed were Chinese guerrilla soldiers, not noncombatants and women.[11]

The debate on Nanking has not been confined to academia or the political arena. When Bernardo Bertolucci's film *The Last Emperor* was released in Japan, it was discovered that the film distributors there had removed a thirty-second scene portraying the Rape of Nanking. Bertolucci was outraged: "Not only did the Japanese distributor cut the whole sequence of the 'Rape of Nanking' without my authorization and against my will, without even informing me, but they also declared to the press that myself and the producer, Jeremy Thomas, had made the original proposition to mutilate the movie. This is absolutely false and revolting." Fumbling for an adequate response, the distributors apologized for the "confusion and misunderstanding," back-peddling behind a defense of ignorance of the larger social issues at hand. One film critic speculated on their motives: "I believe the film's distributors and many theatre owners were afraid these right-wing groups might cause trouble outside the theaters. Some of these people still believe that Japan's actions in China and during the war were part of some sacred crusade."[12]

The similarities to the actions and motives of the Holocaust deniers and their right-wing supporters are, in our opinion, eerie. In the 1980s, during the *Historikerestreit* ("historians' battle") over whether Hitler's actions merely represented a preemptive self-defense against Stalin's intended destruction of Germany and the Jewish "declaration of war" against the Reich, Japanese historians experienced their own *Historikerestreit*. It began in 1984 with the publication of Tanaka Masaaki's *The Fabrication of the "Nanking Massacre,"* in which he argued that "you won't find one instance of planned, systematic murder in the entire history of Japan." Further, he contended, such atrocities could not have been committed because the Japanese have "a different sense of values" from Westerners. A battleline was drawn between the "massacre faction" and the "illusion faction"—the very terms call to mind the Holocaust deniers labeling of Holocaust historians as "exterminationists" and themselves as "revisionists." The more liberal "massacre faction" demanded a public apology on the part of the Japanese government, while the more conservative "illusion faction" claimed that any such apology would be an insult to veterans of the war. And like the Holocaust deniers, who are often their own worst enemy in uncovering evidence of Nazi atrocities against Jews (then are forced to rationalize it by the equivalency argument), Nanking deniers asked for eyewitnesses to present their evidence that the "Rape" was an illusion but were dismayed to find story after story that confirmed the massacre.[13]

How do we know that the Rape of Nanking happened? The same way we know that the Holocaust or any other historical event happened: through a convergence of independent lines of evidence, all pointing to the same conclusion. There is simply no other way to explain all the evidence. This kind of convergence, as we have noted throughout this book, underlies all historical sciences. Indeed, Chang's book is an exemplar of first-rate historical detective work, documenting the crimes committed in Nanking with numerous independent sources, including eyewitness accounts from survivors, perpetrators, and bystanders, correlated with photographs, newsreels, press reports, orders, memos, diary entries, intelligence reports, physical remains, and even documents and press statements from the Japanese government, which initially not only did not deny the crimes, but boasted of them in order to boost slagging public support for the war effort. Only after international condemnation did the Japanese military seal off the city to journalists and the Japanese government start down the path of revising history in a way that would eventually lead to flat-out denial. Piecing together what happened began in March 1944, when the United Nations created the Investigation of War Crimes Committee to collect data on the event, and culminated on May 3, 1946, when the International Military Tribunal for the Far East opened what became known as the Tokyo War Crimes Trial. Two and a half years later (at the end of the longest war crimes trial in history—three times as long as the Nuremberg trials) a 49,000-page multivolume report was issued, presenting no less than 779 affidavits and depositions and 4,336 exhibits documenting the crimes against humanity committed by the Japanese.[14]

What should we make of the parallels between Nanking denial and

Holocaust denial? Are these patterns of denial a repeating social phenomenon? Obviously, we cannot conduct a social experiment with a control group and experimental group, vary the conditions leading to acceptance or denial, and observe the results. Instead, we must use the methods of historical scientists in analyzing natural experiments that have already been run. This is what we have just done in analyzing the Rape of Nanking and the subsequent path to denial. Nanking denial is part and parcel with Holocaust denial in methodologies, arguments, and motivations, and reflects the larger pseudohistorical trends seen in other claims. Since Nanking denial evolved independently from Holocaust denial, it seems safe to assume that Japanese deniers have not been reading the literature of the Holocaust deniers and purposefully mirroring their methodologies and arguments. Rather, we contend that such historical denial is a form of ideologically driven pseudohistory, which adopts techniques designed to undermine historical claims that do not fit with present ideologies and beliefs. We have devoted much of this book to examining what those techniques and ideologies are in relation to Holocaust denial, and we have just reviewed how they operate in a parallel theater of pseudohistory, Nanking denial. Can we extrapolate the lessons we have learned from the Holocaust deniers and the Nanking deniers and apply these to other claims, testing for instances of pseudohistory? And, most important, since historians are in the business of improving (and thus often revising) our understanding of the past and offering new interpretations of history, how can we tell the difference between real revision and dogmatic denial?

REAL REVISION VERSUS DOGMATIC DENIAL

In February 1993 the Wellesley College historian and classicist Mary Lefkowitz attended a lecture at her institution by Dr. Yosef A. A. ben-Jochannan, known for his strong Afrocentrist focus. Among many controversial claims made in the lecture (including that true Jews are African), one of the more surprising was that Aristotle stole his ideas, which became the foundation of Western philosophy, from the library of Alexandria, where Africans had deposited their philosophical works. During the question-and-answer period Lefkowitz asked ben-Jochannan how this could have happened since the library was built after Aristotle's death. "Dr. ben-Jochannan was unable to answer the question," she explained, "and said that he resented the tone of the inquiry. Several students came up to me after the lecture and accused me of racism, suggesting that I had been brainwashed by white historians." If this reaction was not disturbing enough, Lefkowitz discovered a "strange silence on the part of many of my faculty colleagues. Several of them were well aware that what Dr. ben-Jochannan was saying was factually wrong. One of them said later that she found the lecture so 'hopeless' that she decided to say nothing." Moreover, Lefkowitz writes, "When I stated at a faculty meeting that Aristotle could not have stolen his philosophy from the library of Alexandria in Egypt, because that library had not been built until after his death, another colleague responded, 'I don't care who stole what from whom.' When I went to the then dean of the college to explain that there was no factual evidence behind some Afrocentric claims about ancient history, she replied that each of us had a different but equally valid view of history."[15]

Are all views of history equally valid? Or, as the philosopher of science Karl Popper suggests above, are historical interpretations subject to a set of falsification criteria similar to those found in other historical sciences? Herein lies the "boundary problem" between history, revision, and denial. Just where are those boundaries and how fuzzy can they be without our giving up hope of progress in historical interpretation? Can we make a distinction between history and pseudohistory, between legitimate revision and problematic denial? If so, what standards of evidence and interpretation shall we select? How can outsiders to a field discriminate between revolutionary revision and ideological denial?

We do not believe all views of history are equally valid. When a claim—such as the one made for Aristotle's theft from the library of Alexandria—is refuted by just a cursory look at the historical record, it suggests some form of ideological denial is at work. Holocaust "revisionism" falls into this category of pseudohistory, whose purpose is *the denial of the past for present political or ideological reasons*. By contrast, real revision—*the modification of history based on new facts or new interpretations of old facts*—is not only a legitimate activity of historians' profession, it is a necessary tool in our continued search for a true and meaningful past. The prevailing viewpoint on any historical topic, including the origins of Western philosophy, can be questioned and plausibly revised when the participating scholars play by the rules of science, logic, and reason. That is, as long as scholars put their claims forward as testable hypotheses, then those hypotheses can be weighed against the evidence and accepted or rejected in relation to other interpretations.

Cornell University professor Martin Bernal, for example, has presented a revisionist history of the "Afroasiatic influence on classical Western civilization" in his controversial but well-argued book *Black Athena*.[16] Bernal's revisionist history contrasts the "Aryan Model" of Greek history, which views Greece as essentially Indo-European, with the "Ancient Model," which sees it as Afroasiatic, or Levantine and Egyptian. Bernal suggests replacing the Aryan Model, not with the Ancient Model, but with what he calls the Revised Ancient Model. This model, he says, is built on components of both the Ancient and the Aryan Models while at the same time replacing them. This is a good example of a legitimate attempt at revision, of testable historiography, of falsifiable historical hypothesizing. Bernal is not denying anyone's history. Whether his revision is right or not is beside the point. Lefkowitz, for one, believes Bernal is wrong (and makes her case in *Black Athena Revisited*), but she has clarified the difference between this type of revision and the denial practiced by extremists: "We recognize that no historian can write without some amount of bias; that is why history must always be rewritten. But not all bias amounts to distortion or is equivalent to indoctrination. If I am aware that I am likely to be biased for any number of reasons, and try to compensate for my bias, the result should be very different in quality and character from what I would say if I were consciously setting about to achieve a particular political goal."[17] Bernal presented his revision of history, and it was debated in peer-reviewed publications, with the participants, for the most part, abiding by the rules of evidence. Molly Levine, for example, offered a measured and reasoned analysis in the *American Historical Review*, the publication of the American Historical Society.[18]

Differentiating revision from denial and pseudohistory is an ongoing task. A sizable industry of literature deals with claims that the past was not what we think it was. In his book *Frauds, Myths, and Mysteries* the archaeologist Ken Feder tackles just the pseudohistory in archaeology and provides readers with a laundry list of the weird and the strange, including the Cardiff giant, the Piltdown hoax, the lost continent of Atlantis, prehistoric extraterrestrials and ancient astronauts, lost civilizations on Mars, psychic archaeology (using ESP to find buried ruins), pyramid builders, the Shroud of Turin, creationism and Noah's Ark, King Tut's curse, and numerous theories about various peoples who allegedly discovered America before Columbus, including Egyptians, Phoenicians, Africans, Trojans, Carthaginians, Romans, Arabs, Irish, Welsh, Germans, Poles, the lost tribes of Israel, and various groups of Jews (such as the wandering Hebrews, one or more of the Ten Lost Tribes). Feder's point is to ask *why* people distort and deny history. He answers the "why" question six ways, moving from proximate to ultimate causes:

1. Money—from the sale of artifacts, books, lecture tours, T-shirts, mugs, and the like.

2. Fame—by overturning a cherished belief about the past, one may gain considerable attention (and with it money).

3. Nationalism—to show that "we" were first, not "you." The Piltdown hoax was driven by the desire of the British to find an ancient human in Britain. Nazi archaeologists looked for evidence of ancient German settlements in desired territories (and argued that the Poles and Russians were occupying the Eastern territories illegally or unnaturally).

4. Religion—to anchor the belief system in a meaningful and significant history of the faith. As Martin Luther noted: "What harm would it do if a man told a good strong lie for the sake of the good and for the Christian Church . . . a useful lie, a helpful lie, such lies would not be against God; he would accept them."

5. Romantic Past—the belief that the grass is always greener in the other century. Romanticized pasts proliferate in literature. Before the evil Industrial Revolution, some social historians and naive environmentalists would have us believe, life was wonderful, people were happy, and the environment was safe and healthy. Try telling that to the European population during the fourteenth-century Black Death or to the starving folks of centuries prior.

6. Mental Instability—the fact that some people who devise unbalanced ideas are a little unbalanced.[19]

Archaeology seems especially ripe for ideologically driven denial. Consider *Forbidden Archeology* by Michael Cremo (coauthored with Richard Thompson), a research associate of the Bhaktivedanta Institute. The book is published by the Bhaktivedanta Institute in San Diego (a branch of the International Society for Krishna Consciousness) and is dedicated to "His Divine Grace A. C. Bhaktivedanta Swami Prabhupada." Cremo sets out to tell "the hidden history of the human race" and in the process claims that the historical sciences of paleontology, paleoanthropology, and archaeology have conspired—sometimes deliberately, sometimes by default—to cover up evidence that indicates humans have existed in a civilized state, not for tens or hundreds of thousands of years, but for tens or hundreds of *millions* of years.[20] Rather than have dinosaurs living alongside humans ten thousand years ago as "young-earth" Christian creationists do, these "Krishna creationists" (as some call them) have humans living alongside dinosaurs hundreds of millions of years ago. These are very "old-earth" creationists indeed!

Now, why is this denial instead of revision? The archaeologist Brad Lepper illuminates not only why, in his opinion, the authors are wrong but, more important, how he believes they distort and deny the past in order to make it fit their present religious beliefs: "Cremo and Thompson are selectively credulous to an astonishing degree. They accept without question the testimony of nineteenth-century gold miners and quarrymen, but treat with extreme skepticism (or outright derision) the observations of twentieth-century archaeologists. The authors are critical of archaeologists for rejecting the very early radiometric dates for technologically recent stone artifacts at Hueyatlaco, Mexico, but they are as quick to reject radiometric dates which do not agree with their preconceived interpretations." The difference here between denial and revision is not in the extremity of the claim (since radical ideas proliferate in the history of science), but in the purposeful distortion of the past for personal reasons, as Lepper concludes: "Accepting that there is a place in science for seemingly outrageous hypotheses . . . there is no justification for the sort of sloppy rehashing of canards, hoaxes, red herrings, half-truths and fantasies Cremo and Thompson offer in the service of a religious ideology."[21] Undaunted by such criticism, and the many refutations of their theory, in 1998 Cremo published a 569-page volume on *Forbidden Archeology's Impact*, cataloging every review and piece of correspondence related to the book in order to show "how a controversial new book shocked the scientific community and became an underground classic."[22] To us, such braggadocio seems typical of those on the margins of society struggling to get the attention of the mainstream in order to have a part in a conversation from which, by their very methods, they exclude themselves.

At times, as we have indicated, legitimate revision can slip into denial. This happens when a serious and long-term commitment is made to a position for which the evidence is tenuous at best. Science, Karl Popper has demonstrated, depends on the establishment of falsifiable hypotheses that are either definitely rejected or provisionally supported (but never absolutely proved). However, as the philosopher of science Thomas Kuhn has noted, the acceptance or rejection of these testable hypotheses often depends on the psychology of belief established by commitment to a working paradigm and the social dynamics of the community of scholars and scientists working in a particular field.[23] From this perspective, revision may slough into denial when someone refuses to accept the collective rejection of a hypothesis by his or her peers or shifts to a different field and refuses to play by the rules established by a different set of peers.

In *America B.C.*, for example, the retired Harvard marine biologist Barry Fell jumped fields into human history and archaeology.[24] He began with the reasonable hypothesis that various peoples (besides Native Americans) might have visited and lived in the Americas before Columbus (the "B.C." of his title). But instead of testing this hypothesis for each group and then rejecting it if the facts are better explained through other hypotheses (or so ambiguous as to be better left uninterpreted—the "residue" of anomalies not explained by the existing paradigm), it seems that Fell ignored contradictory evidence and stretched interpretative parameters beyond reason.[25] It is not that Druids *could not* have lived in Vermont or Phoenicians in Iowa; it is just that the evidence leads almost all archaeologists to conclude that they *did not*. The historian Ronald Fritze's book *Legend and Lore of the Americas Before 1492* enumerates the countless fallacies of reasoning and bogus "artifacts" used to support such claims.[26] What began as a reasonable (and testable) hypothesis slid from revision into denial when Fell refused to accept the collective rejection of the professionals in the field who examined his hypotheses and interpretations. Instead of playing by the rules of science, Fell seemed focused on elevating a handful of anomalies to full-blown theories, without an appropriate level of evidentiary support.

Why do people distort and deny the past? Fritze answers the question with an appeal to the basics of the human condition: "One reason is that it is a common characteristic of human nature to have a fascination with the strange and fantastic. They also claim to be based on lost or even suppressed knowledge which provides yet a further source of fascination. There are hints and even outright claims of some sort of conspiracy to suppress such knowledge. Sadly, there is also an element of racism. The nineteenth-century supporters of the theory of a lost white race of mound-builders were basically denying that the Native Americans possessed the ability to create a higher civilization."[27] An unwillingness (or inability) to utilize the methods of historical science, especially if tethered to a racist ideology, should sound the same alarm bells that ring for Holocaust denial. It is a dangerous road to go down.

A different road, one exemplifying real revision, can be found in *Lies My Teacher Told Me,* in which the historian James Loewen removes the whitewashing of American history by high school textbooks throughout the 1950s and 1960s. Students were not usually told, for example, that Columbus murdered Native Americans, Thomas Jefferson owned slaves, Woodrow Wilson was antiblack and xenophobic (for example, calling for legislation against German Americans during the Great War), and countless other details that historians now consider to be factual. Why? Nationalism, racism, sexism, xenophobia, ethnocentrism, and classism are all causes that motivate individuals to deny or attempt to alter the history of the United States, a history not particularly worse but certainly not morally better than that of most nations. Loewen also identifies what he considers to be one of the most fundamental reasons for the problems with history textbooks—profit. School boards are often reluctant to adopt controversial textbooks, with the result that we have boring history books, boring history classrooms, and bored students: "Students will start learning history when they see the point of doing so, when it seems interesting and important to them, and when they believe history might relate to their lives and futures. Students will start finding history interesting when their teachers and textbooks stop lying to them."[28] To some—particularly those on the far political right who fear that political correctness has distorted our students' understanding of history by overemphasizing the very things Loewen says are missing—such revision looks like denial.

Women's studies, Latino culture classes, African American history texts, Native American perspectives, cultural studies departments, and multicultural diversity have proliferated on campuses across America, all emphasizing radically different interpretations of history. Some of these interpretations are revisionist, others denial. Some begin by revising but end by denying. How can we know which is which? Native American revisionists, for example, began with the modest approach that the written histories of the Americas had been, for the past several centuries, dominated by a distinct Eurocentrism—"how the West was won" and all that. Revising this form of Whiggish history was long in coming and, after initial resistance, eventually found a permanent place in the academy. Vine Deloria Jr.'s classic 1969 book, *Custer Died for Your Sins: An Indian Manifesto,* for example, provided a needed adjustment of the restricted focus and one-sided bias of the anthropology of Native Americans as it had been practiced up to that time. But a few decades later Deloria changed from scholar to activist, and we believe his 1995 book,

Red Earth, White Lies: Native Americans and the Myth of Scientific Fact,
slides from revision into denial.

Rejecting all the evidence from genetics, physical anthropology, cultural anthropology, linguistics, and history that converges to link Native
Americans to Asian ancestors, and instead basing his theory on Native
American myth and lore, Deloria suggests that American Indians had always been in the Americas, since the time of their creation. His shift away
from scientific evidence dismayed many anthropologists, and caused
some, like Ken Feder, to scrape "the remnants of our 'Custer Died for
Your Sins' bumper stickers off of our aging automobiles."[29] They did so
not because Deloria's revisionism had gone too far but because it equated
myth with science. As indicated in the subtitle of his book, *The Myth of
Scientific Fact,* for Deloria science is no different from other mytholo-
gies, including Native American myths, all of which are equally valid:
"Tribal elders did not worry if their version of creation was entirely different from the scenario held by a neighboring tribe. People believed that
each tribe had its own special relationship to the superior spiritual forces
which governed the universe. . . . Tribal knowledge was not fragmented
and was valid within the historical and geographical scope of the people's
experience."[30] However noble this philosophy of history may sound, we
believe it is vacuous and impotent because if all versions of the past are
"valid," then none are. If there is no method of discriminating between
true and false interpretations of the past, between history and pseudohistory, between revisionism and denial, then there is no point in even
having a discipline of history. With this pseudohistory, historiography
becomes hagiography, science becomes ideology, history becomes myth,
and revision becomes denial.

Like their Native American counterparts, feminist revisionists have
made many important strides in correcting the heavily male-gendered historiography of the past century. In *Telling the Truth about History* the
historians Joyce Appleby, Lynn Hunt, and Margaret Jacob show that in
the generation following the Second World War "women, minorities, and
workers [have come to] populate American and Western histories where
formerly heroes, geniuses, statesmen—icons of order and the status quo—
reigned unchallenged. As members of that generation, we routinely, even
angrily, ask: Whose history? Whose science? Whose interests are served
by those ideas and those stories?"[31] A reasoned and measured example
of a feminist revision of history can be found in *The Death of Nature:
Women, Ecology and the Scientific Revolution,* by the environmental historian and philosopher Carolyn Merchant. She shows how a gendered

perspective allows us to reinterpret the scientific revolution: "Between the sixteenth and seventeenth centuries the image of an organic cosmos with a living female earth at its center gave way to a mechanistic world view in which nature was reconstructed as dead and passive, to be dominated and controlled by humans. . . . In seeking to understand how people conceptualized nature in the Scientific Revolution, I am asking not about unchanging essences, but about connections between social change and changing constructions of nature. Similarly, when women today attempt to change society's domination of nature, they are acting to overturn modern constructions of nature and women as culturally passive and subordinate."[32] Here, we are not passing judgment on the validity of Merchant's thesis. Our point is that she plays by the rules of scholarship.

Such revisionist perspectives on history are refreshing, but the danger of denial looms when, in order to complete some puzzle, an author wedges in fleeting fragments of the past in a way unwarranted by the evidence. Riane Eisler, for example, takes a "journey into a lost world" in search of the beginnings of civilization in *The Chalice and the Blade*. Evidence from Neolithic art and artifacts (primarily from recent archaeological finds unavailable to previous historians, and secondarily from a reinterpretation of known art and artifacts) leads Eisler to this radical conclusion: "In sharp contrast to later art, a theme notable for its absence from Neolithic art is imagery idealizing armed might, cruelty, and violence-based power." In Eisler's reading of the historical record, civilization began peaceably, and for thousands of years most people lived in relative equanimity with a notable lack of hierarchical domination: "There are here no images of 'noble warriors' or scenes of battles. Nor are there any signs of 'heroic conquerors' dragging captives around in chains or other evidence of slavery." Relying heavily on a handful of sources, Eisler concludes that there were few gods but plenty of goddesses, whose symbols represented life, water, the sun, plants, animals, rivers, reproduction, agriculture, and the maintenance of good health. "In Neolithic art," she indicates, "neither the Goddess nor her son-consort carry the emblems we have learned to associate with might—spears, swords, or thunderbolts, the symbols of an earthly sovereign and/or deity who exacts obedience by killing and maiming." More important, she says, "the art of this period is strikingly devoid of the ruler-ruled, master-subject imagery so characteristic of dominator societies." Not surprisingly, Eisler finds this dearth of dominator relationships among people to include that of man over woman. In this egalitarian society—symbolized by the chalice—women had an equal partnership with men. When goddesses were in vogue, men and women shared a worldview "in which the primary purpose of art, and of life, was not to conquer, pillage, and loot but to cultivate the earth and provide the material and spiritual wherewithal for a satisfying life." Eisler infers that a lack of dominator symbols—such as the blade—means a lack of real-world parallels: "If there was here no glorification of wrathful male deities or rulers carrying thunderbolts or arms, or of great conquerors dragging abject slaves about in chains, it is not unreasonable to infer it was because there were no counterparts for those images in real life." For the first several thousand years of civilization, Eisler concludes, society was neither patriarchal nor matriarchal, but "remarkably equalitarian." By 7,000 years ago, however, "we begin to find evidence . . . of disruption of the old Neolithic cultures in the Near East." Archaeological evidence, she claims, indicates "invasion, natural catastrophes, and sometimes both, causing large-scale destruction and dislocation." Goddesses were replaced by gods, the chalice by the blade. Males dominated females. Patriarchy became the norm, egalitarianism and matriarchy the exception.[33]

Amazingly, Eisler extrapolates this radical revision of the distant past primarily from a single archaeological dig at Catal Huyuk in Turkey, which, while a remarkable find, is by no means representative of other cultures. Or other times. Although Eisler claims that Catal Huyuk exemplifies a partnership society at the dawn of civilization, in reality, the culture developed approximately 8,300 years ago.[34] The Paleolithic foundations of civilization were laid between 30,000 and 10,000 years ago, and from the scattered and fragmentary evidence from most sites it is difficult to say whether they were partnership or dominator cultures.[35] Here, it seems to us, we begin to unveil a feminist agenda that drives Eisler's research, rather than the reverse. There is only one ideology, she says, to challenge "the principle of human ranking based on violence" and that "is, of course, feminism. For this reason it occupies a unique position both in modern history and in the history of our cultural evolution." As social ills fall away with the collapse of the dominator society, "our drive for justice, equality, and freedom, our thirst for knowledge and spiritual illumination, and our yearning for love and beauty will at last be freed. And after the bloody detour of androcratic history, both women and men will at last find out what being human can mean."[36] Eisler's thesis, while noble in its efforts to correct possible biases in interpretations of ancient history, looks to us like blatantly 1980s feminism writ past.

Occasionally the accusation of denial is unjustly hurled against a revision of history, and when this happens we see, once again, ideology overwhelming evidence. The Australian anthropologist Derek Freeman, for example, ran into a hailstorm of abuse when he attempted to revise the theories of the most famous anthropologist of the twentieth century, Margaret Mead. Reexamining the research and data on which Mead based her 1928 book *Coming of Age in Samoa,* Freeman concluded in his 1983 book, *Margaret Mead and Samoa: The Making and Unmaking of an Anthropological Myth,* that Mead's Polynesian subjects had duped her. Freeman is a professional anthropologist who wrote his doctoral dissertation based on three and a half years on Samoa (Mead was there for twelve weeks); he then published it as a book with the peer-reviewed and highly respected Harvard University Press (after he went back to Samoa four more times). Despite the many lines of evidence in support of his thesis, Freeman was attacked by the American Anthropological Association at its 1983 meeting, in a special session dedicated to the debunking of his book. One observer wrote to Freeman, "I felt I was in a room with people ready to lynch you." The following day at the annual business meeting a motion was put forward to declare Freeman's book "unscientific." Truth by democratic vote? The motion passed. In December of that year the association's journal, *American Anthropologist,* featured no less than five critical reviews, without a single dissenting voice, not even Freeman's. Of this embarrassing affair, the renowned historian and philosopher of science Karl Popper wrote (in a private letter to Freeman):

> Many sociologists and almost all sociologists of science believe in a relativist theory of truth. That is, truth is what the experts believe, or what the majority of the participants in a culture believe. Holding a view like this your opponents could not admit you were right. How could you be, when all their colleagues thought like they did? In fact, they could prove that you were wrong simply by taking a vote at a meeting of experts. That settled it. And your facts? They meant nothing if sufficiently many experts ignored them, or distorted them, or misinterpreted them.[37]

The issue appeared settled once and for all in 1987 when Fa'apua'a Fa'amu, Margaret Mead's closest Samoan friend, confessed in sworn testimony to the then secretary for Samoan affairs of the government of American Samoa, Galea'i Poumele, that she and a friend had hoaxed Mead about the sexual behavior of Samoan adolescent girls in March 1926, when they were traveling with her.[38] (Franz Boas, anthropology's foremost scientist, had sent Mead to Samoa to undertake "a study in heredity and environment based on an investigation of the phenomenon of adolescence among primitive and civilized peoples."[39] He believed that finding an exception to the alleged universal phenomenon of adolescent sexual turbulence—the universality implying a strong genetic component—would undercut hereditary theories of human behavior and place them squarely in the environmental camp, just where Boas and most anthropologists of that time wanted them.)

The point of this story is not whether Freeman's revision of Mead is valid (there are some nonhysterical, reasoned critiques of Freeman produced by his professional colleagues that indicate his critique of Mead may have gone too far).[40] Rather, it is that this is legitimate revisionism, not dogmatic denial.

DENIAL DETECTION

Again, we ask: What is the difference between real revision and dogmatic denial? When encountering what appears to be revision, how can any of us tell that it is not, in fact, denial? There is no hard-and-fast formula that applies to all claims, of course, and we must look at the details of each before passing judgment (which is why we have enumerated specific examples in this chapter). But there are some questions we might ask when encountering an extraordinary claim that may have crossed the fuzzy border between revision and denial:

1. *How reliable is the source of the claim?* Deniers may appear quite reliable as they cite facts and figures, but closer examination often reveals these details have been distorted or taken out of context.

2. *Has this source made other claims that were clearly exaggerated?* If an individual is known to have stretched the facts before, it obviously undermines his or her credibility. In our interview with Ernst Zündel, for example, he told us that an earlier statement he made about the Nazis housing flying saucers in Antarctica was just a publicity stunt, but it points up the risk of going out on a limb too many times.

3. *Has another source verified the claim?* Typically deniers will make statements that are unverified or verified only by another denier. Ernst Zündel may cite David Cole, who may cite Mark

Weber, who may cite David Irving, and so on. Outside verification is crucial to good science and good history.

4. *How does the claim fit with what we know about the world and how it works?* Consider, for example, the deniers' elaborate conspiracy theories about how the Jews have concocted the Holocaust story in order to extract reparations from Germany and support for Israel from America. As we indicated earlier, these theories ignore the practical realities of modern political systems (e.g., German calculation of reparations by survivors, not victims; American aid to Israel for economic and political reasons, not guilt).

5. *Has anyone, including and especially the claimant, gone out of the way to disprove the claim, or has only confirmatory evidence been sought?* This is what is known as "confirmation bias," or the tendency to seek confirmatory evidence and reject disconfirming evidence.[41] We see no attempt, for example, on David Irving's part to falsify or disprove his own interpretations. Moreover, when confronted with the abundant disconfirming evidence for many of his claims, he seems to evade this, as we described in his rationalizations for the use of the word *ausrotten* and for Himmler's and Goebbels's references to murderous actions against the Jews.

6. *In the absence of clearly defined proof, does the preponderance of evidence converge on the claimant's conclusion or a different one?* Deniers do not look for evidence that converges on a conclusion; they look for evidence that fits their ideology. In examining the various eyewitness accounts of the gassing of prisoners at Auschwitz, for example, we find a consistent core to the stories, leading to a strong theory of what happened. Deniers, in contrast, pick up on minor discrepancies in the eyewitness reports and blow these up as anomalies that disconfirm the theory. Instead of reviewing the evidence as a whole, they focus on any detail that supports their point of view.

7. *Is the claimant employing the accepted rules of reason and tools of research or only ones that lead to the desired conclusion?* Those deniers familiar with the accepted rules of scholarship— like Mark Weber, Robert Faurisson, and David Irving—seem conveniently to abandon them in the service of their ideologies.

Here we are not just talking about the citation of appropriate sources in an article in the scholarly-looking *Journal of Historical Review* or the inclusion of dozens of pages of references in a book. We are talking about the dispassionate employment of scholarship in examining a particular document or translating a certain word or phrase, with strict attention to its historical content and context.

8. *Has the claimant provided a different explanation for the observed phenomena rather than just denying the existing explanation?* Deniers usually have no new theory of history to offer but concentrate instead on knocking down the accepted doctrines of the field. This classic debate strategy—criticize your opponent, never affirm what you believe in order to avoid criticism—is not adequate for research in science and history. Revision may involve legitimate critiques of the existing paradigm or offer a replacement with a new paradigm, but denial rarely amounts to more than attacks on the status quo.

9. *If the claimant has proffered a new explanation, does it account for as many phenomena as the old explanation does?* Occasionally deniers offer new theories of history, but these rarely account for as much of the past as the model they hope to replace. Indeed, evidence to disconfirm the new theories often lies in the unexplained details of the past. If the Holocaust did not happen, as we asked before, then what happened to the millions of Jews unaccounted for after the war? If the Holocaust did not happen, then how do deniers explain all those references to the *ausrotten* (extermination) of the Jews? They do not explain them. They ignore them, rationalize them, or deny them.

10. *Do the claimant's personal beliefs and biases drive the conclusions or vice versa?* All of us are biased. All historians hold personal political and ideological beliefs. The question then becomes: how do those biases and beliefs affect our research? If we try to work in a vacuum, however good our intentions, we may find ourselves searching for facts to fit our preconceptions. But at some point, usually during the peer-review system (either informally, when colleagues read a manuscript before publication submission, or formally, when colleagues read the manuscript and do "blind" critiques), critical feedback helps us root out such biases and beliefs. If not, we see the work rejected for publication.

IN SEARCH OF A TRUE AND MEANINGFUL PAST

These points represent the crux of the difference between revision and denial. There is an unstated understanding among scientists and scholars that they will make every effort to be honest with their data, to put aside personal desires and egos, to look for disconfirming evidence, to verify their claims, to check and recheck the sources, to seek critical feedback from colleagues, and to think through the implications of the results and conclusions. Failure to meet one of these criteria is not *sufficient* to qualify a claim as denial rather than revision, but neither are all ten necessary. Depending on the claim, somewhere between one and ten are *necessary and sufficient* to qualify it as denial. The difference between Holocaust denial and revision, for example, is clear in the debates among the scholars we covered in the last three chapters with regard to the use of gas chambers and crematoria, the number of victims, and the intentional or functional nature of the genocide. Deniers are routinely unreliable in their selection of historical facts. They often make outrageous claims. The claims are rarely verified by other sources, and when they are these sources are often incestuous. Deniers almost never attempt to disprove their claims and, instead, seek only confirmatory evidence. They generally do not play by the agreed-upon rules of historical scholarship, offer no alternative theory to account for the historical data, and thus can muster no convergence of evidence for their nonexistent theory. Finally, as we have demonstrated with a preponderance of evidence, Holocaust deniers' personal beliefs and biases dictate their conclusions.

Holocaust denial is clearly a form of pseudohistory. It is an affront against history and how the science of history is practiced. The solution to the problem of pseudohistory is not *just* in identifying the motives and refuting the claims of pseudohistorians, as we have done here. We must also approach history as a scientific discipline, concerned not only with names, dates, and narratives, but with analyses, methodologies, and theories. As we saw, a convergence of evidence proves the Holocaust. Indeed, a convergence of evidence is what proves *any* historical event, assembling different sources to tell a story. Whether the story is told in a narrative form or an analysis is irrelevant, as long as the facts are presented and the interpretations are made within the boundaries of the evidence. If historians practiced history as the deniers do, there would *be* no history, only competing ideologies screaming to be heard among the cacophony of dogmatic voices.

Pseudohistory thrives because history empowers. For some, it is acceptable to deconstruct the history of those in power and to reconstruct it for those who are not. Questioning the history written by those in power is certainly a legitimate enterprise, but problems arise when the rewriting of history is driven by a particular ideological agenda, without regard for the preponderance of evidence. Many scholars in African American, Native American, and feminist studies have made important contributions enlarging our perspectives on history, but we believe there are a few extremists in these fields who enter into the realm of pseudo-history, whether by seemingly claiming all of Western civilization as African based, by tending to blame white European males for all that is evil in the world, or by constructing a past that seems to fit an ideological worldview rather than the evidence.

Holocaust deniers, in our opinion, find empowerment through the rehabilitation of those they admire and the denigration of those they perceive to be squelching their admiration. Many deniers seem to like the idea of a rigid, controlled, and powerful state. Some are fascinated with Nazism as a social/political organization and are impressed with the economic gains Germany made in the 1930s and her military gains from 1939 to 1941. The history of the Holocaust is a black eye for Nazism. Deny the veracity of the Holocaust, and Nazism begins to lose this stigma. In like manner, denying the atrocity denies any moral authority to victims of the atrocity.

But these are tertiary or secondary levels of explanations. There is something primary about Holocaust denial that touches the wound on the raw as no other extremist claim can. Holocaust denial is shocking because its target is so shocking. To deny the Holocaust is to deny something even deeper—our search to understand extreme acts of inhumanity. Attempts by historians, theologians, philosophers, sociologists, and psychologists to explain the Holocaust have been a deliberate and systematic attempt to get to the core of the human condition by asking the most fundamental question of all: Why did this happen? The deniers' answer—it didn't—is wrong, pure and simple. Others' answers over the past half century, such as those who were involved in the 1980s German *Historikerstreit*—a debate that was really more about German guilt than historical facts—are not so easy to dismiss, although they are by no means proved. These ongoing debates are good examples of revisions, some of which meet outright rejection or eager acceptance, but most of which provide partial truths that we incorporate into the historical narratives to help us find meaning in history. That is, to help us find what really happened in the past and what it means to us in the present.

Consider the brouhaha following the 1996 publication of Daniel Goldhagen's book *Hitler's Willing Executioners: Ordinary Germans and the
Holocaust.* Goldhagen's thesis is that ordinary Germans participated in
the mass murder of Jews because antisemitism was pervasive and nearly
exclusively German. In other words, we cannot blame Hitler and a handful of his extremists in the Nazi Party for the Holocaust. *All* Germans
share the blame. Goldhagen states, "My explanation . . . is that the perpetrators, 'ordinary Germans,' were animated by antisemitism, by a particular *type* of antisemitism that led them to conclude that the Jews *ought
to die.* . . . Simply put, the perpetrators, having consulted their own convictions and morality and having judged the mass annihilation of Jews
to be right, did not *want* to say 'no.'" Thus, he concludes, "an enormous
number of ordinary, representative Germans became—and most of the
rest of their fellow Germans were fit to be—Hitler's willing executioners."[42] No academic work of that year generated more controversy and
debate, with symposia, conferences, television forums, and countless reviews weighing in on the matter of why the Holocaust happened. Even
before it was translated into German the book found itself the subject
of contentious exchanges in Germany. Needless to say, some German citizens today were less than enthusiastic about the implication that they
were and are inherently evil. In 1998 two scholars, Norman G. Finkelstein and Ruth Bettina Birn, responded with an emotionally charged volume entitled *A Nation on Trial: The Goldhagen Thesis and Historical
Truth,* and in a thoughtful *History and Theory* article A. D. Moses succinctly summarized the terms of the Goldhagen debate, the strengths and
weaknesses in both sides, and the implications of each position for our
choice of ethical theories about the ultimate cause of the Holocaust.[43]
Whether Goldhagen's explanation of the Holocaust is right or wrong is
not our concern here. But it is clearly in the camp of revision and not denial. As a source Goldhagen is reliable; he plays by the accepted rules of
historical scholarship; and he accounts for the observed phenomena while
offering a different explanation for them.

Often, revisionist interpretations of the Holocaust over the past half
century tell us as much about ourselves and our culture as they do about
the Nazis and their culture. Two recent books address the problem of
explaining Hitler and the Holocaust and the pitfalls of trying to put them
into a proper historical context. John Lukacs's *The Hitler of History* ex-
plores Hitler and his attempt to exterminate the Jews of Europe through
the eyes of the dozens of biographers and historians who have grappled
with the problem of explanation since 1945.[44] Since Lukacs is a histo-

rian by training, he does not refrain from offering his own theory, albeit
modestly, suggesting how and why Hitler came to order the destruction
of Europe's Jews. Ron Rosenbaum's *Explaining Hitler* provides a critical look at many of these theories and what their differences tell us about
the theorists because, says Rosenbaum, "the shapes we project onto the
inky Rorschach of Hitler's psyche are often cultural self-portraits in the
negative. What we talk about when we talk about Hitler is also who we
are and who we are not."[45] Both Lukacs and Rosenbaum demonstrate
what these Rorschach interpretations tell us, by delving into the political and ideological biases of the various authors who have braved an interpretative narrative. Rosenbaum, a journalist, refrains from attempting an explanation of his own, but in the process offers, we believe, the
stronger work, for both Hitler and the Holocaust, as he notes, seem to
defy explanation.

The explanations for Hitler, and by inference for the Holocaust (as in
Milton Himmelfarb's *Commentary* piece, "No Hitler, No Holocaust"),
have ranged from the ridiculous (Hitler's grandfather was Jewish, or he
had only one testicle) to the sublime (God or Satan willed it). Some insist the explanation has been found (Lukacs places the crystallization of
Hitler's antisemitic personality as early as 1919), that it can be but has
not yet been found (Yehuda Bauer: "Hitler is explicable in principle, but
that does not mean that he *has* been explained"), that it cannot be found
(Emil Fackenheim: "The closer one gets to explicability the more one realizes nothing can make Hitler explicable"), or that it can be found but
should not be (Claude Lanzmann: "There is even a book written . . .
about Hitler's childhood, an attempt at explanation which is for me obscenity as such").[46] The Hitler of the Holocaust ranges wildly between
intentional evil and functional malady. Lucy Dawidowicz's Hitler is the
sole conductor who orchestrated the Holocaust with evil intent, decid-
ing "on his war against the Jews in November 1918, when, at the military hospital in Pasewalk, he learned, in rapid succession, of the naval
mutiny at Kiel, the revolution that forced the abdication of the Emperor,
and finally the Armistice. 'Everything went black before my eyes,' he
wrote. In the ensuing 'terrible days and even worse nights,' while he pondered the meaning of these cataclysmic events, 'my own fate became
known to me.' It was then that he made his decision: 'There is no making pacts with Jews; there can be only the hard: either-or. I for my part,
decided to go into politics.'" By sharp contrast, Christopher Browning's
Hitler stumbles his way hesitatingly into the Holocaust, with "a sense
that in the end he was *scared* of what he was doing. Now I interpret that

as he didn't think it was *wrong,* but he was aware that he was now doing something that had never been done before. Stepping into new territory. Could it be done?"

Rosenbaum's meta-history of Hitler begins with a metaphorical "survival myth." In fictional accounts Hitler somehow escapes the Berlin
bunker and lives out his days in Argentina. Life imitates art, says Rosenbaum, in the sense that Hitler *has* escaped . . . explanation: "The search
for Hitler has apprehended not one coherent, consensus image of Hitler
but rather many different Hitlers, competing Hitlers, conflicting em-
bodiments of competing visions, Hitlers who might not recognize each
other well enough to say *'Heil'* if they came face to face in Hell."[47] If
Hitler can escape explanation in this sense, can the Holocaust? We agree
on the basic facts about the Holocaust, with revisions fine-tuning the technical and demographic details. But interpretations about why it happened
and what it means quickly become entangled in contradictory premises
about human history and human nature. For Claude Lanzmann, the
Holocaust "is a product of the whole story of the Western world since
the very beginning."[48] But what does this tell us? If everything is the cause,
then nothing is the cause. Jacob Talmon would seem to agree with Lanzmann with regard to the question of magnitude and meaning, revision
and redemption, and the evil of those who would deny its impact on the
world historical stage: "What is the meaning of history's greatest horror within the scheme of universal history—what is its sense, its purpose,
its logic? Could the Holocaust be the conclusive proof that history moves
by no law, offers no lesson, and serves no purpose? That it is merely a
succession of irrational accidents, insipid banalities and gratuitous horrors? The mere inclination to accept this point of view suggests a surrender to the mentality of the perpetrators of the Holocaust. After all,
they ended up where they did partly as a result of their desperate denial
of a final station of redemption in history."[49]

Behind the obsession with explaining Hitler and the other leading
Nazis (with or without most of their fellow Germans) is the need to explain the Holocaust. To discover the truth about *why* the Holocaust happened is to give it meaning. Revision of the facts about *how* the Holocaust happened is the bread and butter of historians, and our work on
this project brings us ever closer to knowing what actually happened between 1933 and 1945 in Europe. In this sense, history works as science
does—with the accretion of knowledge item by item until a theoretical
framework nears completion. Revision of *why* the Holocaust happened
and its meaning in history, however, takes place at another level entirely.

Such revision does not bring us closer to an absolute meaning accessible to all; rather, it widens the selection of multiple meanings from which to choose.

We know that the Holocaust happened through the tried-and-true method employed by all historical scientists in the convergence of evidence on a provisional but tenable conclusion. Like criminologists solving a crime, we piece together the myriad bits of evidence until a conclusion emerges from the morass of data. The thousands of pieces of evidence from the thousands of events that happened in thousands of places throughout continental Europe from 1933 to 1945 comprise what is called the Holocaust. No single source proves the Holocaust because this is not how such major historical events are proved. But within the context of events in the second half of 1941 and the first half of 1942 that led the Nazis to change the goal of the Final Solution from deportation to extermination, particular clusters stand out: the Wannsee Protocol of January 20, 1942, and the construction of the death camps that would carry out the new Final Solution. We know the Holocaust happened.

We have a very solid understanding of how the Holocaust happened. The thousands of stories add up to more than a rich narrative of individual suffering and death. They comprise a model, a theory, for how the Final Solution came about—what led to the decision to carry out mass murders, how these mass murders were to be executed, where the killings would take place, when the deportations to the camps would be made, which Jews from which countries would be chosen, which individuals on the train platforms would be selected, and so forth. We know how the Holocaust happened.

Why the Holocaust happened is a question that all who encounter it as a deeply significant historical event must answer in the spectrum of their own vision of history and humanity. The question *why* eludes a consensus answer for the very reason that it is not for the consensus to reason why. It is for the individual. Each of us must look into the well of our soul as we confront the reality of Auschwitz and ask ourselves: what does it mean? It is for this reason, perhaps more than any other, that we believe Holocaust denial is so dangerous and despicable—it is an attempt not just to deny a true past, but to deny a meaningful one. Whatever else it might be, history is the primary story of the storytelling animal, the narrative of our past that offers meaning to our present and, ultimately, our future.

Epilogue

Libel, Denial, and the Holocaust Trial

Holocaust denial is back in the news. The renowned filmmaker Errol Morris recently released his brilliant but dark documentary *Mr. Death,* about Fred Leuchter and his claim to have proved that mass gassings could not have occurred at Auschwitz. As we noted earlier, Leuchter conducted his "research" at Auschwitz by chipping off pieces of brick from gas chambers and submitting this material for chemical analysis. In *Mr. Death* Ernst Zündel, who had commissioned Leuchter's study, recalls, "When my doubts about the Holocaust first came to me, it took me two and a half years, and I was like a reforming alcoholic. I was like one yo-yo, back and forth: believe, not believe, maybe believe, false belief, true belief. Fred was able to purge his own mind within a matter of a week. So I said, 'Fred, what convinced you?' He said, 'Ernst, it wasn't what I found, it was what I didn't find.' That blew me away. It never, ever occurred to me that a man could be convinced by something [Zyklon-B gas residue] that is not there." As we showed in chapter 6, however, the bricks Leuchter examined had been exposed to nearly half a century of weather by the time he took his samples, so his results should come as no surprise. Moreover, Morris found the chemist who tested the samples, James Roth, who confirmed that the gas could not have penetrated deeper than 10 microns (a human hair is 100 microns thick) and indicated that in the samples he was given—big chunks of concrete and brick— any Zyklon-B traces would have been diluted by a factor of hundreds of thousands. Both Leuchter and Zündel seem to ignore this simple explanatory fact, as does David Irving, who told Morris (in the film): "He [Leuchter] came back with these earth-shattering results. The big point: there is no significant residue of cyanide in the brickwork. That's what converted me. When I read that in the report in the courtroom in Toronto, I became a hard-core disbeliever."[1]

"A hard-core disbeliever." That is an interesting choice of words for a man who sued the Holocaust historian Deborah Lipstadt for calling him a Holocaust denier (among other charges). If a hard-core disbeliever in the Holocaust is not also a Holocaust denier, then what does belief or disbelief mean? The Irving-Lipstadt libel trial in England thrust Holocaust denial back into world consciousness, with the major news organizations covering the trial on a regular basis. Although all participants made it clear that the Holocaust itself was not on trial, the veracity of the three major defining points of the Holocaust—six million murdered, the use of gas chambers as one of the killing mechanisms, and the Nazis' intention to exterminate European Jewry—became a subject of contentious debate.

Irving claimed that Lipstadt libeled him in her 1993 book *Denying the Holocaust,* and under British law the burden of proof was on her to show that she did not. Lipstadt refused to take the stand herself, but her attorneys and expert witnesses, including the Holocaust historians Richard Evans and Robert Jan van Pelt, attempted to show that Irving purposely ignored or distorted key documents that prove the Holocaust occurred. In his defense, Irving, who represented himself, countered that these documents do not prove certain key elements of the Holocaust story and therefore there was no distortion on his part. Because of how the trial was conducted, the transcripts (posted on Irving's own Web page) made it clear that the evidence for the Holocaust was indeed on trial here. Hours every day were spent pouring over in excruciating detail the hundreds of documents and letters related to mass killings, mechanisms of mass murder, and the intentions of the major players in the Nazi regime, along with Irving's own intentions.

Intentions are difficult to prove, of course, but what are we to make of Irving's recording in his personal diary that one day he sang this little song to his young daughter: "I am a Baby Aryan / Not Jewish or Sectarian / I have no plans to marry / an Ape or Rastafarian"?[2] It's bad enough that an adult would sing such an offensive ditty to a young child, but to then record the act in his diary makes it difficult for us to believe that Irving does not have some antisemitic leanings that might color his objectivity when dealing with historical documents of what Nazis did to Jews.

When we wrote this epilogue, the trial was still ongoing, so we wondered how the public might react if Irving won. Would a victory for him be nothing more than a personal triumph, or might the Holocaust itself come under additional fire? Perhaps this possibility is what stimulated Israel to release Adolf Eichmann's 1,200-page manuscript penned in 1961, while he was in jail awaiting and during his trial for crimes against humanity. These recollections by Eichmann of what the Nazis did to the Jews during the war make it additionally startling that anyone could deny the Holocaust: "I said [in court] that what happened with the Jews, which the government of the German Reich brought about during the last great war, was the most enormous crime in the history of mankind. And I witnessed the gruesome workings of the machinery of death; gear meshed with gear, like clockwork. It was the biggest and most enormous dance of death of all time."[3]

It seems unlikely that a man on trial for his life would have made such an observation if the Holocaust never happened. Consider also Eichmann's recollection of what his superior, deputy SS leader Reinhard Heydrich, told him in the fall of 1941 about the fate of the Jews: "The Führer has ordered the physical extermination of the Jews. [A Nazi official in Poland] has received from the Führer the necessary instructions. He was told to use the trenches dug as tank traps. I want to know what he does and how far he has come. Go see him and report back to me on what you have seen and heard." Eichmann did just that, witnessing a mass execution in Minsk in Nazi-occupied Belarus in January of 1942: "When I arrived at the place of the execution, the gunmen fired into a pit the size of several rooms. They fired from small submachine guns. As I arrived, I saw a Jewish woman and a small child in her arms in the pit. I wanted to pull out the child, but then a bullet smashed the skull of the child. My driver wiped brain particles from my leather coat. I got into the car. Berlin, I told the driver. I drank schnapps like it was water. I had to numb myself. I thought about my own children. At the time, I had two."[4]

It is worth noting that Irving has seen the Eichmann memoirs, but he seems to have ignored their import. Regardless of the outcome of the Irving-Lipstadt trial, we hope our book has not only provided a thorough and thoughtful answer to all the claims of the Holocaust deniers, but also clearly presented the convergence of evidence for how we know the Holocaust (or anything in history) happened, and how from this we can discover a meaningful past that will help us make sense of the present.

Notes

A NOTE ON TERMINOLOGY

1. Such terms appear throughout the *Journal of Historical Review* (published by the Institute for Historical Review, the leading U.S. Holocaust denial organization), in fund-raising letters for the Institute for Historical Review, and in lectures and presentations at IHR conferences.

2. B. R. Smith, *The Holocaust Controversy: The Case for Open Debate* (Visalia, Calif.: Committee for Open Debate on the Holocaust, 1992), emphasis added.

3. See Y. Gutman and M. Berenbaum, eds., *Anatomy of the Auschwitz Death Camp* (Bloomington: Indiana University Press, 1994).

4. See S. Spector, "Aktion 1005: Effacing the Murder of Millions," *Holocaust and Genocide Studies* 5, no. 2 (1990): 157–173; E. Klee, W. Dressen, and V. Riess, eds., *"The Good Old Days": The Holocaust as Seen by Its Perpetrators and Bystanders* (New York: Free Press, 1992).

5. See F. Piper, *How Many Perished: Jews, Poles, Gypsies . . .* (Kraków: Poligrafia ITS, 1992); C. Browning, *The Path to Genocide: Essays on Launching the Final Solution* (Cambridge: Cambridge University Press, 1991).

INTRODUCTION: WHO SPEAKS FOR THE PAST?

1. Y. Bauer, "'Revisionism'—The Repudiation of the Holocaust and Its Historical Significance," in *The Historiography of the Holocaust Period*, ed. Y. Gutman and G. Greif (Jerusalem: Yad Vashem, 1988), 708.

2. M. Shermer, "Proving the Holocaust: The Refutation of Revisionism and the Restoration of History," *Skeptic* 2, no. 4 (1994): 32–57, and Shermer, "Holocaust Revisionism Update," *Skeptic* 6, no. 1 (1998): 23–24.

3. We recognize the many antecedents to Gutenberg and that, as with most historical figures credited with an invention or discovery, his genius was in synthesizing many components in an original way. See E. Eisenstein, *The Printing Revolution in Early Modern Europe* (Cambridge: Cambridge University Press,

1986) and L. Febvre and H.-J. Martin, *The Coming of the Book* (London: New Left Books, 1976).

4. C. L. Becker, "Everyman His Own Historian," *American Historical Review* 37 (1932): 236.

1. GIVING THE DEVIL HIS DUE

1. Quoted in S. J. Roth, "Making the Denial of the Holocaust a Crime in Law" (London: Institute of Jewish Affairs in association with the World Jewish Congress, research report, March 1982).

2. International Military Tribunal, *Trials of War Criminals before the Nuremberg Military Tribunal under Control Council Law No. 10,* 1: xii (Washington, D.C.: U.S. Government Printing Office, 1946–53).

3. Quoted in Roth, "Making the Denial of the Holocaust a Crime" (1982).

4. D. Butler, "French Research Agency to Seek Ruling on Holocaust Sceptics," *Nature,* April 23, 1998, 745.

5. Quoted in Roth, "Making the Denial of the Holocaust a Crime" (1982).

6. L. Douglas, "The Memory of Judgment: The Law, the Holocaust, and Denial," *History and Memory* 7, no. 2 (1996): 100–120.

7. H. Brin, "Sweden Arrests Top Holocaust Revisionist," *Heritage,* December 31, 1982.

8. J. Rauch, *Kindly Inquisitors: The New Attacks on Free Thought* (Chicago: University of Chicago Press, 1993), 2.

9. Ibid., pp. 1–2.

10. www.fpp.co.uk/online.html.

11. Frank Miele, senior editor of *Skeptic* magazine, was in attendance and reported: "The people outside the door were screaming at Irving and the rest of us inside the room. They tried to force their way in, but the Berkeley police prevented this. At one point an older-looking man with a gray stubbly beard came from the back of the crowd and made his way through the demonstrators and into the room. Irving grabbed his cash box from the display table of books and retreated peacefuly to the wall. The old man pushed the books off the table and then physically pushed and shoved Irving. The Berkeley police finally restored order, moving the crowd out of the building and into the street, where they continued to chant, shout, and demonstrate. When the old man physically assaulted Irving, a muscular young man in a black t-shirt came forward and decked him with one right cross. The young man made no attempt to attack or injure him further, and the Berkeley police took the old man out of the room. I do not know if they pressed charges against him; the young man remained in the meeting the entire time and behaved without incident" (personal correspondence to Michael Shermer, January 2000).

12. R. Post, "Go Home, Irving," *Daily Californian,* February 7, 1995, 1.

13. See S. Samuels and M. Valencia, "Activists Clash over Irving's Revised History," *Daily Californian,* February 7, 1995, 1–4.

14. W. Reich, "Erasing the Holocaust" (book review), *New York Times,* July 11, 1993, 34.

15. See F. Miele, "Giving the Devil His Due: Holocaust Revisionism as a Test Case for Free Speech and the Skeptical Ethic," *Skeptic* 2, no. 4 (1994): 58–70,

and M. Shermer, "Holocaust Denial, Free Speech, and the Burden of Proof," *Skeptic* 2, no. 3 (1994): 13–14.

16. Smith, *The Holocaust Controversy* (1992).

17. See R. Olson, *Science Deified and Science Defied: The Historical Significance of Science in Western Culture from the Early Modern Age through the Early Romantic Era, ca. 1640 to 1820* (Berkeley: University of California Press, 1991).

18. Quoted in Rauch, *Kindly Inquisitors* (1993), 11.

19. Quoted in Joseph Wood Krutch, "Darrow vs. Bryan," *Nation,* July 29, 1925, 136.

20. Reich, "Erasing the Holocaust" (1993), 34.

21. P. Vidal-Naquet, *Assassins of Memory* (New York: Columbia University Press, 1992), 24.

22. Robert Jan van Pelt, personal communication, September 1996.

23. Quoted in N. Cummingham, *In Pursuit of Reason: The Life of Thomas Jefferson* (Baton Rouge: Louisiana State University Press, 1987), 77.

24. Ibid., 49.

2. THE NOBLE DREAM

1. D. D. Eisenhower, *Crusade in Europe* (New York: Doubleday, 1948), 409.

2. See G. Blainey, 1988, *The Causes of War* (New York: Free Press); G. Perret, 1989, *A Country Made by War* (New York: Random House).

3. Quoted in F. Stern, ed., *The Varieties of History: From Voltaire to the Present* (New York: Vintage Books, 1973), 59; see also Peter Novick's splendid history of the historical profession, *That Noble Dream: The 'Objectivity Question' and the American Historical Profession* (Cambridge: Cambridge University Press, 1988).

4. Quoted in Stern, *Varieties of History* (1973), 221–23.

5. Quoted in ibid., 270.

6. B. Croce, *History: Its Theory and Practice,* trans. D. Ainslee (New York: Harcourt, Brace, 1921), 17.

7. Becker, "Everyman His Own Historian" (1932): 221–22.

8. Quoted in Novick, *That Noble Dream* (1988), 269.

9. Ibid.

10. C. A. Beard, "That Noble Dream" (1935), in *The Varieties of History,* ed. F. Stern (New York: Vintage Books, 1973), 323–26.

11. D. LaCapra, *Rethinking Intellectual History: Texts, Contexts, Language* (Ithaca: Cornell University Press, 1983), 42–43.

12. D. Harlan, "Intellectual History and the Return of Literature" *American Historical Review* 94 (1989): 581.

13. K. Marx, "The Eighteenth Brumaire of Louis Bonaparte" (1852), in *The Marx-Engels Reader,* 2d ed., ed. R. C. Tucker (New York: W. W. Norton, 1978), 594.

14. G. Dening, *Mr. Bligh's Bad Language: Passion, Power and Theatre on the* Bounty (Cambridge: Cambridge University Press, 1992), 366.

15. Ibid., 61.

16. K. Windschuttle, *The Killing of History: How a Discipline Is Being Murdered by Literary Critics and Social Theorists* (Paddington, N.S.W., Australia: Macleay Press, 1996), 90.

17. M. Foucault, *The Order of Things: An Archaeology of the Human Sciences* (New York: Vintage Books, 1994), xix.

18. Windschuttle, *Killing of History* (1996), 255.

19. J. T. Kloppenberg, "Objectivity and Historicism: A Century of American Historical Writing," *American Historical Review* 94, no. 4 (1989): 1030.

20. F. Sulloway, *Born to Rebel: Birth Order, Family Dynamics, and Creative Lives* (New York: Pantheon, 1996), and J. Diamond, *Guns, Germs and Steel: The Fates of Human Societies* (New York: W. W. Norton, 1997). See also M. Shermer, "Rebel with a Cause: An Interview with Frank Sulloway," *Skeptic* 4, no. 4 (1996): 68–73.

21. J. W. Schopf, *Cradle of Life: The Discovery of Earth's Earliest Fossil* (Princeton: Princeton University Press, 1999), 304–24.

22. W. Whewell, *The Philosophy of the Inductive Sciences* (London: J. W. Parker, 1840), 230.

23. M. Shermer, *Why People Believe Weird Things: Pseudoscience, Superstition, and Other Confusions of Our Time* (New York: W. H. Freeman, 1997); Shermer, *How We Believe: The Search for God in an Age of Science* (New York: W. H. Freeman, 1999).

24. D. Dwork and R. J. van Pelt, *Auschwitz: 1270 to the Present.* (New York: W. W. Norton, 1996).

25. [Eisenhower committee], *Atrocities and Other Conditions in Concentration Camps in Germany,* report of the committee requested by Gen. Dwight D. Eisenhower through the Chief of Staff, Gen. George C. Marshall, to the Congress of the United States (Washington, D.C.: U.S. Government Printing Office, 1945).

3. WHO SAYS THE HOLOCAUST NEVER HAPPENED?

1. Buchanan, quoted in C. R. Allen, "Patrick J. Buchanan: Master Holocaust Denier," *Reform Judaism* (winter 1996), 23. Although in recent years Buchanan has backed down from some of these statements, as the 2000 election campaign was getting under way in 1999, Buchanan published his controversial book *A Republic, Not an Empire,* in which he argues that initially Hitler had designs only on Eastern Europe and the Soviet Union and that were it not for the intervention of America, much of the death and destruction of the Second World War, including much of the Holocaust in such Western countries as France, Norway, and the Netherlands, could have been prevented.

2. Allen, "Buchanan" (1996), 23–24.

3. See, for example, S. B. Fay, "New Light on the Origin of the World War," *American Historical Review* 25 (1920): 616–39.

4. See, for example, M. R. Konvitz, "Will Nuremberg Serve Justice?" *Commentary* 1, no. 3 (Jaunuary 1946): 11; F. Utley, *The High Cost of Vengeance* (Chicago: Regnery, 1949); P. Rassinier, *Le Mensonge d'Ulysse* [The lie of Odysseus] (Paris, 1950); M. Bardèche, *Nuremberg II ou les faux-monnayeurs*

[Nuremberg II or the counterfeiters] (Paris: Les Sept Couleurs, 1950); H. E. Barnes, "Revisionism: A Key to Peace," *Ramparts* (Summer 1966); A. App, *A Straight Look at the Third Reich: Hitler and National Socialism, How Right? How Wrong?* (Tacoma Park, Md.: Boniface Press, 1974); B. C. Wintzek, *Unssere Väter waren keine Verbrecher: Wie es damals wirklich war* [Our fathers were no criminals: How it really was then] (Asendorf: MUT-Verlag, 1975); M. Weber, "The Nuremberg Trials and the Holocaust," *Journal of Historical Review* 12, no. 2 (1992): 167–213.

5. Arthur Butz, in *The Hoax of the Twentieth Century* (Newport Beach, Calif.: Institute for Historical Review, 1976), provides a classic study in revision turned into denial in his reiteration and documentation of these arguments.

6. M. Hannan, "Scot Who Claimed the Holocaust Was a Hoax," *The Scotsman*, June 1, 1998.

7. All quotations from Ratcliffe are from ibid.

8. Mark Weber, interview with M. Shermer, Altadena, Calif., February 11, 1994 (transcript in Skeptics Society research library).

9. "Letter of IHR to All Interested Parties Intending to Claim $50,000 Reward" (Torrance, Calif.: Institute for Historical Review, April 1, 1982); K. Stimely, "$50,000 Auschwitz Reward Unclaimed; 'Gas Chamber' Myth Continues to Crumble," *IHR Special Report* (Torrance, Calif.: Institute for Historical Review, 1983).

10. See Deposition of William David McCalden, aka Lewis Brandon, *Mel Mermelstein v. Institute for Historical Review, et al.*, Superior Court of the State of California, No. C 356542, Vol. 1, Jan. 16, 1984; Declaration of William Cox regarding the Urgency of Proceedings in *Mel Mermelstein v. Institute for Historical Review, et al.*, Superior Court of the State of California, No. C 356542, Aug. 10, 1981; Statement of Record and Letter of Apology to Mel Mermelstein, signed by G. G. Baumen, Attorney for Legion for Survival of Freedom, Institute for Historical Review, Noontide Press, and Elisabeth Carto, and Mark F. Von Esch, Attorney for Liberty Lobby and Willis Carto, July 24, 1985.

11. See Weber, interview (1994).

12. Personal correspondence from Willis Carto to Michael Shermer, September 22, 1994.

13. Weber, interview (1994).

14. "An Urgent Appeal from IHR" (Torrance, Calif.: Institute for Historical Review, February 1994).

15. Ibid.

16. David Irving, interview with M. Shermer, Altadena, Calif., April 25, 1994 (transcript in Skeptics Society research library).

17. David Cole, interview with M. Shermer, Altadena, Calif., April 26, 1994 (transcript in Skeptics Society research library).

18. Weber, interview (1994).

19. Ernst Zündel, interview with M. Shermer, Altadena, Calif., April 26, 1994 (transcript in Skeptics Society research library).

20. Yisrael Gutman, interview with M. Shermer and A. Grobman, Altadena, Calif., May 10, 1996 (transcript in Skeptics Society research library).

21. Zündel, interview (1994).

22. *Power* (November 15, 1995), 3.

23. Weber, interview (1994).

24. M. Weber, interview, *University of Nebraska Sower* (1989).

25. Weber, interview (1994).

26. Ibid.

27. Weber was introduced by IHR Associate Director Greg Raven, who began the evening with an update and request for donations. Raven reminded the attendees that 1998 marked the twentieth anniversary of the founding of the IHR, then briefly summarized its legal battles with Willis Carto, for which it anticipated a redemptive closure. He also announced that the organization's 501(c)(3) nonprofit status, granted by the IRS after considerable difficulty, allows individuals to deduct donations to the IHR on their tax form. Raven discussed IHR's progress on the Internet, noting that it now has its own domain name—www.ihr.org—and that its goal is to create a research facility where documents can be archived, press clippings organized, and the IHR library made available for research by World War II historians. The IHR plans to be around in fifty years, Raven concluded, but to do so it must raise an estimated $2 million, starting with hoped-for donations from the conference attendees.

28. Weber at IHR conference, March 28, 1998.

29. Cole, interview (1994).

30. Posted on Irving's Web site (www.fpp.co.uk).

31. Ibid.

32. Ibid. Irving's Web page contains a detailed publishing history of this book, as well as many of his other works, trials, arrests, plus his regular journal updates.

33. Irving, interview (1994).

34. Ibid.

35. See D. Irving, *Hitler's War* (New York: Viking, 1977).

36. See, for example, Irving, interview (1994), and Irving, "Revelations from Goebbels' Diary: Bringing to Light Secrets of Hitler's Propaganda Minister," *Journal of Historical Review* 15, no. 1 (1995): 2–21; also Editorial, "Irving: The Truth at Last, or Some of It," *Searchlight* 243 (September 1995). Irving's evolving views can also be tracked on his Web page.

37. Irving, interview (1994) and Irving quoted in Editorial, "Irving" (1995), 2.

38. Irving's Web page, September 12, 1998.

39. Ibid.

40. Ibid. For the legal opinions, see Verdict of the Munich District Court, Criminal Proceedings, no. 432, case 113, main hearing, May 5, 1992. Upheld on appeal, 1993.

41. Quoted in *Vancouver Sun*, October 28, 1992.

42. Irving, interview (1994).

43. Ibid.

44. Irving's Web page, September 12, 1998.

45. Observed by Michael Shermer at 1995 IHR conference.

46. As recounted by Irving at 1995 IHR conference.

47. D. Irving, *Göring: A Biography* (New York: Grafton/Harper Collins, 1989), 238.

48. Ibid., 343.

49. Irving in R. Rosenbaum, *Explaining Hitler: The Search for the Origins of His Evil* (New York: Random House, 1998), 233.

50. Ibid., 224.

51. Ibid.

52. Ibid.

53. Ibid., 225–26.

54. The phrase "the traditional enemy" is found throughout Irving's newsletter, *Action Report*, as well as on his Web page. The description of the conference is based on the observations of Michael Shermer, who attended it (March 28, 1998, at Marriott Suites Hotel).

55. Irving's Web site, December 1, 1997.

56. Irving in Rosenbaum, *Explaining Hitler* (1998), 227–29. During the war, Irving recalls in an *Atlantic Monthly* article, he was sent to "a minor public school," where he was "beaten repeatedly" for his pranks: "The final beating came when I'd hung a twelve-foot hammer-and-sickle flag over the main entrance to the school. They had to call the fire brigade to come and bring it down." Even at this young age, he was interested in Hitler: when he won an art appreciation award and was asked what prize he wanted, he requested a copy of *Mein Kampf*. As he describes it, "I arranged for the local press to be there en masse to take a photograph of the deputy prime minister giving me a copy of *Mein Kampf*. I went up on stage and picked up this prize—and it was a German-Russian technical dictionary" (D. D. Guttenplan, "The Holocaust on Trial," *Atlantic Monthly*, February 2000, 47).

57. Irving in Rosenbaum, *Explaining Hitler* (1998), 227–29.

58. S. Kent and T. Krebs, "When Scholars Know Sin: How New Age Religions Co-Opt Social Scientists," *Skeptic* 6, no. 3 (1998): 36–44.

59. P. Ekman and M. O'Sullivan, "Who Can Catch a Liar?" *American Psychologist* 46 (1991): 913–20; J. H. Barkow, L. Cosmides, and J. Tooby, eds., *The Adapted Mind* (Oxford: Oxford University Press, 1992).

60. Irving in Rosenbaum *Explaining Hitler* (1998), 229–31.

61. See P. Vidal-Naquet, *Assassins of Memory* (New York: Columbia University Press, 1992), 65–74.

62. *Le Monde,* "L'agression contre M. Robert Faurisson revendiquée par 'Les fils de mémoire juive,'" September 19, 1989.

63. S. Roth, "Making the Denial of the Holocaust a Crime in Law" (London: Institute of Jewish Affairs in association with the World Jewish Congress, research report, March 1982).

64. R. Faurisson, "The 'Problem of the Gas Chambers'" (Newport Beach, Calif.: Institute for Historical Review, pamphlet, n.d. [1987]).

65. See Vidal-Naquet, *Assassins of Memory* (1992), 65–74.

66. Story recounted to Michael Shermer at the 1995 IHR Conference and corroborated with the Holocaust Memorial Museum director.

67. B. R. Smith, *Confessions of a Holocaust Revisionist* (Los Angeles: Prima Facie, 1987).

68. See L. Jaroff, "Debating the Holocaust," *Time,* December 27, 1993, 83.

69. Smith, *Confessions* (1987).

70. Ibid.

71. Ibid., 79–80.

72. Ibid., 37, 117.

73. Ad in *Student Life* (February 1992), Washington University, St. Louis.

74. All quotations from *The Revisionist: A Journal of Independent Thought* 1 (November 1999).

75. G. Brewer, "Letter from the Editor," *The Revisionist: A Journal of Independent Thought* 1 (November 1999): 4.

76. *New York Times,* November 17, 1999, B8.

77. B. R. Smith, "The Holocaust Story: How Much Is False? The Case for Open Debate," *Daily Northwestern,* April 4, 1991.

78. Zündel, interview (1994). Unless otherwise noted all quotations in this section are from this interview.

79. Cole, interview (1994). Unless otherwise noted all quotations in this section are from this interview.

80. Editorial, "Rebel Without a Cause," *The Jewish News,* January 21, 1994. A supportive view of Cole can be found in J. Wickoff, "An Interview with 'Holocaust' Revisionist David Cole," *Remarks,* May–June 1992, 1–7.

81. Quoted in H. Roques, "Faurisson and Cole on the Struthof 'Gas Chamber,'" *Adelaide Institute Newsletter,* April 20, 1995, 2.

82. The sixth person is not named.

83. Roques, "Faurisson and Cole" (1995), 2.

84. Quoted in ibid.

85. Quoted in ibid., 3.

86. Robert J. Newman, "David Cole: Monstrous Traitor," www.jdl.org.

87. "Reward for Information," www.jdl.org.

88. "Statement of David Cole." www.jdl.org.

89. Irv Rubin, telephone interview by Michael Shermer, April 6, 1998. All subsequent quotations from Rubin in this section are from this interview.

90. Weber, phone conversation with Michael Shermer, April 7, 1998.

91. M. Weber, *The Zionist Terror Network: Background and Operation of the Jewish Defense League and Other Criminal Zionist Groups* (Newport Beach, Calif.: Institute for Historical Review, 1993).

92. David Cole, phone message to Skeptics Society, April 10, 1998.

93. Theodore J. O'Keefe, letter, *Journal of Historical Review,* October 1999.

4. WHY THEY SAY THE HOLOCAUST NEVER HAPPENED

1. M. Weber, "The Jewish Role in the Bolshevik Revolution and Russia's Early Soviet Regime," *Journal of Historical Review* 14, no. 1 (1994): 7.

2. Irving, interview (1994).

3. The publication ran quarterly from 1980 to 1992, then switched to bi-monthly from 1993 to the present. It was not published at all in 1987, and only six issues were published throughout the two-year span from 1996 to 1997. The issuance of the magazine is quite sporadic, with occasional long lapses between issues.

4. Weber's article appeared in the November–December 1994 issue; the film satire in the May–June 1994 issue; Irving's article in the January–February issue; and the "60 Minutes" piece in the May–June 1994 issue.

5. The "Great Emancipator" story appeared in the September–October 1993 issue, and the two articles on the Inquisition in the January–February 1996 issue. On Pearl Harbor, see, for example, James Martin's "Pearl Harbor's Place in History" and John Mueller's "Pearl Harbor: The Real Infamy Was an Unnecessary War," both in *JHR*, November–December 1997.

6. Our interrater reliability was 83 percent, acceptable by social science standards.

7. Robert Faurisson, "Ah, How Sweet It Is to Be Jewish," *JHR*, November–December 1998, 11.

8. "A Jewish Appeal to Russia's Jewish Elite," *JHR*, November–December 1998, 13.

9. R. Harwood, "'Holocaust' Story an Evil Hoax," *"Holocaust" News* (London) 1 (1982): 1.

10. Quoted in J. C. Obert, "Yockey: Profile of an American Hitler," *The Investigator*, October 1981, 20.

11. Ibid., 20–24.

12. Quoted in T. McIver, "The Protocols of Creationism: Racism, Anti-Semitism and White Supremacy in Christian Fundamentalism," *Skeptic* 2, no. 4 (1994): 76–87.

13. R. Hofstader, *The Paranoid Style in American Politics and Other Essays* (Chicago: University of Chicago Press, 1979).

14. J. Vankin and J. Whalen, *50 Greatest Conspiracies of All Time: History's Biggest Mysteries, Coverups and Cabals* (New York: Citadel Press, 1995).

15. See N. Cohn, *Warrant for Genocide: The Myth of the Jewish World-Conspiracy and the Protocols of the Elders of Zion* (London: Eyre and Spottiswoode, 1967); McIver, "Protocols of Creationism" (1994).

16. Quoted in D. King, *Lyndon LaRouche and the New American Fascism* (New York: Doubleday, 1989), 137.

17. Ibid., 138. For their various theories, see L. LaRouche, *The Power of Reason—A Kind of Autobiography* (New York: New Benjamin Franklin House, 1979); LaRouche, *Will the Soviets Rule during the 1980s?* (New York: New Benjamin Franklin House, 1979); LaRouche, *Basic Economics for Conservative Democrats* (New York: New Benjamin Franklin House, 1980); LaRouche, *LaRouche—Will This Man Become President?* (New York: New Benjamin Franklin House, 1983); M. Lefkowitz, *Not Out of Africa: How Afrocentrism Became an Excuse to Teach Myth as History* (New York: Basic Books, 1996).

18. J. Bacque, *Other Losses: An Investigation into the Mass Deaths of German Prisoners at the Hands of the French and Americans After World War II* (Toronto: Stoddart, 1989).

19. A. Cowdrey and S. Ambrose, "A Review of *Other Losses*," *Canadian Bulletin of Medical History* 7 (1990): 187–191; 8 (1991): 17–20.

20. Quoted in B. Bailer-Galanda and W. Neugebauer, *Incorrigibly Right: Right-Wing Extremists, "Revisionists" and Anti-Semites in Austrian Politics To-*

day (Austria: Stiftung Dokumentationsarchiv des österreichischen Widerstandes, 1996), 45.

21. J. Wikoff in *Remarks* (newsletter) 1990.

22. Ibid., 3; emphasis in original.

23. "How to Cut Violent Crime in Half: An Immodest Proposal," *Instauration,* January 1994.

24. L. A. Rollins, *Lucifer's Lexicon* (Port Townsend, Wash.: Loompanics, 1987).

25. Weber, interview (1994).

26. *Tales of the Holohoax* (Champaign, Ill.: Wiswell Ruffin House, n.d.).

27. Advertisement, *Washington Post,* August 7, 1986.

28. Ibid.

29. D. Brockschmidt, "The Jewish-Nazi Holocaust: The Gloves Are Off," *Adelaide Institute Newsletter,* May 1996, 1.

30. *The New Order,* July–August 1996, 4.

31. J. George and L. Wilcox, *Nazis, Communists, Klansmen, and Others on the Fringe* (Buffalo, N.Y.: Prometheus Books, 1992), 63.

32. Ibid., 58–61.

33. Bailer-Galanda and Neugebauer, *Incorrigibly Right* (1996), 10.

34. D. Bell, *The Radical Right* (New York: Doubleday, 1991), 14.

35. M. Rokeach, *The Open and Closed Mind: Investigations into the Nature of Belief Systems and Personality Systems* (New York: Basic Books, 1969), 6.

36. T. Goertzel, *Turncoats and True Believers: The Dynamics of Political Belief and Disillusionment* (Buffalo, N.Y.: Prometheus Books, 1992), 36.

37. Ibid., 40.

38. Ibid., 367.

39. Richard Nixon, "America Has Slipped to Number Two," *Parade,* October 5, 1980.

40. Quoted in F. FitzGerald, "The Reverend Jerry Falwell," *The New Yorker,* May 18, 1981.

41. Nixon, "America Has Slipped" (1980); see also D. P. Barash, *Beloved Enemies: Our Need for Opponents* (Buffalo, N.Y.: Prometheus Books, 1994).

42. S. P. Huntington, "The Clash of Civilizations?" *Foreign Affairs* 72 (1993): 22, 33.

43. M. Weber, IHR fundraising letter, July 1998. All subsequent quotes in this paragraph are from this source.

44. C. Geertz, *The Interpretation of Cultures* (New York: Basic Books, 1973).

45. S. Freud, *Group Psychology and Analysis of the Ego* (c. 1922), in *Complete Psychological Works of Sigmund Freud,* 18: 126 (London: Hogarth Press, 1940).

46. Barash, *Beloved Enemies* (1994), 137.

47. C. P. Cavafy, *Collected Poems,* ed. G. Savidis, trans. E. Keeley and P. Sherrard (Princeton: Princeton University Press, 1975).

48. L. Christensen, *Skinhead Street Gangs* (Boulder, Colo.: Paladin Press, 1994), 1–16.

49. F. Nietzsche, *The Twilight of the Idols* (1880) (New York: Viking, 1954), 114.

50. *Die Kameradschaft* 4 (August 8, 1990).

51. L. Coser, *The Functions of Social Conflict* (Glencoe, Ill.: Free Press, 1956), 12.

52. Quoted in Anti-Defamation League of B'nai B'rith, *Hitler's Apologists: The Anti-Semitic Propaganda of Holocaust 'Revisionism'* (New York, 1993).

53. Herman Melville, *Moby Dick* (New York: Washington Square Press, [1851] 1964), 391.

5. HOW DENIERS DISTORT HISTORY

1. D. J. Goldhagen, *Hitler's Willing Executioners: Ordinary Germans and the Holocaust* (New York: Alfred A. Knopf, 1996); Rosenbaum, *Explaining Hitler* (1998). See, for example, the exchange of letters in the *New York Review of Books*, May 23, 1996, following the April 4 review of Goldhagen's book—a heated exchange repeated in both print and electronic media throughout 1996.

2. Smith's ad is headlined "The Holocaust Controversy: The Case for Open Debate." Other sources for these ideas include our 1994 interviews with Weber, Irving, Cole, and Zündel; Weber, "Auschwitz: Myths and Facts" (Newport Beach, Calif.: Institute for Historical Review, 1993); and Weber, "The Holocaust: Let's Hear Both Sides" (Newport Beach, Calif.: Institute for Historical Review, 1994).

3. See Shermer, *Why People Believe Weird Things* (1997).

4. Smith, *Smith's Report* 19 (winter 1994).

5. M. Weber, "The Nuremberg Trials and the Holocaust," *Journal of Historical Review* 12, no. 2 (1992): 167–213.

6. Zündel, interview (1994).

7. Cole, interview (1994).

8. Irving, interview (1994).

9. Weber, interview (1994).

10. See E. T. Linenthal and T. Engelhardt, *History Wars: The Enola Gay and Other Battles for the American Past* (New York: Henry Holt, 1996).

11. S. E. Ambrose, *Citizen Soldiers: The U.S. Army from the Normandy Beaches to the Bulge to the Surrender of Germany, June 7, 1944 to May 7, 1945* (New York: Simon and Schuster, 1997).

12. Quoted in B. Russell, *The Record: The Trial of Adolf Eichmann for His Crimes Against the Jewish People and Against Humanity* (New York: Alfred A. Knopf, 1963), 278–79. See also H. Arendt, *Eichmann in Jerusalem* (New York: Compass/Viking, 1965).

13. See P. Rassinier, *Debunking the Genocide Myth: A Study of the Nazi Concentration Camps and the Alleged Extermination of European Jewry* (Los Angeles: Noontide Press, 1978).

14. N. Sagi, *German Reparations: A History of the Negotiations* (Jerusalem: Magnes Press, 1980), 55.

15. Weber, interview (1994).

16. Ibid.; Irving, interview (1994).

17. A. Speer, *Spandau: The Secret Diaries* (New York: Macmillan, 1976), 27.

18. Quoted in Klee et al., *"The Good Old Days"* (1992), 217.

19. Spector, "Aktion 1005" (1990); see also the Jäger report on Einsatz-gruppen activity, discussed in chapter 7.

20. Nuremberg document [N.D.] 3197-PS.

21. Spector, "Aktion 1005" (1990), 159–61.

22. Ibid.

23. R. Breitman, *Official Secrets: What the Nazis Planned, What the British and Americans Knew* (New York: Hill and Wang, 1998).

24. Rassinier, *Debunking the Genocide Myth* (1978), 36.

25. See, for example, Weber's interview (1994) and Bradley Smith's college newspaper advertisement.

26. Browning, *Path to Genocide* (1991); H. Friedlander, *The Origins of Nazi Genocide: From Euthanasia to the Final Solution* (Chapel Hill: University of North Carolina Press, 1995); S. J. Gould, *The Mismeasure of Man* (New York: W. W. Norton, 1981); D. Kevles, *In the Name of Eugenics: Genetics and the Uses of Human Heredity* (Berkeley: University of California Press, 1985).

27. *Donahue* transcript in Skeptics Society research library, Altadena, Calif. All quotations from the show are from this source.

28. T. Blatt, "Soap from Human Fat: Evidence of a Nazi Crime" (1996), man-uscript in collection of Skeptics Society research library, Altadena, Calif.

29. D. Lipstadt, *Beyond Belief: The American Press and the Coming of the Holocaust, 1933–1945* (New York: Free Press, 1986).

30. Blatt, "Soap from Human Fat" (1996).

31. International Military Tribunal, *Trials of War Criminals* (1947), 7:598–601 (LOC D810.J4 F36).

32. T. Blatt, *Sobibor: A Forgotten Revolt* (Issaquah, Wash.: HEP Publishing, 1996), 7.

33. R. Hilberg, interview with M. Shermer, Altadena, Calif., April 10, 1994, transcript in Skeptics Society research library.

34. Gutman, interview (1996).

35. All of these arguments by the deniers come from the 1994 interviews with Weber, Irving, Zündel, and Cole, as well as numerous issue of the *Journal of Historical Review* and such works as Butz's *The Hoax of the Twentieth Century* (1976) and Rassinier's *Debunking the Genocide Myth* (1978).

6. THE CROOKED TIMBER OF AUSCHWITZ

1. I. Kant, "Idee zweiner allgeineinen Geschichte in weltbürgerlicher Absicht," in *Kant's Gersammelte Schriften* 8: 23 (Berlin, 1912).

2. S. J. Gould, *The Flamingo's Smile* (New York: W. W. Norton, 1985), 174.

3. See S. Milgram, *Obedience to Authority: An Experimental View* (New York: Harper, 1969); H. C. Kelman and V. L. Hamilton, *Crimes of Obedience: Toward a Psychology of Authority and Responsibility* (New Haven: Yale University Press, 1989); R. J. Lifton, *The Nazi Doctors: Medical Killing and the Psychology of Genocide* (New York: Basic Books, 1986).

4. See H. Friedlander, *Origins of Nazi Genocide* (1995); E. Kogon, H. Lang-bein, and A. Rückerl, eds, *Nazi Mass Murder: A Documentary History of the Use of Poison Gas* (New Haven: Yale University Press, 1993).

5. See Friedlander, *Origins of Nazi Genocide* (1995).

6. See ibid., for a history of the T4 and euthanasia program.

7. Ernst Klee presents T4 documents confirming these figures, as well as data of so-called mentally ill persons killed in occupied territories in the east, including between 1,800 to 2,200 killed in Riga, Jelgava, and Dvinsk; 544 in Aglona; 545 in Poltava; 836 in Minsk and Mogilev; 1,500 in Dnepropetrovsk; 240 in Markayevo; and 360 in Kiev (Ernst Klee, *"Euthanasie" im NS-Staat: Die Vernichtung "Lebensunwerten Lebens"* [Frankfurt, 1985]). In the Nuremberg trials the number of euthanized persons was estimated at 275,000, although historians place the cumulative figure at roughly 200,000 (see Lifton, *Nazi Doctors* [1986]; F. Mielke, *Medizin ohne Menschlichkeit: Dokumente des Nürnberger Arzteprozesses* [Frankfurt, 1960]; K. Nowak, *"Euthanasie" und Sterilisierung im Dritten Reich: Die Konfrontation der evangelischen und katholischen Kirche mit dem Gesetz sur "Verhütung erbkranken Nachwuchses" und der "Euthanasie"-Aktion* [Göttingen, 1978]; and W. Wuttke-Groneberg, *Medizin im Nationalsozialismus: Ein Arbeitsbuch* [Rottenburg, 1982]).

According to surviving files, the breakdown for the number of people "disinfected" in the "euthanasia" facilities is:

Institute	1940	1941	Total
Grafeneck	9,839	—	9,839
Brandenburg	9,772	—	9,772
Bernburg	—	8,601	8,601
Hartheim	9,670	8,599	18,269
Sonnenstein	5,943	7,777	13,720
Hadamar	—	10,072	10,072
Total	35,224	35,049	70,273

(SOURCE: GStA Frankfurt a/Main AZ: Ks 1/66, judgment of 20 December 20, 1968, 44 [ZSL Coll.: 426]).

8. Dr. Brandt's deposition in "Physicians' Trial," record of evidence, 2419–25.

9. See "Physicians' Trial," record of evidence, 7654, 7661ff; Viktor Brack deposition, GStA Frankfurt a/Main AZ: Ks 1/66 (JS 15/61); depositions by Dr. Hefelmann of August 31, 1960, by Dr. Nietsche of March 11,1948, and by Dr. Heyde of October 12 to December 22, 1961 (AZ: ZSL: 439 AR-Z 340/59, "euthanasia" file, subfiles "Hefelmann" and "Heyde").

10. Quoted in Friedlander, *Origins of Nazi Genocide* (1995), 97.

11. Ibid., 284.

12. See discussion in Kogon et al., *Nazi Mass Murder* (1993), 14–17.

13. A. J. Mayer, *Why Did the Heavens Not Darken?* (New York: Pantheon, 1990), 362.

14. Ibid.

15. See Friedlander, *Origins of Nazi Genocide* (1995), 287.

16. F. Leuchter, *The Leuchter Report: An Engineering Report on the Alleged Execution Chambers at Auschwitz, Birkenau, and Majdanek, Poland* (London: Focal Point, 1989), 10. Since he produced this first report, Leuchter generated *The Second Leuchter Report* on Dachau, Mauthausen, and Hartheim; *The Third*

Leuchter Report: A Technical Report on the Execution Gas Chamber at Mississippi State Penitentiary, and *The Fourth Leuchter Report: An Engineering Evaluation of Jean-Claude Pressac's Book "Auschwitz: Technique and Operation of the Gas Chambers."* All appear to be published in 1989 by Ernst Zündel's Samizdat Publishers in Toronto (no publication dates are given). Interestingly, although David Irving now distances himself from Leuchter (see below), the copy of *The Leuchter Report* in our archives was published by Irving's publishing house (Focal Point), and includes a foreword by Irving.

17. R. Kammerer and A. Solms, eds., *The Rudolf Report: A Discussion of the Rudolf Report on the Formation and Demonstrability of Cyanide Compounds in the Gas Chambers at Auschwitz, with additional research findings on the Holocaust* (Uckfield, Sussex, England: Cromwell Press, 1993), 11.

18. W. Lüeftl, "The Lüeftl Report," *Journal of Historical Review* 12, no. 4 (1992): 391.

19. S. Shapiro, ed., *Truth Prevails: Demolishing Holocaust Denial—The End of "The Leuchter Report"* (New York: Beate Klarsfeld Foundation, 1990); J.-C. Pressac and R. J. van Pelt, "The Machinery of Mass Murder at Auschwitz," in *Anatomy of the Auschwitz Death Camp*, ed. Y. Gutman and M. Berenbaum (Bloomington: Indiana University Press, 1994).

20. *Her Majesty the Queen vs. Ernst Zündel*, District Court of Ontario, 1988.

21. S. Trombley, *The Execution Protocol: Inside America's Capital Punishment Industry* (New York: Crown, 1992), 90.

22. See also Zündel, interview (1994).

23. *Canada News* 1993, 12.

24. *Her Majesty the Queen vs. Ernst Zündel*, District Court of Ontario, 1988.

25. Irving, interview (1994).

26. Leuchter, *Leuchter Report* (1989); Cole, interview (1994), and Faurisson, "The 'Problem of the Gas Chambers,'" (n.d.).

27. One of the best sources of primary documentation on the use of poison gas by the Nazis is Kogon et al., *Nazi Mass Murder* (1993). J.-C. Pressac's *Auschwitz: Technique and Operation of the Gas Chambers* (New York: Beate Klarsfeld Foundation, 1989) also documents the killing process. See also P. S. Choumoff, *Les Chambres á gas de Mauthausen* (The gas chambers at Mauthausen) (Paris, 1972); R. Höss, *Commandant of Auschwitz: The Autobiography of Rudolf Hoess* (Cleveland: World, 1959; original German manuscript in the Auschwitz-Birkenau State Museum); A. Lettich, *Trente-quatre mois dans les camps de concentration* (Thirty-four months in the concentration camps) (Tours: L'Union Coopérative, 1946); Z. Pawlak, *Ich Habe Uberlebt: Ein Häftling Berichtet über Majdanek* (I survived: A prisoner reports about Majdanek) (Hamburg: Hoffman und Campe, 1979); F. Puntigam, H. Breymesser, and E. Bernfuss, *Blausäurekammern zur Fleckfieberabwehr* (Chambers of prussic acid in the defense against exanthematous typhus) (Berlin, 1943).

28. See Leuchter, *Leuchter Report* (1989); *Her Majesty the Queen vs. Ernst Zündel*, District Court of Ontario, 1988.

29. Shapiro, *Truth Prevails* (1990), 45; Pressac, *Auschwitz* (1989), 15–22.

30. Pressac, *Auschwitz* (1989), 53–86.

31. D. Cole, "Forty-Six Important Unanswered Questions Regarding the

Nazi Gas Chambers" (posted on www.codoh.com with cover letter by Bradley R. Smith, October 9, 1995), 2.

32. Ibid., 3.

33. Leuchter, *Leuchter Report* (1989); Cole, "Forty-Six Important Unanswered Questions" (1995); and Faurisson, "The 'Problem of the Gas Chambers,'" (n.d.).

34. Dwork and van Pelt, *Auschwitz* (1996), 272–78.

35. See Gutman and Berenbaum, *Anatomy of the Auschwitz Death Camp* (1994), 485–537.

36. Ibid.

37. Quoted in G. Reitlinger, *The Final Solution* (New York: Beechhurst Press [1953] 1978), 158.

38. Quoted in Pressac, *Auschwitz* (1989), 434.

39. Broad in R. Höss, P. Broad, and J. P. Kremer, *KL Auschwitz Seen by the SS* (Oswiecim: Auschwitz-Birkenau State Museum, 1994), 103–48.

40. Ibid.

41. Cole, interview (1994); Weber, interview (1994).

42. Pressac, *Auschwitz* (1989), 15–22.

43. Quoted in Höss et al., *KL Auschwitz* (1994), 27–102.

44. Ibid., 162.

45. Zentrale Stelle 1945, 6:1148; see M. Tregenza, "Analysis of Majdanek Gas Chambers and Transcript of Sworn Affidavit from Rudolf Reder" (Zentrale Stelle der Landesjustizverwaltungen, Ludwigsburg, 1945, GFR. File No. 208 AR-Z 252/59) (1996 manuscript).

46. Quoted in Klee et al., *"The Good Old Days"* (1992), 254–55.

47. Quoted in Tregenza, "Analysis" (1996).

48. Personal correspondence from Ball to Michael Shermer, December 12, 1995.

49. J. C. Ball, *Air Photo Evidence: Auschwitz, Treblinka, Majdanek, Sobibor, Bergen Belsen, Belzec, Babi Yar, Katyn Forest* (Delta, B.C., Canada: Ball Resource Services, 1992), 37–48.

50. D. Brugioni and R. Poirier, *The Holocaust Revisited: A Retrospective Analysis of the Auschwitz-Birkenau Extermination Complex* (Washington, D.C. Central Intelligence Agency, 1979).

51. Ibid. A complete set of the relevant aerial photographs presented in this book can be ordered through the National Archives in Washington, D.C. They are located in Record Group 373 of the Defense Intelligence Agency, Can D 1508, exposures 3055, 3056; Can C 1172, exposure 5022; Can F 5367, exposures 3182 to 3187; Can B 8413, exposures 6V2, 6V3, 3VI; Can D 1535, exposures 4018, 4019; GX DT/TM-3. Germany-East Auschwitz No. 38; GX 225, 452 SK, exposure 138; GX 12337, 188 SD, exposures 145, 146. The complete cost for the photographs in 1995 was $229.50.

For additional discussions of the aerial photographs and their interpretation, see Aiming Point Report IV.D.4, *I.G. Farben, Oswiecim, Silesia* (Synthetic Rubber), January 21, 1944 (National Archives, Washington, D.C., RG 243, Sec 4–1g [141,142, 163], NND 760124); British Air Ministry, *Evidence in Camera, Photographic Reconnaissance and Intelligence, 1939 to 1945* (London, March 1945); Interpretation Report No. D. 389, *I.G. Farben Synthetic Rubber and Synthetic*

Oil Plant, Oswiecim (Auschwitz), June 9, 1944 (National Archives, Washington, D.C., NND 760129); Interpretation Report No. D.B. 217, *Mediterranean Allied Photo Reconnaissance Wing, Bombing Damage Report,* September 1944 (National Archives, Washington, D.C., NND 760123).

52. See R. J. van Pelt, "A Site in Search of a Mission," in *Anatomy of the Auschwitz Death Camp,* ed. Y. Gutman and M. Berenbaum (Bloomington: Indiana University Press, 1994), and Dwork and van Pelt, *Auschwitz* (1996), 307–54, for references and detailed evidence for these figures and conclusions, as well as those below.

53. The information in this paragraph is from the *Auschwitz Chronicle* [1990]. See also Dwork and van Pelt, *Auschwitz* (1996), 236–306; F. Piper, "The Number of Victims," in Y. Gutman and M. Berenbaum, *Anatomy of the Auschwitz Death Camp* (Bloomington: Indiana University Press, 1994), 61–80.

54. Dwork and van Pelt 1996, 351–54.

55. All listings in the *Auschwitz Chronicle* [1990] are by chronological sequence and we refer to them as such.

56. Irving's Web site (www.fpp.co.uk).

57. Van Pelt, "A Site in Search of a Mission" (1994), 93.

58. Ibid., 94.

59. Dwork and van Pelt, *Auschwitz* (1996), 11.

60. Ibid., 154.

61. Ibid., 158.

62. Ibid., 309.

63. See van Pelt, "A Site in Search of a Mission" (1994), for details of the evolution traced in this paragraph.

64. Quoted in ibid., 148.

65. Quoted in ibid., 149.

66. M. Broszat, "Nationalsozialistische Konzentrationslager 1933–1945," in *Anatomie des SS-Staates,* ed. H. Bucheim, 2 vols. (Munich: Deutscher Taschenbuchverlag, 1967); F. Pingel, *Häftlinge unter SS-Herrschaft* (Hamburg: Hoffmann und Campe, 1978); see also J. von Lang, ed., *Eichmann Interrogated: Transcripts from the Archives of the Israeli Police* (New York: Farrar, Straus and Giroux, 1983).

67. Van Pelt, "A Site in Search of a Mission" (1994), 150–51. See Broszat, "Nationalsozialistische Konzentrationslager" (1967), and Pingel, *Häftlinge* (1978), for further discussions on the multiple uses of the camps.

68. See Dwork and van Pelt, *Auschwitz* (1996), 270–75.

69. J. Marszalek, *Majdanek: The Concentration Camp in Lublin* (Warsaw: Interpress, 1986), 10–35.

70. Van Pelt, "A Site in Search of a Mission" (1994), 114.

71. Quoted in Shapiro, *Truth Prevails* (1990), 49.

72. Ibid., 50.

73. Tregenza, "Analysis" (1996).

74. Ibid.

75. See Marszakek, *Majdanek* (1986); Pawlak, *Ich Habe Uberlebt* (1979).

76. See Marszalek, *Majdanek* (1986).

77. Ibid.

78. Ibid.

79. M. Tregenza, interview with A. Grobman, Altadena, Calif., April 29, 1996 (transcript in Skeptics Society research library).

80. Michael Tregenza, personal correspondence, 1997.

81. Tregenza, "Analysis" (1996).

82. Letter from Faurisson to Michael Shermer, April 12, 1995.

83. Quoted in L. Rosenthal, *"The Final Solution to the Jewish Question":
Mass-Murder or Hoax?* trans. R. Lackner (Berkeley: Institute for Righteous Acts, 1984), 73.

84. Cole, interview (1994).

85. See J. Marzalek, *Mauthausen* (Vienna: Steindl-Druck, 1995). See also E. Dziadosz, *Majdanek* (Lublin, 1980); Z. Leszczynska, *Kronika Obozu na Majdanku* (Lublin, 1980); H. Lichtenstein, *Majdanek: Reportage Eines Prozesses* (Frankfurt am Main, 1979); Z. Murawska, "Kobiety w Obozie Koncentracyjnym na Majdanku," *Zeszyty Majdanka* 4 (1969); C. Rajca, "Analiza Danych Personalnych Wiezniow Majdanka," *Zeszyty Majdanka* 2 (1973).

7. "FOR GOD'S SAKE—TERRIBLE"

1. Rassinier, *Debunking the Genocide Myth* (1978), 278.

2. R. Hilberg, *The Destruction of the European Jews* (Chicago: Quadrangle Books, 1961); Y. Gutman and R. Rozett, "Estimated Jewish Losses in the Holocaust," *Encyclopedia of the Holocaust,* ed. Y. Gutman, vol. 4 (New York: Macmillan, 1990); Reitlinger, *The Final Solution* ([1953] 1978). For the numbers of Jews killed in the extermination camps, see also I. Arndt and W. Scheffler, "Organisierter Massenmord an Juden in nationalsozialistischen Vernichtungslagern," *Vierteljahrshefte für Zeitgeschichte* 24 (1976): 105–35.

3. Irving, interview (1994); Weber, interview (1994).

4. See H.-J. Döscher, *Das Auswärtige Amt im Dritten Reich: Diplomatie im Schatten der 'Endlösung'* (Berlin: Siedler, 1987); E. Nolte, "Vergangenheit, die nicht vergehen will: Eine Rede, die Geschrieben, Aber Nicht Gehalten Werden Konnte," *Frankfurter Allgemeine Zeitung,* June 6, 1986; J. Walk, ed., *Das Sonderrecht für Juden im NS-Staat: Eine Sammlung der gesetzlichen Massnahmen und Richtlinien—Inhalt und Bedeutung* (Heidelberg: C. F. Müller Juristischer Verlag, 1981); and R. Hilberg and U. D. Adam, *Judenpolitik im Dritten Reich* (Düsseldorf: Droste Verlag, 1979).

5. N.D. 2738-PS, 31: 85 ff.

6. W. Benz, *Dimension des Volkermords: Die Zahl der Jüdischen Opfer des Nationalsozialismus* (Munich: Deutscher Taschenbuch Verlag, 1991), 2, our translation.

7. Ibid., 17.

8. Hilberg 1961, 121.

9. G. Wellers, "The Number of Victims and the Korherr Report," in Serge Klarsfeld, ed., *The Holocaust and the Neo-Nazi Mythomania,* trans. B. Rucci (New York: Beate Klarsfeld Foundation, 1978), 145–94.

10. Hilberg, *Destruction of the European Jews* (1961), 173–75.

11. Gutman, interview (1996).

12. Butz, *Hoax* (1976), 10–12.

13. Gutman and Berenbaum, *Anatomy of the Auschwitz Death Camp* (1994), 526.

14. Z. Gradowski, *In the Heart of Hell* (Jerusalem, 1944), 21.

15. L. Langfus, "Horrors of Murder," in *Szukajcie w Popiolach* (Lodz: Committee for Investigation of Nazi War Crimes in Poland, 1965), 361.

16. F. Müller, *Eyewitness Auschwitz: Three Years in the Gas Chambers* (New York: Stein and Day, 1979), 33–34, 61.

17. Released by Thames, the film was produced and directed by Andrew Mollo, with research by Mike Maddison and Pamela Portugall.

18. This quotation, as well as the earlier ones by Elber and Klehr, were transcribed by us from the film *History of the SS*.

19. See C. Browning, *Path to Genocide* (1991), and Browning, *Ordinary Men* (New York: HarperCollins, 1992).

20. Quoted in C. Lanzmann, *Shoah: An Oral History of the Holocaust* (New York: Pantheon, 1985), 53, 54.

21. G. Sereny, *Albert Speer: His Battle with Truth* (New York: Alfred A. Knopf, 1995), 343.

22. For additional documentary reports on large numbers of Jews, including women and children, killed by the Einsatzgruppen, see H. Krausnick and H. H. Wilhelm, *Die Truppe des Weltanschauungskrieges: Die Einsatzgruppen der Sicherheitspolizei und des SD 1938–1942* (Stuttgart: Deutsche Verlagsanstalt, 1981), 117, and A. Streim, "The Tasks of the SS Einsatzgruppen," *Simon Wiesenthal Center Annual* 4 (1987): 309–28.

23. Krausnick and Wilhelm, *Truppe des Weltanschauungskrieges* (1981), 231.

24. Kogon et al., *Nazi Mass Murder* (1993), 228–29.

25. H. Krausnick, H. Buchheim, M. Broszart, and H. Jacobsen, eds., *Anatomy of the SS State* (London: Collins, 1968), 62.

26. Quoted in Klee et al., *"The Good Old Days"* (1992), 173.

27. Ibid., 163–71.

28. N.D. 3363-PS, 891.

29. Ibid., 892.

30. Original document and translation courtesy of National Archives, Washington, D.C., T 992, PS 2233. The German text reads:

Wir haben im Generalgourvernement schätzungsweise 2,5, vielleicht mit den jüdisch Versippten und dem, was alles daran hängt, jetzt 3,5 Millionen Juden. Diese 3,5 Millionen Juden konnen wir nicht erschießen, wir können sie nicht vergiften, werden aber doch mingriffe vornehmen können, die irgendwie zu einem Vernichtungseriolg führen, und zwar im Zusammenhang mit den vom Reich her zu besprechenden großen Maßnahmen. Das Generalgouvernement muß genau so judenfrei werden, wie es das Reich ist. Wo und wie das geschieht, ist eine Sache der Instanzen, Sie wir hier einsetzen und schaffen müssen und deren Wirksamkeit ich ihnen rechtzeitig bekanntgeben werde.

31. All quoted in Broszat, "Nationalsozialistische Konzentrationslager" (1967), 143, our translation.

32. Transcript of Goebbels's speech of September 23, 1942, from British Pub-

lic Record Office; in collection Martyrs Memorial and Museum of the Holocaust, Los Angeles.

33. Irving, interview (1994).

34. From transcript of Goebbels's speech, September 23, 1942.

35. Irving, interview (1994).

36. D. Irving, *Goebbels: Mastermind of the Third Reich* (London: Focal Point, 1996), 387–88 (including quotations from Goebbels).

37. D. Irving, "Revelations from Goebbels' Diary: Bringing to Light Secrets of Hitler's Propaganda Minister," *Journal of Historical Review* 15, no. 1 (1995): 17.

38. Quoted in Irving, *Goebbels* (1996).

39. Originally the book was to be published by St. Martin's Press. However, after the negative publicity, St. Martin's ceased production and distribution, and the book was published by Irving's own Focal Point Publications in London.

40. Irving, *Goebbels* (1996), 388.

41. P. Padfield, *Himmler* (New York: Henry Holt, 1990), 188.

42. Ibid., 334.

43. The tape is archived at the United States Holocaust Memorial Museum, Washington, D.C.

44. N.D. 1919-PS, 64–67.

45. Irving, interview (1994).

46. Quoted in Bauer 1994, 83.

47. N.D. 1120, prosecution exhibit 237.

48. Ibid.

49. Quoted in Y. Bauer, *Jews for Sale?: Nazi-Jewish Negotiations, 1933–1945* (New Haven: Yale University Press, 1994), 105.

50. Quoted in Sereny, *Speer* (1995), 420.

51. All Hitler quotes above from E. Jäckel, "Hitler Orders the Holocaust," in *The Nazi Holocaust,* ed. M. Marrus, vol. 3 (London: Meckler, 1989), 25–31.

52. Quoted in E. Jäckel, *David Irving's Hitler: A Faulty History Dissected* (Port Angeles, Wash.: Ben-Simon Publications, 1993), 29.

53. Quoted in ibid, 32.

54. Quoted in L. Snyder, ed., *Hitler's Third Reich* (Chicago: Nelson Hall 1981), 29.

55. Quoted in Jäckel, *Irving's Hitler* (1993), 33.

56. Quoted in Snyder, *Hitler's Third Reich* (1981), 521.

8. THE EVIL OF BANALITY

1. R. F. Baumeister, *Evil: Inside Human Violence and Cruelty* (New York: W. H. Freeman, 1997), 379.

2. Quoted in M. Berenbaum, *The World Must Know: The History of the Holocaust as Told in the United States Holocaust Memorial Museum* (New York: Little, Brown, 1993), 204.

3. Quoted in Irving, *Hitler's War* (1977), 427.

4. Ibid., 505, 504.

5. Hilberg, interview (1994).

6. Irving, *Hitler's War* (1977), 427.

7. Quoted in Sereny, *Speer* (1995), 362.

8. Translated in H. Friedlander, *Origins of Nazi Genocide* (1995), 67. See "Physicians' Trial," record of evidence, 7654, 7661ff; Viktor Brack deposition, GStA Frankfurt a/Main AZ: Ks 1/66 (JS 15/61); depositions by Dr. Hefelmann of August 31, 1960, by Dr. Nietsche of March 11, 1948, and by Dr. Heyde of October 12 to December 22, 1961 (AZ: ZSL: 439 AR-Z 340/59, "euthanasia" file, subfiles "Hefelmann" and "Heyde"). Although issued in October, the letter was actually predated September 1, 1939, to coincide with the start of the war.

9. Only the copy belonging to Gürtner has survived.

10. GStA Frankfurt a/Main AZ: Ks 1/69, judgment of May 27, 1970 (ZSL Coll.: 435, 42).

11. Ibid., 46.

12. Friedlander, *Origins of Nazi Genocide* (1995), 111; documents presented at GStA Frankfurt a/Main AZ: Ks 2/63 (Js 17/59), indictment, 489.

13. Gutman, interview (1996).

14. Hilberg, *Destruction of the European Jews* (1961), 55.

15. Quoted in P. Witte, "Two Decisions Concerning the 'Final Solution to the Jewish Question': Deportations to Lodz and Mass Murder in Chelmno," trans. B. Richardson, *Holocaust and Genocide Studies* 9, no. 3 (winter 1995): 318.

16. Ibid., 330.

17. Quoted in ibid., 330–31.

18. Ibid., 331.

19. Irving, *Hitler's War* (1977), 397.

20. Irving, interview (1994).

21. See, for example, *Langenscheidt's German-English, English-German Dictionary* (Berlin: Langenscheidt, 1942). Under *ausrotten* the dictionary gives "root out; extirpate, exterminate." Under "exterminate" it lists *ausrotten* and *vestilgen*.

22. Irving, interview (1994).

23. Ibid.

24. Irving, *Hitler's War* (1977), 867.

25. N.D. 2738-PS, 4:355ff.

26. See L. Dawidowicz, *The War Against the Jews, 1933–45* (New York: Bantam, 1975); S. Taylor, *Prelude to Genocide: Nazi Ideology and the Struggle for Power* (London: Duckworth, 1985); G. Fleming, *Hitler and the Final Solution* (Berkeley: University of California Press, 1984); and Goldhagen, *Hitler's Willing Executioners* (1996).

27. See T. Mason, "Intention and Explanation: A Current Controversy About the Interpretation of National Socialism," in *Der Führerstatt: Mythos und Realität,* ed. G. Hirschfeld and L. Kettenacker (Stuttgart, 1981), 21–40. For other functionalists' arguments, see M. Broszat, "Hitler und die Genesis der 'Endlösung,'" *Vierteljarshefte für Zeitgeschichte* 25 (1977): 739–75; K. A. Schleunes, *The Twisted Road to Auschwitz: Nazi Policy toward the Jews, 1933–1939* (Urbana: University of Illinois Press, 1970); and C. Browning, *Fateful Months: Essays on the Final Solution* (New York: Holmes and Meier, 1985).

28. Schleunes, *Twisted Road to Auschwitz* (1970); Broszat, "Hitler und die

Genesis der 'Endlösung'" (1977); H. Mommsen, "Die Realisierung des Utopi-schen: Die 'Endlösung der Judenfrage' im 'Dritten Reich,'" *Geschichte und Gesellschaft* 9, no. 3 (autumn 1983): 381–420.

29. Hilberg, interview (1994).

30. Quoted in J. Fest, *Hitler* (New York: Harcourt Brace Jovanovich, 1974), 392.

31. L. Yahil, *The Holocaust* (Oxford: Oxford University Press, 1987), 5.

32. R. Headland, *Messages of Murder: A Study of the Reports of the Ein-satzgruppen of the Security Police and Security Service 1941–1943* (Rutherford, N.J.: Fairleigh Dickinson University Press, 1992), 194.

33. Gutman, interview (1996).

34. Bauer, *Jews for Sale?* (1994), 252–53.

35. Yahil, *Holocaust* (1987), 62.

36. S. Milton, "The Expulsion of Polish Jews from Germany: October 1938 to July 1939," *Yearbook of the Leo Baeck Institute* 29 (1984): 174.

37. Gutman, interview (1996).

38. Yahil, *Holocaust* (1987), 54.

39. Browning, *Path to Genocide* (1991), 143.

40. A. Speer, *Spandau: The Secret Diaries* (New York: Macmillan, 1976), 27.

41. M. Schmidt, *Albert Speer: The End of a Myth* (New York: St. Martin's Press, 1984), 181, 198.

42. Quoted in Sereny, *Speer* (1995), 354–55.

43. Quoted in ibid., 707.

44. Ibid., 708.

45. R. Harwood, *Did Six Million Really Die?: The Truth at Last* (London: Verrall, [1973]), 1.

46. Bailer-Galanda and Neugebauer, *Incorrigibly Right* (1996), 20.

47. M. Marrus, *The Holocaust in History* (New York: Penguin, 1987), 11.

48. The original document is in Archiv des Auswärtigen Amtes, Bonn (Archives of the Foreign Office of the Federal Republic of Germany). The entire document is reprinted and translated in A. Grobman, D. Landes, and S. Milton, eds., *Genocide: Critical Issues of the Holocaust* (Los Angeles: Simon Wiesenthal Center, 1983), 442–49. For a history and discussion, see also Y. Büchler, "Doc-ument: A Preparatory Document for the Wannsee 'Conference,'" *Holocaust and Genocide Studies* 9, no. 1 (spring 1995): 121–29.

49. For the standard deniers' interpretation of the Protocol, see Butz, 1976, 205–11; for the claim that the meeting might not have taken place, see E. Nolte, *The European Civil War, 1917–1945* (Berlin, 1987), 502–4. Also see the Ger-man publication "Das Wannsee-Protokoll," in *Guttenbriefe: für Dolfstun, Kul-tur, Marhheit und Recht,* June 1992, 2–5.

50. Interview with Michael Shermer, April 23, 1998.

51. See von Lang, *Eichmann Interrograted* (1983).

52. Wannsee Protocol, 1–2. A complete facsimile of the original document, titled *Die Wannsee-Konferenz vom 20. Januar 1942 Analyse und Dokumen-tation,* is available from the Gedenkstätte Haus der Wannsee-Konferenz, Berlin.

53. See J. Delarue, *The Gestapo: A History of Horror* (New York: William Morrow, 1964).

54. As noted in *Die Wannsee-Konferenz*.

55. Ibid.

56. Wannsee Protocol, 2–5.

57. Ibid., 5.

58. Ibid., 7–8.

59. See, for example, the testimonies of Pery Broad, Johann Paul Kremer, and Rudolf Höss in *KL Auschwitz Seen by the SS* (1994). See also Kogon et al., *Nazi Mass Murder* (1993), 174–201.

60. S. J. Gould, *Dinosaur in a Haystack* (New York: W. W. Norton, 1995), 315.

61. Wannsee Protocol, 8.

62. Ibid, 10–11.

63. Ibid., 12.

64. Ibid., 15.

65. H. Friedlander and S. Milton, eds., *The Holocaust: Ideology, Bureaucracy, and Genocide* (New York: Kraus International, 1980), 103–110; see also Krausnick et al., *Anatomy of the SS State* (1968).

66. Korherr Report, Institute for Contemporary History, Munich, ref. F. 12/8, fol. 803–4. Translated in "The First Unabridged Publication of the Two 'Korherr Reports,'" in S. Klarsfeld, ed., *The Holocaust and the Neo-Nazi Mania* (New York: Beate Klarsfeld Foundation, 1978), 165–210.

67. Ibid.

68. Quoted in Russell, *The Record* (1963), 173.

69. A. Hitler, *Hitler's Table Talk, 1941–1944*, trans. N. Cameron and R. H. Stevens (London: Weidenfeld and Nicolson, 1953), 235, emphasis added.

70. G. Barraclough, "Mandarins and the Nazis," *New York Review of Books*, October 19, 1972, 38.

71. W. Laqueur, "The Roots of Nazism," *New York Review of Books*, January 14, 1965, 37.

72. G. L. Mosse, *Nazi Culture* (New York: Schocken Books, 1966), xl.

73. See Kevles, *In the Name of Eugenics* (1985); Gould, *Mismeasure of Man* (1981).

74. H. Ahlwardt, *Reichstag, Stenographische Bericht* (1895), 1297.

75. T. Fritsch, *Antisemiten-Katechismus* (The racists' decalogue) (Leipzig, 1893), 358, our translation.

76. See Gould, *Mismeasure of Man* (1981), 50–68 (on Morton) and 158–73 (on Goddard).

77. See Kevles, *In the Name of Eugenics* (1985), 114–29, including a comparison between American and German laws (114–15); see 108–9 for discussion of the sterilization laws. Also see K. Ludmeier, *Genetics and American Society* (Baltimore: John Hopkins University Press, 1972), and G. Searle, *Eugenics and Politics in Britain, 1900–1914* (Leyden: Noordhoff International, 1976).

78. Quoted in Gould, *Mismeasure of Man* (1981), 335.

79. Quoted in Kevles, *In the Name of Eugenics* (1985), 117.

80. See H. Friedlander, *Origins of Nazi Genocide* (1995), 1–22.

81. A. Hitler, *Mein Kampf* [1925–27], trans. R. Manheim (Boston: Houghton Mifflin, 1943), 286, 291, 294, 296.

9. THE RAPE OF HISTORY

1. These statistics and the others in this section come from Iris Chang, *The Rape of Nanking: The Forgotten Holocaust of World War II* (New York: Basic Books, 1997). Among other sources, Chang cites figures established by the International Military Tribunal for the Far East, "Table: Estimated Number of Victims of Japanese Massacre in Nanking," document no. 1702, court exhibits, 1948, World War II War Crimes Records Collection, box 134, entry 14, record group 238, National Archives.

2. See Chang, *Rape of Nanking* (1997), 6–7. The Nazi quote comes from C. Kröger, "Days of Fate in Nanking" (unpublished diary in the collection of P. Kröger; also in the International Military Tribunal for the Far East judgment, National Archives).

3. See Chang, *Rape of Nanking* (1997), 215. The description of the "Three-all policy" is quoted from R. J. Rummel, *China's Bloody Century: Genocide and Mass Murder Since 1900* (New Brunswick, N.J.: Transaction, 1991), 139. The colonel's remark is quoted from D. Wilson, *When Tigers Fight: The Story of the Sino-Japanese War, 1937–1945* (New York: Viking, 1982), 61.

4. Chang, *Rape of Nanking* (1997), 216. The numerous sources for the total number of deaths are presented in Rummel, *China's Bloody Century* (1991). See also the court records for the International Military Tribunal for the Far East.

5. Chang, *Rape of Nanking* (1997), 219–20.

6. Ibid., 201.

7. Ibid. Quoted from D. Sheff, "Playboy Interview: Shintaro Ishihara—Candid Conversation," *Playboy*, October 1990, 63.

8. Chang, *Rape of Nanking* (1997), 201–2. Based on Yoshi Tsurumi, "Japan Makes Efforts to Be Less Insular," *New York Times*, December 25, 1990; Ishihara Shintaro, in *Journal of Studies of Japanese Aggression Against China*, February 1991, 71.

9. Chang, *Rape of Nanking* (1997), 202–3. Fujio and Okuno quoted from K. Schoenberger, "Japan Aide Quits over Remark on WWII," *Los Angeles Times*, May 14, 1988. Nagano quoted from S. Moffet, "Japan Justice Minister Denies Nanking Massacre," Reuters, May 4, 1994.

10. Chang, *Rape of Nanking* (1997), 207. Quoted from "Truth in Textbooks, Freedom in Education and Peace for Children: The Struggle Against the Censorship of School Textbooks in Japan" (Tokyo: National League for Support of the School Textbook Screening Suit, 2d. ed., June 1995).

11. Chang, *Rape of Nanking* (1997), 209. Noboru quoted from *New York Times*, November 3, 1991; Nobukatsu quoted from S. Efron, "Defender of Japan's War Past," *Los Angeles Times*, May 9, 1997.

12. Chang, *Rape of Nanking* (1997), 210–11. Quoted from R. E. Yates, "'Emperor' Film Keeps Atrocity Scenes in Japan," *Chicago Tribune*, January 23, 1988.

13. Chang, *Rape of Nanking* (1997), 212. See also Yang D. "A Sino-Japanese Controversy: The Nanjing Atrocity as History," *Sino-Japanese Studies* 3, no. 1 (November 1990).

14. Chang, *Rape of Nanking* (1997), 172; see also A. Brackman, *The Other Nuremberg: The Untold Story of the Tokyo War Crimes Trials* (New York: William Morrow, 1987).

15. M. Lefkowitz, *Not Out of Africa: How Afrocentrism Became an Excuse to Teach Myth as History* (New York: Basic Books, 1996), 2–4.

16. M. Bernal, *Black Athena: The Afroasiatic Roots of Classical Civilization*, 2 vols. (New Brunswick, N.J.: Rutgers University Press, 1997).

17. Lefkowitz, *Not Out of Africa* (1996), 171. See also M. Lefkowitz and G. M. Rogers, eds., *Black Athena Revisited* (Chapel Hill: University of North Carolina Press, 1997).

18. M. M. Levine, "The Use and Abuse of Black Athena," *American Historical Review* 97, no. 2 (1992): 440–60.

19. K. Feder, *Frauds, Myths, and Mysteries: Science and Pseudoscience in Archaeology* (Mountain View, Calif.: Mayfield, 1996), 9–10.

20. M. Cremo and R. L. Thompson, *Forbidden Archeology: The Hidden History of the Human Race* (San Diego: Bhaktivedanta Institute, 1993).

21. B. T. Lepper, "Hidden History, Hidden Agenda. A Review of Hidden History of the Human Race," *Skeptic* 4, no. 1 (1996): 100.

22. M. Cremo, *Forbidden Archeology's Impact* (San Diego: Bhaktivedanta Institute, 1998), jacket.

23. See K. Popper, *The Logic of Scientific Discovery* (New York: Harper and Row, 1959); T. Kuhn, *The Structure of Scientific Revolutions* (Chicago: University of Chicago Press, 1962).

24. B. Fell, *America B.C.: Ancient Settlers in the New World* (New York: Pocket Books, 1976).

25. G. Daniel, review of *America B.C.*, by Barry Fell, *New York Times*, March 13, 1977, 8ff.; see also F. Hole, "Saga America" (book review), *Bulletin of the Archaeological Society of Connecticut* 44 (1981): 81–83; M. McKusick, "Contemporary American Folklore about Antiquity," *Bulletin of the Philadelphia Anthropological Society* 28 (1976): 1–23.

26. R. H. Fritze, *Legend and Lore of the Americas Before 1492: An Encyclopedia of Visitors, Explorers, and Immigrants* (Santa Barbara, Calif.: ABC-CLIO, 1994).

27. R. H. Fritze, "Goodbye Columbus? The Pseudohistory of Who Discovered America," *Skeptic* 2, no. 4 (1994): 97.

28. J. W. Loewen, *Lies My Teacher Told Me: Everything Your American History Textbook Got Wrong* (New York: New Press, 1995), 305.

29. K. Feder, "Indians and Archaeologists: Conflicting Views of Myth and Science." *Skeptic* 5, no. 3 (1997): 74–81.

30. V. Deloria, Jr., *Red Earth, White Lies: Native Americans and the Myth of Scientific Fact* (New York: Scribners, 1995), 51–52.

31. J. Appleby, L. Hunt, and M. Jacob, *Telling the Truth about History* (New York: W. W. Norton, 1994), 3.

32. C. Merchant, *The Death of Nature: Women, Ecology, and the Scientific Revolution* (San Francisco: HarperCollins, 1980), xvi.

33. For quotations see R. Eisler, *The Chalice and the Blade* (New York: Harper and Row, 1987), 17, 18, 20, 43.

34. B. Fagan, ed., *The Oxford Companion to Archaeology* (Oxford: Oxford University Press, 1996), 120–21.

35. See Diamond, *Guns, Germs, and Steel* (1996).

36. Eisler, *Chalice and Blade* (1987), 164, 203.

37. Quoted in D. Freeman, "Paradigms in Collision: Margaret Mead's Mistake and What It Has Done to Anthropology," *Skeptic* 5, no. 3 (1997): 66.

38. Ibid.

39. Quoted in ibid., 67. Boas's remark is from 1925.

40. For a critique of Freeman, see J. E. Cote, "Much Ado About Nothing: The 'Fateful Hoaxing' of Margaret Mead," *Skeptical Inquirer* 22, no. 6 (1998): 29–34, and P. Shankman, "Margaret Mead, Derek Freeman, and the Issue of Evolution," *Skeptical Inquirer* 22, no. 6 (1998): 35–39. See also D. Freeman, "On the Ethics of Skeptical Inquiry," *Skeptical Inquirer* 22, no. 3 (1999): 60–61 (for a rebuttal), and J. Cote, "No Evidence Offered Relevant to Points Raised," *Skeptical Inquirer* 22, no. 3 (1999): 61–63, and P. Shankman, "Mead Was Not 'Unevolutionary,'" *Skeptical Inquirer* 22, no. 3 (1999): 63 (for a reply to Freeman's rebuttal).

41. See R. S. Nickerson, "Confirmation Bias: A Ubiquitous Phenomenon in Many Guises," *Review of General Psychology* 2, no. 2 (1998): 175–220.

42. Goldhagen, *Hitler's Willing Executioners* (1996), 14, 454.

43. See N. G. Finkelstein and R. B. Birn, *A Nation on Trial: The Goldhagen Thesis and Historical Truth* (New York: Henry Holt, 1998); A. D. Moses, "Structure and Agency in the Holocaust: Daniel J. Goldhagen and His Critics," *History and Theory* 37, no. 2 (1998): 194–219.

44. J. Lukacs, *The Hitler of History* (New York: Alfred A. Knopf, 1997).

45. R. Rosenbaum, *Explaining Hitler: The Search for the Origins of His Evil* (New York: Random House, 1998), xxv.

46. All quotations in this paragraph from ibid., many from personal interviews he conducted.

47. Ibid., xv.

48. C. Lanzmann, "The Obscenity of Understanding: An Evening with Claude Lanzmann," *American Imago* 48, no. 4 (1991): 473–95.

49. J. L. Talmon, "European History as the Seedbed of the Holocaust," in *Holocaust and Rebirth: A Symposium* (Jerusalem: Yad Vashem, 1973).

EPILOGUE: LIBEL, DENIAL, AND THE HOLOCAUST TRIAL

1. All quotations in this paragraph transcribed by M. Shermer from *Mr. Death: The Rise and Fall of Fred A. Leuchter Jr.*, directed by Errol Morris, distributed by Lion Gates Films.

2. Quoted in Douglas Davis, "Jews Hated for Their Money, Greed, Says Holocaust Denier," *The Jerusalem Post,* February 4, 2000.

3. Quoted in Associated Press translation of Eichmann manuscript, March 1, 2000.

4. Ibid.

Bibliography

Adelsberger, L. 1995. *Doctor's Story: Auschwitz*. Ithaca: Northeastern University Press.

Ahlwardt, H. 1895. *Reichstag, Stenographische Berichte*.

Allen, C. R. 1996. "Patrick J. Buchanan: Master Holocaust Denier." *Reform Judaism* (winter).

Alyishis, G. 1999. *Final Solution: Nazi Population Policy and the Murder of the European Jews*. New York: Oxford University Press.

Ambrose, S. E. 1997. *Citizen Soldiers: The U.S. Army from the Normandy Beaches to the Bulge to the Surrender of Germany, June 7, 1944 to May 7, 1945*. New York: Simon and Schuster.

Amery, J. 1980. *At the Mind's Limits*. Bloomington: Indiana University Press.

Anti-Defamation League of B'nai B'rith (ADL). 1989. *Holocaust "Revisionism": Reinventing the Big Lie*. New York.

———. 1993. *Hitler's Apologists: The Anti-Semitic Propaganda of Holocaust "Revisionism."* New York.

App, A. 1973. *The Six Million Swindle: Blackmailing the German People for Hard Marks with Fabricated Corpses*. Tacoma Park, Md.: Boniface Press.

———. 1974. *A Straight Look at the Third Reich: Hitler and National Socialism, How Right? How Wrong?* Tacoma Park, Md.: Boniface Press.

Applebaum, E. 1994. "Rebel Without a Cause." *The Jewish Week*, April 8–14.

Appleby, J., L. Hunt, and M. Jacob. 1994. *Telling the Truth about History*. New York: W. W. Norton.

Arad, Y. 1987. *Belzec, Sobibor, Treblinka: The Operation Reinhard Death Camps*. Bloomington: Indiana University Press.

Arad, Y., Y. Gutman, and A. Margaliot, eds. 1981. *Documents on the Holocaust*. Jerusalem: Yad Vashem.

Arendt, H. 1965. *Eichmann in Jerusalem*. New York: Compass/Viking.

Arndt, I., and W. Scheffler. 1976. "Organisierter Massenmord an Juden in nationalsozialistischen Vernichtungslagern." *Vierteljahrshefte für Zeitgeschichte* 24: 105–35.

Bacque, J. 1989. *Other Losses: An Investigation into the Mass Deaths of German Prisoners at the Hands of the French and Americans After World War II*. Toronto: Stoddart.

Bailer-Galanda, B., and W. Neugebauer. 1996. *Incorrigibly Right: Right-Wing Extremists, "Revisionists" and Anti-Semites in Austrian Politics Today*. Austria: Stiftung Dokumentationsarchiv des österreichischen Widerstandes.

Ball, J. C. 1992. *Air Photo Evidence: Auschwitz, Treblinka, Majdanek, Sobibor, Bergen Belsen, Belzec, Babi Yar, Katyn Forest*. Delta, B.C., Canada: Ball Resource Services.

Bankier, D. 1992. *The Germans and the Final Solution*. New York: Oxford University Press.

Barash, D. P. 1994. *Beloved Enemies: Our Need for Opponents*. Buffalo, N.Y.: Prometheus Books.

Bardèche, M. 1950. *Nuremberg II ou les faux-monnayeurs* (Nuremberg II or the counterfeiters). Paris: Les Sept Couleurs.

Barnes, H. E. 1966. "Revisionism: A Key to Peace." *Ramparts* (summer).

Barnouw, D., and G. van der Stroom, eds. 1989. *The Diary of Anne Frank: The Critical Edition*. New York: Doubleday.

Baron, A. 1994. *Holocaust Denial: New Nazi Lie or New Inquisition? A Defence of Free Inquiry and the Necessity of Rewriting History*. London: Anglo-Hebrew Publishing/InfoText Manuscripts.

Barraclough, G. 1972. "Mandarins and the Nazis." *New York Review of Books*, October 19.

Bartov, O. 1992. *Soldiers, Nazis, and the War in the Third Reich*. New York: Oxford University Press.

———. 1995. *Murder in Our Midst: The Holocaust, Industrial Killing, and Representation*. New York: Oxford University Press.

———. 1999. *The German Army and Genocide: Crimes against War Prisoners, Jews, and Other Civilians in the East, 1939–1944*. New York: New Press.

Bauer, Y. 1978. *The Holocaust in Historical Perspective*. Seattle: University of Washington Press.

———. 1982. *A History of the Holocaust*. New York: Franklin Watts.

———. 1988. "'Revisionism'—The Repudiation of the Holocaust and Its Historical Significance." In *The Historiography of the Holocaust Period*, ed. Y. Gutman and G. Greif. Jerusalem: Yad Vashem.

———. 1994. *Jews for Sale?: Nazi-Jewish Negotiations, 1933–1945*. New Haven: Yale University Press.

Baumeister, R. F. 1997. *Evil: Inside Human Violence and Cruelty*. New York: W. H. Freeman.

Beard, C. A. [1935] 1973. "That Noble Dream." In *The Varieties of History*, ed. F. Stern. New York: Vintage Books.

Becker, C. L. 1932. "Everyman His Own Historian." *American Historical Review* 37: 231–36.

Bein, A. 1964. "The Jewish Parasite." *Yearbook of the Leo Baeck Institute 9*.

Benz, W. 1991. *Dimension des Volkermords: Die Zahl der Jüdischen Opfer des Nationalsocialismus*. Munich: Deutscher Taschenbuch Verlag.

Benz, W., and B. Distel. 1988–1990. *Dachau Review: History of Nazi Concentration Camps: Studies, Reports, Documents*. 2 vols. Dachau: Verlag Dachauer Hefte.

Berenbaum, M. 1993. *The World Must Know: The History of the Holocaust as Told in the United States Holocaust Memorial Museum.* New York: Little, Brown.

———. Interview with M. Shermer, April 13. Transcript in Skeptics Society research library, Altadena, Calif.

Berlin, I. 1991. *The Crooked Timber of Humanity.* New York: Knopf.

Bernal, M. 1987. *Black Athena: The Afroasiatic Roots of Classical Civilization.* Vol. 1, *The Fabrication of Ancient Greece 1785–1985.* Vol. 2, *The Archaeological and Documentary Evidence.* New Brunswick, N.J.: Rutgers University Press.

The Big Lie: Who Told It? N.d. Arlington, Va.: American Nazi Party.

Blatt, T. 1978. "Blood and Ashes." *Jewish Currents.*

———. 1996a. *Sobibor: A Forgotten Revolt.* Issaquah, Wash.: HEP Publishing.

———. 1996b. "Soap from Human Fat: Evidence of a Nazi Crime." Manuscript in collection of Skeptics Society research library, Altadena, Calif.

———. 1997. *From the Ashes of Sobibor.* Evanston, Ill.: Northwestern University Press.

Braham, R. 1991. "A Changing Landscape of Memory: Eastern Europe and the U.S.S.R." *Dimensions: A Journal of Holocaust Studies* 6, no. 1: 16–21.

Breitman, R. 1991. *The Architect of Genocide: Himmler and the Final Solution.* New York: Alfred A. Knopf.

———. 1998. *Official Secrets: What the Nazis Planned, What the British and Americans Knew.* New York: Hill and Wang.

Brin, H. 1982. "Sweden Arrests Top Holocaust Revisionist." *Heritage,* December 31.

Broszat, M. 1967. "Nationalsozialistische Konzentrationslager 1933–1945." In *Anatomie des SS-Staates,* ed. H. Bucheim. 2 vols. Munich: Deutscher Taschenbuchverlag.

———. 1976. "On the Whitewashers of Nazi Crime." *Patterns of Prejudice* 10, no. 5: 11–14.

———. 1977. "Hitler und die 'Endlösung': Aus Anlass der Thesen von David Irving." *Vierteljahrshefte für Zeitgeschichte* 25, no. 4: 739–75. Translated as "Hitler and the Genesis of the 'Final Solution': An Assessment of David Irving's Theses." In *The Nazi Holocaust,* ed. M. Marrus, vol. 3. London: Meckler, 1989.

Browning, C. 1978. *The Final Solution and the German Foreign Office.* New York: Holmes and Meier.

———. 1991. *The Path to Genocide: Essays on Launching the Final Solution.* Cambridge: Cambridge University Press.

———. 1992. *Ordinary Men.* New York: HarperCollins.

Brugioni, D., and R. Poirier. 1979. *The Holocaust Revisited: A Retrospective Analysis of the Auschwitz-Birkenau Extermination Complex.* Washington, D.C.: Central Intelligence Agency.

Büchler, Y. 1995. "Document: A Preparatory Document for the Wannsee 'Conference.'" *Holocaust and Genocide Studies* 9, no. 1 (spring): 121–29.

Butler, D. 1998. "French Research Agency to Seek Ruling on Holocaust Sceptics." *Nature,* April 23, 745.

Butz, A. 1976. *The Hoax of the Twentieth Century*. Newport Beach, Calif.: Institute for Historical Review.

Caron, V. 1999. *Uneasy Asylum: France and the Jewish Regufee Crisis, 1933–1942*. Stanford: Stanford University Press.

Cavafy, C. P. 1975. *Collected Poems*. Ed. G. Savidis, trans. E. Keeley and P. Sherrard. Princeton: Princeton University Press.

Cavalli-Sforza, L. L., P. Menozzi, and A. Piazza. 1994. *The History and Geography of Human Genes*. Princeton: Princeton University Press.

Cesarani, D., ed. 1994. *The Final Solution: Origins and Implementation*. London: Routledge.

Chang, I. 1997. *The Rape of Nanking: The Forgotten Holocaust of World War II*. New York: Basic Books.

Choumoff, P. S. 1972. *Les Chambres á gas de Mauthausen* (The Gas Chambers at Mauthausen). Paris.

Christensen, L. 1994. *Skinhead Street Gangs*. Boulder: Paladin Press.

Christophersen, T. N.d. *Auschwitz, Truth or Lie: An Eyewitness Report*. Quebec.

Cohn, N. 1967. *Warrant for Genocide: The Myth of the Jewish World-Conspiracy and the Protocols of the Elders of Zion*. London: Eyre and Spottiswoode.

Cole, D. 1994. Interview with M. Shermer, Altadena, Calif., April 26. Transcript in Skeptics Society research library.

———. 1995. "Forty-Six Important Unanswered Questions Regarding the Nazi Gas Chambers." Manuscript posted on Internet (www.codoh.com) with a cover letter by Bradley R. Smith, October 9.

Coser, L. 1956. *The Functions of Social Conflict*. Glencoe, Ill.: Free Press.

Cote, J. E. 1998. "Much Ado About Nothing: The 'Fateful Hoaxing' of Margaret Mead." *Skeptical Inquirer* 22, no. 6: 29–34.

———. 1999. "No Evidence Offered Relevant to Points Raised." *Skeptical Inquirer* 22, no. 3: 61–63.

Cowan, G. A., D. Pines, and D. Meltzer. 1994. *Complexity: Metaphors, Models, and Reality*. Reading, Mass.: Addison Wesley.

Cowell, A. 1996. "Files Suggest British Knew Early of Nazi Atrocities against Jews." *New York Times*, November 19, A6.

Cremo, M. A. 1998. *Forbidden Archeology's Impact*. San Diego: Bhaktivedanta Institute.

Cremo, M. A., and R. L. Thompson. 1993. *Forbidden Archeology: The Hidden History of the Human Race*. San Diego: Bhaktivedanta Institute.

———. 1994. *The Hidden History of the Human Race*. Badger, Calif.: Govardhan Hill Publishing.

Croce, B. 1921. *History: Its Theory and Practice*. Trans. D. Ainslee. New York: Harcourt, Brace.

Czech, D. 1990. *Auschwitz Chronicle: 1939–1945*. New York: Henry Holt.

Daniel, G. 1977. Review of *America B.C.*, by Barry Fell. *New York Times*, March 13.

Dawidowicz, L. 1975. *The War against the Jews, 1933–1945*. New York: Bantam.

———. 1980. "Lies about the Holocaust." *Commentary*, December.

Degler, C. N. 1981. "Bad History." *Commentary*, June.

Deloria, V., Jr. 1969. *Custer Died for Your Sins: An Indian Manifesto.* New York: Macmillan.

———. 1995. *Red Earth, White Lies: Native Americans and the Myth of Scientific Fact.* New York: Scribners.

Dening, G. 1992. *Mr. Bligh's Bad Language: Passion, Power and Theatre on the Bounty.* Cambridge: Cambridge University Press.

Diamond, J. 1993. *The Third Chimpanzee.* New York: HarperCollins.

———. 1996. "The Roots of Radicalism." *New York Review of Books,* November 14.

———. 1997. *Guns, Germs, and Steel: The Fates of Human Societies.* New York: W. W. Norton.

Döscher, H.-J. 1987. *Das Auswärtige Amt im Dritten Reich: Diplomatie im Schatten der 'Endlösung.'* Berlin: Siedler.

Douglas, L. 1996. "The Memory of Judgment: The Law, the Holocaust, and Denial." *History and Memory* 7, no. 2: 100–120.

Dwork, D., and R. J. van Pelt. 1996. *Auschwitz: 1270 to the Present.* New York: W. W. Norton.

Eisenhower, D. D. 1948. *Crusade in Europe.* New York: Doubleday.

[Eisenhower committee]. 1945. *Atrocities and Other Conditions in Concentration Camps in Germany.* Report of the Committee requested by Gen. Dwight D. Eisenhower through the Chief of Staff, Gen. George C. Marshall, to the Congress of the United States. Washington, D.C.: U.S. Government Printing Office.

Eisler, R. 1987. *The Chalice and the Blade.* New York: Harper and Row.

Eldredge, N., and S. J. Gould. 1972. "Punctuated Equilibria: An Alternative to Phyletic Gradualism." In *Models in Paleobiology,* ed. T. J. M. Schopf. San Francisco: Freeman, Cooper.

Engel, D. 1993. *Facing a Holocaust: The Polish Government-in-Exile and the Jews, 1943–1945.* Chapel Hill: University of North Carolina Press.

Evans, R. 1991. "German Unification and the New Revisionism." *Dimensions: A Journal of Holocaust Studies* 6, no. 1: 10–15.

Faurisson, R. 1980. *Mémoire en défense contre ceux qui m'accusent de falsifier l'histoire* (Memoir of defense against those who accuse me of falsifying history). Paris: La Vieille Taupe.

———. 1988. "The Zündel Trials (1985 and 1988)." *Journal of Historical Review* 8, no. 4: 417–431.

———. N.d. [1987] "The 'Problem of the Gas Chambers.'" Newport Beach, Calif.: Institute for Historical Review.

Fay, S. B. 1920. "New Light on the Origin of the World War." *American Historical Review* 25: 616–39.

Feder, K. 1996. *Frauds, Myths, and Mysteries: Science and Pseudoscience in Archaeology.* Mountain View, Calif.: Mayfield.

———. 1997. "Indians and Archaeologists: Conflicting Views of Myth and Science." *Skeptic* 5, no. 3: 74–81.

Feig, K. G. 1981. *Hitler's Death Camps: The Sanity of Madness.* New York: Holmes and Meier.

Fell, B. 1976. *America B.C.: Ancient Settlers in the New World.* New York: Pocket Books.

Ferencz, B. 1979. *Less Than Slaves: Jewish Forced Labor and the Quest for Compensation.* Cambridge, Mass.: Harvard University Press.

Fest, J. 1974. *Hitler.* New York: Harcourt Brace Jovanovich.

Finkelstein, N. G., and R. B. Birn. 1998. *A Nation on Trial: The Goldhagen Thesis and Historical Truth.* New York: Henry Holt.

Fleming, G. 1984. *Hitler and the Final Solution.* Berkeley: University of California Press.

Foucault, M. 1994. *The Order of Things: An Archaeology of the Human Sciences.* New York: Vintage Books.

Foxman, A. H. 1994. "Holocaust Denial: The Growing Danger." *Dimensions: A Journal of Holocaust Studies* 8, no. 1: 13–16.

Frankel, M. 1998. "Willing Executioners?" Review of *Hitler's Willing Executioners* by Daniel Goldhagen. *New York Times,* August 9.

Freeman, D. 1983. *Margaret Mead and Samoa: The Making and Unmaking of an Anthropological Myth.* Cambridge, Mass.: Harvard University Press.

———. 1997. "Paradigms in Collision: Margaret Mead's Mistake and What It Has Done to Anthropology." *Skeptic* 5, no. 3: 66–73.

———. 1999. "On the Ethics of Skeptical Inquiry." *Skeptical Inquirer* 22, no. 3: 60–61.

Freud, S. [c. 1922] 1940. *Group Psychology and Analysis of the Ego.* In *Complete Psychological Works of Sigmund Freud.* 18: 67–143. London: Hogarth Press.

Friedlander, H. 1981. "The Nazi Concentration Camps." In *Human Responses to the Holocaust: Perpetrators and Victims, Bystanders and Resisters,* ed. M. Ryan. New York: Edwin Mellon Press.

———. 1984. "The Deportation of the German Jews and Post-War German Trials of Nazi Criminals." *Yearbook of the Leo Baeck Institute* 29.

———1995. *The Origins of Nazi Genocide: From Euthanasia to the Final Solution.* Chapel Hill: University of North Carolina Press.

Friedlander, H., and S. Milton, eds. 1980. *The Holocaust: Ideology, Bureaucracy, and Genocide.* New York: Kraus International.

Friedlander, S. 1969. *Kurt Gerstein: The Ambiguity of Good.* New York: Alfred Knopf.

———. 1993. *Memory, History and the Extermination of the Jews of Europe.* Bloomington: University of Indiana Press.

Friedrich, C., and E. Thomson. 1977. *The Hitler We Loved and Why.* Reedy, W.Va.

Fritsch, T. 1893. *Antisemiten-Katechismus* (The racists' decalogue). Leipzig.

Fritze, R. H. 1994a. "Goodbye Columbus? The Pseudohistory of Who Discovered America." *Skeptic* 2, no. 4: 88–97.

———. 1994b. *Legend and Lore of the Americas Before 1492: An Encyclopedia of Visitors, Explorers, and Immigrants.* Santa Barbara, Calif.: ABC-CLIO.

Gasman, D. 1971. *The Scientific Origins of National Socialism: Social Darwinism in Ernst Haeckel and the German Monist League.* New York: American Elsevier.

Geertz, C. 1973. *The Interpretation of Cultures.* New York: Basic Books.

George, J., and L. Wilcox. 1992. *Nazis, Communists, Klansmen, and Others on the Fringe.* Buffalo, N.Y.: Prometheus Books.

Gilbert, G. M. 1947. *Nuremberg Diary.* New York: Farrar, Straus.

Gilbert, M. 1981. *Auschwitz and the Allies: A Devastating Account of How the Allies Responded to the News of Hitler's Mass Murder.* New York: Holt, Reinhart and Winston.

———. 1986. *The Holocaust: A History of the Jews of Europe During the Second World War.* New York: Holt, Reinhart and Winston.

———. 1993. *Atlas of the Holocaust.* New York: William Morrow, with Gazetteer.

Goertzel, T. 1992. *Turncoats and True Believers: The Dynamics of Political Belief and Disillusionment.* Buffalo, N.Y.: Prometheus Books.

Goldhagen, D. J. 1996. *Hitler's Willing Executioners: Ordinary Germans and the Holocaust.* New York: Alfred A. Knopf.

Gould, S. J. 1981. *The Mismeasure of Man.* New York: W. W. Norton.

———. 1985. *The Flamingo's Smile.* New York: W. W. Norton.

———. 1989. *Wonderful Life: The Burgess Shale and the Nature of History.* New York: W. W. Norton.

———. 1995. *Dinosaur in a Haystack.* New York: W. W. Norton.

Gradowski, Z. 1944. *In the Heart of Hell.* Jerusalem.

Grobman, A. 1979. "What Did They Know? The American Jewish Press and the Holocaust." *American Jewish History* 68, no. 3 (March): 327–52.

———. 1993. *Rekindling the Flame: American Jewish Chaplains and the Survivors of European Jewry, 1944–1948.* Detroit: Wayne State University Press.

———. 1995. *Those Who Dared: Rescuers and Rescued.* Los Angeles: Martyrs Memorial and Museum of the Holocaust.

Grobman, A., D. Landes, and S. Milton, eds. 1983. *Genocide: Critical Issues of the Holocaust.* Los Angeles: Simon Wiesenthal Center.

Grubach, P. 1992–93. "The Leuchter Report Vindicated." *Journal of Historical Review* 12, no. 4: 445–73.

Gumerman, G. J., and M. Gell-Mann. 1994. *Understanding Complexity in the Prehistoric Southwest.* Reading, Mass.: Addison Wesley.

Gutman, Y. 1985. *Denying the Holocaust.* Jerusalem: Vidal Sassoon International Center for the Study of Antisemitism.

———. 1990. "Holocaust, Denial of the." *Encyclopedia of the Holocaust* 2: 681–87, ed. Y. Gutman. New York: Macmillan.

———. 1996. Interview with M. Shermer and A. Grobman, Altadena, Calif., May 10. Transcript in Skeptics Society research library.

Gutman, Y., and M. Berenbaum, eds. 1994. *Anatomy of the Auschwitz Death Camp.* Bloomington: Indiana University Press.

Gutman, Y., and R. Rozett. 1990. "Estimated Jewish Losses in the Holocaust." *Encyclopedia of the Holocaust,* ed. Y. Gutman, vol. 4. New York: Macmillan.

Guttenplan, D. D. 2000. "The Holocaust on Trial." *The Atlantic Monthly,* February, 44–66.

Hacket, D. A. 1995. *The Buchenwald Report.* Boulder: Westview Press.

Halbreich, S. 1991. *Before-During-After.* New York: Vantage Press.

Hannan, M. 1998. "Scot Who Claimed the Holocaust Was a Hoax." *The Scotsman,* June 1.

Harlan, D. 1989. "Intellectual History and the Return of Literature." *American Historical Review* 94: 581–609.

Harwood, R. [1973]. *Did Six Million Really Die?: The Truth at Last.* London: Verrall.

———. 1982. "'Holocaust' Story an Evil Hoax." *"Holocaust" News* (London) 1: 1.

Hawkins, J. A., and M. Gell-Mann. 1994. *The Evolution of Human Languages.* Reading, Mass.: Addison Wesley.

Hayes, P., ed. 1991. *Lessons and Legacies: The Meaning of the Holocaust in a Changing World.* Evanston, Ill.: Northwestern University Press.

———. 1992. "A Historian Confronts Denial." In *The Netherlands and Nazi Genocide,* ed. G. Jan Golijn and Marcia Littell. Lampeter, Wales: Edwin Mellen Press.

Headland, R. 1992. *Messages of Murder: A Study of the Reports of the Einsatzgruppen of the Security Police and Security Service 1941–1943.* Rutherford, N.J.: Fairleigh Dickinson University Press.

Hertzberg, A. 1998. *Jews: The Essence and Character of a People.* San Francisco: HarperCollins.

Hilberg, R. 1961. *The Destruction of the European Jews.* Chicago: Quadrangle Books.

———. 1993. *Perpetrators, Victims, Bystanders: The Jewish Catastrophe 1933–1945.* New York: HarperCollins.

———. 1994. Interview with M. Shermer, Altadena, Calif., April 10. Transcript in Skeptics Society research library.

Hilberg, R., and U. D. Adam. 1979. *Judenpolitik im Dritten Reich.* Düsseldorf: Droste Verlag.

Hitler, A. [1925–27] 1943. *Mein Kampf.* Trans. R. Manheim. Boston: Houghton Mifflin.

———. 1953. *Hitler's Table Talk, 1941–1944.* Trans. N. Cameron and R. H. Stevens. London: Weidenfeld and Nicolson.

Hofstader, R. 1979.*The Paranoid Style in American Politics and Other Essays.* Chicago: University of Chicago Press.

Höhne, H. 1969. *The Order of the Death's Head.* London: Secker and Warburg.

Hole, F. 1981. "Saga America." Book review. *Bulletin of the Archaeological Society of Connecticut* 44: 81–83.

Horner, J. 1988. *Digging Dinosaurs.* New York: Harper and Row.

Höss, R. 1959. *Commandant of Auschwitz: The Autobiography of Rudolf Hoess.* Cleveland: World.

Höss, R., P. Broad, and J. P. Kremer. 1994. *KL Auschwitz Seen by the SS: Rudolf Höss, Pery Broad, Johann Paul Kremer.* Oswiecim: Auschwitz-Birkenau State Museum.

Huntington, S. P. 1993. "The Clash of Civilizations?" *Foreign Affairs* 72: 22–49.

International Military Tribunal. 1946–53. *Trials of War Criminals before the Nuremberg Military Tribunals under Control Council Law No. 10.* Green Series. 15 vols. Washington, D.C.: U.S. Government Printing Office.

Irving, D. 1977. *Hitler's War*. New York: Viking Press.

———. 1989. *Göring: A Biography*. New York: Grafton/HarperCollins.

———. 1994. Interview with M. Shermer, Altadena, Calif., April 25. Transcript in Skeptics Society research library.

———. 1995. "Revelations from Goebbels' Diary: Bringing to Light Secrets of Hitler's Propaganda Minister." *Journal of Historical Review* 15, no. 1: 2–21.

———. 1996. *Goebbels: Mastermind of the Third Reich*. London: Focal Point Publications.

Jäckel, E. 1989. "Hitler Orders the Holocaust." In *The Nazi Holocaust,* ed. M. Marrus, vol. 3. London: Meckler.

———. 1993. *David Irving's Hitler: A Faulty History Dissected*. Port Angeles, Wash.: Ben-Simon Publications.

Jackson, R. H. 1947. *A Nuremberg Case and Other Documents*. New York: Alfred A. Knopf.

Johnson, E. A. 2000. *Nazi Terror: The Gestapo, Jews and Ordinary Germans.* New York: Basic Books.

Kammerer, R., and A. Solms, eds. 1993. *The Rudolf Report: A Discussion of the Rudolf Report on the Formation and Demonstrability of Cyanide Compounds in the Gas Chambers at Auschwitz, with additional research findings on the Holocaust*. Uckfield, Sussex, England: Cromwell Press.

Karski, J. 1944. *Story of the Secret State*. Boston: Houghton Mifflin.

Katz, S. T. 1994. *The Holocaust in Historical Context*. New York: Oxford University Press.

Kelley, A. 1981. *The Descent of Darwin: The Popularization of Darwinism in Germany, 1860–1914*. Chapel Hill: University of North Carolina Press.

Kelman, H. C., and V. L. Hamilton. 1989. *Crimes of Obedience: Toward a Psychology of Authority and Responsibility*. New Haven: Yale University Press.

Kent, S., and T. Krebs. 1998. "When Scholars Know Sin: How New Age Religions Co-opt Social Scientists." *Skeptic* 6, no. 3: 36–44.

Kevles, D. 1985. *In the Name of Eugenics: Genetics and the Uses of Human Heredity*. Berkeley: University of California Press.

Kielar, W. 1980. *Anus Mundi*. New York: Times Books.

King, D. 1989. *Lyndon LaRouche and the New American Fascism*. New York: Doubleday.

Klarsfeld, S., ed. 1978. *The Holocaust and the Neo-Nazi Mythomania*. New York: Beate Klarsfeld Foundation.

Klee, E. 1994. "History versus Fiction." *Dimensions: A Journal of Holocaust Studies* 8, no. 1: 2.

Klee, E., W. Dressen, and V. Riess, eds. 1992. *"The Good Old Days": The Holocaust as Seen by Its Perpetrators and Bystanders*. New York: Free Press.

Klein, D. B. 1991. "History's Memory Hole." *Dimensions: A Journal of Holocaust Studies* 6, no. 1: 3.

Kloppenberg, J. T. 1989. "Objectivity and Historicism: A Century of American Historical Writing." *American Historical Review* 94, no. 4: 1011–30.

Kochavi, A. J. 1998. *Prelude to Nuremberg: Allied War Crimes Policy and the Question of Punishment*. Chapel Hill: University of North Carolina Press.

Kogon, E., H. Langbein, and A. Rückerl, eds. 1993. *Nazi Mass Murder: A Documentary History of the Use of Poison Gas*. New Haven: Yale University Press.

Konvitz, M. R. 1946. "Will Nuremberg Serve Justice?" *Commentary* 1, no. 3 (January): 11.

Krausnick, H., H. Buchheim, M. Broszart, and H. Jacobsen, eds. 1968. *Anatomy of the SS State*. London: Collins.

Krausnick, H., and H. H. Wilhelm. 1981. *Die Truppe des Weltanschauungskrieges: Die Einsatzgruppen der Sicherheitspolizei und des SD 1938–1942*. Stuttgart: Deutsche Verlagsanstalt.

Kuhl, S. 1994. *The Nazi Connection: Eugenics, American Racism and German National Socialism*. New York: Oxford University Press.

Kuhn, T. 1962. *The Structure of Scientific Revolutions*. Chicago: University of Chicago Press.

Kulaszka, B. 1992. *Did Six Million Really Die? Report of the Evidence in the Canadian "False News" Trial of Ernst Zündel*. Toronto: Samizdat Publishers.

Kulka, E. 1977. *The Holocaust Is Being Denied! The Answer of Auschwitz Survivors*. Tel Aviv: Committee of Auschwitz Camps Survivors in Israel.

LaCapra, D. 1983. *Rethinking Intellectual History: Texts, Contexts, Language*. Ithaca: Cornell University Press.

Langer, L. L. 1990. "Fictional Facts and Factual Fictions: History in Holocaust Literature." In: *Reflections of the Holocaust in Art and Literature*, ed. R. L. Braham. New York: Institute for Holocaust Studies, 117–30.

———. 1991. *Holocaust Testimonies: The Ruins of Memory*. New Haven: Yale University Press.

———. 1995. *Admitting the Holocaust*. New York: Oxford University Press.

Langfus, L. 1965. "Horrors of Murder." In *Szukajcie w Popiolach*. Lodz: Committee for Investigation of Nazi War Crimes in Poland.

Lanzmann, C. 1985. *Shoah: An Oral History of the Holocaust*. New York: Pantheon.

———. 1991. "The Obscenity of Understanding: An Evening with Claude Lanzmann." *American Imago* 48, no. 4: 473–95.

Laqueur, W. 1965. "The Roots of Nazism." *New York Review of Books*, January 14.

———. 1980. *The Terrible Secret: Suppression of the Truth about Hitler's "Final Solution."* Boston: Little, Brown.

LaRouche, L. 1979a. *The Power of Reason—A Kind of Autobiography*. New York: New Benjamin Franklin House.

———. 1979b. *Will the Soviets Rule during the 1980s?* New York: New Benjamin Franklin House.

———1980. *Basic Economics for Conservative Democrats*. New York: New Benjamin Franklin House.

———. 1983. *LaRouche—Will This Man Become President?* New York: New Benjamin Franklin House.

Lefkowitz, M. 1996. *Not Out of Africa: How Afrocentrism Became an Excuse to Teach Myth as History*. New York: Basic Books.

Lefkowitz, M., and G. M. Rogers, eds. 1997. *Black Athena Revisited*. Chapel Hill: University of North Carolina Press.

Lehrer, D. A. 1980. "Rewriting History—Denying the Holocaust." *Backgrounder* (Anti-Defamation League), spring.

Lepper, B. T. 1996. "Hidden History, Hidden Agenda. A Review of Hidden History of the Human Race." *Skeptic* 4, no. 1: 98–100.

Lettich, A. 1946. *Trente-quatre mois dans les camps de concentration* (Thirty-four months in the concentration camps). Tours: L'Union Coopérative.

Leuchter, F. 1989. *The Leuchter Report: An Engineering Report on the Alleged Execution Chambers at Auschwitz, Birkenau, and Majdanek, Poland.* London: Focal Point.

———. N.d. *The Second Leuchter Report: Dachau, Mauthausen, Hartheim.* Toronto: Samizdat Publishers.

———. N.d. *The Third Leuchter Report: A Technical Report on the Execution Gas Chamber at Mississippi State Penitentiary.* Toronto: Samizdat Publishers.

———. N.d. *The Fourth Leuchter Report: An Engineering Evaluation of Jean-Claude Pressac's Book "Auschwitz: Technique and Operation of the Gas Chambers."* Toronto: Samizdat Publishers.

———. N.d. *The Fourth Leuchter Report: An Engineering Evaluation of Jean-Claude Pressac's Book "Auschwitz: Technique and Operation of the Gas Chambers."* Toronto: Samizdat Publishers.

Levi, P. 1986. *The Drowned and the Saved.* New York: Summit Books.

Levin, D. 1995. *The Lesser of Two Evils: Eastern European Jewry under Soviet Rule, 1939–1941.* Philadelphia: Jewish Publication Society.

Levine, M. M. 1992. "The Use and Abuse of Black Athena." *American Historical Review* 97, no. 2: 440–60.

Lichtenstein, H. 1996. "Punctually on the Ramp: The Horizon of a German Railroad Worker." In *The German Public and the Persecution of the Jews, 1933–1945: "No One Participated, No One Knew,"* ed. J. Wollenberg, trans. R. Pribic. Atlantic Highlands, N.J.: Humanities Press.

Lifton, R. J. 1986. *The Nazi Doctors: Medical Killing and the Psychology of Genocide.* New York: Basic Books.

Linenthal, E. T., and T. Engelhardt. 1996. *History Wars: The Enola Gay and Other Battles for the American Past.* New York: Henry Holt.

Lipset, S. M., and E. Raab. 1978. *The Politics of Unreason: Right-Wing Extremism in America, 1790–1977.* 2d ed. Chicago: University of Chicago Press.

Lipstadt, D. 1986. *Beyond Belief: The American Press and the Coming of the Holocaust, 1933–1945.* New York: Free Press.

———. 1991. "Deniers, Relativists, and Pseudo-Scholarship." *Dimensions: A Journal of Holocaust Studies* 6, no. 1: 4–9.

———. 1993. *Denying the Holocaust.* New York: Free Press.

———. 1994a. "Don't Fight the Deniers." *The Jewish Week,* April 8–14.

———. 1994b. "Holocaust Denial: An Overview." *Dimensions: A Journal of Holocaust Studies* 8, no. 1: 3–8.

Littell, F. H. 1986. *The Crucifixion of the Jews.* Macon, Ga.: Mercer University Press.

Loewen, J. W. 1995. *Lies My Teacher Told Me: Everything Your American History Textbook Got Wrong.* New York: New Press.

Lookstein, H. 1985. *Were We Our Brothers' Keepers: The Public Response of American Jews to the Holocaust, 1938–1944*. New York: Vintage Books.

Lourie, R. 1994. "To Combat Denial." *Dimensions: A Journal of Holocaust Studies* 8, no. 1: 9–12.

Lüeftl, W. 1992. "The Lüeftl Report." *Journal of Historical Review* 12, no. 4.

Lukacs, J. 1997. *The Hitler of History*. New York: Alfred A. Knopf.

Macrakis, K. 1993. *Surviving the Swastika: Scientific Research in Nazi Germany*. New York: Oxford University Press.

Marcellus, T. 1994. "An Urgent Appeal from IHR." Letter, Institute for Historical Review.

Marrus, M. 1987. *The Holocaust in History*. New York: Penguin.

———, ed. 1989. *The Nazi Holocaust*. 9 vols. London: Meckler.

Marszalek, J. 1986. *Majdanek: The Concentration Camp in Lublin*. Warsaw: Interpress.

———. 1995. *Mauthausen*. Vienna: Steindl-Druck.

Marx, K. [1852] 1978. "The Eighteenth Brumaire of Louis Bonaparte." In *The Marx-Engels Reader*, 2d ed. R. C. Tucker. New York: W. W. Norton.

Mason, T. 1981. "Intention and Explanation: A Current Controversy about the Interpretation of National Socialism." In *Der Führerstatt: Mythos und Realität*, ed. G. Hirschfeld and L. Kettenacker, 21–40. Stuttgart.

Matthaus, J. 1996. "What about the 'Ordinary Men': The German Order Police in the Occupied Soviet Union." *Holocaust and Genocide Studies* 10: 134–50.

Mayer, A. J. 1990. *Why Did the Heavens Not Darken?* New York: Pantheon.

Mayr, E. 1954. "Change of Genetic Environment and Evolution." In *Evolution as a Process*, ed. J. Huxley, A. C. Hardy, and E. B. Ford. London: Allen and Unwin.

———. 1970. *Populations, Species and Evolution*. Cambridge, Mass.: Harvard University Press.

McIver, T. 1988. *Anti-Evolution: A Reader's Guide to Writings Before and After Darwin*. Baltimore: Johns Hopkins University Press.

———. 1994. "The Protocols of Creationism: Racism, Anti-Semitism and White Supremacy in Christian Fundamentalism." *Skeptic* 2, no. 4: 76–87.

McKusick, M. 1976. "Contemporary American Folklore about Antiquity." *Bulletin of the Philadelphia Anthropological Society* 28: 1–23.

Mead, M. 1928. *Coming of Age in Samoa*. New York: Mentor/New American Library.

Merchant, C. 1980. *The Death of Nature: Women, Ecology, and the Scientific Revolution*. San Francisco: HarperCollins.

Meyerhoff, H. 1959. *The Philosophy of History in Our Time*. New York: Doubleday.

Miele, F. 1994. "Giving the Devil His Due: Holocaust Revisionism as a Test Case for Free Speech and the Skeptical Ethic." *Skeptic* 2, no. 4: 58–70.

Milgram, S. 1969. *Obedience to Authority: An Experimental View*. New York: Harper.

Milton, S. 1984. "The Expulsion of Polish Jews from Germany: October 1938 to July 1939." *Yearbook of the Leo Baeck Institute* 29.

Mommsen, H. 1983. "Die Realisierung des Utopischen: Die 'Endlösung der Judenfrage' im 'Dritten Reich.'" *Geschichte un Gesellschaft* 9, no. 3 (autumn): 381–420.

Le Monde. 1989. "L'agression contre M. Robert Faurisson revendiquée par 'Les fils de mémoire juive,'" September 19.

Moses, A. D. 1998. "Structure and Agency in the Holocaust: Daniel J. Goldhagen and His Critics." *History and Theory* 37, no. 2: 194–219.

Mosse, G. L. 1966. *Nazi Culture*. New York: Schocken Books.

Müller, F. 1979. *Eyewitness Auschwitz: Three Years in the Gas Chambers*. New York: Stein and Day.

Naumann, B. 1966. *Auschwitz: A Report on the Proceedings Against Robert Karl Ludwig Mulka and Others Before the Court at Frankfurt*. New York: Frederick A. Prager.

Nickerson, R. S. 1998. "Confirmation Bias: A Ubiquitous Phenomenon in Many Guises." *Review of General Psychology* 2, no. 2: 175–220.

Nietzsche, F. [1880] 1954. *The Twilight of the Idols*. New York: Viking.

Novick, P. 1988. *That Noble Dream: The "Objectivity Question" and the American Historical Profession*. Cambridge: Cambridge University Press.

———. 1991. "My Correct Views on Everything." *American Historical Review* 96, no. 3: 699–703.

Nolte, E. 1986. "Vergangenheit, die nicht vergehen will: Eine Rede, die Geschrieben, Aber Nicht Gehalten Werden Konnte." *Frankfurter Allgemeine Zeitung*, June 6.

Obert, J. C. 1981. "Yockey: Profile of an American Hitler." *The Investigator*, October.

O'Keefe, T. 1993. "New Books Seek to Discredit 'Growing Threat' of 'Holocaust Denial.'" *Journal of Historical Review* 13, no. 6: 28–36.

Olesker, D. 1995. *"66 Questions on the Holocaust": Examples of a Systematic Distortion*. Jerusalem: Institute for Countering Anti-Israel Propaganda.

Padfield, P. 1990. *Himmler*. New York: Henry Holt.

Pawlak, Z. 1979. *Ich Habe Uberlebt: Ein Häftling Berichtet über Majdanek* (I survived: A prisoner reports about Majdanek). Hamburg: Hoffman und Campe.

Payne, S. G. 1995. *A History of Fascism*. Madison: University of Wisconsin Press.

Persico, J. 1994. *Nuremberg: Infamy on Trial*. New York: Viking.

Petropoulos, J. 2000. *The Faustian Bargain: The Art World in Nazi Germany*. New York: Oxford University Press.

Pingel, F. 1978. *Häftlinge unter SS-Herrschaft*. Hamburg: Hoffmann und Campe.

Piper, F. 1992. *How Many Perished: Jews, Poles, Gypsies . . .* Kraków: Poligrafia ITS.

Popper, K. 1959. *The Logic of Scientific Discovery*. New York: Harper and Row.

Posner, G. 1991. *Hitler's Children*. New York: Random House.

Post, R. 1995. "Go Home, Irving." *Daily Californian*, February 7.

Pres, Terrence des. 1976. *The Survivor*. Oxford: Oxford University Press.

Pressac, J.-C. 1989. *Auschwitz: Technique and Operation of the Gas Chambers*. New York: Beate Klarsfeld Foundation.

Pressac, J.-C., and R. J. van Pelt. 1994. "The Machinery of Mass Murder at

Auschwitz." In *Anatomy of the Auschwitz Death Camp*, ed. Y. Gutman and M. Berenbaum. Bloomington: Indiana University Press.

Puntigam, F., H. Breymesser, and E. Bernfuss. 1943. *Blausäurekammern zur Fleckfieberabwehr* (Chambers of prussic acid in the defense against exanthematous typhus). Berlin.

"Question: How Long Can the Jews Perpetrate the Holocaust Myth?" 1986. *Newsletter* (Washington, D.C., German American Anti-Defamation League), August 7.

Rassinier, P. 1950. *Le Mensonge d'Ulysse* (The lie of Odysseus). Paris.

———. 1978. *Debunking the Genocide Myth: A Study of the Nazi Concentration Camps and the Alleged Extermination of European Jewry*. Los Angeles: Noontide Press.

Rauch, J. 1993. *Kindly Inquisitors: The New Attacks on Free Thought*. Chicago: University of Chicago Press.

Redlich, F. 1999. *Hitler: Diagnosis of a Destructive Prophet*. New York: Oxford University Press.

Reich, W. 1993. "Erasing the Holocaust." Book review. *New York Times*, July 11.

Reitlinger, G. [1953] 1978. *The Final Solution*. New York: Beechhurst Press.

Rhodes, J. 1980. *The Hitler Movement: A Modern Millenarian Revolution*. Stanford: Hoover Institution Press.

Rich, N. 1974. *Hitler's War Aims: Ideology, the Nazi State, and the Course of Expansion*. New York: W. W. Norton.

Robinson, J. 1965. *And the Crooked Shall Be Made Straight: The Eichmann Trial, the Jewish Catastrophe, and Hannah Arendt's Narrative*. Philadephia: Jewish Publication Society.

Rokeach, M. 1969. *The Open and Closed Mind: Investigations into the Nature of Belief Systems and Personality Systems*. New York: Basic Books.

Rollins, L. A. 1987. *Lucifer's Lexicon*. Port Townsend, Wash.: Loompanics.

Roques, H. 1989. *The "Confessions" of Kurt Gerstein*. Costa Mesa, Calif.: Institute for Historical Review.

———. 1995. "Faurisson and Cole on the Struthof 'Gas Chamber.'" *Adelaide Institute Newsletter*, April 20.

Rosenbaum, R. 1998. *Explaining Hitler: The Search for the Origins of His Evil*. New York: Random House.

Rosenthal, L. 1984. *"The Final Solution to the Jewish Question:" Mass-Murder or Hoax?* Trans. R. Lackner. Berkeley: Institute for Righteous Acts.

Ross, J. 1994. "An Update on Holocaust Denial Activities and the ADL Response." *Dimensions: A Journal of Holocaust Studies* 8, no. 1: 44–46.

Ross, R. 1980. *So It Was True: The American Protestant Press and the Nazi Persecution of the Jews*. Minneapolis: University of Minnesota Press.

Roth, H. N.d. *The Big Lie: Six Million Murdered Jews*. N.p.: History Research Unit.

Roth, S. J. 1982. "Making the Denial of the Holocaust a Crime in Law." London: Institute of Jewish Affairs in association with World Jewish Congress, research report, March.

Rummel, R. J. 1992. *Democide: Nazi Genocide and Mass Murder*. New Brunswick, N.J.: Transaction Press.

Rürup, R. 1989. *Topography of Terror: Gestapo, SS and Reichssicherheitshauptamt on the "Prinz-Albrect-Terrain": A Documenation.* Berlin: Willmuth Arenhovel.

Russell, B. 1963. *The Record: The Trial of Adolf Eichmann for His Crimes against the Jewish People and against Humanity.* New York: Alfred A. Knopf.

Sagi, N. 1980. *German Reparations: A History of the Negotiations.* Jerusalem: Magnes Press.

Samuels, S., and M. Valencia. 1995. "Activists Clash over Irving's Revised History." *Daily Californian,* February 7, 1–4.

Schafer, P. 1997. *Judeophobia: Attitudes toward the Jews in the Ancient World.* Cambridge, Mass.: Harvard University Press.

Schleunes, K. A. 1970. *The Twisted Road to Auschwitz: Nazi Policy toward the Jews, 1933–1939.* Urbana: University of Illinois Press.

Schmidt, M. 1984. *Albert Speer: The End of a Myth.* New York: St. Martin's Press.

Searchlight. 1995. Editorial, "Irving: The Truth at Last, or Some of It." September.

Sereny, G. 1983. *Into That Darkness: From Mercy Killing to Mass Murder.* New York: McGraw-Hill.

———. 1995. *Albert Speer: His Battle with Truth.* New York: Alfred A. Knopf.

Shankman, P. 1998. "Margaret Mead, Derek Freeman, and the Issue of Evolution." *Skeptical Inquirer* 22, no. 6: 35–39.

———. 1999. "Mead Was Not 'Unevolutionary,'" *Skeptical Inquirer* 22, no. 3: 63.

Shapiro, S., ed. 1990. *Truth Prevails: Demolishing Holocaust Denial—The End of "The Leuchter Report."* New York: Beate Klarsfeld Foundation.

Shelley, L., ed. 1996. *The Union Kommando in Auschwitz: The Auschwitz Munition Factory through the Eyes of Its Former Slave Laborers.* Lanham, Md.: University Press of America.

Shermer, M. 1991. "Science Defended, Science Defined: The Louisiana Creationism Case." *Science, Technology, and Human Values* 16, no. 4: 517–39.

———. 1993a. "Holocaust Revisionism and Pseudohistory: Does It Warrant Serious Skepticism?" *Skeptic* 2, no. 2: 20–22.

———. 1993b. "The Chaos of History." *Nonlinear Science Today* 2, no. 4: 1–13.

———. 1994a. "Holocaust Denial, Free Speech, and the Burden of Proof." *Skeptic* 2, no. 3: 13–14.

———. 1994b. "Proving the Holocaust: The Refutation of Revisionism and the Restoration of History." *Skeptic* 2, no. 4: 32–57.

———. 1995. "Exorcising LaPlace's Demon: Chaos and Antichaos, History and Metahistory." *History and Theory* 34, no. 1: 59–83.

———. 1996. "Rebel with a Cause: An Interview with Frank Sulloway." *Skeptic* 4, no. 4: 68–73.

———. 1997. *Why People Believe Weird Things: Pseudoscience, Superstition, and Other Confusions of Our Time.* New York: W. H. Freeman.

———. 1998. "Holocaust Revisionism Update." *Skeptic* 6, no. 1: 23–24.

———. 1999. *How We Believe: The Search for God in an Age of Science.* New York: W. H. Freeman.

Simon Wiesenthal Center. 1993. *The Neo-Nazi Movement in Germany.* Los Angeles.

Smith, B. R. 1987. *Confessions of a Holocaust Revisionist.* Los Angeles: Prima Facie.

—. 1991. "The Holocaust Story: How Much Is False? The Case for Open Debate." *Daily Northwestern,* April 4.

—. 1992. *The Holocaust Controversy: The Case for Open Debate.* Visalia, Calif.: Committee for Open Debate on the Holocaust.

—. 1993. "Writer Claims Holocaust a Hoax." *Ohio State Lantern,* September 5–6.

—. 1994. *Smith's Report* 19 (winter).

Snyder, L., ed. 1981. *Hitler's Third Reich.* Chicago: Nelson Hall.

Spector, S. 1990. "Aktion 1005: Effacing the Murder of Millions." *Holocaust and Genocide Studies* 5, no. 2: 157–73.

Speer, A. 1976. *Spandau: The Secret Diaries.* New York: Macmillan.

Steinlauf, M. C. 1997. *Bondage to the Dead: Poland and the Memory of the Holocaust.* Syracuse, N.Y.: Syracuse University Press.

Stern, F., ed. 1973. *The Varieties of History: From Voltaire to the Present.* New York: Vintage Books.

Stern, K. 1993. *Holocaust Denial.* New York: American Jewish Committee.

Stimely, K. N.d. "$50,000 Auschwitz Reward Unclaimed; 'Gas Chambers' Myth Continues to Crumble." Special report, Institute for Historical Review, Torrance, Calif.

Stivelman, M. 1998. *The Death March.* Rio de Janeiro: Nova Frontiera.

Streim, A. 1987. "The Tasks of the SS Einsatzgruppen." *Simon Wiesenthal Center Annual* 4: 309–28.

Sulloway, F. 1996. *Born to Rebel: Birth Order, Family Dynamics, and Creative Lives.* New York: Pantheon.

Supreme Court of Canada. 1991. *Ernst Zündel, Appellant; v Her Majesty the Queen, Respondent, and the Attorney General of Canada, the Attorney General of Manitoba, the Canadian Civil Liberties Association, the League for Human Rights of B'Nai Brith Canada and the Canadian Jewish Congress, Interveners.* Supreme Court of Canada File No. 21811.

Swiebocka, T. 1993. *Auschwitz: A History in Photographs.* Bloomington: Indiana University Press.

Tales of the Holohoax. N.d. Champaign, Ill.: Wiswell Ruffin House.

Talmon, J. L. 1973. "European History as the Seedbed of the Holocaust." In *Holocaust and Rebirth: A Symposium.* Jerusalem: Yad Vashem.

Taylor, S. 1985. *Prelude to Genocide: Nazi Ideology and the Struggle for Power.* London: Duckworth.

Tec, N. 1993. *Defiance: The Bielski Partisans.* New York: Oxford University Press.

Teitelbaum, S. 1993. "Who Needs Enemies?" *The Jerusalem Report,* October 21.

Tregenza, M. 1996a. "Analysis of Majdanek Gas Chambers and Transcript of Sworn Affidavit from Rudolf Reder (Zentrale Stelle der Landesjustizverwaltungen, Ludwigsburg, 1945, GFR. File No. 208 AR-Z 252/59)." Manuscript.

—. 1996b. Interview with A. Grobman, Altadena, Calif., April 29. Transcript in Skeptics Society research library.

Trombley, S. 1992. *The Execution Protocol: Inside America's Capital Punishment Industry.* New York: Crown.

United States Holocaust Memorial Museum. 1996. *Historical Atlas of the Holocaust*. New York: Macmillan.

Utley, F. 1949. *The High Cost of Vengeance*. Chicago: Regnery.

Van Alpern, E. 1997. *Caught by History: Holocaust Effects in Contemporary Art, Literature, and Theory*. Stanford: Stanford University Press.

Vankin, J., and J. Whalen. 1995. *50 Greatest Conspiracies of All Time: History's Biggest Mysteries, Coverups and Cabals*. New York: Citadel Press.

van Pelt, R. J. 1994. "A Site in Search of a Mission." In *Anatomy of the Auschwitz Death Camp*, ed. Y. Gutman and M. Berenbaum. Bloomington: Indiana University Press.

Vidal-Naquet, P. 1992. *Assassins of Memory*. New York: Columbia University Press.

von Lang, J., ed. 1983. *Eichmann Interrogated: Transcripts from the Archives of the Israeli Police*. New York: Farrar, Straus and Giroux.

Walk, J., ed. 1981. *Das Sonderrecht für Juden im NS-Staat: Eine Sammlung der gesetzlichen Massnahmen und Richtlinien—Inhalt und Bedeutung*. Heidelberg: C. F. Müller Juristischer Verlag.

Weber, M. 1992. "The Nuremberg Trials and the Holocaust." *Journal of Historical Review* 12, no. 2: 167–213.

———. 1993a. "Auschwitz: Myths and Facts." Newport Beach, Calif.: Institute for Historical Review.

———. 1993b. *The Zionist Terror Network: Background and Operation of the Jewish Defense League and Other Criminal Zionist Groups*. Newport Beach, Calif.: Institute for Historical Review.

———. 1994a. "The Holocaust: Let's Hear Both Sides." Newport Beach, Calif.: Institute for Historical Review.

———. 1994b. Interview with M. Shermer, Altadena, Calif., February 11. Transcript in Skeptics Society research library.

———. 1994c. "The Jewish Role in the Bolshevik Revolution and Russia's Early Soviet Regime." *Journal of Historical Review* 14, no. 1: 4–14.

Weimann, G., and C. Winn. 1986. *Hate on Trial: The Zündel Affair, the Media, Public Opinion in Canada*. New York: Mosaic Press.

Wellers, G. 1978. "The Number of the Final Solution Victims." *Aus Politik und Zeitgeschichte* 29, no. 7: 22–29.

Westermann, E. B. 1998. "'Ordinary Men' or 'Ideological Soldiers'? Police Battalion 310 in Russia, 1942." *German Studies Review* 21: 41–68.

Whewell, W. 1840. *The Philosophy of the Inductive Sciences*. London: J. W. Parker.

Wiesel, E. 1982. *Night*. New York: Bantam Books.

———. 1995. *All Rivers Run to the Sea: Memoirs 1969*. New York: Alfred A. Knopf.

———. 1999. *And the Sea Is Never Full*. New York: Alfred A. Knopf.

Wiesenfeld, S. 1984. "Antisemitism and the Denial of the Holocaust." Ph.D. thesis, Department of Religion, Concordia University, Montreal.

Wikoff, J. 1990. *Remarks: Commentary on Current Events and History* (newsletter, Aurora, N.Y).

Windschuttle, K. 1996. *The Killing of History: How a Discipline Is Being Mur-*

dered by Literary Critics and Social Theorists. Paddington, N.S.W., Australia: Macleay Press.

Wintzek, B. C. 1975. *Unssere Väter waren keine Verbrecher: Wie es damals wirklich war* (Our fathers were no criminals: How it really was then). Asendorf: MUT-Verlag.

Wistrich, R. 1991. *Antisemitism: The Longest Hatred.* New York: Schocken.

Witte, P. 1995. "Two Decisions Concerning the 'Final Solution to the Jewish Question': Deportations to Lodz and Mass Murder in Chelmno." Trans. B. Richardson. *Holocaust and Genocide Studies* 9, no. 3 (winter): 318–45.

Wood, T. E., and S. M. Jankowski. 1994. *Karski: How One Man Tried to Stop the Holocaust.* New York: John Wiley.

"Would Challenger Have Blown Up If German Scientists Had Still Been in Charge?" 1986. *Newsletter.* Washington, D.C.: German American Anti-Defamation League, August 7.

Wyszogrod, M. 1999. *A Brush with Death: An Artist in the Death Camps.* Albany: State University of New York Press.

Yahil, L. 1987. *The Holocaust.* Oxford: Oxford University Press.

Yerushalmi, Y. H. 1982. *Zakhor: Jewish History and Jewish Memory.* Seattle: University of Washington Press.

Young, J. E. 1988. *Writing and Rewriting the Holocaust: Narrative and the Consequences of Interpretation.* Bloomington: Indiana University Press.

Zentrale Stelle der Landesjustizverwaltungen, Ludwigsburg. 1945. GFR File No. 208 AR-Z 252/59: Case against Josef Oberhauser (Belzec case).

Zündel, E. 1994. Interview with M. Shermer, Altadena, Calif., April 26. Transcript in Skeptics Society research library.

Zuroff, E. 1994. *Occupation: Nazi Hunter. The Continuing Search for the Perpetrators of the Holocaust.* Hoboken, N.J.: KTAV Publishing House.

Index

Text:	10/13 Sabon
Display:	Akzidenz Grotesk and Franklin Gothic
Design:	Nicole Hayward
Composition:	Integrated Composition Systems
Printing and binding:	Data Reproductions